THE MANAGEMENT

Scotland's Great Football Bosses

THE MANAGEMENT

Scotland's Great Football Bosses

Michael Grant and Rob Robertson

BIRLINN

First published in 2010 by
Birlinn Limited
West Newington House
10 Newington Road
Edinburgh
EH9 1QS

www.birlinn.co.uk

ISBN: 978 1 84158 819 3

British Library Cataloguing-in-Publication Data
A catalogue record for this book is available from the British Library

Typeset by Iolaire Typesetting, Newtonmore
Printed and bound by MPG Books Ltd, Bodmin

For Sharon, Tom and Charlie, and for
Donald and Ruby Grant, with love and thanks.

And with love to Claire, Kirsten, Clare and Bruce Robertson.

Contents

Contents

Acknowledgements

To all of the great Scottish managers over the years: thanks for the memories, thanks for the results, thanks for the great quotes and stories, thanks for making our clubs and country proud.

The authors of *The Management* would like to thank: Mike Aitken, Richard Bath, Ralph Brand, Craig Brown, Peter Burns, Sandy Busby, George Cheyne, Bryan Cooney, Stuart Cosgrove, Harold Davis, Tom Devine, Tommy Docherty, Tom English, Tom Forsyth, Glenn Gibbons, George Graham, Darren Griffiths, Mark Guidi, Roger Hannah, David Hay, Tony Higgins, John Hutchinson, Jim Jefferies, Jonathan Jobson, Alex Knight, John Lambie, Jim Leishman, Craig Levein, Hugh MacDonald, Kenny MacDonald, Graham Mackrell (and others at The League Managers Association), Alastair MacLachlan, Rhona MacLeod, Archie Macpherson, Richard McBrearty, Kevin McCarra, Ally McCoist, Peter McCloy, Graham McColl, Robert McElroy, Mark McGhee, Derek McGregor, Hugh McIlvanney, William McIlvanney, Danny McGrain, Andy McInnes, Shaun McLaren, Jim McLean, Alex McLeish, Ruth McLennan, Billy McNeill, Doug McRobb, David Mason, Jody Megson, Willie Miller, Neville Moir, James Morgan, David Moyes, Michael Munro, Bill Murray, Jonathan Northcroft, Alan Pattullo, Stephen Penman, Gary Ralston, Jimmy Reid, Lawrie Reilly, John Roberts, Ian Ross, Alan Rough, Andy Roxburgh, Robin Russell, Alex Salmond, Brian Scott, Ron Scott, Jimmy Sinclair, Alex Smith, Tommy Smith, Walter Smith, Graeme Souness, Graham Spiers, Kevin Stirling, Gordon Strachan, Kenny Strang, James Traynor and Eddie Turnbull. Also a very special thanks to Mrs Margaret McDade and Mrs Jessie McNeill, the sisters of Jock Stein, for giving so much of their time, and also to Sir Alex Ferguson and Kenny Dalglish for their best wishes.

Foreword

Scotland is a country which has influenced what people are doing all over the world. Look through history: Scottish people keep popping up all over the place, whether as inventors, heading multinational companies, or in politics, science or engineering. Scotland always seems to produce leaders, people who do exceptional things. Especially when it comes to football management.

If Sir Matt Busby hadn't been a football manager but had been, say, a captain in the army you just know that he would have been distinguished and would've come home with medals. If he'd been a politician he would have risen to a position of power. There is a quality to leadership that is hard to quantify, but part of it is all the little things that go into making a man and which end up radiating something that makes others think 'wait a minute, this guy's worth following'.

Players have to look at you and think you are invincible. They have to think that you believe 100 per cent in your own ability. You have to be able to pull people with you. If any of the great Scottish managers had been weak in any way, or there was a chink in their armour, the players would have been able to detect it. Players just get a sense of that from any leader. You have to show you are strong and you know what you are doing. The great Scottish managers gave off that aura.

I think a working-class background brings values and makes people understand what it means to achieve something. It makes you understand the value of winning. It's not romanticising things to say many Scottish leaders and football managers have had to fight their way out of situations to improve themselves.

I'm from a working-class, council-house background in Fife. My grandfather was a blacksmith, my dad was an electrician in the dockyard at Rosyth. My wife's father was a miner. Don't get me wrong – I'm not saying we lived in a cardboard box in the middle of the road – but things weren't easy. There wasn't an awful lot of money. And when you're a kid you want things. I think when you have that fire in your belly it can lead to great things. Our great managers had that, that real desire to prove themselves.

Think of Sir Alex Ferguson. He has leadership qualities that are tied into that idea of protecting 'his' people. He protects the people who do well for him, the people who represent him. It's like trade unionism. Then look down in England at the teams that are punching above their weight. For me that is an indication of who is doing well in management. You look at Davie Moyes. He has that about him, the same sort of qualities as Sir Alex.

You would not say that most of the great managers were great players. They come to the fore more as managers than they did as players. It's sometimes not about knowing the game, it's about understanding the intricacies of people. To me, that's management. Understanding people rather than understanding football. That's what all our great managers could do.

There is no single stereotype of 'the great Scottish manager' but there are common themes. I think Scots are always trying to prove themselves, trying to prove they are better than people think they are. I don't know where that comes from but, again, it's about having that fire in the belly.

I don't think there is a logical reason why Scottish managers should have all these 'magical' qualities which come together, but an inordinate amount of them have done well in English football. We haven't done so well abroad. I've wondered about that in the past. Did they go to England and think that was the pinnacle? Are we reluctant to learn another language? Possibly. Or are we trying to prove something? It's as though we have conquered England . . . but that's as far as we've wanted to go.

I like listening to other managers after a game when they start talking about things. I'm always looking to find out who's a threat to me. I think if you can get something over on another manager then your team's got a chance of getting on top of them. You learn a lot from other managers before and after games, and you can use that down the line.

I aspire to be anywhere near where our great managers reached in the past. The Scotland manager's job is not seen as the best job in the world. Some people might not even see it as the best job in Scotland. So it's far removed from what Busby, Ferguson, Bill Shankly and Jock Stein have done. But only Shankly did not manage Scotland at some time during his career and I am sure he would have been hugely proud to do so.

In the history of football there are only so many people who have had the opportunity to manage their country. It is a burden at times; you do feel the weight of everyone's expectations. But I have a real desire to improve things. And I felt enormously proud to have been given the chance.

Craig Levein

Chapter One

The Master Race

How the pits, the shipyards and the mean streets created football's great managers

Fear is one of the first things that comes to mind. The fear of being on the receiving end of a Fergie hairdryer. The fear, just as awful in its own way, of losing Busby's approval and sensing you had disappointed him. The fear of being injured and knowing that you were no use to Shankly, to the point that he would ignore you if you passed him in the corridor. You didn't exist to him until you were fit again. The fear of getting a Smith stare in the Rangers dressing room and feeling the temperature drop a few degrees. The fear of Stein, full stop.

The great Scottish football managers have never done hugs and kisses. They've never done touchy-feely, holistic, New Age or alternative therapies. Or, if they ever did, they frightened their players into keeping their traps shut so we didn't find out about it. They've never shrugged their shoulders when their team's been beaten. They've never put up with a player talking back to them. Never understood or sympathised when a referee made a mistake which hurt them. Never thought it was a fair point when a journalist criticised. Never written anything off as a bad day at the office. Never felt sorry for themselves. Never backed down. Never, ever, been good losers.

The great Scottish managers have come to represent something in football. They have become the epitome of the tough, aggressive, no-nonsense gaffer. Disciplined, strict and controlling. Hard as nails. Old school. Not to be messed with, not to be crossed, streetwise and armed with every trick in the book. They love hard graft. Their hair is short, their clothes neat, their shoes polished, their posture straight. Ready for anything, be it pinning a player against a dressing-room wall or psychological warfare against opponents, officials, the press or anyone who might constitute 'them' against 'us'. They stand up for themselves, their players, their club and their supporters. They simmer after a setback. They boil. Their temper explodes. Around them, anger management has a different meaning entirely.

And all of that is only a part of the picture. The great ones also innovate. They inspire, they experiment, they take calculated risks. They can charm the birds from the trees or crack a line which makes a room dissolve into laughter. They know football inside out and are also informed by a wider, worldly intelligence. They have an eye for a player. Their judgement is as close to flawless as any managers can get. They see things that others don't. They are knowing and well-connected, with armies of informants quick to lift a phone and whisper in their ear if one of their players is spotted in a pub or nightclub. But they aren't always intimidating men who rule with an iron fist. Their genius has often graced the game with the lightest of touches.

For the greatest of them all, genius is not too strong a description. In 2007 *The Times* published a comprehensive article on the all-time top 50 managers in world football. These sorts of lists are great newspaper material: highly subjective and guaranteed to provoke a row and a reaction from readers. This one was better than most: impressively researched and confidently presented. The top 20 made for compelling reading. It comprised a couple of Englishmen, a couple of Italians, two Dutchmen, two Spaniards, two Brazilians, and one representative each from Germany, France, Argentina, Austria, Portugal and Hungary. That accounted for 16 of the 20.

And then there was the country which made up the rest. The country which produced the most managers of all, twice as many as any other. The country with the smallest population of any of the nations represented on the list. No prizes for guessing which one. Four of their twenty greatest football managers were Scots.

Neglecting to include Sir Matt Busby, Bill Shankly, Jock Stein and Sir Alex Ferguson would have reduced the poll to a comedy item. Those four head a field of Scottish managers who have shaped, dictated and dominated football – occasionally in Europe and almost continually in Britain – since day one. It goes without saying that along the way they collected a mountainous haul of trophies in Scotland, England and Europe.

The volume of silverware gathered by Scottish bosses at club level is breathtaking. The European Cup has been lifted by a Scottish manager's hands four times. Stein was the first from Britain to hold it with Celtic in 1967, and a year later it came into the possession of Busby at Manchester United. Ferguson brought it back to United in 1999 and then became the only Scot to win it twice, with another triumph for the club in 2008.

Ferguson, this colossal personality, is the most successful manager in the history of the European club competitions. He also has two European Cup Winners' Cups and two Super Cups to his name (winning each trophy with both Aberdeen and United). Europe has not limited him: he has an Intercontinental Cup and a FIFA Club World Cup success too.

Ferguson, Stein and Busby are among six Scottish managers to have won the big European trophies. Willie Waddell and George Graham took the European Cup Winners' Cup for Rangers and Arsenal respectively and Shankly delivered the UEFA Cup for Liverpool.

For a country with a production line of managerial excellence it was predictable that there would be these spikes of high achievement on the continent. But it is the hold Scots have had on British football which has confirmed a mastery of the skills required to assemble, organise and inspire hugely successful teams. For decades the domestic trophies within Scotland itself were harvested only by home-grown managers. Men like Celtic's Willie Maley (who was born in Northern Ireland but moved to Glasgow at the age of one and played at international level for Scotland) and Rangers' Bill Struth ruled Scottish football from the 1890s to the 1950s. These two giant figures of Old Firm history won 60 leagues and major cups between them.

With Maley, Struth and other natural, charismatic leaders who emerged at clubs like Hearts, Hibs, Aberdeen, Dundee United, and Motherwell, it was little wonder that for almost a century Scottish club chairmen hardly saw the need to appoint an English manager, let alone one from overseas. Few non-Scots have managed in Scottish football. Only in the 1990s did it become fashionable to begin appointing men like Liam Brady, Wim Jansen, Dick Advocaat, John Barnes and Martin O'Neill. Up until then the frequent conquering of England by Scottish managers seemed to amount to compelling evidence that there wasn't much to learn from anyone else. The country has always regarded management as a serious business. It was a Scot who invented the manager's dugout, an idea which spread around the world.

Scooping up all the trophies in their own back yard could never have given Scottish managers worldwide respect. The country is too small for its domestic scene to be regarded as a major stage or proving ground. Scottish managers had to broaden their horizons and follow the money. That meant moving south of the border. They did so at the very beginnings of the professional game – the first paid 'manager' in the world was a Scot, George Ramsay, appointed by Aston Villa in 1886 – and the drain of talent became relentless. It continues to this day. Oddly, the migration usually extended only as far as England: with only a few notable exceptions, Scots have tended not to take charge of European clubs. Of the four giant figures, Busby and Shankly never served Scottish clubs as either a player or a manager and Ferguson gained full recognition only when he began to deliver trophies for Manchester United. Stein is the exception to the rule: the one manager who achieved full international respect and status for what he accomplished while working only in Scotland.

It is what Scots achieved in charge of English clubs that truly marked them out. By the end of the 2009–10 season England's top division had been won 65 times by an Englishman and 39 times by a Scot. Given that the population of England is ten times greater, that is a mighty level of overachievement for the wee country.

The most successful manager in English league history is a Scot. The most successful manager in FA Cup history is a Scot. No Englishman has won their League Cup more times than its most successful Scot. The big four clubs in English football were all shaped to varying extents by Scottish managers. The only managerial legends in Manchester United's history are Busby and Ferguson. Shankly is the most popular and iconic boss Liverpool has ever had. Arsenal's first manager was a Scot. So was Chelsea's.

When the 2009–10 season ended the Champions League was 18 years old and only three men born in England had ever been the manager of a club in its group stages: Ray Harford, Sir Bobby Robson and Stuart Baxter (who is the son of a Glaswegian, spent much of his childhood in Scotland and doesn't mind being described as a Scot). Three managers in 18 years? In the 2008–09 tournament Scotland had three managers in a single Champions League group: Ferguson, Gordon Strachan and Bruce Rioch.

These statistics are trotted out not to belittle the achievements of English managers – men like Herbert Chapman, Bob Paisley and Brian Clough were outstanding leaders who stood comparison with anyone – but to provide a context for the staggering contribution Scots have made in their own country and in the more demanding arena of their larger neighbour. Busby, Shankly, Stein, Ferguson and a supporting cast including George Ramsay, Tom Mitchell, Maley, Struth, Scot Symon, Tommy Docherty, Eddie Turnbull, Jim McLean, Kenny Dalglish, George Graham, Walter Smith, Gordon Strachan, Alex McLeish and David Moyes amount to a remarkable concentration of managerial talent to emerge from a country with roughly the same population as Eritrea or Singapore.

Why the Scots? Why should a small country previously respected for its excellence in finance, engineering, medicine and
science turn out to be such a cradle for football managers? How
did four of the greatest the sport has seen – Busby, Shankly,
Stein and Ferguson – come to be born within 44 miles of each
other?

One approach is to consider the qualities and character traits
which are found in all of the great football bosses. What makes a
manager? No two are exactly alike. There is no textbook for
managerial excellence. All that can be said is that there are shared
characteristics. All of the greats possess a formidable combination of
presence, authority, charisma and toughness. Every one of them
enjoys a certain streetwise intelligence and imagination. Most have
excellent communication skills and a way with words. They show
a fanatical attention to detail. Their thirst for success is unquench-
able.

Scotland has a limitless resource of another quality found in the
greats, namely a deep-rooted obsession with football itself. The
game has held Scotland's imagination for more than 125 years and
the deteriorating quality of her footballers has not weakened the
infatuation. 'In Scotland, football is the game,' said former Scotland
national manager Craig Brown. 'In England there can be the
distraction of cricket and maybe rugby. In Scotland it's only
football.' His predecessor, Andy Roxburgh, held the same view:
'We have had an environment in Scotland, a breeding ground,
which almost encouraged an obsession with football. Football has
been the lifeblood.'

If all great managers have to be football obsessives then a few are
bound to emerge from a country which is populated with fanatics.
'Football is the number one sport in Scotland by a country mile,'
said Tony Higgins, the former Hibs player who became the
Scottish representative of FIFPro, the international players' union,
'The country as a whole is obsessed with it. Eddie Turnbull used to
talk football, football, football. All day long. The best managers I've
known are obsessive characters. Completely obsessed by football. I

remember once having the chance to go into management and a couple of jobs came up. I spoke to the likes of Alex Ferguson and Alex Smith for advice and they said: "If you're going to do it you have to forget your family." They were quite clear. To be a successful manager was a 24–hour-a-day job.'

Jim McLean has said that when he was at the peak of his powers with Dundee United in the 1980s he used to set aside only one hour a week to spend with his wife and two sons. He would meet them at a steakhouse at 4 p.m. on a Thursday and return to work at 5 p.m. A man prepared to make that level of personal sacrifice could not be anything other than a formidable opponent.

For almost a century in Scotland professional football was one of the few realistic means of escaping from a hard, unforgiving, dirty life working down coal mines, in shipyards, or in other forms of heavy engineering. Hundreds of thousands of working-class men left school at 14 or 15 years old without a complete formal education. The majority used football as an exciting way to spend their Saturday afternoons and expose themselves to some rare fresh air with friends. For some it was more than that. For those with the talent, it was their lifeline to social improvement. A better life.

Busby, Stein and Shankly all worked down the pits before earning full-time contracts to play football. The game was Ferguson's way out of a career as a Clydeside toolmaker in the shadow of the shipyards. Each of them was determined that he was never going back. It was the same story in England. Nearly all of England's great managerial figures were hewn from the same mining or heavy industry backgrounds as the Scots. Paisley was a miner. Chapman and Sir Bobby Robson were the sons of miners. Clough and Don Revie were from industrial Middlesbrough.

Every truly exceptional managerial achiever from Britain has emerged from Scotland or the north of England, with the exception of Sir Alf Ramsey from Dagenham. This suggests a correlation between the creation of outstanding leaders and their formative years being spent in the hard, tight, interdependent communities found in coalmining regions or other areas reliant on heavy industry. Why no great sporting managers from the mining heart-land of Wales, then? Well, some argue that the greatest of them all was Welsh: Carwyn James, another miner's son from a pit village. Wales had all the ingredients seemingly required to create great dugout leaders except for the essential obsession with football itself. Her game was rugby union, so James blossomed as the legendary coach of the 1971 British Lions.

It seems that the qualities often found in Scottish people are conducive to creating great football men. Others often portray Scots as being dour, joyless and thrifty, fuelled by hard graft and self-denial. Dundee United beat Motherwell 6–1 in a 1981 Scottish Cup tie and manager McLean withheld the bonus they were due for an exceptional performance. 'There were times when we were sluggish,' he said, 'We might have gone out of the cup.' That appeals to people's perception of the Scots.

The American satirist P.J. O'Rourke thought the whole of Scotland saw its glass as half empty. He wrote: 'Racial character-istics: sour, stingy, depressing beggars who parade around in schoolgirls' skirts with nothing on underneath. Their fumbled attempt at speaking the English language has been a source of amusement for five centuries, and their idiot music has been dreaded by those not blessed with deafness for at least as long.' P.G. Wodehouse was more succinct: 'It is never difficult to distinguish between a Scotsman with a grievance and a ray of sunshine.' Scots would be a sorry bunch if there were no more to them than that. But the satirists are having a laugh. They know the bigger picture.

Many of the great football bosses were shaped by a Scottish upbringing which seemed to arm them with the necessary psy-chological equipment to cope and excel in the job. 'Think about the Scottish psyche,' said Roxburgh, 'Hard-working, conscien-tious about what they're doing, obsessive about what they're doing, with a winning mentality and real competitiveness. Alex Ferguson has always wanted to win at absolutely everything he's ever done. It's like seeing a ten-year-old Scottish kid crying if he doesn't win at a game of cards. There is a whole chemistry of the environment, of where we're brought up, the passion for football, the hard-working mentality. We're not alone in having these qualities. The Italians, the English and so on have these qualities and produce great coaches too. But there are 50 million of them. There are only five million of us.'

So, obsessed with football, hard, competitive and driven by an unremitting work ethic. But what else is in Scotland's favour? The peerless sports writer Hugh McIlvanney, who himself moved from Scotland to conquer his field in England, pointed to a sense of collective self-assurance and the Scots' refusal to be belittled or taken for granted.

'I don't think it's silly to suggest that part of the explanation of Scotland's production of strong, successful managers is the Scots' ingrained inclination to refuse to think that anyone is superior to us,' he said, 'I don't mean the "wha's like us" rubbish. That belongs to another section of our collective personality, and it's a pest. What I'm talking about is the idea that you don't let anyone shit on your head. You don't see any reason to let people be presumptuous towards you and you believe that you will be even money with the best of them. If you are aware of having certain talents you are never going to be intimidated about trying to apply them. It may seem less plausible to mention a profound gift for promoting teamwork as another strength the Scots bring to football manage-ment, given that whenever we get together, even in twos and threes, our fondness for argument is liable to come to the fore. But we're also pretty good at sticking together under pressure and nobody can doubt that the lessons in interdependence Busby, Shankly and Stein learned in the pits, and that Ferguson absorbed in his factory days as a trade union activist, gave them a funda-mental understanding of the value of teamwork. It was reflected in the teams they fielded.'

Teamwork was certainly prominent among the qualities cham-pioned by those Scottish missionaries who helped popularise football around the world a century ago. Scots were at the forefront of the British Empire. Her sailors, engineers, bankers, teachers, scientists and ministers fanned out across the world and that provided a platform to spread education, capitalism, the Bible . . . and football.

'Successful Scottish football managers are part of a much wider trend,' said the leading Scottish historian, Professor Tom Devine, 'It is easy to fall into what I call an "ethnic conceit", but there's no doubt that globally the Scots have punched above their weight in a whole variety of areas, and football management is one of them. It's the same in medicine, in science, in engineering. They played a pre-eminent role, for better and for worse, in the empire. And remember the line "Beam me up, Scotty"? There's significance to that. In *Star Trek* the only ethnic groups on Starship *Enterprise*, apart from the Americans, were a Russian, a Japanese and a Scot.' If there had been an Enterprise XI, Scotty would have been the manager.

In the late 19th and early 20th centuries Scots arrived in South America, Asia and mainland Europe and taught the innovative 'Scottish' football style of short passing and teamwork. At that time the game in England revolved around long kicking or players simply dribbling with the ball until they were dispossessed.

The world was receptive to Scottish ideas. They were hugely significant in establishing football as the sport of the masses in Brazil, Argentina and Uruguay, three countries which would go on to win many World Cups between them. Modern football was introduced to China by a Scot in 1879. Other Scottish coaches worked in Holland, Italy, Hungary and Czechoslovakia. And they flooded into England.

Long before the era of 'tracksuit managers' like Shankly and Stein, men with suits, bowler hats and Scottish accents were in charge of clubs such as Aston Villa (George Ramsay) and Blackburn Rovers (Tom Mitchell). Between 1894 and 1920 Ramsay, a Glaswegian, won six league titles and six FA Cups and Mitchell, from Dumfries, won five FA Cups. Scotland's managerial stamp was on English football from the very beginning.

The early success of Ramsay and Mitchell and the frequency of

Scotland's victories over England in the annual international fixture meant that Scots were seen as having knowledge and understanding of the game. Over the following decades the contribution of Busby, Shankly, Stein, Ferguson and others set that reputation in stone. The modern deterioration of Scotland's playing standards has not affected the common perception that Scots 'know the game'.

'In an odd way the English love the idea of "the Scottish manager",' said the broadcaster, cultural commentator and St Johnstone fan, Stuart Cosgrove, 'That might be to do with national stereotypes and myths. A friend of mine is a Blackpool fan. He once said to me "What Blackpool need is a disciplinarian in charge, they need a hard taskmaster, they need a Scottish manager!" He was just grabbing an available stereotype but he wasn't associating a Scottish manager with talking about diets or psychology or iced baths or whatever. They see the Scottish manager as the solution when players need to be reeled in and disciplined. They see the gnarled, grizzly Jock.'

It is true that Scottish managers are usually perceived as all being gruff, unyielding and pugnacious. Able to handle themselves. 'Even real hard men would not challenge them,' said Hugh McIlvanney, 'Take Paddy Crerand, a real Gorbals guy. Denis Law used to say, "When Paddy starts, put out the lights and lie on the floor . . ." But one glance from Busby could have Paddy quaking, because he didn't want to embarrass himself in Busby's eyes.'

The sense of being a crew of formidable characters has resulted in comparisons being drawn between Scotland's great managers and her most powerful politicians, those at home in the adversarial bearpit of Commons debates. 'All Scottish managers I meet seem to be frustrated politicians,' said spin doctor Alastair Campbell after Ferguson, his friend, gave a 2007 speech about Labour Party values.

Scotland's First Minister, Alex Salmond, could understand what he meant. 'There are certain similarities in character traits between our managers and our politicians,' he said, 'Scottish politicans often come from a debating background, they are disputatious. It would be difficult not to recognise a Scottish debater, and it would be difficult not to recognise a Scottish football manager. Neither of whom would you probably wish to meet on a dark night . . .'

In his autobiography the broadcaster Alan Green devoted a chapter to his fractured relationship with Ferguson and compared him to his predecessors: 'I'm told that Bill Shankly and Jock Stein were both men it was best not to cross. And Matt Busby's withering silences disguised a cut-throat manner when he deemed it necessary. You'll notice, all of them Scots.'

Whatever their field of expertise, leading Scots know how to look after themselves. The author William McIlvanney, the brother of Hugh, once saw a flash of Busby's understated but intimidating power when he somehow struck the wrong note with a question during an interview. 'I still don't know what I said, it was totally innocent, but I must have tread on a toe somehow because he said "But we'll no' be talking about that." He had such strongly fixed parameters. He must have thought I was angling to ask him about something. I don't know what it was. I never got to find out, either. I knew instantly I had to back off. I don't know anyone who would have been keen to take on Bill Shankly, or big Jock, or Alex, and certainly not Matt Busby.'

How could they be anything other than hard men, given the upbringings they had? Their formative years were moulded by tragedy or danger, gnawing hardship, or their parents' worries about money or ill health. They also shouldered heavy responsibility at a young age. Busby was six years old when his father was killed in the First World War. By age twelve he was walking five miles every morning to get to school. He left at fifteen and went down the pits at sixteen. His mother also took a job at the pit head to supplement her widow's pension. Shankly was born within five years and thirty miles of Busby. One of ten children, he left school at fourteen and spent two years as a miner until the pit closed and he was unemployed. Stein was only nine years younger than Shankly and born five-and-a-half miles from Busby. Stein was in the mines by sixteen, working in a pit where a three-month sequence of accidents claimed the lives of seven of his colleagues.

Mining united those three. In 1913 there were 140,000 miners in Scotland and 200 pits in Lanarkshire alone. The industry – this fertile source of great football managers – was gradually wiped out by various factors including the rise of alternative fuels. The last deep mine in Scotland closed in 2002, ending the miner-to-manager route.

'The hardness of their existence and their environment made them challenge and be challenging figures,' said Archie Macpherson, the broadcaster and biographer of Stein, 'It's so obvious, isn't it? They were brought up hard, they remained hard, and their focal point was being able to transmit that hardness in a sport that they knew inside out. That's why all of these men seemed to be able to reach the heights.'

It's no coincidence that Busby, Shankly, Stein and Paisley served time in the dirty, dark and dangerous world of coalmining. The sense of solidarity and comradeship among miners was unsurpassed in any other workforce. Men effectively placed their lives in the hands of their colleagues every time they entered a cage and were lowered down the shaft to the seam. They might be suffocated, crushed by a pit collapse, trapped in an underground fire or killed or injured some other way. The unity of purpose, the shared exposure to death and danger, hardened the miners and enabled them to deal with any other difficulty life might present to them. When they emerged blinking into the daylight at the pit head they rejoined a local community entirely united by reliance on the mine.

'We all know that, without any desire to over-romanticise mining communities, there is no question at all that they had a great spirit and an imposed spirit of togetherness,' said Hugh McIlvanney, 'Men underground had to believe in teamwork of the most basic kind because their lives could depend upon it. I don't think it's too fanciful to suggest that the values of mining contributed seriously to the approach that men such as Stein,

Shankly and Busby had to their later work in football. A lot of people would possibly sneer at the connection I'm making, but I think they would be foolish to do so. These are not the only men who drew their wisdom for working in football from a background in mining. Jock worked underground until he was 27. He once said to me that he knew that when he was working in the pit that wherever he went, and whatever he did, he would never work with better men.'

The McIlvanney brothers, journalist Hugh and author William, can talk with some authority about miners given that their father spent part of his working life down the pits. 'Jock once said "If you've been down a pit you're not going to worry too much about a wee kerfuffle in a football club",' said Hugh, 'It gave them terrific perspective on life. They had that experience in the wider world. So when it came right down to it was a football player ever going to bother them that much? Not only had they had to confront real physical danger, but there was the fact they had dealt with really hard men who would be hard with them if they didn't handle themselves properly. So if a football player might have tried to act the goat with them it really didn't have much of an effect.'

Archie Macpherson used to detect an attitude when he saw his friend, Stein, engage some adversary or other in an argument. 'When you saw Stein taking swipes at people he gave a sense that he was thinking "You don't know what you're talking about, you haven't had to face the challenges that I've had". That mining background bred self-confidence bordering almost on arrogance, as it did in Shankly's case, albeit a pleasant, almost comedic arrogance. It's maybe too obvious to pick up the mining community thing and dismiss it, say it can't be that which shaped the great managers, but there is little doubt that Stein spent the early part of his life feeding the rats his piece down the mines. He also had men die beside him in an accident down Bothwell pit. I don't think miners went down consciously thinking that they might not get out alive, but I think the awareness existed. Life was about survival, making ends meet, and with it an aspiration to get out of that. Anything else in life is probably relatively easier to cope with after that.'

Given the aspects of trust, loyalty, solidarity, resilience and pragmatism required to survive life in the pits, or the shipyards, Tom Devine has said that great human qualities were forged there. 'These places were universities.'

Ferguson's upbringing was steeped in shipbuilding. His father and brother worked in the Govan yards and although Ferguson himself did not, the yards were on his doorstep. He was an apprentice toolmaker and the sense of community around the noisy, bustling Clydeside yards was a constant source of wonder to him. At the peak of production 100,000 men were employed in 33 yards on Clydeside. Today there are only three yards and fewer than 4000 workers. Ferguson has talked of the 'intensity of shared experience' found when a community is reliant on a single industry. He has left no one in any doubt that Govan made him. If he were born today he would be in a different Govan and he could not evolve as quite the same character.

'I grew up accepting that shipbuilding was part of the fabric of my existence,' Ferguson has said. 'It has been said that the values great managers like Jock Stein, Sir Matt Busby, Bill Shankly and Bob Paisley brought to their jobs in football were rooted in their mining background. I have no doubt it is true and I am sure, too, that any success I have had in handling men, and especially in creating a culture of loyalty and commitment in teams I have managed, owes much to my upbringing among the working men of Clydeside.'

William McIlvanney has admired Ferguson's sense of 'Don't forget where ye come fae'. He said: 'I was at a game at Old Trafford once and the match programme had small biographies of the two managers. It said "Alex Ferguson, born Govan". Not "born Glasgow", but Govan. It was that precision of knowing where he really came from. Not a Glasgwegian, but a Govanite.'

Football became Ferguson's lifeline to escape. Not to escape Govan – never that – but to escape the uncertainty, monotony and limitations of life as a toolmaker. The lives of working-class Scottish males seemed predetermined and unalterable in the first half of the 20th century. The sons of miners became miners themselves. The sons of shipyard workers became shipyard workers. Further education was all but closed to the majority of the working-class population and there was an accepted inevitability about leaving school, taking a place in the prevailing industry of the region, and settling into the same hard, subsistence existence their parents had gone through.

Professional sport offered the prospect of a better life for the precious view with the talent to merit full-time status. Boxing became a doorway for some but many more used football. Imagine how precious a footballer's contract would be to someone whose alternative was the darkness, dirt and danger of a life down the pits . . .

'For unskilled, semi-skilled and skilled labour in Scotland, as Shankly said, football is much wider and deeper than simply a game,' said Tom Devine. 'Almost all of these guys left school at 14 or 15. Their aspirations in their particular cultural or social milieu were to excel in the area or areas they knew best, and one of those areas was football.'

Busby left the pits behind when he joined Manchester City, aged 18. Shankly signed for Carlisle United when he was the same age. Stein once said 'You don't want to be underground all your life'. A less talented player than the other two, he had to wait until he was 27 before Llanelli became the first club to offer him full-time professional status. When the Welsh club ran into financial difficulties Stein feared losing his full-time status and having to go back down the pits. He was spared that when Celtic offered a contract to return and play in Scotland.

'People would not have thought that men coming from those areas could become successful businessmen or successful football managers,' said Macpherson. 'But they did. I think they cared less about the consequences of their actions. They took chances, and taking those chances was part of the gamble that they took in life.

They took chances that perhaps someone from a more protected, or middle-class or even upper working-class environment wouldn't take, because there the taking of chances simply wasn't necessary. Nobody cushioned them or mothered them. Some might have gone on to boxing but the sensible and athletic ones saw football as an opportunity to show what they were capable of doing.'

Serving time in 'real' jobs before entering football was enormously significant in determining the attitudes, priorities and sense of perspective that men like Busby, Shankly and Stein brought into management. Footballers tend to emerge from the working class, even today, and here were men who knew what it meant to graft for a living.

Ferguson was cut from a similar cloth, born during the Second World War and now the last of his kind in top-class British football management. 'Alex does represent much the same background and much the same values as the great managers of previous generations, especially those three ex-miners, Stein, Busby and Shankly,' said Hugh McIlvanney, 'Having served his full apprenticeship as a toolmaker he knows about earning a living outside football. That's pretty rare for managers now. These days they usually come through from within the insular world of football and they are not directly acquainted with what goes on in more ordinary workplaces. I'm not suggesting they don't have enough imagination to realise what it is like to make a living elsewhere, but they don't have the personal experience of "earning your keep" in any area other than football. And a narrower background tends to mean narrower perspectives.'

Mining and the yards were universities which produced a handful of extraordinary football managers and hundreds of thousands of socialists. Labour was the default party of the Scottish working class for decades. The political sympathies of men like Busby, Shankly, Stein and Ferguson were left-wing, aware and supportive of the issues and concerns affecting the common man. Even a younger manager such as David Moyes has talked of being 'dead against' private schools. There was a minute's silence at the Labour Party conference in 1981 when Shankly's death was announced. Busby and Stein were interested in miners' issues for decades after they left the pits.

Stein and Ferguson walked together to a game at Hibs' Easter Road Stadium during the 1984 miners' strike. There were collection buckets outside for the striking miners. Ferguson, his thoughts occupied by the game he was about to see, walked past. Stein stopped, flashed his younger friend a challenging stare and asked 'Here, are you not forgetting something?'. Ferguson had forgotten himself, no more than that. He was as sympathetic to the miners as Stein was and quickly dug out a fiver for the bucket.

'The miners have been crucial in the evolution of socialism,' said William McIlvanney, 'They needed communal values. If you didn't have a cup of sugar you'd be given a cup of sugar. If you didn't have a suit for a funeral you'd be lent a suit for a funeral. There was that sense of mutual deprivation that led to a sense of mutual sharing. Remember Shankly saying "If you get them [footballers] to pool all the things they can do for each other, it's a form of socialism: without the politics, of course . . ." That giving of respect and demanding of respect would be crucial in a managerial position. Now you have players with manic self-esteem because of the money they get. If you have someone like Ashley Cole crying in his car because he thought Arsenal were offering him "only" 50 grand a week, I just find that pathetic. If values have been distorted to such an extent that you are emotionally distraught at not getting the other 30 grand a week they should also be giving you, it's time to forget it. Abdicate the species.'

The four pre-eminent managers were instinctively drawn to the charismatic Govan trade union leader Jimmy Reid, and vice-versa. Here was a gruff, strong, articulate, hugely impressive man cut from the same cloth as themselves. When Reid led a work-in in a proud attempt to spare the Upper Clyde Shipbuilders (UCS) yards from government closure in the early 1970s the great football figures supported his cause financially and emotionally. 'They were

all of the left, insofar as they had any politics in them at all,' said
Reid, talking to the authors in one of his last interviews before his
death in August 2010. 'They were proud of their origins, they
identified with the Scottish working class and that never changed,
no matter how successful they were. They were good guys. If you
knew them they were very open and if they could help in any way
they would do so. I know you have to be able to be a bit of a
bastard to be a good football manager, but these guys were all good
working-class men and proud of that. Shankly talked about football being a form of socialism. You could argue that in the Scottish
working class a huge proportion of men you might call "natural
leaders" went into trade unionism or football.'

It is an intriguing idea, that fate might have delivered Shankly or
Ferguson into a career in trade unionism or politics, or a charismatic leader like Reid into football management. Ferguson quickly
became the representative of the players' union at whichever club
he joined. It was common for the union leader in any club's
dressing room to be a Scot.

'There was the idea of that generation being inextricably linked to
trade unionism, to the nationalised industries, to industry itself,' said
Stuart Cosgrove, 'Just like today every player has an agent, in those
days every player had a relationship to a place of work that wasn't
football. Because Scotland had the big ones – coal, shipyards, steel,
all the big, physical industries – it had a culture of organised labour.
I'm convinced if you look at any of the big English clubs it would
have been Scots who were among the first players' union leaders,
whether it was Jimmy Sirrel or Shankly or whoever. I think the
Scottish dressing-room leaders would also have been anti-"the
system" or anti-the directors or whatever. Anti-establishment.
Within a year of being at St Johnstone Alex Ferguson had already
fallen out with the club. You get the feeling they would often be in a
tense relationship with the directors. Ferguson at some of his clubs,
Shankly at Preston, Docherty throughout his career.'

When Sir Alf Ramsey took over as manager of Birmingham
City one of his first acts was to say: 'There's one thing in this

dressing room I don't like . . . there are too many Scots.' This was not a criticism of the quality of players like Kenny Burns, Jimmy Calderwood and John Connolly. Ramsey was acknowledging that the Scots would be strong characters, unionised barrack-room lawyers who were liable to give him trouble if they thought he was taking liberties.

'Mining and the shipyards developed a strong background of solidarity,' said Salmond, 'Us against the world. United we stand. Community. There's that streak in our great football managers. Maybe a lot of great motivators have that in one way or another. I don't think it's necessarily the fact that they came from mining, it's much more about the solidarity issue. A football manager has to be able to speak to a predominantly working-class group of football players. There are some very smart guys who made it as players – Davie Weir, Maurice Malpas, Alex McLeish are clever men – but even now the number of them who have degrees would be quite low. Craig Levein is an intellectual guy but he also knocked out Graeme Hogg with a punch in a game at Stark's Park. So intellectual or not, you've got to be able to communicate in a language the squad understands. We know that Sir Alex Ferguson does – often with some force – and we know that Jock Stein did. We also know that both of these men and others have the ability to control the uncontrollable. Who else could have managed Jimmy Johnstone?'

Shankly made endless connections between football and socialism. Stein had been a pit delegate representing the concerns of his fellow miners. During his apprenticeship as a toolmaker Ferguson served as a shop steward in the Amalgamated Engineering Union and was actively involved in two Clydeside strikes in 1960 and 1964.

Busby's leanings were similarly left-wing. 'Any time I went to Manchester, if there were any posters up saying "Jimmy Reid speaking" or whatever it was, Matt would be on the phone saying I'd to come down to Old Trafford on the Saturday and be a guest of the club,' said Reid. 'It was like being part of a Clydeside Mafia!

They looked after their ain. In my experience they were very supportive and sympathetic towards whatever problems were affecting the men of the yards. I got to know them all very well. Walter Smith is cut from similar cloth. He has a kind of Scottish working-class character. Although they don't make a song and dance about it, they are proud of it and they hold on to it. They are principled guys. They represent values that the Scottish working class used to hold quite dear. The funny thing was that when they became managers they would all have their wee fall-outs with the players' unions!'

Stein and Shankly were teetotal, in defiance of the heavy-drinking environments in which they were brought up. Busby drank in moderation but saw his greatest playing talent, George Best, reduced by the bottle. Ferguson likes a fine wine and owned a pub while he was manager of St Mirren. Perhaps Bryan Robson, Norman Whiteside and Paul McGrath believed that would mean he would turn a blind eye to their drinking when he arrived at Manchester United. Instead, Ferguson identified the 'drinking club' as a massive problem and obliterated it by getting rid of Whiteside and McGrath. Robson would have gone too, but his skills were indispensable.

Busby, Stein, Shankly and Ferguson were all spared the predisposition towards heavy drinking which grips so many working-class Scots. At the level they reached, drunkenness and hangovers would be incompatible with the energy, drive and focus required to deliver relentless achievement.

Ferguson brings sharpness, vitality, commitment and competitiveness to all his passions. His 1999 autobiography, *Managing My Life*, was an enormous undertaking and he went about it with the ambition and thoroughness that he has brought to management itself. At almost 500 pages it was far larger than most sports biographies, albeit he had rather more to fit in than most. It won the 2000 British Book Awards book of the year. The pages reveal the intelligence, the hunger for knowledge, and the range of interests that Ferguson shares with all the truly exceptional managers.

Leaving school early or missing out on further education was no impediment to them. They could hold their own in any company. It can be no coincidence that every one has been refreshingly free from the curse of religious prejudice which still pollutes the west of Scotland. Stein, Shankly, Ferguson, Graham, Smith, Dalglish, McLeish and Moyes all emerged from Rangers-supporting families, of varying passion, and Busby and Docherty from Celtic ones. All were blessed with wise, principled parents who drummed it into them that there was no place for sectarianism in their lives. That open-mindedness was the intellectual equivalent of having a goal of a start.

'A lot of the Scottish managers are self-taught,' said Tony Higgins, 'It's like the days of the old Communist Party in Scotland, the Jimmy Reid thing of being self-taught, self-educated. Guys like Fergie read books on being managers and tried to understand it, not from attending a course in university but by reading books about leaders and things like that. He would read about Fidel Castro, or whoever, to absorb lessons about leadership.'

The football historian, broadcaster and journalist Bob Crampsey – a former 'Brain of Britain' and semi-finalist on *Mastermind* – described Stein as having 'the most powerful intelligence' he had ever encountered.

Hugh McIlvanney described Stein as a sort of 'uneducated intellectual'. 'Many Scots are quick to develop a certain world-liness, a useful freedom from naiveté,' he said, 'Along with an alertness to human foibles, there's often the sense of keen intelligence applied in a practical way. Jock Stein had those advantages, and lot of others. He had a very special mind. Nothing about the game could fool him. He was a complex man, capable of being melancholic, of sinking into moods that took him to depths of introspection. And, naturally, he was too thoughtful not to have serious interests beyond the game. But his passion for football was immense and when he committed himself to it the quality of his mind meant he was a master of team management.'

This form of street intelligence, gained in the rough-and-tumble of their neighbourhoods or the mines or the yards, gave the great managers the priceless advantage of understanding what made men tick. Alex McLeish said, 'A lot of us have tried to copy big Jock and Fergie and might think it's about making up fancy words and bamboozling our players with tactical stuff and making long-winded speeches. But then you hear them and you remember that they made it really simple.'

The greats have always been able to strike the balance between encouragement and intimidation. They could sense which of their men responded to an arm around the shoulder and which needed a kick up the backside. Ferguson has always been selective about who was on the receiving end of 'The Hairdryer', the ferocious, nose-to-nose bawling he administers to a player who has displeased him.

'You have to look at the forthright honesty and integrity of these guys,' said Craig Brown, 'The blunt truth from the Shanklys and Steins of the world. If you speak from the heart and you know the game it's impossible for anyone to dispute those qualities. Davie Moyes embodies those qualities right now: straightforward, right down the line, no flannel. There's an awful lot of bullshit in English management but the Scottish guys are right down the line. They are complimentary when required, critical when required. And there's a wee touch of humour about them all too. I think a wee sense of humour is useful in a dressing room.'

It has been said that all Scots have a great sense of humour because it is a free gift. Very droll. What's certainly true is that men like Shankly, Tommy Docherty and Gordon Strachan have enriched football with some great lines over the years. Scottish managers as a whole are seen as having the gift-of-the-gab and being more than capable of holding their own if a rival or journalist tries to put one over on them.

Shankly once claimed that the fact continental Europe was on different time zones to Britain was a conspiracy to inconvenience Liverpool Football Club in the European and UEFA Cups. He once told his players that Manchester United's Paddy Crerand, whom they were about to face, was 'slower than steam rising off a dog turd'. When United's players arrived at Anfield before a game he emerged in their way holding a raffle ticket and told them: 'Guess what, boys? I've had a go on the tickets that give the time when the away team will score. And it says here "in a fortnight".'

On what it felt like to play for Scotland, he said: 'You look at your dark blue shirt, and the wee lion looks up at you and says "Get out after those English bastards!"'

No manager has ever delivered a line like Shankly could, although there have been others who knew how to produce quite a quote. Docherty used to craft and rehearse some of his one-liners before delivery. When a reporter once asked Strachan what he took from the game, he got the reply: 'I've got more important things to think about. I've got a yoghurt to finish, the expiry date is today.' The charismatic former Partick Thistle manager John Lambie produced one of football's greatest quips when his physio told him during a match that their concussed player, Colin McGlashan, didn't know who he was. 'Tell him he's Pele and get him back on.'

It helped that all of these lines were delivered in that rich, resonant accent. The accent is one of Scotland's great little gifts. Though Scots may be mocked for being incomprehensible to others, in fact the ability to communicate has taken many to the highest positions in broadcasting and, it seems, has been an advantage in management. 'I've said this to people at the BBC,' said Gordon Strachan, an occasional pundit himself, 'There's something about the accent that sounds authoritative.' Players know that their Scottish manager's seductive burr can switch, instantly, to a deep and rumbling sense of menace.

Salmond will always remember the power of McLeish's voice – and his deliberately sparing use of it – as he spoke to the Scotland players before the final, all-or-nothing Euro 2008 qualifier against Italy at Hampden in 2007. 'One of the privileges of being First Minister was that I was in the dressing room before that Scotland–Italy game. I was just watching Alex. I was very impressed by his non-verbal motivational techniques before they went out. It wasn't King Henry at Agincourt, or Robert the Bruce at Bannockburn, or William Wallace/Mel Gibson in *Braveheart*, but it was very effective. It was just "The folk are here, let's go and do it". Very short, staccato, very effective. That was just before kick-off.'

Attaching some significance to the accent is not as flippant as it may seem. 'I think people hear the Scottish accent and they associate that with someone who won't be fucked around in the dressing room,' said Cosgrove.

'Maybe the gruff accent frightens people,' said Jimmy Sinclair, the SFA's former head of youth development who later joined Rangers, 'Even now I listen to Scottish accents down in England and they are so different. A Scottish accent brings its own football authority. You often hear Scottish pundits on television or radio and so the accent is associated with opinions on the game and – more importantly – knowledge of the game. Fergie sets the tone right away. With the pundits you have Alan Hansen, Gordon Strachan, Andy Gray. There is an association between knowledge of football and Scottishness. The perception is that a Scottish guy is going to know his football.'

In the end there can be no single explanation for Scotland punching above its weight in the production of excellent football managers. Management, like the men themselves, is too complex for that. If it was as simple as saying 'great managers used to work as miners' then there would be tens of thousands of them, not a handful. The great forces of background, upbringing, hardship and discipline which shaped them were also be found in cities and regions which created no exceptional managers. Over the past century and more there have been millions of intelligent men who were obsessed with football and devoted endless time and energy to it. None of them became great managers. Hundreds of hard-working, streetwise, former players have tried management and found they couldn't do it to any noteworthy level.

No two great managers are entirely alike. In terms of their friendship Busby and Shankly were as thick as thieves but in some respects their personalities were polar opposites. There is a vast archive of fantastic, funny, imaginative Shankly quotes; Busby did not trade in quotes. Shankly's brother, Bob, was a successful manager who said even less. Docherty was a showman who buzzed with life in front of cameras and microphones; Dalglish would have enjoyed his career even more if he had never had to do a press conference. There is no textbook for managerial excellence, at least not one in which the entire checklist must be completed. It is each to his own.

The inescapable fact is that these Scots – Busby, Shankly, Stein, Ferguson, all the others – surely would have been strong, impressive and successful in any walk of life. The influence of mining or the shipyards or poverty or natural empathy with others or an obsession with football simply added more layers to formidable personalities who always had the potential for greatness.

It just so happened that Scotland could offer the perfect brew of conditions for these charismatic figures to blossom into natural leaders. Scotland's obsession with football meant that talented men were channelled towards the game. Working-class poverty gave them a ferocious drive to better themselves socially and economically. Exposure to danger in traditional Scottish industries like mining or the shipyards hardened them, made them fearless about comparatively trivial decisions, and it made them ferociously disciplined. Socialism – the prevailing political ethos of the Scottish working class – gave them a precious affinity with supporters and their own hungry young players. They instinctively gave and commanded respect.

Stuart Cosgrove has an amusing theory that the quintessential Scottish manager once popped up in a context which had nothing to do with football. 'Look at the prison warden in the sitcom *Porridge*. Prison Officer Mackay, played by Fulton Mackay. He looks the part, he comes in, he cuts through the shit, he knows Ronnie Barker's Fletch is at it, he knows who the jokers are, and it always feels like he's walked into the equivalent of a dressing room. He's got the accent, the gnarled looks, the disciplinarian style. He's the greatest manager Scotland never had . . . And the thing is, that character couldn't have been in *Porridge* unless it was recognisable to an English audience as a stereotype – and actually quite a positive one – of Scots. I think there are still a lot of English people who see exactly that sort of guy when they think of a Scottish manager.'

Strachan took the idea one step further. 'I think Prison Officer Mackay is based on Shankly. Think about it. Disciplined. Everything about him was spotless. Fergie was always like that, his shoes were always spotless. They look the part. We like that. When my players are training I do the running with them. I'm asking players to be disciplined. So they won't see me carrying fat, they won't see me smoking or taking a drink. Never. Because it isn't good for you.'

The greatest Scottish manager of them all is Ferguson. There is a phrase he comes out with now and again which is delivered with a satisfied grin to an audience, usually, of English football journalists. It is a joke intended only to put them in their place, but in the context of management few would entirely dismiss it as a hollow description. He calls Scots 'the master race'.

Chapter Two

The Pioneers

How Scottish managers have won in England for 100 years

It all began one summer's day in 1886. What seemed like a small, unremarkable advertisement appeared in the pages of a local newspaper in the English Midlands. 'Wanted: manager for Aston Villa Football Club, who will be required to devote his whole time under direction of committee. Salary £100 per annum. Applications with reference must be made not later than June 23 to Chairman of Committee, Aston Villa Club House, 6 Witton Road, Aston.'

Readers of the Birmingham *Daily Gazette* might have been slightly puzzled about what it meant. Football clubs were still quite new and unfamiliar in those days but those that did exist were led by a secretary. Why did they need 'a manager'? More to the point, what *was* a manager? The job description in their advertisement was unusual, but Aston Villa then did something which was to become very familiar indeed. They gave the position to a Scot, a Glaswegian called George Ramsay. The decision made a minor piece of history. It meant that technically the first paid 'manager' anywhere in world football was Scottish.

This was no leap into the unknown for Aston Villa. Ramsay had been in with the bricks at the club long before the formality of applying for and receiving the position of manager. He had been living in Birmingham since 1871, having arrived to work as a clerk in an iron merchant's. Some years later he was out for a stroll when he saw some men thrashing a football around Aston Park with enthusiasm and strength but little skill. Ramsay asked if he could play – at first the group strained to understand his Scottish accent – and when they agreed they were immediately startled by his ability. He could control the ball, dribble it and pass far more skilfully than any of them. Here was precisely the sort of fusion of English and Scottish styles which was happening all over Britain. The unskilled group was connected with Villa Cross Wesleyan Chapel and when the kickabout was over they surrounded Ramsay, bombarding him with questions, one of which was 'Will you join our club?'. They became Aston Villa.

Ramsay soon became Villa's captain and, as word spread about how fine a player he was, spectators began turning up to watch the little man nicknamed 'Scotty'. He helped identify an area of ground in the city where it would be possible to charge people a small admission fee. That contributed to the club's growth, as did his organisational skills and ability to coach the other players in training. Soon Villa were fine exponents of the 'passing game'.

The club converted from amateurism to professionalism in 1885 and the newspaper advertisement to which Ramsay responded was placed in June of the following year. Although the wording of the advertisement described the position as 'manager' the convention of the time was followed and Ramsay was generally referred to as the club's secretary.

Villa's teams were picked each week by their committee – including another Scot, William McGregor, the founder of the English Football League in 1888 – but as the secretary of that committee Ramsay's contribution was immense. He looked after the players, coached and trained them, and was the primary figure in recruitment and transfers. Archie Hunter, the famous Villa centre forward and Ayrshireman, said: 'It was in the 1886–87 season that Mr George Ramsay, the first Villa captain, became our manager. In that season we practically carried everything before us.'

It was the start of what is still known as Aston Villa's 'Golden Age', a period so influenced by their Scots – Ramsay, Hunter, McGregor et al – that they adopted a Lion Rampant on their club badge. Under Ramsay Villa won the FA Cup in his first season, 1887, and did so again in 1895, 1897, 1905, 1913 and 1920. With six victories (from eight cup finals) Ramsay remains the most successful manager in the history of the FA Cup.

There were league titles, too. Villa proved themselves to be the finest team in England in 1894, 1896, 1897 (making them only the second club to win the league and cup double), 1899, 1900 and 1910. These days football does not know or recognise Ramsay. But in terms of winning the major English trophies his haul is second only to Sir Alex Ferguson. His chairman, McGregor, described him as 'The little, dapper, well-built laddie.' Ramsay held his position as secretary (ie, de facto manager) of Villa until 1926, when he was 71, and then became an advisor and vice-president. Nine years later he passed away, ending a fifty-nine-year association with a football club that he came across by chance during a stroll in a Birmingham park. On his headstone he is described as 'Founder of Aston Villa'.

The evolution of the football 'manager' was a vague and unscientific business. Some clubs appointed a manager, essentially in the form that we would recognise them today, years or even decades ahead of their rivals. Others were slower to adapt, or even resistant to change. In the early 1870s all football clubs existed on amateur terms as a vehicle for youths and men to play the game as a pastime. Matters such as fitness, training, organisation, coaching and the trading of players seemed much too trivial for any club to go to the bother of employing someone to deal with them.

As football's popularity increased and the clubs grew in size, their owners and directors began to find more and more of their own personal business time being occupied by what they had intended to treat as an enjoyable hobby. As the day-to-day running of clubs became too onerous, these chairmen and directors appointed secretaries to deal with the administration and eventually secretary-managers who could also take charge of team affairs. The process was accelerated by the widespread change from amateurism to professionalism in the 1880s. Eventually the directors' selection committees relinquished control of picking the team at all. At last the role of manager was distinct and established. This chain of events happened at every club, although for some it was well into the 20th century before the manager actually picked the team.

There was no mystery as to why some of the first secretary-managers and managers at English clubs were Scottish. From as early as the 1870s English clubs had offered inducements to sign the leading Scottish players, whose intricate passing, movement and teamwork elevated the game to a level which was not evident elsewhere. It was seen as a sophisticated approach and they were nicknamed 'The Scotch Professors'. When England accepted professionalism in 1885 Scottish players flooded south to earn from football. Villa, Sheffield Wednesday, Arsenal, Liverpool, Bolton, Newcastle United, Sunderland, Middlesbrough and especially Preston North End had significant Scottish representations. And so did Blackburn Rovers.

Tom Mitchell was born in Dumfries and moved to England in his 20s. What became a glorious relationship with Blackburn began soon after they were formed in 1875 and he was appointed as their secretary-manager in 1884. They won the FA Cup that year, the first of five occasions in which they would do so over the next eight seasons under Mitchell. It was no coincidence: the best players of the day were Scottish, and appointing a Scot in charge gave Blackburn an advantage when it came to recruitment.

Mitchell, an imposing, formidable man who had been a highly respected referee, resigned from Blackburn late in 1896. Twelve years was enough. His reputation was such that the following year he moved to Arsenal to become the great London club's first professional manager. He resigned there early in 1898, without adding to his haul of trophies, and returned to Blackburn.

Others followed Ramsay and Mitchell. In 1901 John Cameron, from Ayr, did something no other manager has ever achieved.

Tottenham's victory in the FA Cup final that year remains the only time a club from outwith the English League has won that trophy. Spurs were in the Southern League at the time. Cameron began as their player/manager in 1899 – he scored in their FA Cup final replay win over Sheffield United – and remained in charge until 1907. He was a cool customer. He was the last Spurs player to walk onto the field for the cup final and did so nonchalantly, his hands in his pockets.

Cameron had what would later seem like typical Scottish socialist instincts: he was the first secretary of the Association Footballers' Union, aimed at improving footballers' terms. But he was also aware of a manager's place in the social order. 'The manager is not the sole governing authority,' he once said. 'As regards his status, he is indubitably the servant of the club directors.'

Scots were everywhere, represented extensively at almost every major club and occupying many of the positions of power in English football. Sunderland were the champions of England in 1902 under the management of Alex Mackie, from Banff. They scored only 50 times in 34 games but their defence was excellent. In 1904 there was the unique distinction of the Scottish and English FA Cups being won by a pair of brothers. After Willie Maley had harvested one of his multiple Scottish Cup wins with Celtic, seven days later his brother, Tom, delivered the first major trophy in Manchester City's history by lifting the FA Cup with a final win over Bolton. The following year, 1905, John Robertson, from Dumbarton, was appointed as the first manager of Chelsea.

Official records show that Newcastle United teams were picked by a selection committee until 1930. The club secretary, though, was Frank Watt, another Scot, and most 'Toon' historians would recognise and appreciate his primary role in the organisation, coaching and selection of the sides which won the English title in 1905, 1907, 1909 and 1927, and the FA Cup in 1910 and 1924. Officially Watt was not the manager, because he did not pick the team, but unofficially he is acknowledged as the longest-serving and most successful the club has ever had. Newcastle were in the

old Second Division when he joined in 1895 and he served them
for 36 years. He was replaced as the man in charge of team affairs by
another Scot, Ayrshireman Andy Cunningham, who won another
FA Cup for Newcastle in 1932.

The only major trophy in Bradford City's history was the 1911
FA Cup, won under the management of Peter O'Rourke, another
Ayrshireman, who was in charge for 16 years. Lengthy spells at the
helm of a club were by no means unusual at the time. Peter
McWilliam, from Inverness, took charge of Tottenham in 1912
and did not leave until 1927. During that period he led them to
promotion, won the 1921 FA Cup, and finished second in the
championship the following season. A quiet but popular figure, he
was said to be so trusting of his players that he did not bother to
explain the revised offside law to them. He figured that they could
work it out for themselves.

Matt McQueen was only three months short of his 60th
birthday, and a member of Liverpool's board of directors with
no previous experience of management, when he was asked to take
over on a temporary basis in February, 1923. He had previously
played for the club, as well as for Hearts and Scotland, and had
subsequently served as a qualified referee. Liverpool were defend-
ing English champions and top of the league when previous
manager David Ashworth surprisingly resigned, but McQueen
saw them over the line to win the 1923 title and he remained
in charge for another five years.

Johnny Cochrane was a character. He had won the Scottish Cup
for St Mirren, his home-town club, in 1926 before taking over at
Sunderland two years later. In more than 500 games over 11 years
on Wearside he made them champions of England in 1936 and
won the FA Cup for the first time in their history the following
season. Short, round, dapper, fond of a bowler hat, a cigar and a
dram, Cochrane had a singular attitude to preparation. The
Sunderland and England star of the day, Raich Carter, once fondly
recalled: 'Team talk? Johnny used to stick his head around the door
at five to three and, in a cloud of cigar smoke, ask: "Who are we

playing today, lads?" We'd chorus: "Arsenal, boss". And he would just say: "Oh well, we'll piss that lot". Then he'd close the door and be gone. The manager's job in those days was to assemble a good team and then let it play.'

It worked. Cochrane was the last Scottish manager to win major trophies in England before the outbreak of the Second World War. But the art of management was changing. Cochrane's charming, laissez-faire attitude could not succeed when football resumed after the war. By the time Scottish managers Doug Livingstone and Les McDowall were winning the FA Cup for Newcastle United and Manchester City respectively in the mid-1950s the game was beginning to fall under the spell of a new breed of manager; hard, powerful figures who would stand up to interfering directors, insist on total authority, and impose their will and force of personality on a club from top to bottom.

The great Yorkshireman Herbert Chapman had shown elements of this with his meticulous, innovative, open-minded and highly-successful approach to managing Huddersfield and Arsenal in the 1920s and '30s. Now society as a whole was changing. The old class divisions were being broken down and football was on the brink of its next step.

It would be taken by a Scot, from the wreckage of a bombed-out ground in the southwest of Manchester.

Chapter Three
The Four Kings

Sir Matt Busby

*'Let the angels help him make a team that will give
divine pleasure to all the souls in heaven, just as his
boys gave joy here on earth.'*

Busby said he would be waiting in a car outside Manchester
Airport. Over the phone the voice had been heavy, strong,
familiar: 'What time are you due to get down from Glasgow,
son? Twelve? That'll be fine. I'll be there, son.' He had been kind
enough to agree to a rare interview about his upbringing, his
family, and all those wonderful years around Manchester United.
At twelve he called again to say he was parked outside the airport in
a black Mercedes, bang on time. Busby was a polite, busy, sociable
man in his mid-70s. The first thing you noticed about him was the
top of his head and its thick covering of wild grey hair. Momen-
tarily it seemed wrong, but then this was another Busby. The son,
not the father.

Sandy Busby led an enormous army of mourners when his dad
died in 1994. It was Manchester's equivalent of a state funeral. The
people braved a cold wind and lined the streets in their thousands
to pay their last respects as Sir Matt Busby's funeral cortege drove
from Chorlton to Old Trafford and finally on to the city's Southern
Cemetery. They began arriving three hours early to claim a good

vantage point along the route. United colours hung from lamp-posts and railings. A scarf was draped across the coffin. Men, women and children stood in silence, watching the hearse or briefly bowing their heads. For the older ones, who saw Busby and his football in the flesh as well as in vibrant television footage, there were tears.

Busby's funeral was a re-enactment of one aspect of his extra-ordinary life. Men had always fallen silent around him. The defining characteristic of this enormous football figure was an effortless authority. No manager has ever exuded such stature and aura, and he had it long before he won a league or the European Cup. Any who came close – Jock Stein being the most obvious candidate – did so with the help of some occasional demonstrations of black temper. Busby commanded a room with-out uttering a word. A blethering group would hush and look towards him as soon as he walked through a door. He was not a bully and he didn't swear. It was unusual for him to even raise his voice. A glance was enough. He controlled a vast football club in a way that no other manager has ever done. Being around Busby was like being in the presence of a good and popular king.

Players dreaded his disapproval. Even the greatest and the hardest of them got a knot in their stomach if they felt they had let him down. They wanted to please him. He quietly understood that and used it. He was able to transmit confidence and belief to his men. All through his life Busby somehow exuded a sense of force and power behind an unchanging façade of genial composure. Everyone knew the toughness which lay beneath that gentle exterior. There was never any need for him to prove it. Anyone who didn't instinctively respect Matt Busby needed their head examined.

'It wasn't a physical thing with me dad,' said Sandy, 'He did it with his tongue. I was on the receiving end a couple of times. He was always right, in the end. I knew that I hadn't to get into trouble with him. If I did it was his tongue that did the damage, he didn't do it physically. He looked after his lads, the players, and he looked after me.'

Physically he was strong and imposing, with large features and a kind, intelligent face. He treated people as his equal even when they knew that it was not the case. Others were made to feel as though they mattered around Busby. He was modest and humble, a man of humanity and warmth. That amounted to an array of attributes which would have elevated him to greatness in any walk of life. But he had more than that. He possessed an exceptional knowledge and understanding of football and an imaginative and innovative approach to how it should be coached. And so he became the first true giant of post-war management. He could be cunning and he was a formidable and unyielding adversary for foes inside the club and out, but he built Manchester United and established them on the purest of football principles. 'The old man always told us that football is more than a game,' said Sir Bobby Charlton, 'It has the power to bring happiness to ordinary people.'

There is no mystery to why Busby thought footballers dancing across a pitch could illuminate a working man's life or provide a temporary escape from the humdrum grind of his existence. The game had lit up his own, and Busby had experienced deprivation and tragedy in his early years

He was born in 1909 in one of thirty-two two-room cottages in a 'miners' row' in Old Orbiston, near Bellshill in Lanarkshire. The cottage was more than 100 years old, had gas lighting and a cold-water tap outside. The communal toilets were 75 yards away. Heat and hot water came via a fire behind the large cast iron fireplace. There was a zinc bathtub in the kitchen where his father, Alex, would have to scrub himself from black back to white after every shift down one of the eight nearby pits.

Such descriptions of hardship can seem almost hackneyed these days. By the time Busby was watching Ryan Giggs play for Manchester United towards the end of his life his existence had changed to the extent it is hard to appreciate how basic and unforgiving conditions were when he was a child. They became a whole lot worse in 1916, when word returned from Arras that his father had been killed by a sniper in the First World War. Busby was six years old, the only male in a house also occupied by his mother and three younger sisters. He felt vulnerable and unprotected but reacted in a way which offered the first evidence of an innate strength of character. He realised that a great responsibility had fallen on him, and he began dealing with it.

By the age of twelve he was walking five miles every morning to get to school in Motherwell, and the same back in the afternoon. Friends and family called him 'Mattha'. His mother was enthusiastic about education and Busby – well-mannered, studious and clever – did so well in class that teachers wanted him to stay on at school. 'It was me dad who said "No, we need money coming into the house, I'm going to go down the pits." ' said Sandy, 'That's a strong thing to say at that age. The pits were so dangerous in those days. They propped up the mine shafts with a bit of wood and he was down at the pit face. He was very, very strong-minded. He really started building his character from going down the mines at an age when kids these days are still at school.'

He left school at the age of 15 and coalmining brought in £2 a week for the family, now swollen by a step-father and a half-brother and half-sister. Naturally his mother, Nellie, was reluctant to see Matt descend into the mines – the family had planned to emigrate to America – but the industry dominated their area and she, too, took a job at the pithead to supplement her widow's pension. It was effectively the teenage Matt, as the bread-winner, who got his way. The talk of emigrating across the Atlantic petered out.

'I think a lot of his character came from his mother.' said Sandy, 'She was very strong. A very strong woman. Many years later when he had made it as a footballer they were having a drink and me dad poured himself a glass. His mam watched him doing it then said "Matt, what are you doing?" Like a little lad he said, "But mam, I'm the captain of Scotland." She said: "Oh, I just don't know what you're going to be up to next."

'He never spoke a great deal to me about his upbringing. I often wish I could have asked him about me granddad, who was killed early on in the First World War. I don't know where me dad got his character from. Well, I do really, but it would have been nice to hear about his dad.'

As a young Lanarkshire boy it was as inevitable that football would become as precious as oxygen to Matt Busby. The game was his pastime, his first love and his escape. He progressed from the village team to the finest local youth side and then to junior football at Denny Hibs, where for some away fixtures they kept their clothes near the side of the pitch so that if they won they could do a runner before getting battered by angry locals.

'He was a Celtic man and hoped Celtic would come for him,' said Sandy. The Busbys were Catholics and his faith sustained Matt throughout his life. 'Then out of the blue Rangers invited him for a trial. He thought he did well, but they found out he was Catholic, so that was that. The next thing, Celtic invited him for a trial. Great! He thought he did well and then they said "You've been for a trial with Rangers, haven't you?" So that was it, in those days, kiboshed. It was all about religion. Disgraceful.'

Busby never served any senior Scottish club, although many years later there was an offer from Celtic for him to become manager. His escape from mining to full-time football came at the age of 17 in 1928 when he received an offer to join Manchester City. After a slow start at the club – he initially said 'I feel out of my sphere in football' – he stayed for eight years and built a reputation as an intelligent and efficient right half, appearing in the side which won the 1934 FA Cup after losing the final in 1933.

In 1936 he joined Liverpool, becoming captain and latterly a mentor to many, including a young Durham lad called Bob Paisley. Busby became a Scotland international. When he left Liverpool his career wound down to a natural end during the Second World War. Already his authority and stature had been noticed. He was posted in the Army PE corps and given command of the British Army team sent to entertain troops behind Allied lines in Italy. The time had come. Matt Busby was ready for management. He turned down the Ayr United job – having decided he had no wish to return to Scotland – and the assistant manager position at Reading. He was on the point of accepting a coaching role at Liverpool when a handwritten letter arrived in the post.

Sandy has bundles of newspapers cuttings, photographs and other memorabilia from his father's life. Among it all is that letter addressed to 'Dear Old Matt' from Manchester United official Louis Rocca. It is dated 29 December, 1944, and made the first, unexpected contact between the club and Busby about the manager's job at Old Trafford. Busby and Rocca had been friends since the latter had unsuccessfully tried to sign him for United in 1930. A decade and a half later the offer being made was far, far more substantial. 'The job here would be £500 a year and I suppose bonuses for results,' wrote Rocca, 'I know you are the real man for the job.' Note the casual mention of bonuses '*I suppose*'. Doubtless Busby was canny enough to get a bonus figure in writing. There would be a few coming his way over the following 24 years.

The contract was signed on 22 October, 1945. The *Manchester Evening News* broke the story with the following, sober opening paragraph: 'Company Sergeant-Major Inspector Matt Busby, left centre-half back and Scotland captain, today signed an agreement to become manager of Manchester United when he is demobilised.'

Anyone familiar with Manchester United knows the story by now. Old Trafford had been extensively bombed in the war and United, heavily in debt, were playing out of neighbouring Maine Road. Busby's astute handling of the club, his judgement and eye for a player enabled him to construct an efficient side so quickly that United finished second in their first postwar season, missing out on the title by one point.

He was strong-minded and sure of himself from the start. When United struggled in the early months of the following season, 1947–48, their chairman, James Gibson, demanded that they sign some star players (vast postwar attendances had quickly removed their financial worries). Busby refused because he thought no one who was available was right for his team. It was his first standoff, his first power struggle, but Gibson trusted his instincts and backed down. This was a significant episode for United and, eventually, football in general, a subtle but important shift in the balance of power between chairman and manager. Busby's status grew. They climbed the league to finish as runners-up again and won their first major trophy for 37 years: the 1948 FA Cup.

Busby had his first silverware as a manager. United paid him an enhanced bonus and he spent it imaginatively. It had always slightly troubled him that he had let his mother down years earlier by insisting that he would leave the pits to join Manchester City rather than supporting her wish that the family would emigrate to Pittsburgh. 'When he won his first FA Cup at Old Trafford he got a bonus,' said Sandy, 'He gave it to his mum so she could go to Pittsburgh and see relatives she had over there. When she came back he asked her how it was. She said "Oh Mattha, thank God we didn't go to that crazy country!" Me dad was delighted. He didn't need to feel guilty any more.'

He also managed the Great Britain team at the 1948 Olympics. In 1949 United were back at a rebuilt Old Trafford. By 1952, after several seasons as the bridesmaids, they became the champions of England for the first time in 41 years. Busby was already showing vision and boldness. With their defence of the title faltering the following season he made a remarkable declaration at a United board meeting: 'I'm going to make the move which will make or break Manchester United.' The act he had in mind was the essence of Matt Busby. He meant tearing out almost half of the first team and replacing them with untried young reserves who had been impressing him behind the scenes. His 'Babes'. In came Duncan Edwards, Bobby Charlton, David Pegg and Eddie Colman. More would follow. He complemented the young ones by signing Tommy Taylor from Barnsley. The deal was done for £30,000, but Busby even had a sense of good public relations. He told Barnsley: 'Let's make it £29,999 because £30,000 sounds a lot.'

Trusting an emerging crop of young players was not a whim

from Busby. It was the inevitable end product of a calculated and truly revolutionary programme he had implemented soon after becoming manager. Busby did not merely embrace youth development and widespread scouting, he effectively invented it. Young talent was cheap, he figured, and it could also be moulded and shaped into the way of playing he wanted to see from United teams. He told his board of directors that the young ones were United's future. A backroom team of formidable quality was put in place (led by brilliant chief scout Joe Armstrong and assistant manager Jimmy Murphy) to find, develop and educate the young players who would take United to the next level. With Busby's knowledge, the club was not beyond using financial inducements to land the best young prospects if that was what it would take. The entire concept was brilliant. Clubs all over the world have copied it ever since.

United won the league again in 1956, their young side running away with it to the extent of winning by eleven points in the era of two points for a win. Old Trafford had undergone an incredible £200,000–worth of improvements, including the introduction of floodlights. The Football League had not welcomed the introduction of the European club tournaments in the mid-1950s and told their champions not to participate. Chelsea bowed to that request in 1955. The following year Busby did not. He knew European competition was the way forward and defied the governing body by declaring that United would be taking part. In 1956–57, their first attempt, they reached the European Cup semi-finals. They won the league that season by eight points.

This was the 'Busby Babes' in their majestic pomp. The best team in England, with an average age in the early 20s. The possibilities were limitless. And then came Munich. On February 6, 1958, the plane carrying the United squad crashed and caught fire as it made an unsuccessful attempt to take off from a slush-covered runway at Munich Airport. It was an unimaginable tragedy.

Sandy Busby remembers how he first heard about the air disaster which cut down eight members of that fine side and almost killed his father. 'I was coming back from Blackburn and it was on a newspaper bill at the station. It just said "Manchester United in plane crash". It didn't hit me until about 10 yards further on. Plane crash? Not "fright", but "crash". That's when I ran to the phone. I got home straight away.'

Edwards, Pegg, Colman and Taylor died, along with Roger Byrne, Billy Whelan, Mark Jones and Geoff Bent. Jackie Blanch-flower and Johnny Berry survived but never played again. In all there were 23 fatalities among the 44 people on board the flight. Busby was almost a 24th. A punctured lung was among his serious injuries and as he lay in an oxygen tent at a Munich hospital the last rites were read to him twice. Busby held on and came through. It was two months before he was well enough to return to England. 'I flew to Germany the morning after it happened,' said Sandy, 'I went out for four, five, six days and then me mam said "You have to come back and go to as many funerals as you can to represent the family" '.

'When I went to Munich the first time me dad was in intensive care in this little room. When I went back again later he was in a room on his own. They couldn't believe what a constitution this man had.'

Busby's wife, Jean, talked him out of his black depressions and out of retiring from football, appealing to his loyalty to his dead boys by stressing that they would have wanted him to carry on. Slowly, his strength returned and so did the will to rebuild the team and the club which had been cruelly shattered. He even briefly agreed to take charge of Scotland on a part-time basis later in 1958, albeit lasting only two games before conceding that the job at United was too demanding.

Busby was already a giant in the game, a figure revered by all other managers. His great friend Shankly once said of him: 'Matt Busby is without doubt the greatest manager that ever lived. I'm not saying that I *think* he is the greatest manager. I'm saying he *is* the greatest manager.'

Busby once talked Shankly out of resigning as manager of

Liverpool during one of his rows with the Anfield directors. Sandy said, 'One time Shanks came to me dad and said "I'm resigning from Liverpool, packing it in. The directors are driving me crazy." Dad said: "Have you got a job to go to?" Shanks didn't. Dad said: "Well wait 'til you get a job to go to, and then you can tell them to go stick their job!"

'Shanks thought the world of me dad. The players at Huddersfield [when Shankly was manager there] were in the dressing room getting ready for a match one time when Shanks walks in. He's got a Trilby hat on. He goes in front of the mirror. And he's adjusting it, and he's looking at himself, and he's adjusting it again, and he's checking himself out. The lads are looking at him and then looking at each other, as if he's mad. But no one's mentioned the Trilby. All of a sudden Shanks turns around and with that gruff voice of his he says: "Hey, do you like the Trilby?" Someone says "Aye, it looks great." Shanks goes: "Do you no' think I look like Matt with it on?"'

Probably even Shankly found it remarkable that United could finish as high as second in the campaign after Munich. The following few seasons proved more predictable – United fell away in the championship and were understandably mediocre – but another rebuild was underway and it would be every bit as spectacular and celebrated as the first. In 1960 youth player Nobby Stiles made his first team debut. In 1962 Busby signed the 22-year-old Denis Law for a record British transfer fee. In 1963 he signed Pat Crerand and gave a debut to another youth player, George Best. And he still had Bobby Charlton.

After five barren seasons post-Munich they won the 1963 FA Cup and finished second in the league in 1964. In 1965 they were back for good. They won the league again. If the Busby Babes side had broadened the club's appeal enormously and given it depth, emotion and folklore, the 1960s team gave United style, swagger, flamboyance and sheer sex appeal. The football of Law, Best and Charlton was utterly electrifying.

They were champions again in 1967 – Busby's fifth league title –

and began another assault on a trophy which he had begun to suspect was beyond them, The European Cup. On this, at least, he was mistaken. In the *pièce de résistance* of Busby's career and of English club football in the 1960s, Manchester United won the 1968 European Cup, removing the great trophy from the hands of Busby's fellow Scot, Jock Stein, whose Celtic had won it in 1967.

They beat Benfica 4–1 in the final at Wembley. Busby went into the game without his injured predator, Law. He used the tigerish Stiles to nullify Benfica's great Eusebio. It was a tactical triumph. As the Portuguese side tired Best began to run riot. Busby finally had the trophy he felt had been stolen from his cherished young boys, along with their lives, ten years earlier.

United were huge. Best was a phenomenon. A pop star in shorts and football boots, his unprecedented fame and popularity meant he would have required careful handling regardless of his temperament. But a self-destructive addiction to drink and nightclubbing slowly eroded his talent and transformed the job of managing him from a privilege into a problem. Busby cared about Best as though he were his own son. The affection was genuinely mutual, but Best could not help himself. He was the individual who came to define and shape the final phase of Busby's management. The great man was perceived as being a little too lenient with this superstar variously referred to as El Beatle, The Fifth Beatle, The Belfast Boy or simply Georgie Boy. Best was from a different generation, one with which Busby could not easily identify.

Sandy Busby believes his father may have been more tolerant towards an alcoholic because of a close relationship he had with a kindly relative who was a heavy drinker during his own childhood. In any case, no manager had ever had to deal with someone like Best, who was as much a celebrity as he was a footballer.

'Bestie was the first to get that level of pressure,' said Sandy, 'Good looks, a great footballer, he must have put 10,000–20,000 on the gate everywhere they went. Me dad used to know about everything that was going on. He used to hear it all. I don't know if people phoned him, or what, but he had a sense of everything. He called for Bestie to come and see him one day and said "I hear you're knocking around with a married woman. How old are you, 18, 19? I'm telling you now, knock that on the head. Cut it out. Go and get yourself a nice young girl." So Bestie said he would. Next thing he goes away to Sweden on a pre-season tour and before long it was splashed across the front of the papers: "George to get married to a 19-year-old Swedish girl!" So me dad had to call him into the office again. "That's not what I meant, George!"

'He probably did give Bestie more leeway, later on. I know Bestie thought the world of me dad but he couldn't stop the behaviour. He was a sheer alcoholic. Me dad liked his whisky, later on. He used to take a whisky before he went to bed. But I can't honestly say that I saw me dad drunk. When I went to the reception when we won the European Cup he was full of the joys, but I couldn't say that he was drunk.'

Busby learned he was to be knighted within a month of the European Cup victory and a few months later he announced that after 24 years as manager of Manchester United he would stand down at the end of the 1968–69 season. There was nothing more for him to prove or achieve. He became the club's general manager when Wilf McGuinness succeeded him, but was temporarily back in the dugout when McGuinness was sacked in December 1970, and continued there until the end of that season, when Frank O'Farrell was appointed.

Busby became a director and remained so until taking over as club president in 1992. He had not left United when there were alternative offers to take over at Roma, Real Madrid and Celtic, among others, so he wasn't about to do so in retirement. The shadow he cast over Old Trafford during the 1970s and 1980s was enormous and, such is the way of these things, many felt that his mere presence was inhibiting and unhelpful to his successors. Busby meant well, of course, but it was natural for lesser managers to feel uncomfortable while he was around and he did become a magnet for any dissenting voices around the club. United went into decline. O'Farrell, Tommy Docherty, Dave Sexton and Ron Atkinson all followed McGuinness as managers who came and went without making them champions of England, let alone Europe.

Then United looked to Scotland again and made another appointment. In the autumn of 1987, a few months after they had done so, Matt quietly told Sandy that he sensed United had finally found his natural heir. 'I swear on my life that this is true,' said Sandy. 'After eight months or so me dad said "I think we've got the man".'

The man was Sir Alex Ferguson. At last, in his 80s, his health failing and a widower after Jean passed away in 1988, but still sharp and perceptive, Busby saw trophies begin to trickle back into Old Trafford. He witnessed Ferguson win the FA Cup in 1990, the European Cup Winners' Cup and Super Cups in 1991, the League Cup in 1992 and then, gloriously, in 1993, for the first time since he had done so himself in 1967, the league title. Busby passed away eight months later.

He had been thrilled by Ferguson. 'Oh, Dad was delighted. He had a little office at Old Trafford and Fergie would walk by, give a knock on the door and say "How are ye, auld yin?" Ferguson has gone into orbit with Manchester United. Me dad will be there looking down today and saying "This is marvellous, marvellous!"' Ferguson admired Busby immensely, and not just because the old man steadfastly stood by him during the rocky early years of his United management.

Today the club president's seat in the Old Trafford directors' box is permanently reserved for Sandy Busby. In 1993 Warwick Road North outside the stadium was renamed Sir Matt Busby Way. A bronze statue of Busby is placed outside the ground's East Stand. Back in Bellshill there is the Sir Matt Busby Sports Complex and, in 2009, a Sir Matt Busby Scholarship was launched for coach education in Lanarkshire along with the Sir Matt Busby Shield, contested between Motherwell and a young Manchester United side. A United supporters group paid £8000 for 16,000 plastic sheets to spell out "For Sir Matt" and show a portrait of his face at the 2009 Champions League final in Rome on what would have been his 100th birthday. Respected Manchester artist Harold Riley gave Sandy a limited edition print of his father. On the back was a dedication, part of which read: 'Let the angels help him make a team that will give divine pleasure to all the souls in heaven, just as his boys gave joy here on earth.'

There were chances for Sandy Busby to follow his father into management – he played for Blackburn Rovers before working as a bookmaker, publican and the manager of United's souvenir store – but their temperaments and talents were different.

'I wish I'd had his character and personality. But what he had was special. He was one of the few who stood out. I got a few offers, non-league of course. I got an offer to be the manager at Burton Albion. So I phoned them. I agreed to come for an interview and then he said: "Your dad would help you of course, wouldn't he?" That was it. I said "Do you want me or do you want me dad?" I put the phone down soon after that.'

Busby virtually invented professional scouting and youth development. He insisted on playing the game with style and grace. He embraced European competition from its infancy. Under him the role of manager was redefined from servant to boss. Interfering directors were put in their place. He had the wise and calculating mind of a cardinal, and people routinely say that he had the stature to silence a room merely by entering it. His judgement was sound. As an elderly man, at the start of the 1990s, he predicated that wildly inflated players' wages would be the 'ruination' of the game.

And this great man, this legendary manager, innovative thinker and visionary, also happened to be a kind and loving father. There was an occasion when a Manchester United European trip meant he had to be away from home over Sandy's birthday. He sent his boy a telegram which said: 'Happy Birthday. Sorry I'm not with you. Love, Dad.' The birthday was Sandy's 22nd, the date was February 4, 1958. Two days after that telegram arrived Sir Matt boarded a flight in Munich.

Mercifully, for his family and for football, he survived. His legacy survives still.

Jock Stein

'He was a good judge of character. He used to joke that he had a smell test to work out whether he liked someone or not. He would sniff the air near that person and say to us "There's a bad smell coming off him."'
Danny McGrain

The pair of them had a rich seam of wonderful stories and insights into Jock Stein's life and no one with a tape recorder or notebook had ever turned up to hear them. Poignant tales which had been locked away in their memories for more than a quarter of a century, untold.

They remembered the heart scare which forced him to stop on his way to Parkhead one day, made him get out of the car and lean against a wall to get his breath back. That was years before he died. They remembered that awful night in Cardiff when they innocently switched off the television as they saw him being helped up the tunnel at the end of the Wales game: they knew he had a bad ankle and merely assumed he'd taken a kick to it. When they put the telly back on his face was on the screen and the newsreader was saying he was dead. No-one had telephoned to tell them.

They remembered not being present when a bust of Jock Stein was unveiled at Parkhead. When they did visit the ground one day they went on the official stadium tour and had their tickets booked under a different name. No-one realised who they were. They didn't want to make a fuss. They even remembered the happy wee lad who celebrated every goal by swinging on the clothes poles.

Few in his life knew him better, even fewer meant as much to him. And he was never Jock to them. His name was John.

One spring morning in 2010, almost 25 years after his death, two elderly ladies in Burnbank, Jessie McNeill and Margaret McDaid – Stein's two surviving sisters – put on a pot of tea and made themselves comfortable in the front room. And then they spoke publicly about their extraordinary brother for the first time.

Jessie: There were five of us – four girls and John – plus our dad, George, and mother, Jane, all growing up together in a wee house in the miners' rows at Burnbank. Two of our sisters died young which left John as the oldest, me and then Margaret. Mum and dad lived at 339 Glasgow Road, Burnbank when John was born but we moved to 89 Albert Buildings, which wasn't far away, when the family got bigger.

Margaret: The block of flats where we live now is not far from our original house and is on the site of the old railway track that used to take the coal back down from Earnock Colliery where our dad and also John – or Jock, as folk kept calling him – worked. He only got called Jock when he started playing football. We never called him that.

Jessie: I remember you used to be able to hear from our old house the sound of the coal wagons trundling past. Those were very different days. We had a really happy household and a really good upbringing. Being the only boy John was doted on by our mum. She loved us all but especially John. He was her boy.

Margaret: We used to laugh a lot. John always liked to smile and he never lost that. Even when he was a manager and maybe under a bit of stress he never lost his sense of humour.

Jessie: Our dad was a really big football man. He loved the game and was involved with Blantyre Vics. You could say that is where

John got his interest but really where we grew up there was no escape from football. The boys played it morning, noon and night. John used to play on the green near the house and when he scored a goal he used to swing on the clothes poles where people hang their washing, which were sometimes used as goal posts. Our dad used to say that John would have to have clothes poles put on any pitch he played on so he could swing on them to celebrate any goals he scored.

Margaret: Dad enjoyed having a son to share his interest in football. He played a bit himself for Blantyre Vics and I remember him and John playing in games near the house. Some of the matches used to be between the married men, with my dad on one side, and the single men with John in their team on the other. These games used to go on forever.

Jessie: My dad was a big Rangers man and supported them all his life. Even when John played for and managed Celtic our dad's team was still Rangers. Of course he wanted John's team to do well but he was Rangers daft. A Rangers man through and through and John was brought up in a Rangers-supporting house.

Margaret: When John played for Celtic my dad still went to see Rangers on a Saturday. John sometimes had to make sure there was a place on the local Rangers supporters' bus to Ibrox for Dad before he got his things together and headed to Parkhead to play for Celtic. Whenever John went to play for Celtic my mother used to always say good luck to him.

Jessie: And my dad, who would have his Rangers scarf on on a Saturday, also used to wish him luck. But always used to say "I hope you just draw". That made John laugh every time. He was fine with it. He knew his dad was a Rangers man and nothing would change that. He always wanted Rangers to do better than Celtic whether John was playing or not. Dad would never change his team but we all knew he was also incredibly proud of his boy. When my dad had his stroke John was playing regularly for Celtic at centre-half. Whenever John used to go to see him either in hospital or back at the house he used to ask him who was the best centre-half in Scottish football. He used to always say George Young of Rangers! Never, ever John. My dad died aged 72 a few years before John's team won the European Cup in 1967. That was a tragedy. He was a proud, proud man and would have been made even prouder by what John had achieved. He may have been a Rangers supporter but he would have been the proudest man in Scotland to see his son with the European Cup.

Margaret: John enjoyed being at Glenlee Primary School and then the main Greenfield School like the rest of us. He was a clever boy but left school to work in a carpet factory for a wee while and then went down the pit. He also played for Albion Rovers and then went to Wales to play for Llanelli and then Celtic. Wherever he went he kept in touch with us. He was good like that. As a brother there was never any nonsense with John. He was straightforward. He never smoked or drank and could work out if someone was good or bad pretty quickly. He was a very kindly man. Maybe too kind, because when he became successful in football he had a lot of hangers-on. He had his family and some close friends, like the bookie Tony Queen, but there were a lot of people who wanted to be his pal because of what he had achieved, not because of who he was. He was wise to those folk.

Jessie: John liked good company and all his mates could tell so many funny stories. John never needed alcohol or cigarettes to have fun. In fact when he lived in Queen's Park he never even brought drink into the house. He always kept it in the garage. There was so much that one freezing winter night all the bottles of wine and whisky burst and they made a huge puddle on his garage floor. It stank for weeks. He hated smoking and said if you were meant to smoke you would have a chimney coming out the top of your head. His wife smoked and if they had had a few folk round on a Saturday night he would come to see us the next morning and always be complaining about his house stinking of cigarettes.

Margaret: His first love was his family and then football. I never bothered with the game, even when John was involved. I didn't watch any matches at Parkhead. One of the few I did watch was the European Cup final in 1967 but that was on the television. It never crossed my mind to go.

Jessie: We went to the celebrations when Celtic arrived back in Glasgow. That was brilliant. Even after that win John never changed. He used to still come up to see us and our mother after our dad died. He never got too big for his boots. I know a lot of folk think he should have got a knighthood after Celtic won the European Cup and I agree with them. He should have got one but I don't think he would have liked one.

Margaret: Aye, you're right. Oor John wouldn't have liked all that fuss. In saying that when you see some of the folk that get knighted nowadays, it's ridiculous. They must be scraping the bottom of the barrel. John would have been much more deserving, although not getting knighted would have been no big deal for him.

Jessie: He did get the CBE, which he picked up at Buckingham Palace. My mother asked him what Buckingham Palace was like and John said that her house in Burnbank was a bigger palace. He said the Queen's house wasn't any better than my mother's and the carpets were worn. John also got an invite to the Queen's Garden Party at Holyrood. My mother said that was nice, but he wasn't going.

Margaret: He had us all laughing when he said he had been at her hoose and she hadn't been to his so he couldn't go into her garden until she visited him.

Jessie: "I cannae go to sit in her garden on her chairs and eat her food until she's come to visit me first." John used to say. He had no airs or graces about him. He used to be up seeing our mother all the time after my dad died, even when he was really busy with Celtic or Scotland. One day when he was up at my mother's two wee boys came up and knocked on the door and asked for his autograph. John, who was Celtic manager at the time, signed and said to them both "So what team do you pair support?" One said Celtic the other said Rangers. And John said to them, and I'll always remember it: "You pair stick together and love one another, whatever happens." He had no time for all that religious nonsense. He loved football. He couldn't understand all the rubbish about Catholics and Protestants supporting different teams.

Margaret: A long time after our dad died, my mum finished up staying with me. When she came to stay she put a picture she had of John in his office at Parkhead on top of the television and used to talk to it all the time when he wasn't there. Maybe John's wife Jean would phone down and say he couldn't come to visit because he had a board meeting. Mother would talk to the picture and say, "John, you may have gone up in the world but you can come down just as quickly." She didn't mean it, but liked to keep her boy's feet on the ground, not that it was really necessary.

Jessie: He used to come round every Sunday to see her and that was when he could really relax. Most pictures you see of him he's either in a tracksuit on the training ground or in a shirt and a tie in his office or on business for club or country. When he came round on a Sunday he was always casually dressed. I think one time he even came round in his slippers. He used to say he was really pleased to get his collar and tie off. He never felt comfortable in it. John treated people with respect and expected to be treated in the same way. He was a lovely man but absolutely hated being kept waiting. Time was precious to him. If he said he would be there at a certain time he would be there. Whether it was for a training session or to meet us for a cup of tea. He had no time for people who kept him waiting. He had no patience with that. He thought it was really rude for someone to turn up late.

Margaret: The night he died in Wales was terrible. He had slight heart problems long before that and once I remember he had to stop his car and stand against the school wall on his way to Parkhead. When he got there the club doctor asked him to go to hospital. He did go but he was murder in there. I remember visiting him on a Saturday and he was in bed and there was a television in another room and he was in and out the bed getting the football results. He was not very good at resting. He never wasted a minute of his life.

He was not really well the day he went away to Wales for the World Cup qualifying match in 1985. I was down his house the night before he went to the Macdonald Hotel to meet the players. His wife Jean said that he had not been well. He had been at Celtic Park, because someone had been injured, then he had to go with Scotland to play Wales.

Jessie, me and our husbands were in my house the night of the Wales game. We were delighted Scotland had won and saw John coming out of the dugout at the end and when he went down we thought someone had kicked his ankle as he always had a bad ankle. We turned the television off at the final whistle to have a cup of tea and a chat. When we put the television back on John's picture was up on the screen saying he was dead.

Jessie: We could not believe it. We were out that door straight away and Margaret's daughter, Janice, ran us down to John's house. His wife was there, Ernie Walker's wife, other folk from the SFA, Jean's brother and John's daughter, Rae, was in a terrible state. She loved her dad so much.

Margaret: John's funeral was a fitting tribute to him. There were thousands of people out on the street on the way to the crematorium. There was a man at the top of a hill near the crematorium with a Rangers scarf on as the hearse went in. We were in one of the cars and called him the Lone Ranger. John would have loved that. He would have laughed at that description. The fact that man and lots of other Rangers fans lined his funeral route was great. He would have been really touched.

Jessie: Through his life John always kept his private and public life separate. So much so that when Bob Crampsey brought a book out on his life two years after he died he wrote that he only had one sister left alive. Margaret and I went up to see him and asked which one of us was deid!

Margaret: He gave us a free book!

Jessie: We weren't at the unveiling of his bust at Parkhead. The first time we ever saw it was when we went to Parkhead for my 70th birthday and paid for a stadium tour. It was Margaret's son-in-law who booked the table in the name of Simpson so they had no idea who we were, and we didn't tell them.

Margaret: We didn't want to make a fuss. John never traded on his name when he was famous. He was a humble man who treated everybody the same.

Jessie: We still miss him to this day. He was a great brother.

It was a measure of the managerial talent of Jock Stein that he brought success to Celtic using local talent and without dipping too extravagantly into the transfer market. He trusted his instinct about the players he brought to the club and nine times out of ten he was spot on. Famously the Lisbon Lions, who won the European Cup in 1967, were all born within a 30-mile radius of Parkhead.

Apart from the European Cup, when Stein was at Celtic he also won ten Scottish League titles, eight Scottish Cups and six Scottish

League Cups. Before that he had won the Scottish Cup with Dunfermline, who beat Celtic 2–0 in a replay back in 1961.

He further enhanced his reputation during his one year at Hibernian and then left in March, 1965, to take over from Jimmy McGrory at Parkhead. He transformed a club that had not won a trophy for eight years to the extent that the famous European Cup win came just two years after his arrival. Such was the supremacy of his team that they went on to win nine Scottish League titles in a row.

Stein was born in Burnbank in South Lanarkshire on October 5, 1922, the only son of George and Jane Stein. He went to the local Glenlee Primary and then Greenfield School and left there in 1937, just before his 15th birthday, to work in Stevenson's carpet factory before going down the local Earnock Colliery while playing part-time junior football with Blantyre Victoria. He joined Albion Rovers in 1942 and helped them to promotion to the First Division in 1948.

In 1950 he moved to Wales to sign for non-league Llanelli, being paid £12 a week, but stayed there only for a year before Celtic bought him for £1200. He was made captain before he retired due to persistent ankle injuries in 1956. In his time as a player he led them to the Scottish League and Scottish Cup double in 1954.

On his retirement he coached the reserve and youth players under McGrory and his first success as a manager came in 1958 when he led the reserves to the Second XI Cup with an 8–2 aggregate triumph over Rangers. His work with the Celtic second string got him noticed and he became manager of Dunfermline on March 14, 1960. They were in danger of relegation but he helped them escape with six wins in their last six league matches.

The following year he took the East End Park club to their first-ever Scottish Cup final victory when they beat Celtic 2–0 after a replay. In their first time in the European Cup Winners' Cup they made the quarter-finals, where they lost to Ujpest Dozsa 5–3 on aggregate.

In April 1964 Stein moved to Hibs, whom he helped lead to the Summer Cup before his rapid rise up the managerial ladder led him back to Parkhead just 11 months later.

Within six weeks of his arrival at Celtic, in March 1965, his team had beaten his former club Dunfermline 3–2 to win the Scottish Cup, their first major success for seven years. He released 20 players in those first few months and also enthusiastically encouraged the launch of a club newspaper, *The Celtic View*, which is still with us today.

Because of his early success with Celtic he was earmarked as the temporary, part-time replacement for Ian McColl as Scotland coach in the final few games of the campaign to qualify for the 1966 World Cup. He did well, with the highlight being Scotland's 1–0 win over Italy at Hampden thanks to a John Greig goal, but in the must-win return match in Naples they lost 3–0, which meant his team would not be crossing Hadrian's Wall to take part in the finals that were hosted and won by England. He was relieved in the end to get away from the bureaucracy of the SFA where a selection committee nominated the players for the Scotland squad and the manager picked his starting 11 from them.

Still, he learned a lot from his short time with Scotland and when he had the chance to solely concentrate on Celtic he put together a side that in 1966 won the first of their nine consecutive league titles. The year of 1967 will remain the most famous in the history of Celtic Football Club. They won every competition they entered, which meant the European Cup, the league title, Scottish Cup, League Cup and Glasgow Cup all had pride of place in the packed trophy room.

Three years later Celtic once again reached the final of the European Cup but were defeated by Feyenoord of Holland. In that year Stein was linked with a move to Manchester United. It would be highly unlikely he would have moved south, even to a club of that stature, because he felt settled at Celtic and his family wanted to stay in Scotland. Stein received a CBE in the

Honours List, which many still argue was scant reward for his efforts.

Government papers released under the Freedom of Information Act in 2007, on the orders of the Scottish Executive, revealed that Stein had in fact been dropped from the 1968 New Year's Honours List because his players were involved in a violent brawl during an infamous Intercontinental Club Cup game against Argentine champions Racing Club. During the match – their third meeting after the two-legged final ended in a 2–2 draw on aggregate – six players were sent off, four from Celtic, who lost the game 1–0. Papers show that the Home Office mandarins stopped him from being knighted because they claimed, rather unusually, that someone whose team had been involved in such a match should not be honoured in such a way.

Matt Busby, who guided Manchester United to the European Cup in 1968 was knighted, as was Alex Ferguson, who led the Old Trafford team to their famous last-minute victory in the Champions League final of 1999 over Bayern Munich. Stein, the first manager from Britain to lift the European Cup, never received that honour. There are still moves afoot to have him knighted but so far the authorities have not moved on the issue.

From 1966 to 1974 Stein led Celtic to nine Scottish league championships in a row and was at the peak of his powers. Many feel he was never the same man after a serious car crash in 1975 in which he was nearly killed. He was driving his Mercedes on a stretch of the notorious A74 road near Lockerbie on a bright Sunday morning when it was in collision with a Peugeot. His wife Jean, close friend Bob Shankly – who took over from Stein at Hibs – and Shankly's wife Margaret came out of the wreckage relatively unscathed. Stein and his close friend, bookmaker Tony Queen, were badly injured.

All five had been coming back from holiday in Menorca and were the innocent parties as the other car had driven up the wrong side of a dual carriageway. Stein had the reputation as a fast but essentially safe driver, and in this case could do nothing to stop the crash. Three years later he raised an action in the Court of Session against the driver of the Peugeot but it was another two years before he received a substantial out of court settlement.

The 1975–76 campaign started without Stein at the helm of Celtic and with his assistant Sean Fallon in charge. Stein returned occasionally during the season but was far from fit and had to go into hospital in Manchester for a toe operation, a legacy of the car crash. Without him not a single trophy was won as Rangers won the treble.

It was only at the start of the 1976–77 season that Stein returned to full health and was able to lead Celtic from the start of the campaign with a new assistant, Davie McParland, the former manager of Partick Thistle. He brought in some top signings, like Pat Stanton from Hibs and former Rangers player Alfie Conn from Tottenham Hotspur. Both men helped the Parkhead club win the league title as well as the Scottish Cup. It looked like the good times were back for Celtic, but the following season proved otherwise. The 1977–78 campaign proved to be a disaster as Celtic failed to win a trophy. To make matters worse they finished a dreadful fifth in the ten-team Scottish Premier League. To add to Stein's woes Kenny Dalglish, the club's prized possession, had left to join Liverpool.

For once some of the Celtic fans voiced their anger at Stein who, up until that point, had been untouchable. Looking back, it could be interpreted as a knee-jerk reaction by the Celtic board that after Rangers appointed former captain John Greig as their manager – on May 24,1978 – Celtic replaced Stein with Billy McNeill four days later.

For 13 years' service Stein was given a place on the Celtic board, in charge of fund-raising. John Fairgrieve, the late, great sports writer with the *Sunday Mail*, said the greatest Scottish football manager of his generation had been given the job as 'a ticket vendor for the Celtic Development Fund'. To try and keep him sweet Stein was honoured with a testimonial against Liverpool, when 60,000 people turned up and gate receipts totalled £80,000. To rub salt into the wounds of losing Dalglish the striker returned to Parkhead to play and was booed by some sections of the Parkhead crowd for leaving them.

An indication of the standing Stein had in the game, despite him being replaced as Celtic manager, came in a section of the match programme written by Bill Shankly. 'A great man with a heart of gold who would give you his last shilling. Aye, Stein knows it all. He's the best. And that's me, Billy Shankly, once of Liverpool, saying so. I ken you'll agree.' Inside Parkhead on the night of 14 August 1978, there was not a dissenting voice.

They fully expected to have Stein around their club for many years, a talismanic figure to the masses who knew that as long as he was around Celtic would be fine. Imagine, then, the outcry, just weeks after his testimonial, when it emerged that he had decided to move to Leeds United. It came as a huge shock to the Celtic fans and also to the general footballing public who had seen Stein turn down a move to Manchester United in 1970 and again in 1974.

It seems the decision was based on the fact that he had realised he didn't want to spend the rest of his days involved in fund-raising for Celtic. He wanted to be back in the cut and thrust of the game, which is why he moved south. He lasted just 44 days before being tempted back to manage Scotland on 4 October 1978 – the day before his 56th birthday – after the sacking of Ally MacLeod. Luckily for the SFA, Stein had never been one to sign contracts or rush to put pen to paper.

Because of that he had yet to sign his three-year contract at Elland Road for a basic pay packet of £85,000 when the SFA came calling. That meant they did not have to pay compensation for his services. During his short time at Elland Road his team played just seven league games of which they lost three, won three and drew the other. When he left Leeds they were in thirteenth position in the league and finished fifth at the end of the season. He was embarrassed at leaving a club of Leeds' size so quickly. An indication of that came from the fact that his entry in *Who's Who* completely omitted the episode.

Stein inherited a Scotland team that had lost their first European Nations Cup match 3–2 against Austria. Initially his appointment didn't help the cause much, with his team finishing a disappointing fourth in the five-team group. Still always keen to learn, the visit to Scotland by the 1978 World Cup winners Argentina proved to be a great experience.

He was in awe of the skill of the South American side that beat Scotland 3–1 at Hampden. A team that included established stars like Luque, Houseman, Passarella and Tarantini was always going to be tough to beat. Added to the mix was a young man called Diego Maradona, who scored his first goal for his country, and it was obvious to Stein how much work he had to do with Scotland to even get close to the best in the world. He soon realised that he could never afford to play the sort of free-flowing football with Scotland that he had with Celtic. At international level the opposition players were of a higher standard and would counter-attack at pace and with ruthless efficiency.

When the draw came for the 1982 World Cup he was in luck. FIFA had agreed to increase the number of finalists in Spain from 16 to 24 for the first time. That meant two countries would qualify from the section of five that Scotland found themselves in which included Sweden, Northern Ireland, Israel and Portugal. As it turned out, the increased number of qualifiers did not really matter to Scotland. They topped their group.

Nowadays it would be the World Cup campaign that would be the most important tournament but back in the 1980s the Home International series was also still a big deal. Stein misread the mood of the public during the Home Internationals when he treated them as a semi-competitive event in the lead-up to the more important World Cup in Spain.

His team narrowly beat Wales, drew with Northern Ireland, and worst of all lost 1–0 at home to England. Stein tried to rationalise away his decision for fielding a weakened team in the fixture that most Scots fans at the time felt was the biggest game of them all. The fans felt short-changed because he played five across the back at home and refused to bring on Gordon Strachan, who was the form player of Scottish football at the time. The fact that Stein made it clear that Strachan had had a long, hard season cut no ice.

The poor showing in the Home Internationals meant that Stein went to Spain under pressure and knowing the only way he could win back the fans was through some improved performances in the World Cup. His team won their first game 5–2 against New Zealand then against the mighty Brazil in the Benito Villamarin stadium in Seville they took an unlikely lead. Described by BBC pundit Jimmy Hill as a 'toe-poke', David Narey's goal in 18 minutes had a nation in raptures. Unfortunately it only angered the Brazilians who went on to score four goals through a Zico free-kick and further efforts from Oscar, Eder and Falcao.

A win was essential in their final match against Russia, but a comedy of errors put paid to that. Joe Jordan put Scotland ahead after just 15 minutes, but again they could not retain their lead. Russia equalised with a half-hit shot from Chivadze which Alan Rough didn't cover himself in glory in his effort to keep out. Next Alan Hansen and Willie Miller bumped into each other just inside their own half which allowed Shengelia to run 40 yards to score. In the final minutes Graeme Souness scored to make it 2–2 but it wasn't enough. For the third World Cup in a row Scotland had been eliminated from their group on goal difference.

Despite having a top-class group of players to choose from Stein failed to take Scotland to the next European Championships in France in 1984. Belgium, Switzerland and East Germany, weren't the toughest opponents but Scotland still failed to qualify.

Past his 60th birthday, questions started to be asked over his ability to guide Scotland through to the 1986 World Cup. Was he a man past his best? He was still hugely respected but did he still have the drive and energy to take his team through an arduous qualifying campaign? He liked the look of Scotland's World Cup section which included Iceland, Wales and Spain. One team would automatically qualify with the second place team facing a home and away play-off against the winners of the Oceania Group.

Not surprisingly Spain won the group, which left Scotland travelling to take on Wales at Ninian Park knowing a draw would be good enough to secure them second place and take them into a play-off against Australia. The night of September 10, 1985 was an evening of mixed emotions for the Tartan Army.

Stein's last involvement with the Scotland fans perfectly showed the affinity he had built up with them through the years. Before the game Wales goalkeeper Neville Southall had been having trouble getting the balls back from the crowd at the end of Ninian Park where the majority of the Scots fans had gathered. He asked Stein for help and as the big man stood in front of the crowd one ball, then another, came flying out. As he left the field it was with a friendly arm round Southall and a big smile on his face.

The match was a tight affair, with Wales taking the lead in 13 minutes through a strike from Mark Hughes, and they had chances to increase their lead. Stein, not a man to lose his cool, did so at half-time when he realised that the reason that Jim Leighton had looked all at sea at times was because one of his contact lenses had fallen out. Leighton had left his replacement pair back at the hotel in Bristol, which gave Stein no alternative but to take him off and replace him with Rough.

In the second half Wales missed more chances and in an attempt to change things Stein took off Strachan and brought on Davie Cooper. Nine minutes from time the extra width Cooper gave to the Scotland attack paid off. David Speedie hit a ball against the arm of Welsh defender David Phillips in the box, which won his side a penalty. Up stepped Cooper to put the ball past Southall and salvage the point Scotland needed to take them to the play-offs. Stein got up to acknowledge the goal but sat down straight away. The only time he got up before the final whistle was to try and move a persistent photographer who would not get out of his way.

At the whistle, amid all the celebrations, Stein remained on the bench, and once the television cameras panned back to the touchline the viewing public saw the police carrying him up the tunnel. The dreaded news was confirmed by SFA secretary Ernie Walker, who left the players' tunnel distraught along with Graeme Souness, who had missed the match through suspension.

Later it was revealed that Stein had not taken his regular pills that stopped excessive water getting into his lungs because he was worried taking them might affect his sharpness and ability to deal with the pressure of the big match build-up. He was such a professional he did not want anything to interrupt his preparations. Had he taken the drugs he might have survived.

Cardiff, so vibrant in the wake of Scotland's win, fell silent when news of Stein's death emerged. He was buried three days later, on Friday, 13 September 1985, at Linn Crematorium in Glasgow with a crowd of more than 10,000 lining the route. The Reverend Doctor James Martin of High Carntyne Parish Church said during his oration: 'Of the many moving tributes that have been paid to the man we mourn, none moved me more than the one given by a Scottish fan interviewed on television in Cardiff, just after the sad news became known last Tuesday night. He said it was a great result but every Scottish fan would rather Scotland were out of the World Cup and Mr Stein was still with us. That fan was speaking for us all.'

Never a truer word had been spoken. It was the fitting end to a tribute for a man who gave so much to Scottish football.

Danny McGrain worked under Stein more than any other player, a total of eleven years at Celtic and four with Scotland. He has fond memories of the man he still calls 'Mr Stein', the biggest influence on his football career. McGrain, a world-class full-back who spent 20 years as a Celtic player and was capped 62 times for Scotland in the 1970s and 1980s, became reserve team coach at Celtic.

'The first time I really came face to face with Mr Stein was in his office a few months after Celtic won the European Cup in 1967. I was a seventeen-year-old part-time player who had been training two nights a week at Parkhead along with the likes of Paul Wilson,

Kenny Dalglish, Jim Brogan and Vic Davidson. Mr Stein was busy with the first team and never really came to watch the youngsters train so I knew his assistant, Sean Fallon, who signed me and other players like Kenny, a bit more.

'I was an apprentice mechanical engineer at the time but wanted to be a full-time footballer, which meant I had to pluck up the courage to go in to see Mr Stein and ask him for a full-time contract. Imagine me, a 17-year-old on £5 a week, going in to see Mr Stein, whose team had just won the European Cup. I was terrified. Even thinking back to me walking in to see him still scares me to death. I was in complete awe of him. I thought things would be easier to go with my pal Kenny, who was a trainee joiner at the time but who also wanted to go full-time. We decided we would both ask for a meeting with him, one after the other.

'Neither of us wanted to go in first so we tossed a coin which Kenny lost and that meant he went in first. He was supposed to come out and tell me what kind of deal he had been offered but when he left Mr Stein's office he buggered off without telling me anything. That meant I headed in not knowing how Kenny had got on or what kind of deal he had been offered. So I went into Mr Stein's office for the first time ever without any idea what I was going to say or ask for. It wasn't great.

'Mr Stein had a tiny room which made him look even bigger than he actually was. I had not seen him close up until that moment. I could hardly speak. To see this great man towering over everything in this small room was nerve-racking. He asked me what I wanted despite the fact he knew exactly what it was. There were no agents back then in the late 1960s so I didn't know how much extra to ask for. I wasn't going to nip out and ask Billy McNeill, who I had never met, or any of the other Lisbon Lions who had just lifted the European Cup how much they were on, now was I?

'I said I wanted what Kenny had got and Mr Stein put a contract in front of me which I signed without discussion and left on his desk. This was in November 1967, and he said I would continue to train two nights a week until the end of the season and he would see me in the summer and that was it. I was going to be a full-time Celtic player. I nipped out to the bottom of the road at Parkhead and jumped on the bus to my girlfriend's flat in the Kingsway area of Glasgow. Her mum and dad were there and we opened a bottle of sparkling wine to celebrate me getting a full-time contract. I had a couple of glasses and then my girlfriend Laraine, who is now my wife, asked how much I would be getting. I stared at her for a moment then realised I hadn't a clue. I had no idea whatsoever. I was just delighted to be offered a contract with Celtic by Mr Stein. That had been good enough for me. The next day I had to phone up Mr Stein's secretary to make an appointment so I could go back and see him to find out what I was earning. I can't remember for the life of me what my rise was but it was more than the £5 a week I was getting.

'More important than the money was the fact I was training as a 17-year-old with the Lisbon Lions who had just won the European Cup. It was a dream come true. I was training with McNeill, Craig, Gemmell, Auld, the lot of them. I was tackling Bobby Lennox. I learned more being trained by Mr Stein and working with these guys in a few sessions than most players do in a lifetime. I still remember running out on the training pitch and Mr Stein would have his tracksuit on and Sean Fallon would be beside him. Whether you had been there for a few months or a few years Mr Stein used to show his disgust in the same way if you failed to play him a decent one-two when he wanted one.

'He would simply belt the ball out of the park and you would have to go running for it and go back to the end of the queue. It was doubly embarrassing when it happened to me early in my career when legends like Billy McNeill or Bobby Lennox were watching.

'Mr Stein also liked to make sure the goalkeeper's reflexes were spot on because he realised their value to a team. He used to stand in front of the goalie and you would hit shots towards Mr Stein who would deflect it by his hands, his head, any part of his body to change the flight of the ball to make the goalie react.

'His training flowed. It was never stop-start. Kenny and I and the rest of the young guys training with the first team were in awe. The Lisbon Lions obviously loved Mr Stein because of what he had done for the club and for them as players. They called him the manager or maybe a few of them "Big Jock". Never, ever, just "Jock". I couldn't even bring myself to call him that. He was always "Mr Stein" to me. The only time I called him "Jock" was when I introduced him at the top table of my testimonial dinner when I retired and it almost killed me. I never, ever thought I was on the same level as Mr Stein. Nobody was.

'I worked with him for 15 years in total and I must admit I did see him go mad in the dressing room more than a few times. He would only pick on players who he thought were not doing the job for him on the park that he had asked them to. He put his faith in you and you wanted to repay him. If you failed he would not miss you.

'He was very intelligent, a football-minded guy who had been in the game long enough to know how to handle a young boy like me coming into the game. He would tell me to keep it simple and more often than not play it to Jimmy Johnstone. He was very big on players thinking all the time, of looking for different options when they came to pass the ball. He gave me so much to think about on the park. Sometimes I used to come off the pitch with my head throbbing. I had a spell in the Celtic reserves in a group of players called "The Quality Street Gang" because Mr Stein realised they weren't too bad a mix. There was George Connelly, John Gorman, who went on to be assistant manager at England, Lou Macari, Davie Hay, Kenny and myself.

'I made my Celtic debut against Dundee United at Tannadice in 1970 and worked with Mr Stein for another 12 years at club and international level from then. Two years after my debut, just when things were going really well, I fractured my skull playing against Falkirk at Brockville. Doug Somner came in from the side and hit me on the head. I got smelling salts to bring me round and I lasted for about another ten minutes until half-time.

When I got to the dressing room I collapsed and was rushed to hospital.

'It was a long road back to fitness for me but Mr Stein never forgot me and encouraged me all the way. I remember when I was well enough to jog and jump he took me onto the training ground and produced some balloons. Now Mr Stein had not had any training on how to rehabilitate players who had a head injury but he showed his ingenuity by having me head these balloons.

'To begin with I felt really daft. But such is the respect I had for Mr Stein I would have headed balloons all week if he had asked me. It did get a bit silly as the minute I headed a balloon it would float off somewhere and I would be left running after it. From balloons one day we graduated the next onto plastic balls, which I had to buy a supply of myself because Celtic didn't have any. It was all about me getting my jumping right and feeling confident about heading the ball. Mr Stein persevered with me till I got my timing in the air back, and for that I was eternally grateful to him.

'He helped any player he rated and the better the player the more attention he got. Especially if he went off the rails. Mr Stein had most of his problems with wee Jimmy Johnstone. He loved wee Jimmy as we all did, but his drinking had him tearing his hair out. Mr Stein didn't drink and to have wee Jimmy smelling of drink in the changing room at times really got his back up. He used to give wee Jimmy dog's abuse because of it. Jimmy must have apologised 3000 times and he would have meant it every single time. He was playing in an era when drink was prevalent and with a bit more money in his pocket than the average man Jimmy couldn't resist having a few.

'People would phone Mr Stein – bar owners, bouncers, punters – to tell him if they had seen a Celtic player worse for wear. Usually it was Jimmy and Mr Stein did go and get him out of the boozer a few times. Behind his efforts to keep Jimmy on the straight and narrow was his realisation that he was worth the effort. Mr Stein wasn't daft. He knew it was in his best interests to keep wee Jimmy fit as he could win him games.

'He was a good judge of character, and not just with Jimmy. He used to joke that he had a smell test to work out whether he liked someone or not. He would sniff the air near that person and say to us "There's a bad smell coming off him". He sized people up by the questions they asked and how they asked them, especially journalists. If anybody was disrespectful to Mr Stein they were being disrespectful to Celtic Football Club and they would be frozen out.

'I never once remember anybody talking back to him in the dressing room. I used to even hate it when he asked me a question about tactics in case I got the answer wrong. I used to get so flustered as Mr Stein was sharp as a knife and he didn't just want the right answer, he wanted a quick answer.

'I'm sure he had a bit of a soft heart, as everybody keeps telling me he had one, but there was also this big, hard bit that made him such a successful manager. If he hadn't had that hardness about him he would have been crucified, as the players would have picked up on it. He always treated me the same way. Just because I worked with him for years didn't mean I got any special attention. He was straight down the middle with us all. It was his way or the highway, even when it came to the events he arranged to keep us occupied between matches.

'Football was his life and he was never much of a golfer, which meant we never saw him at many players' outings. He liked gambling and he also liked lawn bowls. In the days before it was trendy to go in for team-bonding sessions Mr Stein used to get us together to play bowls. At Celtic it was at a bowling green in South Street in Glasgow and when we were on Scotland duty it was at a green near the Marine Hotel in Troon. You had folk like me, Kenny Dalglish, Alan Hansen, Willie Miller, all trying to be taught bowls by Mr Stein. I was useless but had to keep playing because he was in charge. Nowadays they go go-karting, which would be much easier.

'He was a very private person and although I worked with him longer than most I didn't know anything about his family or home life. He kept that separate. The only change I saw in his personality was after he was severely injured in a car crash in 1975. He got a lot quieter than he used to be after that. He also got thinner and a bit more ratty. On top of that, around the same time he lost players like Kenny Dalglish, who went to Liverpool, and he could only watch as the team he had built fell apart. It must have been hard for him. When he left Celtic himself in 1978 it was a tough time for me because he had made me the player I was. He was a huge influence.

'I still met up with him when I was on Scotland duty and although he made me captain for the 1982 World Cup in Spain that was only because he felt I was the best man for the job. It was no old pals' act. He just wasn't like that. He was always a great communicator who could explain tactics to you simply. He made you feel good about yourself and when he was on your side, by God, he was on your side. He would defend you to the death.

'He also had that working-class drive that many Scots have, and it never left him. They talk about Sir Alex Ferguson being the Mr Stein of today and I would not argue with that. But you can't forget their circumstances are different. Sir Alex, despite the fact he is the greatest living manager, had a lot of money to spend putting together his team. Mr Stein's greatest ever side, the Lisbon Lions, were put together on a budget and was made up of Scottish players all born within a 30–mile radius of Parkhead. That is incredible. As a man Mr Stein was a giant. As a football manager an absolute genius. The best there ever was.'

Bill Shankly

*'Listen, son, I'm Bill Shankly and I take no shite
from anybody.'*

Bill Shankly's charisma was magnetic. People were electrified by him. The legendary Radio One disc jockey and ardent Liverpool fan, John Peel, told a story of how it felt to be in Shankly's presence. 'I once carried his bag from the hotel to the bus after Liverpool had beaten Real Madrid in the European Cup final at the Parc des Princes. It was genuinely one of my proudest moments. It was like being able to go up to the Pope. He meant enough for one of our children to be named after him: Florence Victoria Shankly Peel.'

Peel had plenty of fellow disciples. Brian Clough, a manager with an ego the size of Anfield, revered Shankly too. Liverpool men like Ian St John and Kevin Keegan still talked of him with awe decades later. The former Conservative Party leader Michael Howard, another serious Liverpool supporter, was another among the mass of fanatics, not that Shankly would have welcomed a Tory's endorsement.

Clough is arguably the only other British manager who had quite such a messianic impact on his people. Shankly wasn't just liked or appreciated or respected by Liverpool supporters, he was worshipped. And while Sir Matt Busby and Jock Stein brought enormous success to their clubs, of Scotland's trio of heavyweight 1960s leaders only Shankly created a lasting dynasty. Today Liverpool is an enormous, global football 'brand'. It was all started by one little Ayrshire miner.

He protected and encouraged the legendary Anfield 'boot room', a tiny neuk in the bowels of the stadium where the Liverpool backroom coaches would gather to drink tea and discuss every aspect of their own club and everyone else's. Shankly's managerial successors Bob Paisley and Joe Fagan, and later Roy Evans and (briefly) Ronnie Moran, were all 'boot room' men. Shankly himself was not always present. He let his staff discuss tactics, ideas and any gossip they had picked up from opponents without him being around to dominate proceedings. They usually met on a Sunday and would pour everything out to Shankly. It was simple, straightforward and beautifully effective. Shankly was the motivator and figurehead, Paisley the tactician and go-between with the players. Both were qualified physiotherapists: Liverpool had fewer injuries than most teams.

There will never be another Bill Shankly, the eccentric, fire-cracker product of a mining village which no longer exists. It was no exaggeration to say that the hold he had on much of Merseyside in the 1960s and early 1970s bordered on a sort of religious devotion. In terms of actual trophies his haul seems modest – three league titles, two FA Cups and one UEFA Cup in 15 years – but he transformed, reinvented and pumped up Liverpool Football Club. Famously, he once said he wanted to make them seem unbeatable. He wanted opponents broken and defeated from the moment they turned up. 'I want to build a team that's invincible, so that they have to send a team from bloody Mars to beat us,' he said in that unmistakeable, rasping, theatrical delivery, 'My idea was to build Liverpool into a bastion of invincibility. Napoleon had that idea. He wanted to conquer the bloody world. I wanted Liverpool to be untouchable. My idea was to build Liverpool up and up until eventually everyone would have to submit and give in.'

The masses lapped it up. Shankly gave them wins, trophies, wonderful players, outstanding teams and unforgettable quotes. He was one of them, proud to be an uncomplicated man of the people. They loved him back, of course. For him the two best teams in the city were Liverpool and Liverpool reserves. That was genuinely his opinion, not a jibe at Everton. He would come in to address his players before a game, rubbing his hands together gleefully. Guess what? He had just seen the opposition and they looked scared stiff about playing Liverpool. A different opponent had felt the same way the previous week, and another the week before that.

He had travelled a long, hard road from his childhood in Glenbuck, where he was one of ten children, including five boys who all went on to play professional football. His brothers initially played for the village's famous team, Glenbuck Cherrypickers. Shankly never did although he was always on the periphery of the first team. The brothers were steeped in football. One of them, Bob, became a title-winning manager too, steering a wonderful Dundee side to the Scottish championship in 1962.

The Shanklys' tough upbringing formed the basis of the version of socialism which drove Bill, one based on basic humanity, collective effort and shared rewards. He did not regard that as a set of beliefs which were necessarily political, just normal and decent. He epitomised the qualities, characteristics and views of the working-class Scot of his time. Behind the gnarled exterior, the bravado and the wit, he was a compassionate and caring man. Like so many of his generation in Glenbuck, he worked down the coal mines. Mercifully for him, and for Liverpool, his talent as a footballer brought him up and out into the light.

He was playing for the Scottish junior team, Cronberry Eglinton, when he was spotted by a scout from Carlisle United. The offer of a professional contract began his football career, and ended his mining one, at the age of 18 in 1932. Within a year he joined Preston North End and was their player in 1938 when he won the FA Cup and earned the first of five Scotland caps in a 1–0 win over England. The Second World War – during which he served in the RAF and made guest appearances for eight clubs, including Arsenal and Partick Thistle – coincided with what would have been his peak years as a footballer, although he did return to play again for Preston after the hostilities.

He finished playing in 1949 – by then he was a qualified masseur – and immediately moved into management at Carlisle. He thought the club promising but unambitious. The Shankly work ethic was quickly apparent: he helped the young players with their duties, swept the floors, cleaned boots, painted the walls. No task was too small for him, yet he expected total control.

He was interviewed for the Liverpool job in 1951 but talks broke down when he was told the directors would have final say on his team selections. Instead he moved to Grimsby Town that summer, taking a pay cut to do so but lured by a larger budget for signings, and then to Workington at the start of 1954. His was not a career of instant, uninterrupted success like those of Busby, Stein and Sir Alex Ferguson. He was at his fourth club, Huddersfield Town at the end of 1956, before something began to stir. He joined as assistant manager to Andy Beattie but they were in the First Division and Shankly wanted to experience life in the top flight again.

Denis Law, a skinny striker wearing NHS glasses and with a squint, had been brought south from Aberdeen as a 15-year-old by Beattie. Shankly recognised Law's talent immediately and placed him on a diet of milk and steaks to build him up. 'Get out your diary and write this down,' Shankly declared, 'One day Denis Law will be transferred for £100,000.' Law joined Manchester City for £55,000 in 1960, setting a new British record fee, before he moved to Torino. In 1962 he joined Manchester United. The fee? £115,000.

Shankly became Huddersfield manager when Beattie resigned. He did well, but not exceptionally so. It was surprising when Liverpool called on him again. Until then he had talked a good game at every club but his results were only moderate. He negotiated with the Anfield board for nearly a month before agreeing to join at a salary of £2500 a year, £500 more than he was getting at Huddersfield. It was December, 1959. Liverpool were in the Second Division and slow to invest in their team. Anfield was not the impressive stadium it is today – Shankly described it as 'a toilet' – and the training ground at Melwood was dreadful.

Shankly's managerial doctrine was to keep things simple – pass and move – and he used that as his basis for all of Liverpool's future success. He would exhaust his players in training then give them the time to recover. There were two-a-side, three-a-side and five-a-side games to work the players' technique, passing and control. He wanted them turning and twisting, like a boxer. Players had it drummed into them that they were at the best club in the land. Opponents were not praised in team-talks. Shankly sometimes asked an old fellow in the stadium to hand the visiting teams toilet rolls when they walked through the door. He was full of devilment.

Squabbles with directors continued. He nearly resigned when Johnny Morrissey, a quick outside left, was sold to Everton without his authority. Only the intervention of his good friend, Busby, stopped him handing in his notice.

The real Shankly transformation of Liverpool took hold from the summer of 1961. That was partly down to a clearout of what he regarded as some dead wood from the squad, but equally significant was the arrival of Eric Sawyer as a club director. Sawyer was an accountant in the Littlewoods empire which was run by John Moores, who was a shareholder in both Everton and Liverpool at the time. He was made managing director at Anfield and funds were released to him by Moores to allow Shankly to buy new players. Shankly's first major capture was Scotland internationalist Ian St John from Motherwell for £37,500. Weeks later Ron Yeats arrived from Dundee United for £30,000. Two Scots signings fell within what he claimed to be his unofficial policy on buying any of his strong-willed countrymen: 'If you've got three Scots in your side you've got a chance of winning something. If you've got any more, you're in trouble.'

Shankly was captivated by Yeats in particular and expected that others would be too. When the 6ft 2in defender signed, Shankly was so impressed at his physique that he told journalists: 'Go on, walk around him, he's a colossus!' He told them Yeats had once worked in an abattoir and killed a raging bull with his bare hands. It was bull all right – from Shankly – but Liverpool were buying quality at last and easily won the Second Division title in 1961–62. The revolution was underway.

In their first season back in the First Division they finished eighth, which might have pleased Shankly had it not been for the fact Everton won the championship. Later he would be memorably dismissive of the neighbours, although always with tongue in cheek: 'When I've nothing better to do, I look down the league table to see how Everton are getting along.'

Emulating his city rivals was an early Shankly motivation. Ian Callaghan, Peter Thompson and Tommy Smith were added. The improvement continued. By 1963–64 they were First Division champions. Shankly was now a winner, and a one-of-a-kind talisman. On an end-of-season tour of America he steadfastly refused to acknowledge being in a different time zone, seeing that as a nonsense and an affront to Britain. He was appalled when the locals did not recognise his Liverpool FC club crest. He had a distrust of foreigners, which some felt inhibited his interest in doing well in the European tournaments. Even so, in the following season's European Cup they reached the semi-finals to be eliminated by Inter Milan. In the league they dipped to seventh.

Liverpool had never won the FA Cup. In 1965 Shankly delivered it for them. The cup final victory over Leeds United showed the level of commitment he was able to draw out of his players. Gerry Byrne went down under a heavy tackle in the third minute and broke his collar bone. Substitutions had not yet been introduced to football so Byrne had to continue. He even set up Roger Hunt's opening goal. Although Leeds equalised, St John scored in the second period of extra-time for a famous win. Shankly claimed that half a million people gathered in Liverpool to welcome the team home from Wembley. It was the period when Shankly and the Kop fell in love with each other, not to mention Shankly and the media. He was the biggest managerial personality around until Clough followed suit.

They had qualified for the 1966 European Cup Winners' Cup and defeated Juventus, Standard Liège, Honved and Celtic on the way to a final against Borussia Dortmund. Shankly was beside himself with excitement: the final was being played at Hampden Park. To win a European trophy in Scotland would have meant everything.

Before the match he was nervous as he met friends and members of his family who had travelled up from Ayrshire for the game. This time he did not want to let down just the Liverpool fans but all of the Scots in the crowd who were supporting the team because of him. What might have been arguably the greatest moment of his Liverpool career never materialised. Dortmund were gifted two easy goals, which gave them a deserved 2–1 victory. Over the following couple of years his two great friends, Stein and Busby, enjoyed the European success which had just eluded him. Shankly travelled to Lisbon in an open show of support for Stein at the 1967 European Cup final. After Celtic's win he burst into their dressing room, embraced Stein and shouted: 'John, you're immortal!' The following year Busby won the same competition with Manchester United.

Liverpool were champions again in 1965–66. Although there was some criticism of him for being overly loyal and slow to refresh his tried-and-tested side, new faces did begin to emerge, notably Emlyn Hughes from Blackpool early in 1967. Ray Clemence took the goalkeeper's jersey away from Tommy Lawrence and Larry Lloyd replaced Yeats in defence. Out of the reserve team, players like Brian Hall and Phil Boersma started to make an impression. John Toshack arrived from Cardiff City for £110,000 in November 1970. Steve Heighway began to make a stir on the wing. When he was unsuccessful in signing Celtic's Lou Macari, Shankly told his players 'Ach well, I only wanted him for the reserves.' Still, Liverpool had been generally eclipsed by Leeds United.

Shankly's 'new' side reached the FA Cup final of 1971 but came up against an Arsenal team which won to complete the double. Liverpool had booked an open-topped bus to tour the city the folllowing day, just in case they had won the cup. Rather than cancel it Shankly insisted they took part in the Sunday afternoon procession. Thousands turned up to cheer their beaten team, something which made a lasting impression on the players, just as Shankly hoped it would. As he stood on the balcony at the city chambers he took the microphone and in that growling, captivating voice he said: 'At Wembley we lost the cup. I have always drummed it into my players that they are playing for you, the greatest public. If they did not believe it then, they will now by you all turning out today.'

Shankly knew he needed one last ingredient for his team to be great and he signed a young man from Scunthorpe United the week before that 1971 cup final: Kevin Keegan. When the new season began Keegan scored in front of the Kop within 12 minutes of his debut. The double act he went on to form with fellow striker

Toshack became legendary. Liverpool missed out on the 1971–72 league title when they only drew with Arsenal in the final game of the season. They had a goal disallowed with five minutes left, which meant Clough's Derby County pipped them to the championship. Shankly had not delivered a trophy for Liverpool in six years, but the fundamentals were right.

The following season was the best of his career. They narrowly won the league title with a goalless draw against Leicester City at Anfield on the final day of the season. He used only 14 players during the entire campaign. There was European glory too. Liverpool made the UEFA Cup final after wins over Eintracht Frankfurt, AEK Athens, Dynamo Berlin, Dynamo Dresden and Tottenham.

West German football was on a high in the early 1970s and a two-legged final against Borussia Monchengladbach was a formidable proposition. Borussia had Berti Vogts, Gunter Netzer, Rainer Bonhof and Jupp Heynckes who would all go on to be World Cup winners with their country the following year. Liverpool won 3–0 at Anfield, enough to see them win the trophy despite being outplayed and losing the second leg by two goals. Shankly was a European trophy winner at last.

Despite the victory some tentative questions were being asked as to whether Shankly, after 14 years in charge, was still up to the task of leading Liverpool for much longer. Early in 1974 chairman John Smith issued a statement stating that he could stay as manager for as long as he liked. That appeared to be the end of the speculation over his future. In 1973–74 Liverpool finished second in the league and beat Newcastle United 3–0 to win another FA Cup. In the civic reception to honour the team he came out with another great Shankly one-liner. As he looked at the tens of thousands of fans around St George's Hall, he said: 'Chairman Mao has never seen a greater show of red strength than today.'

And then came his bombshell. No newspaper got an exclusive on the story, no player had an inkling of what was to come. On 12 July 1974, Liverpool called a press conference. The journalists did not know what chairman Smith was about to say: 'It is with great regret that I as chairman of Liverpool Football Club have to inform you that Mr Shankly has intimated that he wishes to retire from active participation in league football. And the board has with extreme reluctance accepted his decision.'

The news rocked Merseyside and beyond. The fans who trusted him, had faith in him and looked up to him were stunned and distraught. Supporters jammed the Anfield switchboard with telephone calls, pleading for reassurances that the news was untrue. Shankly revealed that at the age of 60, and after 43 years in the game, he wanted a break. At the time he felt tired, perhaps weary even of having to 'perform' by living up to his image as a great orator and wag. In an emotional press conference he said: 'My wife thought at one time that I would not finish until the coffin came in the house but I think maybe I will have years now before the coffin arrives. I'm not saying the game would kill you, but being a manager is often like steering a ship through a minefield.'

Shankly promised to continue to live on Merseyside and to continue coming to games as a fan, maybe even to return to football in some other role in the future, although definitely not as manager of Liverpool. He had regretted not giving more time to his family. He admitted that his wife, Nessie, had had to put up with long periods on her own as he travelled the country with the team or on scouting missions. It was time to make things up to her. During that stressful period he appeared not to have lost his sense of humour, at least in public. When Adidas wanted to award him a Golden Boot for his contribution to football they asked him his size: 'If it's in gold, then I'm a 28.'

Strangely, having announced his retirement, he agreed to lead out the Liverpool team for the Charity Shield at Wembley and was also in the dugout for a testimonial match played for Celtic captain Billy McNeill at Parkhead. He even took the first day of pre-season training three days after retiring because no new manager had been appointed. Because retiring had been in his mind for over a year he had planned to recommend Paisley. If the Liverpool board decided to look externally for his successor Shankly's choice was Jack Charlton.

The club went with Paisley, the man who had tried to talk Shankly out of retiring in the first place. That proved to be an inspired appointment but, unfortunately for Paisley, retirement and Shankly did not mix. He couldn't get Liverpool out of his system and used to turn up to watch their training sessions at Melwood. Unintentionally, he was doing Paisley no favours. Even the players called Shankly 'boss' while Paisley was 'Bob'. Eventually the club informed him that it would be better if he stopped showing up at Melwood. It was one of several little moves which, unthinkably, drove a wedge between Shankly and Liverpool. He was not the type to ask for favours or turn up where he felt unwanted. When the new season began he spent his first Saturday as a retired manager watching Everton play Derby County: movingly, Goodison Park gave him warm and sustained applause.

There was talk of giving him the role of general manager or a place on the Liverpool board, just like Busby had been given at Manchester United. Neither offer materialised. As the months rolled on unsatisfactorily Shankly came to the conclusion that he was not being given the respect he deserved. There was a train of thought that he had made a major misjudgement and had regretted handing in his notice only hours after doing so. Because he was such a proud man he felt he could not go back on his decision. Liverpool did give him a testimonial match but he gradually felt marginalised and excluded.

In December 1976, he turned down an offer to be general manager at Derby and then had a short informal spell advising Wrexham. He helped John King at Tranmere Rovers and was actively encouraged by Everton manager Howard Kendall to come to their training ground. Kendall knew he still had a lot to offer football.

Shankly had always been a fitness fanatic. Although he still played five-a-side football and looked good for his age at 68, eight years after he retired he was taken into hospital following a heart attack in September 1981. Although financially able to do so, he did not opt for private treatment. That would have been against his socialist principles. He was treated in an ordinary ward of

Liverpool's Broadgreen Hospital. But then, on 29 September 1981, he was gone. A second heart attack proved fatal.

News of his death brought Liverpool to a standstill. Even the Labour Party conference held a minute's silence for the lifelong socialist. Busby, his longtime friend and confidant, was too upset to give an initial reaction to his death. Shankly was cremated and his ashes buried at the Anfield Crematorium. A memorial service at Liverpool Cathedral saw tens of thousands of people line the streets to honour 'Shanks'. Keegan, Paisley and Tom Finney – Shankly's favourite player – spoke during an emotional service which was concluded by Gerry Marsden singing the Liverpool anthem, 'You'll Never Walk Alone'.

The famous Shankly gates were erected at Anfield soon after on his wife Nessie's wishes. She wanted a tribute which was accessible for his people. In December 1997 a bronze statue of Shankly, complete with Liverpool scarf around the neck, was erected outside the stadium. The pose, chosen by Liverpool artist Tom Murphy, depicted a moment in 1973 when Shankly and his team were parading the league championship trophy in front of the Kop. A young supporter tossed his scarf onto the pitch in front of Shankly and an over-eager policeman kicked it away. He was admonished by the great man. 'It's only a scarf to you, but it's somebody's life.' Shankly picked up the scarf and wrapped it around his neck.

He was not remembered fondly only by Liverpool. When Preston North End rebuilt their ground in 1998 they renamed one stand the Bill Shankly Kop. It was designed with different coloured seats that created an image of his face. On 18 December 1999, a parade of legends gathered at Anfield to mark the 40th anniversary of the day Shankly walked in as manager for the first time. They were all there, Keegan, St John, Yeats, Smith and many more. Nearly all of the 1965 and 1974 FA Cup winning teams paraded on the pitch, where they stood in silence as two bagpipers played 'Amazing Grace'. Then 12,000 on the Kop gently sang the name 'Shankly' to the tune as they held up a mosaic bearing his face and the Saltire.

For all the very public tributes to Shankly over the years perhaps the most poignant is an elegant granite monument back at Glenbuck. The words on the memorial, paid for by a Liverpool supporters' club and Scottish Coal among others, read: 'Seldom in the history of sport can a village the size of Glenbuck have produced so many who reached the pinnacle of achievement in their chosen sport. This monument is dedicated to their memory and to the memory of one man in particular, Bill Shankly. The Legend. The Genius. The Man.'

Tommy Smith was one of Shankly's first signings at Liverpool. Shankly once said of him: 'Tommy Smith wasn't born, he was quarried', although when Smith turned up for training one day with a bandaged knee Shankly snapped: 'Take that poof bandage off, and what do you mean you've hurt your knee? It's Liverpool's knee.' Under Shankly the teak-tough defender won two league championships, two FA Cups and one UEFA Cup.

'Liverpool would not be the football club it is today if it had not been for Bill Shankly. He transformed its fortunes and made the careers of many players, including me. I first came across him when I went with my mum Margaret up to Anfield as a 15-year-old to sign for the club on 19 May 1960.

'It was a dream come true. I had gone to Cardinal Godfrey High School in Liverpool and had idolised Billy Liddell. To be honest, I was more excited about meeting him at that stage than I ever was about meeting Shanks. I ended up playing alongside Billy in the reserves as I was a centre-forward back then and it was one of the biggest thrills of my life.

'I went onto the ground staff, which turned out to be a blessing in disguise for the simple reason that out of the nine of us, five were from Scotland. That meant that when I broke through into the first team and worked with Shanks every day I had no problem picking up his quick Scottish accent because I had heard similar ones among my mates on the ground staff.

'Shanks was a private man who you never really got to know.

Probably the only time I was at his house was when I was on the ground staff. Not because he had invited all of us round, but because he absolutely hated doing his garden. It was his pet hate, so he got the boys on the ground staff to do it for him. In fact he hated it so much that years later, when I got married, I asked the club for a loan to buy a house and tidy up the garden. Shanks looked at me with disgust and said: "Son, I'll give you the money to buy paving stones to put down over the grass and money to buy the paint to paint them green. You're a footballer, son, not a gardener."

'I was well looked after at Liverpool and went from the C team to the B team to the reserves. I was in the reserves for a while. I thought I was doing okay and kept knocking on his door asking him when I would get my chance in the first team. I think he respected the fact I had the confidence to fight my corner, but my logic was that because I was playing well what better time to push myself forward for selection? You're not going to do it if you're playing badly, are you?

'I finally wore him down. Shanks gave me my debut against Birmingham on 8 May 1963. I was as high as a kite and played my part in a 5–1 win. I may have just been 18 years old but thought I would get a good run in the side after that. The complete opposite happened. In the 1963–64 season, when Liverpool won the title, I never got a game. I spent my time in the reserves. He said he didn't think I was ready for an extended run in the team, which I didn't agree with. I felt he was doing it to show me who was boss. I was really angry because I was bigger than most of the other young boys at the club and knew I could cope in the first team. I got into an argument with Shanks, which I had no chance of winning.

' "Listen, son, I'm Bill Shankly and I take no shite from anybody!" he said as he ordered me out of the office. Through the years the phrase "I take no shite from anybody" was one I used a lot. "I was Tommy Smith. I played for Liverpool. I take no shite from anybody." I became a regular in Shanks's team in the 1964–65 season. What a team we had! Players like Tommy Lawrence in goal, Ron Yeats in defence, Ian St John up front. I could go on. Shanks could certainly pick a player.

'He was also an innovator. Tactically he was away ahead of others of his generation, although he didn't go on and on about tactics all the time like some managers. A lot was made about England winning the World Cup in 1966 playing with an "innovative" 4–4–2 formation. What a lot of rubbish! Shanks was playing with that formation long before Alf Ramsey introduced it to England.

'He also did his homework on players. He could tell us what wingers preferred to go down the line and which ones always came inside. He would pinpoint the best player in the opposition and tell us to watch him but would never ask us to man-mark whoever it was. He kept it simple. If he pushed up on the right, our left back would watch him. If he drifted inside our centre-backs would pick him up. If he moved to the left, our left-back would pick him up. By never man-marking players we never thought any of the opposition were terribly frightening. It took the pressure off us as we didn't have to concentrate on anybody long enough to worry about them. As Shanks would say, he wanted the opposition to worry about us.

'He would leave no stone unturned as he tried to bring success to Liverpool. Despite the fact I was a defender he got me to play with number ten on my back when we played foreign opposition to try and confuse them. It usually worked for a while until they twigged that there was no point man-marking the number ten because he never usually crossed the half-way line. Putting that little bit of self-doubt into foreign opposition always made Shanks smile.

'Training-wise, he introduced techniques that helped improve my skills and fitness. Talking to some of the older guys when I first arrived at Liverpool, it seemed that all the players did in training before Shanks arrived was to run round the pitch or up and down the steps in the stand. He even brought boxers up to Anfield to talk to us about their training regimes so we could learn about the miles they put in every day and the hard graft they did between bouts. Out on the training ground, when there were fights between players Shanks would be delighted. He used to stand there and say "Look at them . . . imagine what they are going to be like on Saturday."

'If we won on Saturday we were off Sunday and Monday but if we had been beaten we were back in on the Monday for training. You could gauge how angry Shanks had been with our performance from whether or not he joined us in the sauna after the Monday training session. Now I don't think many managers, if any, would follow their players into the sauna, but Shanks knew he had a captive audience. Our hearts used to sink when he used to jump in and started laying into whatever poor soul was in there at the time. Woe betide you if you left the sauna early before he had finished shouting you out.

'We used to take his criticism on the chin and on a personal level me and him got on pretty well, to the extent he gave me the captaincy in 1970 when he was rebuilding the side and Ron Yeats was about to leave for Tranmere Rovers. When I took over he told the press I wasn't "born", I was "quarried", not because I was big but because he thought I was gobby and my mouth was as big as a quarry.

'It was no secret at Liverpool that I never got on with Emlyn Hughes and it was when Shanks gave the captaincy to him ahead of me that we fell out a bit. Shanks called me and said Hughes wanted the captaincy off me and if he didn't get it he was leaving the club. He felt it was worth giving in to him and he made him on-field captain but he tried to keep me sweet by making me club captain.

'It didn't really work and I remember we were playing against Arsenal and I wasn't picked so I packed my bag and headed out of the stadium. Shanks followed me out and said he would have done the same thing himself, which took a bit of the sting out of the moment. You always knew where you stood with him, even when I lost the captaincy. He never let things fester. He confronted things head on and you respected him for it.

'The long-standing joke between the pair of us through all my years at Liverpool was the fact that Alf Ramsey only picked me once for England. Just the bloody once! I used to get really upset about that and whenever the latest squad came out Shanks used to come up to me and put his arm round me. "I see he's done it again, son. I canna' believe he hasn't picked you. But don't worry about it, son. What does Alf Ramsey know? He's only won one cup." The fact that the one cup was the World Cup didn't bother Shanks. He saw one of his boys a bit down and wanted to encourage him. That was the great thing about Shankly. He was always on your side.'

Sir Alex Ferguson

*'If God came alongside him, Fergie would tell him
what he thought of him.'*

Everyone always says that Sir Alex Ferguson is behind his desk at Manchester United's training ground at the crack of dawn. Every-one always says he prides himself on his punctuality. He's never late for a meeting. Well, he was this time. A four-hour drive from Scotland, an overnight stay in a Manchester hotel and an early rise to beat the rush-hour traffic: all to be in Carrington in plenty of time for the scheduled 9 a.m. interview with Fergie. And he was nowhere to be seen. His car wasn't even in the car park.

Eventually his secretary confirmed that he was running late. A few minutes later this was extended to 'He's phoned to say he'll be a while yet' and eventually, 'You might as well go away and come back around 11 o'clock.' Two hours later than arranged, in other words. From the point of view of the interview this was good, an obvious icebreaker. Fergie would feel bad about having kept a fellow Scot waiting after coming down to see him. It might soften him a little; increase the likelihood of him opening up. Better quotes. It was a nice idea.

What actually happened was this: Ferguson suddenly burst in, made a beeline for this author, offered the firmest of handshakes, sat down, clapped his hands together and said 'Right, fire away!' No apology, no small talk, no 'How was the trip down?' Would he have some time for the photographer after the interview? 'Naw. He can fire away as we're talking.'

Much later, on the cusp of another question being blurted out, he abruptly clapped his hands together again and stood up. Interview over. No negotiation, no checking of the watch, no fourth official holding up a board saying three minutes left, just an abrupt final whistle. Ferguson quickly said 'Well done' (a phrase he has a habit of using at the end of an interview) and then managed the tiniest morsel of chit-chat: 'You driving back up the road just now? That's good. Right, cheerio.'

Brusque, unapologetic, unconcerned, and now disappearing behind a door which was closing firmly behind him. Gone. There hadn't even been an opportunity to reminisce about the first time we'd met, when the author was one of a coachload of schoolboys taken to visit Pittodrie and Ferguson had stood at the bus door and patted each of us on the back and thanked us for coming. It had been only 20 years earlier. He was bound to remember. And the interview itself? Lengthy, wide-ranging, opinionated, funny and rewarding. A joy from start to finish. The entire episode had been in turn unnerving, fascinating and compelling, like Ferguson himself. And the photographer got a lovely picture of him, laughing.

Where do you start with Sir Alex Ferguson? This epic personality, a footballing Ali or Churchill, has had around 20 books written about him, including hagiographies, hatchet jobs and his own compelling autobiographies. He's never off the back pages. Television laps him up. There have been documentaries and DVDs. Because everyone in the land knows about Ferguson the vast majority – who don't watch his football and recognise only the caricature of a purple-faced touchline Taggart – assume that everything his wonderful teams have achieved has been down to a hard bastard from Glasgow shouting and bawling at them from the dugout. Furious, angry, raging Fergie: putting the fear of God into his players until they're too scared to come back to the dressing room unless they've won. Well, yes, that's part of it. There's no denying the man's intimidating temper and ruthless competitiveness.

'Fergie's strong,' said Sandy Busby, son of the great Sir Matt, 'If God came alongside him, Fergie would tell him what he thought of him.' But football management has seen plenty of bullying sergeant-majors come and go without leaving a trace. Ferguson has become the greatest manager Britain has ever produced – with a strong claim to be the most exceptional the game has ever seen – because of an unprecedented range of qualities, influences and characteristics. He is an extraordinary individual who just happens to be a football manager.

Romantic eulogies to a Govan childhood and the shipyards might account for his hard, unflinching temperament, but they don't begin to explain his football instincts, man-management and cunning. Who put it into his head to motivate East Stirlingshire players by telling them the local press was against them in 1974? What inspired him to go around Paisley in a van with a loudhailer, like a politician at election time, encouraging St Mirren fans to turn out? Or to keep records of how many times the leading Glasgow-based journalists travelled to Aberdeen to watch his team? These are all hackneyed Ferguson stories by now, but what's interesting is that he had never worked under a manager who had done any of this. They were all inspired, brilliant stunts. He thought them up.

And then there is the longevity. He has been around forever. Every book on him is quickly rendered out of date by some fresh accumulation of silverware. By the end of the 2010 season he had won 34 major trophies: 24 with United (including 11 league titles and two European Cups) and ten with Aberdeen (including three league titles and the European Cup Winners' Cup). People respond to his teams: every club he has managed has experienced huge increases in attendances. United's average crowds were

46,000 the season before Ferguson; now they fill 76,000 every week. His consistency means United's status as a superpower has been taken for granted. It is down to him. In the mid–1980s they could have slipped away to become another Newcastle United or Leeds United. Even then, when they had gone 20 years without winning the league, he correctly judged that they could be far, far bigger than their financial turnover or attendances suggested.

'When I think back to when I was in cahoots with him in the 1980s and was talking to him all the time, one of the things that struck me was the enormity of his vision for Manchester United,' said Mark McGhee, who was close to Ferguson for several years after playing for him at Aberdeen, 'He spoke of wanting the capacity to be 75,000. Now this was at a time when gates were struggling a wee bit and the capacity would have been about 50,000. He had this much bigger vision of the club being global. Man United has turned out to be the perfect job for him. He needed something as big as that in order to be a vehicle for the size of his vision. He wanted a job that could enable him to make a club the biggest club in the world. Manchester United was able to give him that.'

Who else might Ferguson have worked for? He seems inextricable from the red, white and black, but Sheffield United, Wolves, Rangers, Arsenal and Tottenham (whom he came very close to joining in 1984) all made offers when he was at Aberdeen. There was interest from Barcelona and Inter Milan. After he joined United there were offers from Real Madrid, Inter Milan, Barcelona, Monaco and the Republic of Ireland, and he was sounded out by England more than once. The latter would have had no appeal to him beyond its use as a bargaining tool to lever a more appropriate salary out of United. Ferguson has always adopted loud, almost comedic displays of his patriotism around United and in front of the English media.

'They [his fellow players] call him my dad or granddad,' said United's Scottish midfielder, Darren Fletcher, 'He is just one of those guys who are very patriotic about Scotland. Any Scottish team, any Scottish sportsman. It puts a lot of pressure on me, actually, all these little side bets he puts on during international week. There's nothing like going off to play France with the manager shouting ' "If you lose, don't come back!" ' Ferguson makes insulting remarks about the English media – in front of them, and with next to nothing coming back at him – when Scottish reporters arrive to cover a United game against Rangers or Celtic in the Champions League. When United's European ambitions were hampered by UEFA's 1990s insistence that a club must play eight home-based players in European and UEFA Cup ties, he said: 'I never thought I'd see the day when I'd say we needed more Englishmen in our squad.'

Scotland has been proud of Ferguson at United, but essentially he has been committed only to a red crusade. He has done things his way and held English football by the scruff of the neck for two decades. There is that iconic quote about arriving to unseat the dominant club in the land – 'My greatest challenge was knocking Liverpool right off their fucking perch . . . and you can print that' – but that was said in 2002 and the job was already done by then. More revealing of his steely self-belief was a remark at the beginning of his second full season. 'This isn't just a job to me, it's a mission. I am deadly serious about it. We will get there. Believe me. And when it happens, life will change for Liverpool and everybody else. Dramatically.'

It did. Ferguson was still in his 40s the last time Liverpool won a title. The greatest achievement of all was to slowly rewrite football history and become the fourth man on a podium which only had room for three. The Holy Trinity of Scottish management used to be Busby, Bill Shankly and Jock Stein. Now he stands above them all. 'He's virtually the shop steward down here,' said his rival and friend David Moyes. 'He's the man. Not just for Scottish managers, but any of them.'

Trying to copy Ferguson would be of limited value to a younger manager. He was born with natural assets which cannot be imitated. He was blessed with an analytical and incisive mind, a restless intellectual curiosity and an exceptional memory for facts, faces, telephone numbers and, crucially, the minutiae of how moves unfold during a passage of football. No dulling of the brain, no forgetfulness, crept in as he approached 70. He can still discuss the seductive tribalism of English football – Geordies, Yorkshiremen, Scousers, Mancs, the Midlanders, Southerners – and sound like an enthusiastic youth. And then there's Europe.

'That tribalism forces you to do well in the Premier League but the real excitement comes in European games. The Wednesday night atmosphere when you maybe go to Madrid or Barcelona and you can smell the cigars and there's perfume in the stands. It's wonderful, it's different. I love it. You go to Milan and everyone's so stylish. Every woman who passes you by is Miss World.'

He is seen by some as unyielding and 'old school' but if there was nothing more to him than that he would have been redundant in modern management years ago. His open-mindedness and ability to adapt to the enormous sea changes in football over nearly four decades have ensured his astonishing longevity, his continued relevance, and his success. When Ferguson was first appointed as a manager, in 1974, Don Revie was still in charge of Leeds United, Harold Wilson was Prime Minister and Richard Nixon was in the White House.

An explosive temper was bound to become the most recognisable element of his autocratic personality. For much of his career he ruled by fear, although that aspect diminished as he became successful at Manchester United and was able to control young, multi-millionaire footballers through more sophisticated techniques. Ferguson's qualities are legendary: hardness, aggression, a confrontational nature, ferocious competitiveness, insatiable desire, ambition and a relentless work-rate. Some have affectionately referred to him as 'Furious' since the late 1970s. After his visit to the palace in 1999 he became 'Sir Furious'. Search the internet for the words 'Fergie' and 'hairdryer' and headlines will pop up along the lines of 'Fergie turns hairdyer on FA' or 'Wenger gets Fergie hairdryer treatment' or 'Man City get the Fergie hairdryer'.

Anyone who has played under him would snort at such nonsense. Those headlines allude to impossible stories. The 'hairdryer' has never been experienced by a rival manager, a governing body, or another club.

Some newspaper headline-writers make the mistake of using the word as shorthand for any show of anger from Ferguson. The real thing was always much more terrifying, stressful, personal, un-pleasant and humiliating than that. A few journalists have been on the receiving end of it over the years but by and large it has been reserved for those who served under him at East Stirlingshire, St Mirren, Aberdeen and Manchester United. A memorable account was given by Colin Gibson, who became the scapegoat after United lost 4–0 to Tottenham.

' "Where the fuck is Gibson? Where is that little cunt?" That's the welcome I got when I got into the dressing room. Then he just fixed his eyes on me and started saying "You think you can play for England, do you? You wouldn't get picked to play for England's women's hockey team!" He was trying to humiliate me in front of my team-mates.'

Ferguson had been at United for only six months at the time. The club didn't know what had hit it. He confronts those who have challenged or angered him in a literal, physical way. He moves across the room until he is right in their face. His nose is two or three inches from theirs, the chin up, the shoulders back. The body language is aggressive and unflinching. His eyes fix on to theirs like a bird of prey locking on to a field mouse. Now that he has them pinned he is in position to let rip with his remorseless, expletive-driven barrage of criticism, abuse and intimidation. He might openly question their ability or even their future at his club. He is so red and angry and close that the player can feel his breath. Tiny flecks of Fergie saliva might spray from him during the ordeal. All of this usually goes on against a dressing-room wall in clear view and hearing – naturally he unloads at full volume – of the hapless player's silent team-mates. They avoid eye contact. They shift uneasily in their seats. They are sorry for their mate but they're just glad it's someone else's turn this time. He does it as soon as possible so that it's out of the way, especially at half-time when every minute is precious. For the poor sod on the receiving end it seems to last a lifetime. Mark Hughes was the one who experienced the up-close heat, noise and intensity of an uninterrupted Ferguson blast and realised that it felt as though his hair had been blown back. Hence he coined the phrase 'the hairdyer', although not until after he had left Manchester United. 'He would stand nose-to-nose with you and just shout and bawl, and you would end up with your hair behind your head,' said Hughes.

Ferguson takes any mention of it with a sort of gently amused exasperation. He once consulted United's lawyers to see if he could sue for defamation when a newspaper wrote that he used to go behind a stand to practice screaming. Generally he accepts that there's no smoke without fire. It is accepted that some of his rants were for effect rather than born out of genuine anger. It's all part of the 'Furious Fergie' persona, and just as horrifying for the un-suspecting victim. In his time he has kicked football boots at his players in the dressing room and hurled a tray of tea cups towards them after hurting his hand when he smacked a tea urn. It is misleading to see these histrionics as part of his weekly repertoire, even though that is often the impression given in the media. Twenty-two years passed between him throwing tea cups towards Gordon Strachan and kicking a boot towards David Beckham.

'He could be a frightening character,' said Strachan, 'It was almost a test of character when he had a go at you. He wanted to know if you had enough bottle to stand up to him . . . and that would prove that you had the same bottle to help you succeed on the park. Fergie's thing was anger. He works on anger. You look at the year when he decided to pack it in at the end of the season [2001–02]. There wasn't a fire in that United team because there was a bit of magic missing from the man at the top, that real drive and determination was missing for a while.'

That was a commonly held view at the time and the speculation was not lost on Ferguson himself. 'The critics were saying I'd lost my hunger and desire,' he said later, 'You bet that hurt. I'd never had my desire questioned before. That's what really wound me up.' It was inevitable that he would take any criticism of his focus and professionalism as a personal affront. Bobby McCulley, who played under him at East Stirlingshire, said: 'He owned a pub in Glasgow called Shaw's Bar and I used to go in after he'd moved to St Mirren. I'd find Fergie inside playing dominoes with all the old men, slamming his pieces down, deadly serious, trying to win.' The veteran journalist Glenn Gibbons has long been used to receiving unexpected telephone calls from Ferguson seeking an answer on some piece of trivia. A film title, perhaps, or the name of a singer. Doubtless he was in a quiz or had made a wager. 'Alex's competitiveness is legendary and it's so comprehensive: it's physical, it's cerebral, it's everything,' said Gibbons. 'Anything he does has to be fully committed. I don't know how he finds the time in the day. He always says decisiveness is the most important part of the job. You have to be decisive, even if you get some wrong. His whole career is littered with big decisions that he got mainly right.'

Physically Ferguson has always had the resilience and stamina to put the hours in. He has rarely been ill and can operate at optimum levels after only four or five hours' sleep. It nourishes him to be up at 6 a.m. and, usually, at his desk by 7.15. He was treated for a heart condition late in 2003 and had a pacemaker fitted a few months later. It was barely mentioned again. He is of pensionable age and a grandfather several times over, yet there is no sense of physical frailty about him. The 'stress' of managing Manchester United seems to energise him like a mobile plugged into its charger. 'I've been blowing up since I was five years old,' he has said, 'Probably it helps that I'm able to get rid of pressure by losing my temper. And once I've lost it, I don't usually think much about the issue afterwards. I can put the problem out of my mind and life is wonderful again.'

His friend and biographer, Hugh McIlvanney, says Ferguson's energy has always seemed remarkable. 'One of the things about Alex that isn't always emphasised sufficiently is the bestial energy he has brought to his work. The energy and drive and stamina have been phenomenal throughout his career. He hasn't just been relentless in bursts. He's been relentlessly relentless. When he was working on his autobiography Alex wrote 250,000 words on foolscap as a basis for the text I produced. On the day United won the Champions League final in Barcelona in 1999 he phoned me and said: "I'm just sitting here on the balcony writing about some stuff we should cover in the book." I said: "Alex, haven't you got other matters you should be attending to?" He said, "Ach well, I had a wee bit of time and thought I'd make use of it." Now that could be regarded as slightly unusual behaviour.'

Although he has been consistently competitive and uncompromising, Ferguson is generally an unpredictable individual. When one of his dark moods seems inevitable, he can turn out to be unnaturally chirpy. He often goes around singing to himself. When a result would suggest he should be sunny, he will emerge in a thunderous mood. He cannot be second-guessed. The banter and craic around a football club stimulates him and can bring out the devilment. One seasoned Ferguson watcher said: 'People wouldn't understand this but he has them in stitches. He's hilarious with these young lads. Some young lad will pass him at Carrington [United's training ground] and say "hello gaffer" and Alex will say to anyone nearby "What about this boy, have you ever seen an uglier boy than this?" And the boy will be killing himself laughing. It's daft stuff, really, but can you imagine how those boys feel when Alex talks to them? It's the man himself!'

Interestingly there has been no consistency – either in temperament, attitude, background or even nationality – in the men Ferguson has picked to be his assistants over the years: Ricky McFarlane, Pat Stanton, Archie Knox (twice), Willie Garner, Brian Kidd, Steve McClaren, Carlos Queiroz (twice), Walter Smith and Mike Phelan. During his decades in the spotlight Ferguson has often been invited to analyse his own qualities. 'The one thing I always felt I had when I was young is that I was always prepared to be decisive. Whether or not that was in instinct or impulsiveness, I had it in me to do that. I was a wee bit bossy when I was younger. I'm not saying this as a promotion of myself, but you get some guys who stand out in that way. It's just a characteristic thing about me: being decisive and go-ahead, at times even aggressive. I've always been like that, never changed. That aggression is a Glaswegian thing, especially with guys of my generation. I meet guys throughout the world and hear the Scottish accent and I say "Where are you from?" and they're "I'm frae Glasgow". It's amazing how many are out there. They go out there because they have the determination to do well.'

Ferguson still controls, dominates and scares people. His own players, other managers, governing bodies, referees and especially journalists are wary of him. Age has not lessened the sense of menace he gives off. There are countless witnesses to the more rounded, warmer aspects of his complex personality. He is a natural raconteur and a high IQ ensures that he can be lively, easy company, knowledgeable on a variety of subjects and full of laughter. It is significant that the less appealing aspects of his nature express themselves only within football. There are no tales of him being rude, disrespectful or arrogant with members of the public. On the contrary, he is at ease with people and social conversation flows naturally. He can be friendly and charming. He is capable of showing great compassion and humanity. His time and energy are kindly given to charities, or to attend funerals for distant friends or associates, or to telephone another manager, or even occasionally a reporter, who has lost his job. There have been many little personal gestures, unreported, which speak volumes for the man. Youth and other initiatives in Manchester, Glasgow and elsewhere have benefited hugely from his public patronage.

Sandy Busby still recalls with great gratitude something that happened a few months after Sir Matt had passed away: 'The first Christmas after my dad died, my sister and I got a bunch of flowers, each. They arrived from the club, but we knew that would have been down to Fergie.' He has been an enthusiastic champion of the League Managers Association and a comforting voice on the end of a telephone for struggling managers or even successful ones in need of advice.

'This is a business,' said David Moyes. 'If you're from Glasgow you have to stand on your own two feet. But I've been to see him a few times about jobs I've been offered. I remember him phoning me and saying I should sell a player. It was good advice he was trying to give. He was trying to help. He wants to see people who are hungry and driven to succeed in the same way he was. He has to be admired but, make no mistake, he's as tough as he's ever been. He wouldn't give you a result in a million years.'

A Scottish accent may help, but Ferguson does not discriminate when it comes to offering help to fellow managers. 'There's no doubt it's an advantage to have Fergie's ear,' said Alex McLeish, who has followed him from Aberdeen into top flight management in England, 'But I think a lot of English managers are very close to Fergie too. He has been mentor to loads of young managers. It's amazing how generous he is with his time.' That is the lesser-known Ferguson.

On the other hand, the extreme significance he attaches to personal loyalty means he will cut people dead if he feels they have crossed him. He doesn't so much carry a grudge as absorb it into his marrow. When he discards someone it is as though he is a jockey or a boxer shedding unwanted fat. Some snubs or setbacks fuelled his ambition. He felt victimised towards the end of his time as a Rangers player and left the club in sour circumstances: 'The feeling of rejection and failure when I was discarded by Rangers was a real bad one. Yet, out of that adversity, I found a sense of determination that has shaped my life. I made up my mind then that I would never give in.' Years after being dismissed as the manager of St Mirren he said: 'I felt degraded by being sacked. After all I'd done for them I was obsessed with getting back at them. I wanted to humiliate them the way they had me.' Curiously, as a member of the heroic quartet with Busby, Shankly and Stein and arguably the greatest of them all, he is the only one to have experienced being sacked.

The list of individuals whose previously close relationship with Ferguson became strained or irreparably damaged is long and contains a high percentage of his former assistant managers (McFarlane, Garner, Kidd and Knox) as well as players who served under him such as Strachan, McGhee, Jim Leighton, Neil Webb, Paul Ince, Jaap Stam, Beckham, Roy Keane and Ruud van Nistelrooy. Being dropped by Ferguson for the 1990 FA Cup final replay was incredibly wounding for Leighton, who had been playing under him for club and country since 1978. 'There is not a hope in hell of that friendship ever being revived,' Leighton said later, 'I have promised myself that I will never again speak to him. I cannot find it in my heart to forgive him.' Yet it had been purely a football decision and many would see it as a textbook example of the sort of clinical, unsentimental act which has been part of Ferguson's managerial genius. He later explained it in a way which revealed much about his ability to sense the right course of action and pursue it, whatever the price. 'It was an animal instinct, nothing else. You smell danger and that depth of feeling burns inside you and tells you precisely the next move. Believe me, it really hurt. My conscience is absolutely clear.'

The 'danger' he could smell was losing the replay. Instead United won it without Leighton and Ferguson had his first trophy at the club after three and a half uncomfortable years. He lost a friendship but probably saved his own job. And in the final reckoning his loyalty was to United. McGhee returned to speaking terms with Ferguson but a previously long, close relationship hit the buffers when McGhee was manager of Wolves. Ferguson had recommended him to the club – his own son, Darren, was a player there at the time – but it had not worked out. Suddenly the telephone calls from Manchester were at an end. McGhee never quite understood why, but he knew Ferguson well enough to roll with the punches. 'People often talked to me about the fact our relationship was suddenly at an end. They said to me "Phone him" but I said no, because I knew him too well. That's not how he works or how he thinks. He doesn't take the huff with you. It's just that that relationship is at an end, for whatever reason. And that's permanent. It was with me. We do speak, but I don't have a relationship with him. I used to speak to him about once every three weeks. The end of our relationship was my loss. I don't have any hang-ups about it. I was grateful for the help he gave me at the beginning of my career. For whatever reason he made a decision that I was no longer a member of his privy council and because I knew him well enough I knew there was no fucking point phoning him up. So I just took it on the chin and tried to go and be successful anyway. I have phoned him a couple of times, so I don't have a problem. But I wasn't phoning to say "What have I done to upset you?" '

Strachan has described him as a 'complex' character. 'Even the people who get close to him will never really know him. They never get the chance. Players certainly don't get inside his head. He'll mingle with them one day, and then the next he won't say a word.' Journalists recognise that description. Reporters or entire newspapers are routinely banned from his press conferences. His interviews and briefings can be the best in the business. The media hangs on his every word, not just because of who he is but what he says. His opinions and analysis are perceptive, stimulating and original, even if they come unfailingly from a United perspective. He said United's fortress of a training ground at Carrington was good because 'It keeps those fuckers from the media out'. He has often closed a press conference with the parting shot: 'Away and write your shite!' When he was once asked if he would fly over to attend a World Cup he replied: 'None of your business. Do I ask if you're still going to those fucking gay clubs?'

In 2004 he stopped speaking to the BBC after a documentary investigated the relationship between United and his agent son, Jason. No wrongdoing was found and Ferguson has always insisted he was owed an apology by the BBC. 'People think there are degrees of loyalty,' he has said, 'There are no degrees of loyalty. If someone lets me down once, there's no way back.' Ironically, Jason has worked as an agent and in the media, two professions his father largely distrusts. 'It's not easy negotiating with agents,' he once said, 'Because every one of their players is the best in the world. So you have to go through all this shit before you have a sensible discussion.'

Ferguson was born in his grandparents' council house in Drumoyne, Glasgow, on Hogmanay, 1941. Famously, he was chiselled into shape by the vibrant, noisy shipbuilding community of Govan, close to Ibrox stadium and the giant cranes beside the River Clyde. His father, also Alex, was a shipwright in the yards. He was an intelligent, impressive figure of quiet authority, but demanding, occasionally fiery, not easily impressed and intolerant of weakness. He was a Protestant who married a Catholic, Liz; an energetic, determined, strong woman. Ferguson's father worked a lot of overtime and both parents lived carefully, so the family was relatively comfortable. There was no car, television or telephone, but they had an inside toilet and as an unusually small family – there was only one other sibling, Martin – they lived in two rooms, with a third rented to another family.

Ferguson does not regard himself as having been raised in poverty. 'Growing up in Govan at that time, it was a real hub. I grew up opposite Harland and Wolff [shipbuilders] so I had to live through the noise of the night shift workers banging around. The hammers going all night. You didn't have a lot but I never call it poverty, because I don't think it was poverty. You always had your meals, you never missed school, and you were always clean and tidy. We didn't have a bathroom but we did have a big zinc bath and you'd have your bath once a week and be scrubbed clean. It was a great upbringing.' The appreciation of his roots is palpable. He is still in touch with pals from primary school.

Although his father was chairman of the local Celtic Supporters' Club branch Ferguson's independent streak was quickly revealed and he chose Rangers. Mostly his free time was spent playing football himself. 'All we ever did was play football. Every day, all the time. We grew up in tenements so we spent all our time outside. Our mothers would say "Get out there and get some fresh air" so you were always out the back fighting with the gangs up the road and playing football. That was your life. Nowadays I'm in a 20–storey hotel and I look down and go "Oh for fuck's sake!" but when you're young nothing worries you.'

He left school at sixteen and began a five-year apprenticeship as a toolmaker, not in the Govan shipyards but four miles away at Hillington. Immediately, he became active in the trades union movement, joining the Amalgamated Engineering Union and becoming a shop steward. He was prominent in two apprentices' strikes. 'In most cases, and particularly in my case, your political views are formed by your parents' ideology or the way they want to see you brought up. My father was a strong Labour man and my mother was Labour too. I think my inner instinct is to be a socialist and a Labour man and no matter how much money I've got I will never change that.' Both of his parents had been shop stewards too.

Later Ferguson became close to two Prime Ministers, Tony Blair and Gordon Brown. 'I went to do a documentary of myself. I went to Glasgow and down to the shipyards. We went on to the deck of this ship and it was absolutely freezing. Honest to God, the wind was howling down the Clyde. It was just a young interviewer and he said "What do you think has shaped your character?" And I says "Do you feel that flipping wind?" Glasgow people are very down to earth. The things that make Glaswegians are the climate, and it was the tobacco, and then it became the shipbuilding. We were world famous. When they said "Clyde-built" they meant excellence.'

Ferguson qualified as a toolmaker aged 22 but eventually gave it up for a career as a footballer which began at Queen's Park, St Johnstone and Dunfermline. His ability tends to be downplayed. He was a prominent player of his time and joined Rangers in 1967 for a fee, £65,000, which was a record between Scottish clubs at the time. His 29 months at the club he supported became demoralising but had lasting significance. The manager he respected and who had signed him, Scot Symon, was quickly replaced. Soon Ferguson was made a scapegoat for a heavy defeat to Celtic in the 1969 Scottish Cup final and felt it was held against him that his new wife, Cathy, was a Catholic. Rangers' institutionalised sectarianism at the time was an open secret.

Ferguson's career wound down at Falkirk and then Ayr United. He scored 222 goals in 432 career appearances. Curiously, none of his six clubs ever made him captain. He was a natural leader, a strong voice in the dressing room, and a barrack room lawyer. His intelligence, energy, unfulfilled ambition and obsession with football meant an attempt at management was inevitable. He read *World Soccer* magazine when no other player did. He asked questions of his own and other managers relentlessly. He made note of the impact when Celtic manager Stein cleverly said Rangers could only throw away the title when they had a large lead in the closing weeks of the 1967–68 campaign. The comment seemed to wobble Rangers and they won only three of their final six games. Celtic snatched the title by two points. Similar 'mind games' would become a hallmark of Ferguson's own managerial formula. He had come to know Stein through a restaurant they both frequented with their wives and inevitably the Celtic genius was a major influence. Ferguson's final season had been under Ally MacLeod at Ayr and he found his irrepressible enthusiasm 'stimulating'. From Rangers men Symon and Bill Struth (who he had admired as a young supporter) there was a sense of the discipline and standards required at a truly professional club. And Symon never criticised his players in public.

The managerial jigsaw was coming together. Ferguson had become a qualified SFA coach in 1966 and was one of the few who frequently returned for refresher courses. He was hungry. After a recommendation from MacLeod to a contact at East Stirlingshire, Ferguson's managerial career began at that tiny club at the end of June 1974. It was a lifetime ago. Bobby Moore was still playing football and Carlisle United were briefly at the top of the league. Manchester United were in the second division. Ferguson was 32 years old and paid £40 a week (his livelihood came from running a pub). He stayed at 'The Shire' for only 117 days – long enough for one fall-out with directors and one threat to resign – which were successful and revealing. Players were told to turn up in collar and ties, training was restructured, briefings on the opposition were thorough, the team rose to third and average attendances leapt from 400 to 1200.

'I'd never been afraid of anyone but he was a frightening bastard from the start,' said one of the players, Bobby McCulley. A classic Ferguson trick was revealed for the first time. The players were told the local paper was biased towards the town's bigger club, Falkirk. He must have had a ruler out to detect a couple of extra column inches.

Poor old St Mirren. They had the vision and insight to appoint Sir Alex Ferguson as their manager in October 1974, and how are they remembered for it? As the stupid clowns who sacked him in 1978. He took the job on Stein's advice. St Mirren were sixth in the second tier and playing in front of 1900. When he left they had been promoted to the Premier Division, had 11,200 average gates and had assembled an excellent side without any transfer fees.

Ferguson's confidence and profile grew. More innovation: he wanted a full-time public relations officer for St Mirren, he launched a weekly club newspaper, and once or twice he went around the streets of Paisley with a loudhailer to drum up interest. The sacking had nothing to do with football. The board felt he had become a law unto himself at the club and directors were unhappy with unauthorised bonus and expenses issues. They suspected he had been tapped up by Aberdeen. The chairman at the time, Willie Todd, was mocked for the rest of his days about sacking Ferguson but it had been a unanimous decision by their five-man board. Ferguson was appointed by Aberdeen the following day.

Hurt and embarrassed by the stigma of being sacked, he claimed unfair dismissal at an industrial tribunal but lost the case a few months later. Coverage of the tribunal said the panel had concluded that he was a good team boss but a bad general manager of day-to-day club affairs and 'petty, immature, possessing neither by experience nor talent any managerial ability'. The author of that verdict had more to be embarrassed about than Todd. Aberdeen and Alex Ferguson were made for each other in 1978. Both were ready for take-off. Scotland's north-east felt vibrant as it transformed from a rural farming and fishing economy to the oil capital of Europe. Pittodrie had become the first all-seated, all-covered ground in Britain and one of the first with executive boxes.

The club had a very strong squad and an excellent crop of emerging young players but lacked self-belief and tended to 'freeze' when it mattered against Celtic and Rangers. They needed Ferguson's nerveless leadership. He sensed he was at a club with the fan base, resources and stable board – led by calm old chairman Dick Donald, whom he admired hugely – to take on the Old Firm and win major trophies. Ferguson, who had never won one of the three major competitions in Scotland, needed Aberdeen. He swept through the place like a hurricane, surviving a near-mutiny from some players in his first season and winning the league title in his second. He transformed an inferiority complex into arrogance. More titles and cups followed. Now Aberdeen expected to go to Glasgow and win, and they did.

They evolved into one of the outstanding teams in Europe in the first half of the 1980s. Ferguson bought only two members of the team which beat Real Madrid to win the 1983 European Cup Winners' Cup in Gothenburg but it was unmistakably a side in his image: mentally strong, resilient, organised, brimming with energy and character, and capable of moments of inspired brilliance. Aberdeen won eight major domestic trophies in Ferguson's eight years there, the same as they managed in more than 90 years without him. Success fed Ferguson. It reinforced his beliefs and convinced him his methods were right.

He was already a major personality in Scottish life. Young, eager, impatient, and ready to take on the world. Aberdeen players suffered him at his most formidable, his most furious. On long coach trips to away games they would watch the good films on the way down, just in case they played poorly and Ferguson denied them access to the video recorder on the way back. At a reserve match at Forfar he angrily kicked a laundry basket and spilled its contents all over the dressing room, including a pair of pants which landed on a young player's head and sat there like a hat. The lad was too scared to remove them. Ferguson continued his outburst before noticing. 'And you can take those fucking pants off your head. What the hell do you think you're playing at?'

Perhaps the key aspect of that anecdote is the setting: a reserve match at Forfar. He tore into his team minutes after the 1983 Scottish Cup final. 'It was a disgrace of a performance,' he said, so consumed by anger that he talked over the questions being put to him by a television interviewer on the Hampden pitch. 'I'm no' carin' – winning cups disnae matter – our standards have been set long ago and we're no' gonnae accept that from any Aberdeen team.' They had just beaten Rangers 1–0 in Glasgow to win the cup, 10 days after the astonishing triumph over Real Madrid. Ferguson realised he had overstepped the mark and apologised the following day, but the incident epitomised how he had utterly revolutionised Aberdeen. The only thing he couldn't change was the weather. 'Minus 18, on that beach, the wind's hitting your face, freezing your knackers off. You never get used to the cold.'

It was with Aberdeen that he perfected the indoctrination of players with a siege mentality. In this case the manufactured 'cause' was sticking it to west coast journalists who would rather report favourably on the Glasgow clubs. On one occasion Ferguson entered the press room at Motherwell after Aberdeen had dropped points there. His eyes happened to fall on the first reporter he saw, Hugh Keevins. 'You fucking cunts!' Ferguson bawled at him. 'You don't know fucking anything about Aberdeen. We never see you up at Pittodrie!' The season was around six weeks old. It so happened that Keevins, although based in Glasgow, had already been to Aberdeen four times. Much later the point was quietly made to Ferguson. 'I know. He just happened to be the first in my line of vision, so I shouted at him!' Ferguson has always been able to do premeditated rage better than anyone.

The press men genuinely were harming Aberdeen in another way, though, simply by alerting the wider world to this force of nature who had shattered the Old Firm's domination of Scottish football (it was quickly restored when he left). His chairman and mentor, Donald, tried every trick to keep him, including making him a director and offering him outright ownership of the club, but they both knew Ferguson had outgrown Aberdeen and that his team had peaked. Donald's wise but mournful face was across the Scottish media when Ferguson left on 6 November 1986. 'Manchester United have agreed to compensate us for the un-fulfilled portion of Mr Ferguson's contract,' he said, 'But how can you evaluate the loss of his services?'

Ferguson's reign as part-time caretaker manager of Scotland had been short but revealing. Taking over after witnessing the fatal heart attack of his friend and mentor Stein, Ferguson had eight months, ten games and the 1986 World Cup finals as an international manager. The six current or former Aberdeen players he took to the Mexico finals could not entirely comprehend what they saw: he was much calmer with the Scotland squad. There were no hairdryers. International players would not react to bullying, he had calculated, so he softened his approach. He made an unlikely visit to Sir Alf Ramsey for advice on acclimatising to Mexico (Ramsey had been at the 1970 finals there). Scotland were eliminated at the opening group stage but performed creditably against West Germany, Denmark and Uruguay. Ferguson con-troversially omitted Alan Hansen – Liverpool's double-winning captain – from the 22–man squad and days later his team-mate and extremely close pal, Kenny Dalglish, pulled out citing an injury. In Mexico Ferguson dropped captain Graeme Souness, by then the player/manager of Aberdeen's great rivals, Rangers, for the final game against the Uruguayans. He judged that heat exhaustion had diminished Souness's impact. The gamble with Souness backfired and Ferguson later admitted it had been a mistake. Still, Man-chester United were impressed by the bravery of the decision-making.

In all the years that Sandy Busby was in charge of the club shop beside Old Trafford, only one newly appointed Manchester

United manager went to the bother of coming in and introducing himself to everyone. 'Fergie and Archie Knox came walking in one day and introduced themselves,' said Busby. 'And he bought every book in the shop.' The visit had twin purposes. First, it was part of Ferguson's early process of familiarising himself with the club's staff of 140 or so, on a first-name basis. How could he make United feel like a family without knowing them all? Secondly, it helped him size up and get a feel for what he had joined. 'He has this thing about wanting control,' said Mark McGhee, 'We used to talk about it at Aberdeen. He wanted to control everything. So how could he possibly go to Man United and know how many toilet rolls were being used, or whatever? But that's the thing. You get the impression he still does.'

United were going nowhere when Ferguson arrived. They had finished fourth the previous season under Ron Atkinson and the general vibe was rudderless, complacent and half-hearted. Ferguson's impact was predictable: harder training sessions to improve their inadequate fitness, earlier starts to the working day (so the players would be caught in rush-hour traffic, inconveniencing but attuning them to the idea they were going to their work), days off were reduced, and players were told to get haircuts. Blazers and flannels were provided. They dropped into the relegation zone when they lost his first game, 2–0 at Oxford United on 8 November 1986, and his mother passed away a month later (his father had died early in 1979 during Ferguson's difficult first season at Aberdeen). United rallied a little to finish 11th. 'You can't go into a club and tell people their fitness is terrible, that they're bevvying, they're playing too much golf, and their ground is filthy. You simply have to improve things bit by bit,' said Ferguson. He might not have told them, but he thought it instantly.

The first three and a half years are remembered as the period when United almost did a St Mirren and sacked him. There is no evidence that their board of directors had any intent to do so, although supporters' pressure could have driven them to it in 1990 had he not won the FA Cup. The period tends to be lazily recalled as a period of unremitting failure. United actually rose to finish second in his first full season, behind Liverpool's outstanding John Barnes/Peter Beardsley side of 1987–88. Important arrivals were reshaping the first team – Brian McClair, Steve Bruce, Lee Sharpe, Mark Hughes – but corrosive flaws still ran through what often seemed like Manchester United Drinking Club. It took him two and a half years to move Paul McGrath and Norman Whiteside – great players, but prodigious boozers – out of Old Trafford. He had also sent rockets through the club's youth structure, resulting in some early success.

On Ryan Giggs's 14th birthday Ferguson turned up at his front door. Visiting the home of potential youth signings has always had multiple rewards for Ferguson. He can judge their character from a glimpse of their upbringing and they are usually so awed by his appearance that they pledge themselves to his club. One other benefit: Ferguson secretly sizes up the parents to gauge how big their lad will become. Gary Pallister and Paul Ince were signed. Paul Gascoigne turned him down.

But he was not delivering on the field. Under him they finished 11th, 2nd, 11th and 13th between his arrival and early May, 1990. That month's FA Cup final victory over Crystal Palace spared the United board from what might have become irresistible pressure to dismiss him. 'When is Mr Ferguson going to realise that he doesn't know what he is doing and return to that quiet backwater Aberdeen?' the *Red Issue* fanzine asked in 1989. A message scrawled on a bed sheet at one game read: '3 years of excuses and it's still crap . . . Ta-ra Fergie'. There were 'Fergie out!' chants after a 5–1 humiliation against Manchester City in 1989. Ominously, the season's FA Cup run began at Nottingham Forest. The vultures circled above, sensing Ferguson's head. 'Fergie, Fergie on the dole' taunted the Forest fans. Mark Robins's winning goal brought a reprieve. Going on to win the cup turned the tide in his favour. It bought him time. Just like that, the darkest days were behind him.

'If I hadn't had success at Aberdeen I definitely couldn't have done it at United. Unless you have a store, a surplus of experience, knowledge, talent and, just as important, guts, you wouldn't have a prayer. To be at Manchester United you have got to have bottle and real character. I had to dip deep into my personal resources.' The scouting was better, the youth coaching was better, the facilities were better, the discipline was better, the fitness was better, the organisation was better, the attitude was better, the players were better. The vast oil tanker of Manchester United had slowly been turned around. They rose to finish sixth and won the European Cup Winners' Cup in 1990–91.

Andrei Kanchelskis came into the side and Peter Schmeichel was signed. Giggs made a debut at 17. The media was all over the latest 'new George Best' but Ferguson allowed them virtually no access to the spectacular prodigy. It was powerful media management which helped shape Giggs' career and personality. United's 26-year wait for a league title ended in 1992–93. Eric Cantona was the catalyst: a strutting, imperious conductor who epitomised the flair and power Ferguson had assembled. 'It was the day I truly became manager of Manchester United,' he said of winning the champion-ship, 'There was a sudden, overwhelming realisation that I was master of my own destiny.' Busby, a kindly figure in the back-ground, swelled with pride: United, his baby, was in safe hands at last. The great old man died a few months later.

Ferguson has a habit of describing this or that squad or team as 'my best ever' but the claim is particularly valid for the 1993–94 side: Schmeichel; Paul Parker, Pallister, Bruce, Denis Irwin; Kanchelskis, Ince, Roy Keane, Giggs; Cantona, Hughes. They won United's first league and FA Cup double. 'The team of '94 was fabulous,' he said, 'There were a lot of different ingredients in it and it had a combustible nature. They'd fight anyone. They were physically strong and could deal with anything. If you wanted to play football, we'd play football. If you wanted to fight us, we'd fight you.' At the start of that season Ferguson had told them he had an envelope containing the names of six players he feared were not up to the job and told them it was their duty to prove him wrong. Later he joked that the only name in the envelope had been his own.

Roy Keane would become, like Cantona, an iconic United figure. Ferguson's genius lay in infecting outstanding players with his own insatiable desire for relentless success. None reflected him on the field more than Keane. Life at United became a soap opera, with Ferguson the director even if he could not always dictate the script. His brilliant man-management of Cantona included protecting and reassuring the Frenchman when he was banned for nine months for a kung-fu kick on a supporter. In the summer of 1995, having finished behind champions Blackburn Rovers, Ferguson caused consternation by allowing Hughes, Ince and Kanchelskis to leave. He was infuriated by an entirely unscientific *Manchester Evening News* poll which claimed to show 53 per cent of United supporters felt it was time for him to go. The season began with a defeat at Aston Villa and Alan Hansen's 'You can't win anything with kids' line. Paul Scholes, Gary Neville, Phil Neville and Nicky Butt had started the match for United, with Beckham coming on as a substitute. That coltish team went on to win a league and cup double and form the backbone of triumphant United sides for more than a decade. Ferguson's judgement was sound. Having the courage of his convictions and the bravery to throw them all in collectively was extraordinary.

His success in English football has long since elevated him beyond credible criticism in that arena, although under him United have punched below their weight in the European Cup. By 2010 he had launched 16 assaults on the Champions League, won it twice, lost a final, and gone out in three semi-finals and five quarter-finals. United have been knocked out by moderate opponents like Galatasaray, Borussia Dortmund, Monaco and Bayer Leverkusen and twice failed to get past the group stage. 'We definitely should have at least a couple more [European Cups].' At 90 minutes of the 1999 Champions League final they seemed beaten again, losing 1–0 to Bayern Munich as the game eased into stoppage time. What followed were the greatest 103 seconds of

Ferguson's career. Teddy Sheringham equalised from a corner and almost instantly Ole Gunnar Solskjaer jabbed in an impossibly dramatic winner. Fergie had won the European Cup, emulated Busby, and completed an unprecedented treble with the league and FA Cup. He unscrambled his senses long enough to capture the raw theatre of it all in four words: 'Football, eh? Bloody hell!' It is one of his most-repeated quotes, along with referring to the closing stages of a title race as 'squeaky bum time'. 'When I won my first European Cup I said "Thank fuck that's out of the road!"', because that was always a criticism of me. Then we went through a dry zone and we had to wait another nine years to do it.' His second success did not register so high on the Richter scale, as Chelsea were beaten on penalties in the 2008 final in Moscow. Ferguson has often claimed that great clubs are defined by how often they win the European Cup. Only by that standard can he feel a little unfulfilled.

In 2001 he became the first manager ever to win three consecutive English titles (Huddersfield and Arsenal had changed bosses during their earlier hat-tricks). In 2009 he completed another three-in-a-row. United's form dipped when it was known he was retiring at the end of the 2001–02 season, before he changed his mind. The accusation that he and/or the players had taken their eye off the ball resurfaced during 2003–04 when he became embroiled in an ugly legal claim against the Irish horseracing magnate John Magnier. Ferguson had been gifted co-ownership of the champion horse 'Rock of Gibraltar' and believed he would also have half of its future breeding rights. Magnier said this was not the case and their friendship abruptly ended when Ferguson sued him for over £50 million. Eventually, after an escalation of distracting and unpleasant exchanges, the matter was settled out of court.

United rolled on under him. Allowing Beckham and Keane to leave and signing the likes of Juan Sebastian Veron, Rio Ferdinand, Cristiano Ronaldo and Wayne Rooney maintained United's profile and Ferguson's position as the undisputed *capo di tutti capi*.

For two decades he has been the manager by which all others in England are judged. From 1993 to 2010 George Graham, Kenny Dalglish, Arsene Wenger, Kevin Keegan, Gerard Houllier, Jose Mourinho, Rafa Benitez and Carlo Ancelotti won seven titles between them. Ferguson won 11. He met, head-on, the challenge from Roman Abramovich's enriched Chelsea when plenty rushed to write obituaries for him and United. He has enjoyed playing a cat-and-mouse game with one managerial rival after another, adopting a deliberately confrontational attitude and seeming to revel in lingering feuds as if they fuel him and his players. His ability to pick fights, lob verbal grenades and get into the minds of his competitors is unsurpassed. Curiously, that was not an approach he used in Scotland, where he saw Dundee United manager Jim McLean as a co-conspirator to help bring down the Old Firm. He was not disrespectful to the Celtic and Rangers managers of the time.

At one point relations were so hostile with Wenger that government ministers and the Metropolitan Police expressed their concerns and the FA wrote to both United and Arsenal demanding a truce. Keegan and Benitez were others who have wriggled on the hook although, perhaps surprisingly, there was mutual respect and admiration between Ferguson and Mourinho. Such is the interpretation placed on everything Ferguson says that when he began to discuss Wenger more fondly it was seen as a sign that he no longer regarded Arsenal as a primary threat.

Ryan Giggs broke the record for the number of United first team appearances when he pulled on the colours for the 758th time in 2008. Every one of them had been under Ferguson. The feat was astonishing for both men, an indication of breathtaking longevity from player and boss. Giggs has now heard Ferguson's pre-match addresses well over 800 times, sat through 800 of his half-time team-talks. He has heard every anecdote, knows every turn of phrase, has witnessed every hairdryer, can anticipate what the manager's likely to come up with next. How can Ferguson still motivate someone like Giggs? How does he keep it fresh? How can a manager keep the tap dance going at the same club for a quarter of a century?

'When I was there I remembered hearing the same thing he'd said about eight years earlier in a game at Motherwell,' says Gordon Strachan, who served him at Aberdeen and United. 'At the age I was at I got upset with it. So I had to motivate myself. He can't say anything new when you are that age. It's probably the same with Giggs. He probably won't speak often to Giggs now. Giggs will self-motivate. When you're younger it's about hammering in that winning mentality. After six or seven years of that you know you're hearing the same thing. What he has to do then is change the bodies, so that it's fresh to them. He's got boys that only need a couple of sentences now. We used to have meetings that lasted for hours and hours and hours. Now he's got the ability to say "This, this and this", and that's it. Ferguson always has different players coming into the dressing room and that keeps things fresh.' When that boot whacked into Beckham's face in the United dressing room in 2003 it was interpreted by some as a sign of Ferguson's rage against the dying of the light. Men didn't wear a sarong in Govan or at East Stirlingshire. Here was Ferguson lashing out the only way he knew how, some said; angry and violent against someone who had grown away from his control and come to embrace and represent football's takeover by celebrity, pop culture, crass commercialisation and unfettered freedom for players. That analysis underestimated Ferguson completely.

The ability to anticipate, act and react to the changing landscape of his working environment has been the quality which distinguished him as the greatest manager of all. He has been great for longer than anyone. Relentlessly great, barring the odd inevitable hiccup. Even those who sang his praises the loudest at Aberdeen or in the early years at United could not have anticipated that he would be still ready and able to answer the call a couple of decades later. His own explanation is predictably straightforward: 'Management is all about control. Success gives you control and control gives you longevity.'

He might sound curmudgeonly about how society has changed, and mourn the lost values of his own upbringing, but he has adapted like a chameleon. 'Manchester United is a massive club. The club I joined in 1986 is nothing like the one it is today. The modern man has changed. There's a need to be recognised, a need to be known. You see that with earrings, tattoos, the way that dress sense and hairstyles change every six months. Probably when I was in my teens I was the same. I remember buying an LP, Dean Martin, *Deano Latino*. It was lying on the kitchen table in Govan. My dad comes in and says "Jesus God! Who the hell is he?" '

Being around footballers young enough to be his grandsons keeps Ferguson feeling youthful, not old. There have been no meaningful signs of ageing. A doddery Fergie is unthinkable. He gives off no sense of frailty, mental or physical. His judgement still stands up to scrutiny. 'Jock [Stein] had already shown signs of decline before his car crash in 1975,' says Glenn Gibbons, 'Most of the great ones do. It's one of the extraordinary things about Ferguson; the longevity, to have maintained it for as long as he has. Most of the great ones start to hit the wall in their middle to late 50s. One of the things they do, which contributes to that, is that they begin to think they can walk on water. They sign bad players and say "He'll be a good player for me".'

'You can only think that the intensity of it over the years must have some kind of effect. I think their sense of themselves becomes distorted. It happened to them all: Stein, Shanks, Brian Clough. Old Bob Paisley got away with it because he started so late. Ferguson is the first one I have ever known who has not been subjected to that kind of erosion.'

Ferguson has always been such a formidable character in every regard that it is jarring when he admits to feelings of vulnerability or nervousness. During his Aberdeen days he claimed. 'I'm not a confident person at all, I worry like hell about all sorts of things. Team talks, for instance.' His players came to recognise a Ferguson cough which seemed more frequent ahead of big games. His later habit of chewing gum seemed to cure the cough. Peter Davenport described him as looking nervous at his very first United team-talk (so much so that he called Davenport 'Nigel') and said he was 'like a kitten'.

When he's in the mood he will happily tell stories against himself. He has one about being caught at traffic lights near Leeds United's ground. 'This bunch of supporters, 20 or 30 of them, they see me and go "Ferguson!" and start running across the road. The lights are still red. I'm almost shitting myself and they're getting nearer, then the light goes to amber [impersonates screeching tyres] and I'm away!' He remembers a moment of self-awareness while delivering a ferocious half-time bollocking to Peter Schmeichel. The Dane, 6ft 4in, and 22 years younger, was just as angry as Ferguson and, unusually, gave him both barrels back. Two hair-dryers facing each other. 'He was towering over me and the other players were almost covering their eyes,' said Ferguson. 'I'm looking up and thinking "If he does hit me, I'm dead".'

It seemed genuinely shocking when Ferguson was the victim of an unprovoked street attack in London in 2007, when he was kicked several times. The assailant turned out to be a drunk from Fife who then said: 'I'm sorry Fergie . . . I didn't know it was you.' Clearly. Family, friends and multitudes of admirers have always suspected that more significant damage to Ferguson might be self-inflicted. He announced in May 2000 that he intended to retire at the end of the 2001–02 season but was talked out of doing so by his wife Cathy and their three grown-up sons. They sensed that he had plenty more to give and still needed a meaningful outlet for his energy. Ferguson didn't need much persuading.

There are grandchildren to attend to. He finds the time to be a voracious reader of biographies – Muhammad Ali, Nelson Mandela, Tony Benn, Elvis, Sinatra, JFK. He plays the piano, he plays golf, he frequents the best restaurants, appreciates and collects fine wine, still likes the horses and owns a few. After years of feeling financially under-rewarded by United and bickering with the club over money his terms eventually improved. From 2005 he was on an annual rolling contract worth £3.6m and his personal wealth has been estimated at £24m. He can do what he likes.

Whatever the final tally of trophies, his legacy is secure. Sir Alex Ferguson's teams have played attacking, fast, powerful, relentless football. He likes width and aggressive, goalscoring midfielders. The sides have had guts, character and indomitable spirit, driven by a Willie Miller, Bryan Robson or Roy Keane. He has kept United at the front of the pack throughout the enormous commercial expansion of football during his time. His successor will inherit a superpower.

He is woven into any tapestry of the four great Scottish managers. He was inspired and mentored by Stein, worked under United club president Busby for seven years, and was a manager in a dugout for the first time in August, 1974, the very month when Shankly led out Liverpool for the last time. Is he the best ever? He has improved every club he served. He came to Aberdeen and turned them into champions after a 25-year wait. He came to United and they won their first title in 26 years. He is the only manager to win all the major trophies in Scotland and England. He has won more trophies than anyone else, full stop. Appreciation will eventually spread when he retires and his image is softened by time. The rougher edges will be smoothed into a fonder caricature of the ultimate gritty Scottish manager.

On this matter some voices hold more credibility than others. 'I've got to be honest; I think Fergie's the best manager we have had in this country, not just in Scotland but in Great Britain. I can't see anyone else. He is ahead of "Big Jock" because of the length of time he's been there and his ability to go from one club to another and still create success. You have to admire him totally because of the manner in which he develops clubs. He's different class.' The words are from Billy McNeill, the captain who helped Stein win the European Cup.

Ferguson has had years of people telling him he should have quit while the going was good. Since 2005 the timing of his retirement has periodically bubbled to the surface as the issue of the day in

English football. Everyone knows what happened to the others. Shankly was tormented by resigning too soon. Busby was a frustrated witness to the decline of the club he built. Stein died in a wee medical room in the bowels of Cardiff's Ninian Park. Ferguson's final demonstration of greatness will not be lifting another league title or cup. It will be masterminding the personal exit and the long, satisfying retirement which eluded the others. When it comes to tapping his watch and acknowledging that time is up, he can take on one last challenge for the sweetest victory of all.

Chapter Four
In a Dugout Far, Far Away

Scots who managed abroad

World Cups won by Scotland: none. European Championships won by Scotland: none. Scotland's major influence on football has never been demonstrated by anything as vulgar as lifting international trophies. But there has been no shortage of claims made on football around the planet by some of the country's most interesting and adventurous managers. One Scottish boss led another national team to a third-place finish at a World Cup; another masterminded one of the greatest World Cup shocks ever witnessed.

Scotland's football men fanned out across the globe from the very beginning. It is no exaggeration to say Brazil and Argentina – multiple World Cup winners – have Scottish coaches to thank for the development of their national game. The football communities in China, Canada and the USA owe a debt to the men who became known as 'The Scotch Professors'.

At club level, from Sao Paulo to Shanghai, from Pennsylvania to Prague, Scottish managers have made their presence felt. Even a member of football's aristocracy such as Juventus has turned to Scottish managers in the past (twice), as have clubs everywhere from the Middle East, the Far East, Australia and the Americas.

This was no accident. What else was there to expect when, from the late 19th century onwards, some Scots were prepared to travel the world with a football literally packed in their luggage?

'With the ever-expanding British Empire it meant that Scots took their industrial work skills abroad and also the pastime which they loved, which was football,' said Richard McBrearty, of the Scottish Football Museum at Hampden, 'English commentators referred to the early Scottish players who first came to England as "The Scotch Professors". The term was also used to describe the players, coaches and even groups of Scots workers living abroad who introduced the passing game, and sometimes even football itself, to a host of nations like Germany, France, Italy, Argentina, Uruguay, Brazil and Mexico. Rudimentary forms of football existed in many of these countries but it was improved by the visiting Scots coaches who demonstrated their advanced technical style of play and the short passing game. They went about their work to introduce football abroad with a missionary zeal.'

Among those 'professors' was Charles Miller, the son of a Greenock shipyard worker from Fairlie in Ayrshire, who is credited with teaching Brazil how to play the beautiful game. In 1894 he travelled to Brazil, where his father had gone in search of a better life, from his boarding school in Southampton. In his suitcase he had a football and a set of the game's rules. He helped establish Sao Paulo Athletic Club and was one of the men who set up Liga Paulista, the first official football league in Brazil, in 1901.

Six years later, in 1907, former Ayr United defender Jock Hamilton became Brazil's first professional manager when he took over Club Atletico Paulistano in Sao Paulo while on a sabbatical from his role as Fulham head coach.

Hamilton set in place such an impressive coaching scheme at Paulistano, from youth level upwards, that it was copied through-out Brazilian football. For the first time in the country's history proper coaching structures were put in place that would lay the foundations for the future success of one of the greatest football nations in the world.

Scots were also hard at work in other areas of South America. The so-called 'Father of Argentine Football' was former Glaswegian schoolteacher Alexander Hutton, who worked at St Andrew's School in Buenos Aires in the early 1880s. In 1891 he established the inaugural Argentine football league – the first of its kind outside Britain.

John Harley, a railway engineer from Springburn in Glasgow, was held in high regard for his work in Uruguayan football. As manager of club side Penarol, and then the Uruguayan national team for a year in 1909, he changed the way football was played there. Harley brought a short passing game that was hugely popular and effective, just as Hamilton had in Brazil.

John Prentice, from Glasgow, similarly introduced a modernised version of football to China in 1879 and was involved in establishing and coaching the first football club in Shanghai. David Forsyth, a schoolteacher from Perthshire, helped set up the first leagues in Canada and managed their national representative team on a successful tour of Britain in 1888.

Some of those men were missionaries and administrators, but as the game evolved around the world Scots rose to prominence as clearly defined managers as they would be recognised today. In the USA, Paisley-born former St Mirren player Robert Millar managed their national team to the 1930 World Cup semi-finals. They beat Belgium and Paraguay, both by 3–0, before losing 6–1 to Argentina in front of an 80,000 crowd in Montevideo. Having taken all that tournament's results into account FIFA officially recorded the USA as having finished third under Millar in the 1930 World Cup.

Four years later David Gould, who was born in Galston, East Ayrshire, was in charge and took the USA to the 1934 tournament. It was a straight knockout event, without groups, and the USA immediately lost 7–1 to eventual world champions Italy. A third Scot to manage the USA was Paisley-born Andrew Brown, who had a year in charge of their national team from 1947.

And then there was the manager who could lay claim to orchestrating the greatest international result ever recorded by a Scot. Books have been written and a film made about what Bill Jeffrey's team pulled off at the 1950 World Cup finals in Brazil.

Jeffrey was born in Edinburgh in 1892 but in his early 20s he left to live with a relative in America, working as a mechanic in

Pennsylvania and becoming manager of the company football team. When they played an exhibition game against Penn State University the university officials were so impressed they offered him the job as their manager. He held it for a remarkable twenty-seven years and won ten national college championships. But that's not what secured his footnote in football history.

Jeffrey was the manager of the USA when they played England on 29 June 1950. The result seemed like a foregone conclusion. Even Jeffrey said the Americans had no chance: 'Sheep ready to be slaughtered,' he said. It didn't seem like kidology. England's record was formidable and their team included outstanding players including Tom Finney, Billy Wright, Stan Mortensen and Wilf Mannion. The USA had lost their previous seven games and cobbled together their team at the eleventh hour. Jeffrey himself had been offered the job only a fortnight before the World Cup began. Spain beat them 3–1 just days before the England fixture.

Not a single American journalist was sent to Belo Horizonte to cover it; the only one present was on holiday and paid his own way there. England dominated but just before half-time Joe Gaetjens, who worked part-time as a dishwasher, scored the only goal of the game. England were humiliated and the USA had the first stunning result in its football history. The Reuters wire service accurately reported the result as 1–0 but several newspapers assumed this to be a mistake and published the result as 10–1 or 10–0 to England.

The USA lost their next game 5–2 to Chile, were eliminated, and did not make it back to a World Cup for 40 years. But Jeffrey's status as an American hero was established. He is a member of their National Soccer Hall of Fame.

Oddly, Jeffrey was not the only Scot in that great triumph. Ed McIlvenny, from Greenock, had moved to America the previous year to stay with his sister and was eligible to play for the USA team because he had – innocently and honestly – informed their football authorities that he intended to become a US citizen. As it turned out, he never did. But he captained the USA in a game American sports journalists still refer to as 'The Miracle on Grass'. A Scottish manager and captain bringing down the mighty England: no wonder England's right-back that day went on to show a coldness for all things Scottish. His name was Alf Ramsey.

Ramsey would win the World Cup as England manager only 16 years later, but Jeffrey was not around to witness that. He suffered a fatal heart attack at a football clinic in Pennsylvania in January 1966.

In Europe there has always been a demand for Scottish managers. Arbroath-born William Maxwell moved to Belgium after his playing career and had spells managing the Belgian national team from 1910 to 1913 and again from 1920 to 1938. In 1954 former Celtic and Everton player Doug Livingstone – who had just spent three seasons as manager of the Republic of Ireland – became a hero in Belgium after guiding them to the 1954 World Cup. They drew 4–4 with England at the finals. Even the Dutch had a Scot in charge of their national side once: Billy Hunter in 1914. Ten years later Hunter was manager of Turkey and introduced professional coaching methods there.

In Sweden a founding member of its first football club was John Lawson, a lacemaker from Newmilns in Ayrshire who had gone to work at a sister factory in Gothenburg. He managed the football section of the Örgryte Idrottssällskap (ÖIS) sports club. In 1892 the first ever game in Sweden took place between Örgryte FC, who included six Scots, and IS Lyckans Soldater.

Arguably the most successful Scottish manager ever in club football overseas was John Madden. As a player he had won championships with Celtic in 1893 and 1894. What hinted at something different in Madden's make-up was the fact he was bold enough to take up his first managerial appointment in Czechoslovakia.

Dumbarton-born Madden first arrived in Prague in 1905 at the age of 40 to take over as manager of Slavia Prague. He had been to the Czech capital before with Celtic and it is assumed that was when first contact was made. But there is a theory, outlandish as it may sound, that after visiting Prague he was so desperate to return that he effectively conned the Slavia Prague committee into giving him the job and paying for his fare back over to eastern Europe.

A relative, Tom O'Neill, who has researched his life, said there had been suggestions that Slavia were impressed by the Rangers team under William Wilton and wanted one of their players to take over. According to O'Neill, Rangers players Jacky Robertson and Findlay Speedie, from Madden's home town of Dumbarton, gave Madden some Rangers clothing. Then they took a photograph which they sent to Prague along with a curriculum vitae of his coaching experience, which did not amount to very much at the time.

Whatever the reasons behind his appointment, he turned out to be a huge success. Although he could not speak Czech, he surrounded himself with good local coaches and an interpreter and was able to get his football philosophy across.

He was a disciplinarian, which was hard to impose in bohemian Prague. He banned his players from smoking – albeit for only three hours before the game – and also stopped them drinking the night before a match, which was a new and unpopular move in that era. Madden also imported the tough training regime he had experienced at Celtic and used freezing water to treat muscle strains, another idea which was not widely used at the time.

Madden's techniques were copied by other Czech coaches, who acknowledged him as the master. Indeed his success, which included three league titles, meant there were attempts to lure other Scots across to eastern Europe to manage Czech clubs.

One who decided to go was John Dick, from Eaglesham near Paisley, who took over at Sparta Prague when Madden was still in charge at Slavia. When the former Arsenal centre-half arrived in Prague in 1912 Albert Einstein was studying at the university and Vladimir Lenin was in the city helping set up a branch of his Bolshevik Party. In the middle of all of that were Madden and Dick, the two straight-talking Scots who went head-to-head in local derby matches between Slavia and Sparta.

Dick drifted away from Prague after a couple of years but Madden remained as a major figure in Czech football. He took their national football squad to the Paris Olympics of 1924 and during 25 years at Slavia Prague he won the Czechoslovakian league title in 1925, 1929 and 1930 and the local Prague Cup four times between 1908 and 1912.

An indication of the quality of the team Madden had assembled came from their performance in the Coupe des Nations held in Geneva in 1930, which was an early prototype version of the Champions League. Organised by Swiss champions Servette, it was for the league or cup winners from European nations which had not attended that year's World Cup finals in Uruguay.

All of the other major European football nations of the time were invited except for the British associations, who were not yet part of FIFA. Slavia Prague beat Cercle Bruges of Belgium, Real Union of Spain and First Vienna of Austria on their road to the final, where they were defeated 3–0 by Ujpest of Hungary. Madden's team was one of the best in Europe.

He retired soon after the Coupe des Nations at the age of 66. He remained in Prague for the rest of his life, was a national hero, and had a statue erected in his honour. In 1948 his funeral cortege was accompanied by players dressed in team strips. Flowers are regularly left on his grave, and 'The Madden Award' is seen as their equivalent of a player of the year trophy.

In Italy, Juventus twice appointed a Scottish manager. Edinburgh-born George Aitken and Willie Chalmers from Bellshill have a permanent place in the Turin club's archives alongside other former managers such as Fabio Capello, Carlo Ancelotti, Giovanni Trapattoni and Marcello Lippi.

Aitken was in charge of Juventus for two seasons from 1928 and led them to a third place finish in the first ever season of Serie A. Chalmers, a former QPR and Newcastle United player, had just the 1948–49 season in charge and made only a limited impression.

Although none of the legendary Scottish managers ever worked overseas – Sir Matt Busby turned down an offer to take over Real Madrid – the increasing familiarity with other cultures and improved transport led to many Scots taking over foreign clubs.

Another success was former Hearts, Tottenham and Scotland midfielder Dave Mackay, who made such an impact with club side

Al–Arabi in Kuwait in the 1970s and 1980s that he won six league titles and was latterly referred to as the 'Sir Alex of Kuwait'. Mackay also managed the Qatar national youth side and had a spell in Egypt as head coach of Zamalek.

In Australia Eddie Thomson, the former Aberdeen player, was manager of their national team for six years in the early 1990s before moving to club football in Japan. The late Ian Porterfield was another who embarked on a fascinating nomadic international career incorporating the national jobs in Zambia, Zimbabwe, Oman, Trinidad & Tobago and Armenia, and club jobs in the Far East. Stuart Baxter is frequently held up as another managerial ambassador for Scotland although he was born and raised in England, to a Scottish dad. Graeme Souness managed Galatasaray in Turkey, Torino in Italy and Benfica in Portugal during the 1990s.

Scottish coaches are more frequently appointed in Australia, America and Canada – Tommy Docherty and former internationals Steve Nicol and Mo Johnston among them – but now and again one will pop up in the most unlikely environment. In 2008 Uganda appointed Kilmarnock's 1997 Scottish Cup-winning manager, Bobby Williamson, as their national boss.

For some Scottish managers, a sense of adventure endures.

Danny McLennan

The untold story of football's most travelled boss

'I was wearing a watch one day when I was doing supply teaching in Pittenweem. This lad came up to me and says "Hey, is that no' that bad man?" I looked down and realised it was a watch with Saddam Hussein's face on it. I'd forgotten I was wearing it.'
Ruth McLennan

Tucked away in a lovely house in the Fife village of Crail there is a blue suitcase and a battered brown briefcase. Neither of them seems to be worth a second look, which goes to show that appearances can be deceptive. They contain souvenirs, photographs and newspaper cuttings which celebrate an astonishing life in football. They tell the story of the Scot who became a managerial missionary.

Some reckon there should be a place in the *Guinness Book of Records* for Danny McLennan. As far as anyone can work out he managed more international sides than anyone in the history of the game; ten different countries. The man himself had no need for such an accolade. Football, travel and adventure were rewards enough.

McLennan was a restless, engaging, bold character who skipped from country to country at the end of every contract. He moved especially through the Middle East and Africa and would earn his next post by word-of-mouth because he was doing such an impressive job in his current one. He won friends and influenced people everywhere he went, and he would take any challenge going.

To thousands of football supporters and the children and players he coached he was 'Mr Danny'. At one point there was even an advertising campaign in Africa with the slogan 'Drink Pepsi, Danny Does . . .' In Scotland he could have walked down any street in the country without being recognised.

He was a tall, handsome, powerful figure. There was something of the Hollywood leading man about him. He had presence and charm. 'You are either born with that or you're not,' said his wife, Ruth, opening those cases full of memories as the sunshine flooded into her living room, 'Everyone had great respect for him and sort of idolised him. He didn't have to assert his authority much because people naturally listened to him. He drew people in. Every time he went for a job interview I knew he'd get it. He would always charm them.'

Central to the McLennan story was the streak of individuality in his character. He had been born and brought up in Scotland and spent his entire playing and early managerial career there. It was an ordinary tale that he made extraordinary by deciding that life could be bigger. Scotland was too suffocating. He wanted to uproot, spread his wings and experience the world. And once he started, there was no looking back.

It was no easy decision to make. There were no mobile phones, no internet, no quick, cheap or plentiful flights when McLennan began crisscrossing the planet. When he took his first job in the Philippines he didn't see Ruth, who he had recently married, for a year. Much later they worked in Middle Eastern countries without adequate secondary schooling so the couple dealt with the stress of putting their two daughters into a boarding school back in Scotland.

McLennan endured it all — the isolation, the language difficulties, the travel problems, the everyday inconveniences and occasionally the danger — because the rewards and the satisfaction were greater than anything Scottish football could offer. Early in the 1970s he rejected an approach by secretary Willie Allan to work for the SFA. McLennan had been unimpressed a couple of years earlier when the Scotland job was advertised with the caveat that it need not necessarily be full time. He also was unconvinced that the SFA was committed to a genuine national youth policy, a view he still held decades later. Allan offered a £6000 annual salary and a Rover car. McLennan turned him down.

Compared to Scotland he found other countries exciting, challenging and open to ideas. He would write newspaper columns to spread the word wherever he went. In Africa he would have film reels of *Match of the Day* sent by a contact at the BBC and would show them on outdoor screens. Large crowds would gather to watch.

In 1971 he was manager of Zimbabwe (then called Rhodesia) when he wrote an article for a sports magazine. There was a paragraph in the piece which captured the verve, enthusiasm and ambition he brought to every national football association which employed him. 'Since coming to this country I have put the training of coaches high on my list of priorities. The time has come to think bigger and better. This applies not just to coaching but to planning with regard to stadiums, training grounds and flood-lighting. Rhodesian soccer has been sleeping for many years! A great awakening is now evident!'

His talent was in generating enthusiasm and raising participation levels in football. He built teams and gave them respectability and structure. The training ground was a natural home. 'He was very serious about his football,' says Ruth, 'He was like Alex Ferguson: everyone knew their limits and how far they could go with him. He stood no nonsense. But away from football he had a real big personality.'

McLennan was born in Stirling in 1925. He was a left-half for Rangers, Dundee and, most memorably, East Fife where he was a member of the team which won the 1953 League Cup. A knee injury ended his career prematurely and he drifted into management with Berwick Rangers, Oldham and Stirling Albion. It was an enjoyable career, but a routine and unremarkable one. He wanted more. When he lost out to Jock Stein for the Dunfermline job in 1961 he began to realise it was time for his life to take a new turn.

Through the British consul in Manila he got the job as national coach of the Philippines. It was a year-long contract and through-out it he never returned home nor saw his new wife Ruth, who had to stay behind in their Stirling flat to complete her teacher-training course.

McLennan was hooked. 'Life was difficult for him there. There were robberies and all sorts of dangerous elements to his life,' said Ruth. In one match he noticed that the linesman happened to be the local chief of police, running the line with a gun on his hip. On another occasion the pitch was entirely washed away during a typhoon.

'But he enjoyed it hugely. He wasn't homesick or anything, he enjoyed the coaching side of it. It was great when I got the letter saying he had got a job in Mauritius, again through the British consul, and that I should go out there and join him. He came home for a wee bit and then we set off together for Mauritius. It was absolutely marvellous there.'

McLennan was blessed: he had a wife who shared his sense of adventure and was willing to throw herself into the life he wanted. 'I was quite keen on travelling the world too,' she said, 'Danny was a maverick and I became one!' They never looked back. After three years in Mauritius, where their eldest daughter Rosemary was born, they moved to Africa when Sir Stanley Rous helped McLennan into the post of Zimbabwe manager in 1968. The couple stayed for five years and their second daughter, Louise, was born there in 1972.

'The football coach was like a god in the countries where there was poverty and so on. It used to open all the doors. All the little kids along the road would shout "Mr Danny, Mr Danny". Apartheid was still in place in those days. Danny became friendly with Garfield Todd, the old prime minister who opposed white minority rule.'

It went without saying that McLennan was open-minded and inclusive. 'He liked working with different races and handling them. He really loved the Arabs. He got friendly with sheikhs who would invite us to their homes. I think he found Scottish football too restrictive. He was more his own boss abroad. Here there would have been directors and a system and I don't think that suited him. Abroad he was free to do his own thing a bit more. He didn't like a rigid regime.'

After a temporary contract to take charge of Bahrain in 1973, Rous helped him into another job which confirmed McLennan's readiness to take on any challenge. Rous warned him that being the manager of Iran would be no picnic. McLennan understood and took it on. Tehran was an uncomfortable place to bring up two young girls, their accommodation was poor, and one evening Danny and Ruth walked to post a letter and were approached by a policeman who drew a gun on them and demanded to know why they were out at night.

'Iran was very hard. It was harder for Danny too. There were spies and informers everywhere. You had to watch what you said. It wasn't that there was wariness towards Westerners as such, it was just the way they were out there. It was like Russia in that sense. You couldn't go walking to the shops or anything. Going to the supermarket for the weekly food was a real nightmare. It took ages to get there. You stood out as strangers in Iran. But Danny still enjoyed the football.'

McLennan coached Iran from 1973 to 1974 and was hugely influential in developing and shaping the players who would play against Scotland at the World Cup finals in Argentina four years later. 'He knew all the players in that team. It was the team Danny had moulded and coached. So when Scotland were drawn against Iran Danny wrote to Ally MacLeod and gave him information on every one of them.' Who knows if MacLeod took any notice? Iran pulled off a shock 1–1 draw which effectively knocked Scotland out of the World Cup.

The McLennans spent most of the 1970s in the Middle East. After Iran they moved to Iraq. 'He was getting well known in the Middle East so he would be approached and asked "Will you come to us once your contract is finished?" And he would take the offer. Iraq was the most famous time of his life, his golden years. He had been coaching for a while by that time and handling all sorts of Africans and Filipinos. He really loved Iraq and so did I. It was primitive but not difficult like Iran was. People were open. It was just a great place to live although Saddam Hussein was just beginning to emerge. I remember going north of Mosul to the borders of the Kurdish areas and noticing that there were lots of tanks and military vehicles. When Saddam came to power he put his two sons in charge of the football and it became terrible, with talk of the players being tortured if they lost games. Thankfully Danny wasn't around then. That wasn't the Iraq we experienced.'

Ruth was a talented tennis player. She was a decade younger than Danny and when they met he acted as her tennis coach and for a considerable time their relationship was platonic. But they were soul-mates. When they married she embraced new cultures as much as he did, maybe even more so, given that his time was consumed by football. When not teaching or raising the children she painted or visited historical sites. 'It was just luck that it was a way of life that worked for both of us. It was really a good partnership. It would have been difficult for some wives but I really liked just about every aspect of it.' She won open tennis championships in Bahrain, Iraq and Jordan.

When they left Baghdad McLennan spent 1978 coaching the Norwegian club Kongsvinger and then the couple moved to Jordan. They spent two years there before moving to Saudi Arabia in 1980 when McLennan accepted a job with a leading club side.

More moves followed: club football was never more than a means of filling time between international jobs and in 1983 they returned to Africa so he could become the national coach of Malawi for a year. The 1980s saw even more moves than the decades before it: back to Jordan and then Malta for club sides, the Mauritius national job (again) from 1986 to 1988, two years with the Kenya Breweries club in Kenya and then the same spell in charge of Fiji.

'He went all over the islands in Fiji. In other countries like Iraq or Iran you were taken by bus or cars or whatever, but in Fiji it was these tiny little aeroplanes. Microlights. He always felt that he was going to crash in one of them! He would come back and tell me he'd been somewhere out of a Somerset Maugham novel with all these old fogeys just sitting about, waiting to die . . .'

At the age of 67 McLennan agreed to take charge of Libya. He was there 1992–93, dates that were to be profoundly significant because of something that had happened in, of all places, Scotland. The bombing of Pan Am Flight 103 over Lockerbie took place in 1988 but it was during McLennan's spell in Tripoli that two UN Security Council resolutions were passed to impose sanctions against Libya. McLennan's team were not allowed to play anyone.

'They put an embargo on them and they weren't allowed to play any countries. He was coaching but had no matches to play! That was a real adventure. I was waiting to go and join him but there was no point because the national team couldn't play anybody.' The man later convicted of the Lockerbie bombing,

Abdelbaset Ali Mohmed Al-Megrahi, had lived near Libya's national training ground. 'Danny used to pass that Al-Megrahi's house every day when he was walking to the training ground in Tripoli. I remember him saying he didn't believe the man could have done it.'

McLennan was almost 70 when he took over at the Churchill Brothers club in Goa, India. The couple had four enjoyable years there before he became restless again and returned for what would be their last spell in Africa. They had a year in Tanzania and disliked it. 'That was the worst place we lived. We were in Dar es Salaam. It was really terrible, worse than Iran. You couldn't go out without gangs trying to steal your shoes or whatever. We were there for a year: it was a year too long. I never felt in such a dangerous environment. People would try to steal your watch even as you sat at a table with your arm on the side.'

They returned to the peace and tranquillity of Goa and a second spell with Churchill Brothers. It turned out to be McLennan's last post. They had bought their house in Crail in 1975 as a permanent base between jobs and were back there in 2004, planning a trip to Mauritius where they would look for a house they could finally retire to, when McLennan suffered a massive stroke. 'It was so strange, what happened. Danny's body was very fit. He was a keen golfer. Everyone always thought he was ten years younger than he was. I think it must have been the strain of football management. The stroke was so severe that he only lasted a week in Dundee's Ninewells Hospital.' On 11 May 2004, the most travelled manager in the history of football passed away just an hour's drive from where he was born. He was 79.

Ruth collected a lifetime's worth of anecdotes from her marriage to a unique football man and free spirit. 'I was wearing a watch one day when I was doing supply teaching in Pittenweem. This lad came up to me and says "Hey, is that no' that bad man?" I looked down and realised it was a watch with Saddam Hussein's face on it. That's what all the players and the coach had been given as gifts. I'd forgotten I was wearing it!'

It was Saddam's only recorded appearance in Pittenweem. Without Danny as her travelling companion and fellow adventurer Ruth was forced to retire to a quiet life in Crail. Thankfully she retains a sharp memory for detail, because nothing beats the evidence of a loving eye-witness. The contents of the blue suitcase and the battered brown briefcase could only scratch the surface of Danny McLennan's great adventure.

Chapter Five
The Great Old Firm Managers

The Great Celtic Managers

Willie Maley

'Willie Maley was his name/He brought some great names to the game/When he was boss at Celtic Park/ Taught them how to play football/Made them greatest of them all'

In any discussion of Scotland's greatest football managers, a question mark rests against the name of Willie Maley which applies to none of the others. What makes any manager 'great' can be a subjective matter up to a point where a level of achievement makes the point unarguable. Jock Stein or Bill Shankly might not have been everyone's cup of tea, but no one could doubt their ability. Maley reached that same point early in his long, epochal reign as manager of Celtic. It's not whether he was great that is in question, but whether he was Scottish.

Maley's nationality was a cloudy, vague issue because he made it so himself. In 1868 he was born in army barracks in Newry, Northern Ireland, where his southern Irish father was a serving soldier in the British army. Before Willie had reached his second birthday his father, Thomas, had taken his honourable discharge from the army and decided to begin a better life for the family by moving them to Cathcart in Glasgow. Maley therefore spent all his school and working life in Scotland and lived in the country for 87 of his 89 years.

And he regarded himself as Scottish. Maley was proud enough of his Irish roots and was more influential than any other individual in Celtic's history in shaping the club as, first, a charitable force to help poor Irish children in Glasgow's east end, and then as an enormously popular and successful football club. But he was no misty-eyed romantic. Thomas Maley came to Scotland with the intention of integrating fully and immersing himself in Scottish culture and it was an attitude shared by Willie, the third of four sons. Young Maley saw no reason why there couldn't be a proud and vibrant Irish Catholic community existing harmoniously within an accepting, tolerant Scotland. Being Scottish or Irish, Catholic or Protestant, were distinctions that Maley hoped would eventually blur into meaninglessness.

Long before he left school at the age of 13 he had decided he wanted to play international football in a Scotland jersey. He was 24 when it happened. There was some disquiet about his selection, given that he had been born in Ireland, as had his father, but Maley stressed that he had spent nearly all his life in Scotland and that his family was Scottish on his mother's side. The Scottish Football Association was persuaded. Maley won the first of his two caps – against Ireland, ironically – and consequently proved his credentials for inclusion in any list of Scotland's great managers.

He was an extraordinary character. He played for Celtic in the club's first-ever match, on 28 May 1888, and did not leave the payroll until January 1940. Of those 52 years' service 43 of them were spent as manager. Nothing about Maley is more breathtaking than that, not even his accumulation of 16 Scottish League titles and 14 Scottish Cups.

Willie Maley was a true giant of Scottish football. Would he have been an exceptional manager if he had lived a century later? There is no reason to doubt it. Maley was a product of the Victorian age. He was a deeply religious man, fastidious in his dress – a suit, soft hat and overcoat were de rigueur for managers of the day – disciplined and paternalistic. Mostly he was caring and protective of his players and humane and compassionate in general. He was not given to praising them publicly or even in private, though, and it was not beyond him to be cold and bullying. Money was a frequent cause of friction between him and the players and many were moved on, sometimes prematurely or against their will, because Maley had some sort of problem with their level of pay. Anyone who knew him also knew to keep out of his way if Celtic had been beaten. He could be frightening when roused. But for the most part, and certainly in the first two thirds of his term of management, the dozens of players who served under him responded to his dictatorial style.

Like all managers of his era he approached the job in a way which would be unrecognisable today. His time on the training ground was limited and he was not a believer in pre-match or half-time team-talks. Nor was he prone to talking up the opposition to his players, lest his men be inclined to doubt themselves. They would not always know in advance if they had been picked to play in any given game and sometimes had to read it in the morning newspapers. Still, his knowledge of football in general and tactics in particular were excellent. He was a sound judge of a player and an expert team-builder. There is no question that he was the architect of all the glories achieved during his reign.

His interests and knowledge were broad. Like all great leaders, he was intelligent and inquisitive. In his excellent biography, *Willie Maley, The Man Who Made Celtic*, David W. Potter wrote: 'On train trips to Aberdeen, for example, he would sit with supporters and other passengers talking about football, politics, the king's various illnesses and indispositions, the Liberal government with its changes to society, the rising Labour movement, South Africa and other subjects, impressing everyone with his knowledge and affability.' Maley would have been a deeply impressive man regardless of his chosen line of work. It moved him when he saw the level of poverty in the east end of Glasgow and beyond, and the charitable motivation for Celtic's foundation struck him as being correct and necessary.

His height and stature gave him a natural presence which, like Stein decades later, somehow made people in a room aware of his entrance even if they had their backs to the door. Maley could hold court and charm a company with his conversation and affability. If the mood was right, he liked a song. He was way ahead of his time in making the wives, girlfriends and family of his players feel important and looked after, although that may have said more about his essentially sociable nature than any calculating attempt to benefit his own squad.

He could be stern, inflexible and stubborn. He had a temper, and woe betide any player, or opponent, who defied him or somehow stepped over the line. Again, those qualities tend to be found in the greats of any era. He had the traits, good and bad, which are found in all of football's outstanding leaders.

Maley was there at the very genesis of Celtic. It is a part of the club's lore that its founder, Brother Walfrid, visited the Maley home to recruit his brother, Tom, as a player for the very first game. Brother Walfrid was on his way out of the house when he paused and asked, almost as an afterthought, if Willie fancied coming along too. Willie had preferred running and cycling up until then – Scottish athletics records note that at one point he was the national 100–yard sprint champion – but helping to establish Celtic appealed to him. Little could he have suspected that it would become the passion and cornerstone of his life. He initially served Celtic as a player but the club committee knew he was studying to be an accountant and were impressed by his attention to detail and administration skills. At 20 he became Celtic's match secretary, a role he fulfilled with increasing enthusiasm and effectiveness.

As Celtic grew as a focal point for the Irish immigrant and wider Catholic communities in Scotland no one was quicker than Maley to sense the size of the potential fanbase and therefore how big the club could become. Although he was a devout Catholic he saw no merit or appeal in drawing Celtic players from only that section of society. In his mind the club should be inclusive of all, regardless of religion. Some of Maley's beliefs did not always sit comfortably with sections of the supporters on the Parkhead terraces. Here was an Irish-born Catholic and seemingly the quintessential Celtic man, yet he was the son of a British Army soldier, and later allowed wounded ex-servicemen into Parkhead for half-price or even free. At times he allowed the army to recruit there on match days, granting them permission to make loudspeaker appeals for volunteers. Maley was also a Royalist. In some ways he was the ultimate Celtic man, yet he was also untypical of many who served or follow the club.

It was Maley who established Celtic's commitment to attacking football. His attitude was straightforward: an attractive style of play would appeal to more people and accelerate the club's rise to popularity. He organised successful tours to England, Ireland and then Europe to help spread the word. He engineered the club's move to a larger stadium with the scope for future expansion and he lobbied for Scottish international fixtures and cup finals to be staged there because it would reflect well on Celtic. The furtherment of Celtic was one of the abiding motivations of Maley's life.

By the age of 29 he was such a powerful figure that he became the club's first secretary-manager. In his first full season he won the 1897–98 championship and in the second he delivered the Scottish Cup. And so it continued for the next 42 years. In all that time Celtic never went more than three seasons without winning the league or the cup. He was the first man to achieve the league and Scottish Cup double, and did so three times. There was a spell when he won eleven out of fifteen championships including six-in-a-row, a run which was not equalled until Stein did so six decades later.

At the beginning of that spell Maley assembled a team of young, unproven players, some of whom would go on to become Celtic's earliest heroes. Jimmy Quinn was taken from junior football and would become a rampaging bull of a centre-forward who scored 216 times in a 14-year Celtic career. Patsy Gallacher and Jimmy McGrory were others who became iconic figures.

Maley was periodically touched by tragedies which served to deepen his emotional connection to Celtic. He grieved when a couple of men who had played for him, Peter Johnstone and Donnie McLeod, lost their lives in the First World War. There was a personally traumatic incident to cope with in 1931 when his goalkeeper, John Thomson, died on a hospital operating table hours after suffering a major head injury when he dived at the feet of the Rangers forward Sam English in an Old Firm game. As Thomson lay motionless for seconds and then minutes after the accidental collision Maley left his seat in the stand to come to the Ibrox touchline and then on to the pitch itself to help attend to his man. Years later Maley demonstrated his compassion when he invited English to the unveiling of a Thomson memorial at Parkhead. He was a big man in more ways than one.

For the second half of his reign he was up against a man who was every bit his equal, the stentorian Bill Struth of Rangers. From 1921 to the outbreak of the Second World War was a remarkable period for Scottish football, the only time when two colossal figures have clashed over an extended period of time. Struth and Maley were huge, hard, formidable, iconic Glasgow managers. Each was the unmistakeable leader of his tribe. Theirs was a truly titanic battle for supremacy. Between Struth's appointment in 1921 and Maley's dismissal at the start of 1940 the pair of them harvested 30 of the 38 national trophies contested. Together they won 18 out of the 19 championships.

Struth was the clear victor, with fourteen league titles to Maley's four and they evenly shared twelve Scottish Cups, although the statistics slightly flatter the Rangers man. Maley was already showing signs of being battle-weary when Struth arrived on the scene – after all, he had been coping with the pressure of managing Celtic for 24 years by then – and his judgement and decision-making became less reliable in his latter years. Struth was not up against Maley at his best. Coupled with Rangers' improved professionalism and ambition under Struth, and the willingness to release substantial funds for him to enhance his team, the challenge to Maley was stronger than before and he and Celtic could have reacted more effectively. Often they had to accept second best.

Even so, the duel was compelling. In the modern media age, with its fascination with personality, conflict and controversy, Maley versus Struth would be relentlessly hyped as an epic heavy-weight contest. Typically, there was understanding and enormous respect between the men themselves. Celtic and Rangers need to be led by big characters and there were none bigger or more domineering than those two. Although most of Maley's reign took place before Struth emerged, and the Rangers boss continued for a few years beyond his great rival's removal, they were essentially men of the same era whose careers were bound together. They died within a couple of years of each other at the end of the 1950s.

When the Maley family arrived from Ireland it had craved admission and acceptance in Scottish society, and Willie in particular received that. He was a major figure within Scottish football and Glasgow as a whole, very much part of the establishment. The three years he spent as president of the Scottish Football League afforded him huge influence on the governance and politics of the game. Equally important, in its own way, was his long ownership of a restaurant in Glasgow's city centre called 'The Bank'. That became a meeting point for all sorts of prominent characters, from football managers and players to journalists, politicians, business-men, bookmakers and various dubious hangers-on. Maley would often arrange for the Celtic first team and reserves to have meals there. Benny Lynch, Glasgow's famous boxing son, was a regular.

'The Bank' was precious for Maley as a source of news and gossip. He was quick to appreciate the value of an extensive network of contacts. He had friends and confidants at all levels throughout the game and plenty around the pubs and clubs of Glasgow too, who would let him know if his players were stepping out of line. Maley had that great managerial gift of appearing to be all-knowing. Although he was not teetotal, he drank rarely and moderately and was intolerant of excessive drinking by footballers. Players did not take liberties with him because they sensed they would not get away with it, and usually they were right.

It was age rather than Struth that did for Maley in the end. Problems began to mount as Rangers replaced Celtic as the country's dominant club and Maley's response was unconvincing. If the players still trusted him they didn't always show it in performances. Results became erratic. In the 1930s Celtic won only two championships and three Scottish Cups. Supporters became restless.

In 1939–40 Celtic were struggling at the wrong end of the wartime league and the board of directors was ready to take a stand against Maley for virtually the first time in half a century. When the club gave him a cash sum to mark its golden jubilee there was a squabble over who should pay the tax, a minor row which rumbled on and soured relations between the parties. Directors had grown exasperated by the extent of Maley's control, his methods and his apparent belief that he was answerable to no one. Results were no longer good enough to save him. The board swallowed hard and told Maley that he would be bundled into retirement with effect from 1 February 1940. The world at large had greater matters on its mind, but it was an enormous moment for Celtic in general and Maley in particular.

He was 71 and prone to melancholy and feelings of depression and insecurity. His modus operandi was no longer delivering the same results and Struth was an imposing, victorious presence across the city. The Celtic directors had done the right thing for the club, but it hurt Maley and he resented the way he had been treated. This man who had lived and breathed Celtic from teenager to pensioner walked out of Parkhead one day and did not set foot in the place again for 14 years, by which time he was a frail 85-year-old who returned only for a testimonial match held in his honour. He died in a Glasgow nursing home in 1958, just a few weeks short of his 90th birthday.

At Parkhead these days supporters can often be heard singing 'The Willie Maley Song'. Yet Maley's name does not immediately leap to the lips of many modern supporters. Ask them to name the most influential member of the club's founding fathers and Brother Walfrid would probably receive more mentions. Ask them to name the most celebrated manager and most would surely say Jock Stein. Younger fans would probably assume that the next best was Martin O'Neill or Gordon Strachan. Maley is not revered like Walfrid, Stein, Jimmy Johnstone or the other Lisbon Lions. There is no statue of him outside the Parkhead entrance, no stand named after him, but no one did more for Celtic.

Billy McNeill

'It was desperate by the end, all the arguments with the chairman. It wasn't easy for me to leave Celtic. I spoke to my dad. My dad just said "You're in a situation where this man just doesn't respect you so I don't think there's a future for you." That's what I felt too.'

Of the tens of thousands of photographs taken during Billy McNeill's career, perhaps only a handful could be said to be truly iconic. And one of them makes him grimace at the very sight of it. It does not show a defeat, nor an injury, nor capture any sort of low moment in his career. Quite the opposite. Even so, it became a truly memorable image and McNeill has never been comfortable with it. He simply did not like what it appeared to show.

Supposedly a picture paints a thousand words, but that doesn't guarantee an accurate portrayal of the story. The photograph in question is the one which caught McNeill's appointment as the man Celtic chose to succeed Jock Stein. It was 28 May 1978, and a photographer on bended knee took a snap of McNeill and Celtic chairman Desmond White shaking hands across Stein's chest as the great man stood between them, looking down mournfully at their clasped hands.

It is a great shot which seemed to poignantly catch a moment in history. It appeared to show the isolation and marginalisation of Stein while White and McNeill, seeming to ignore him, cemented their new, shared future. White and McNeill tower over Stein. They look conspiratorial. White is facing forward with his left arm out, almost invading Stein's personal space to reach across him for McNeill. Archie Macpherson has written of this 'awkward hand-shake', adding, 'In this tableau a humbled giant could not avoid the chilling role of outcast.'

Here is how McNeill regards the picture: 'That was rubbish. That was misleading, to be quite frank with you.' Even now, decades later, a look of pain crosses his face at the memory. 'Desmond did not have the use of his right arm. He had been in the Royal Air Force and apparently he had walked into a propeller which had damaged his arm. So he couldn't use that hand. But that picture gave totally the wrong impression. Desmond White used his left hand to shake my hand because he had this twisted arm that didn't work for him. Twisted brain as well, mind you!'

If one image truly defines Billy McNeill it is a far happier, more famous one. It shows him thrusting the European Cup in the air when Celtic became the first British club to win it, in 1967. That was the pinnacle of an extraordinary playing career in which he was a commanding, regal presence through almost 800 appearances for Celtic, his only club. Further achievements came his way in management. So many, in fact, that it is startling to remember that he was only 51 when he decided he had had enough of being a manager. Considering the longevity of bosses like Sir Alex Ferguson, Giovanni Trapattoni and Craig Brown, McNeill could have had another couple of decades in the front line.

Instead he turned down any approaches to return to management after being sacked by Celtic in 1991. 'I got several offers but I was gone. I'd lost the appetite to be a manager. I got an offer a couple of weeks later to go to Dundee. I was on my way up to talk to the chairman that morning and I just woke up at 5 or 6 a.m. and thought "Naw, why go to Dundee?" So I picked up the phone, spoke to the chairman and said "Look, sorry, but I'd be coming for the wrong reasons and I don't want to disrespect you in any shape or form."

'I got newspaper work, so I was still involved in football and I enjoyed that aspect. Then I had an offer from Hibs, but not to be manager. If that had come earlier I would have been delighted. By that time the momentum had disappeared.' In 1998 he had a short spell as football development manager at Hibs which included a single game as caretaker manager. On 7 February 1998, he was a manager for the very last time and his Hibs team lost 3–0 at Aberdeen, the club where his managerial career had taken off two decades earlier.

McNeill signed for Celtic in 1957, at the age of 17. He was 35 when he left them in 1975. In between he harvested nine league championship winner's medals, seven Scottish Cups, six League Cups, and the European Cup. The only club managers he served were Jimmy McGrory and Stein.

The son of a former Black Watch soldier, McNeill's tall, imposing stature and aristocratic appearance gave him the look of officer material. Management material, in other words. In the sort of dormant period which would be unthinkable for a player of his profile today, he retired and spent almost two years doing no more than coaching Celtic Boys Club's under-16s, attending to some business interests and doing the odd bit of media punditry. Finally Clyde were the club which woke up to this sleeping giant on their doorstep and offered him the job as their manager. The ball was rolling. Three months later Jock Stein telephoned to sound him out on Aberdeen's behalf and in the summer of 1977 he took over at Pittodrie.

He won nothing in his only full season as a manager. Nothing but friends and admiration. Aberdeen finished second in both the league and the Scottish Cup but there was an unmistakeable vibe that this was a club, and a city, on the up. McNeill enjoyed the north-east immensely and the working relationship he had with chairman Dick Donald would never be equalled. His first major misjudgement as a manager was to leave Aberdeen after only 11 months.

Stein had been back on the phone. This time the question sent the blood rushing to McNeill's head: did he fancy taking over at Celtic? Against all reasoned analysis which told him he was on a better bet where he was – as Alex Ferguson proved as Aberdeen's next manager – McNeill succumbed to the impulses of his Celtic DNA and accepted. He collected his assistant, fellow Lisbon Lion John Clark, and they drove away from Pittodrie. 'I remember we left Aberdeen and stopped at a wee village before Stonehaven, a smattering of houses, and we blethered and blethered about what we were going to do. Neither of us was really prepared for what we were going to face at Celtic. To come in after big Jock meant the demands were going to be enormous. But neither of us – myself in particular – could have said no to the offer.

'I felt very, very guilty. I remember going to speak to Dick about it. He said "You'll nae enjoy working with that Celtic board as much as you've enjoyed working with us." I thought maybe that was the thing you'd expect him to say. But he was absolutely right.'

The sequence of events which took McNeill to Celtic drains some of the supposed power from that infamous handshake photograph. Stein may have been unwilling to give up the reins as manager of Celtic but he knew the time had come, and he was the architect of McNeill's selection as his successor. And McNeill never conspired against Stein. On the contrary, he accepted the job only because the initial offer had come from Stein himself.

If Desmond White's twisted arm explained their positioning for that uncomfortable photograph, what McNeill called his 'twisted brain' was to become far more significant. McNeill was only 38 when he took over at Parkhead. Rangers had just won the treble. 'I wasn't ready for it. It was difficult. Everything was demanding. And you had the image of big Jock immediately behind you. I often wish that I had stayed at Aberdeen because I would have gotten an education up there that would have been absolutely brilliant. If I had had any sense I would have stayed there. My worry was that I might never be offered the Celtic job again.

'My whole career had been Celtic. I knew the demands of the club. They are always enormous. What Celtic always has is that magnificent fanbase. They are always there to support the club. They don't walk away from it. Their demand is that they see good football and an end result.

'But I found the board to be difficult. It was almost like it was us against them. I always thought a board would want to support your attempts to take the club on but it didn't work out that way. They were difficult to work with. I couldn't honestly tell you what the board wanted when I was at the club.

'And after Jock's car accident he lost something. It took something away from him. That was understandable. But it didn't help me when I went to take over from him at Celtic. I had to make my own way. It was a strange situation. Then he was away very quickly. He was away to be manager of Leeds United, just like that. I thought Jock would be around Parkhead. That would have been ideal. I thought he was pushing himself to get into the Celtic hierarchy, almost like a director of football role. That would have made my life so much easier. It would have been brilliant, fabulous for Celtic to have that man there. Big Jock would have done that job so well because he didn't like things not being done well. But it never happened. Looking back, I don't think he was treated as well as he should have been at Celtic.'

McNeill soon felt the same description applied to himself. Today he uses words like 'difficult' and 'desperate' to describe his first spell as Celtic manager between 1978 and 1983. He was up against the traditional threat from Rangers and a new, enormous challenge coming from Dundee United and the club he'd left behind, Aberdeen. And there was one other obstacle to overcome: the chairman of Celtic.

McNeill and White were never close. There was little warmth between them. McNeill felt unappreciated and undermined even as he delivered the title in 1979, 1981 and 1982, with a Scottish Cup and a League Cup along the way. He signed influential players like Davie Provan and Murdo MacLeod and brought through talents like Paul McStay and Charlie Nicholas. Yet he felt his every decision was questioned. 'It was desperate by the end, all the arguments with the chairman. I just went "keys up" and got away. It wasn't easy for me. That wasn't easy at all. I remember I went up and spoke to him. I spoke to my dad. My dad just said "You're in a situation where this man just doesn't respect you so I don't think there's a future for you." That's what I felt too.' Incredibly, the managers of Rangers, Aberdeen, Dundee United and even St Mirren were paid more than McNeill was by Celtic in 1983. When White pushed through the sale of Nicholas to Arsenal against McNeill's wishes, the beleaguered manager looked for the first available escape route.

'I just dived into Manchester City when they offered me their job. Just dived in. Desmond White said to me "If you want to go to Manchester City you may as well go." There was no effort to keep me. City were skint. They'd just been relegated to the old second division. I spoke to Sir Matt Busby for advice and spoke to Tommy Docherty. They were fantastic. They were hesitant about whether Man City was the right club for me to go to because they were virtually penniless. And my first season [1983–84] was a real hard season because we didn't have the quality of players. But then we got promotion, which was brilliant.

'I had three smashing years at Man City. I made a massive mistake by leaving them to join Aston Villa in 1986. I'd had another fall-out with the board at City. Three years at City were really demanding, exhausting. But overall I loved the experience and I loved the fans. Again I spoke to Sir Matt Busby and asked him about the job and he was very cautious. He said "That Doug Ellis [Villa's chairman] doesn't have the best reputation, watch what you're doing." Tommy Docherty told me "He's a fucking arse-hole." So I had the advice and I disregarded it. I took it on myself. I asked for advice, got it, and didn't listen to it.'

McNeill, this titan whose three spells at Celtic totalled 27 years, lasted only seven and a half months at Aston Villa. The club was heading towards relegation when he was appointed and he was unable to halt the slide. Unhappy with his circumstances and distrustful of his chairman, he was sacked. There was a lucrative offer to become involved in football in the Middle East. Instead he accepted another job in a different sort of gulf. He returned to Celtic – under a different chairman – in 1987 in a brave attempt to narrow the widening gap with rich, Graeme Souness-driven Rangers.

'Souness wasn't just bringing in players, he was bringing in England internationalists. England's captain. England's goalkeeper. I knew the scene I was coming back to, but again I just couldn't say no to Celtic. No regrets.'

In his first campaign back at Celtic he stemmed the blue tide and delivered the Premier Division and Scottish Cup in 1987–88, a particularly special achievement because it was the club's centenary season. McNeill had won round one against Souness but he knew how Rangers would respond.

'That was where the mistake was made. That double was great, it was terrific. But that's where the difficulty with dealing with that Celtic board came into being. I knew how Rangers would respond, by bringing in new, outstanding players. They had a helluva lot of money available. Whatever else Graeme Souness did, he bought bloody good players.

'After we won the double I said to the Celtic directors "Listen, we can't stop here, we can't think this is enough because they are going to go out and strengthen themselves". I knew Rangers wouldn't stand still. I never realised they would be able to do things to the extent that they did, but that's what happened. They bought real quality players.

'I didn't have a fraction of their resources. I had bought in players for that first season, Frank McAvennie, Andy Walker, Billy Stark, but we didn't then follow it up and build on it. That was frustrating. Aw, it was murder. The board said to me "well done, well done" but "well done" disnae mean anything if you're not improving the squad you've got.'

White was not the chairman for McNeill's second spell but the essential problem – a Celtic board unwilling to spend – was worse than before. Celtic retained the Scottish Cup in 1989 but it was McNeill's last honour. The confirmation of Celtic being second best in a two-horse race deepened when Mo Johnston chose to sign for Rangers instead of Celtic when both clubs wanted him. Celtic were falling way behind in every aspect. Rangers were bankrolling their 'nine-in-a-row' era and when he went two seasons without any trophy the unthinkable happened: Celtic sacked Billy McNeill.

'I saw it coming. But the manner in which it was done . . . I don't think I got any respect. There is a manner to do things if you're parting company with somebody, somebody who's played 18 years for you, somebody who has been your manager for nine years over two periods. You should get a bit of respect. That didn't happen to me. The fans were always great with me. They under-stood. They understood Rangers were spending and our board wasn't.'

McNeill was bitter about his dismissal but was sustained by the knowledge that he had been a successful manager of Celtic twice over: four titles, three Scottish Cups and one League Cup. What if he had taken the job and failed? 'I would probably have shot myself!' By 2009 time had healed the wounds. McNeill had been off Celtic's payroll for 18 years and was now aged 69. Celtic's board of directors were all new, ambitious and progressive. When an offer was made to him to become an ambassador for Celtic, McNeill happily accepted.

The move was warmly received throughout football. In one sense, of course, it was no more than a formal declaration of the obvious. For all his adult life, McNeill had never been anything other than the ultimate ambassador for Celtic.

Davie Hay

'Hearts had printed T-shirts saying "Champions" or
something. I remember saying "Right lads, let's make
that an obsolete item, so nae bastard is buying it."'

There have been more famous Celtic managers than Davie Hay.
More successful ones, too. Over the years many have been better
paid and plenty were indulged with much more money to spend
on new signings. Hay is not the type to envy any of them. Some
who have come and gone through the job cannot claim to have
something that he enjoys. They cannot walk the streets of Glasgow
and be met by the sort of quiet, knowing respect which washes
over this tough, likeable 'Celtic man'.

Hay is in his 60s and his business commitments and social circle
often take him into the centre of Glasgow. If he pops in for a pint
somewhere there will be a few in the pub who recognise him. A
quiet murmur might spread that a former Celtic manager is in their
midst. Hay won the Scottish Cup and then the Premier Divison
with Celtic. He bought exciting players and produced flamboyant
football, and he was sacked only because the Parkhead board of
directors panicked about the early impact made by Graeme Souness at Rangers.

Hay left with dignity and sympathy from knowledgeable supporters, which still endures decades later. He achieved something
that was beyond the likes of John Barnes, Paul le Guen and Tony
Mowbray: he met the challenge of managing an Old Firm club,
held his ground, delivered and survived to tell the tale with his
integrity intact.

'I do enjoy it, being able to go around Glasgow and feel
appreciated,' he says. 'It's nice if someone comes up to you. It
doesn't always have to be a Celtic supporter. Strangely enough,
sometimes a Rangers fan might come up and tell me they admired
me as a player, even if they tend to mean when I played with

Scotland. You appreciate that when it happens. Although you don't realise it at the time, there is an appreciation out there and you can think to yourself "Maybe I wisnae too bad". On the whole, you can come into a pub and people come up and are friendly and respectful. That's nice. I feel grateful about that.'

Hay was an excellent footballer. He was a formidably hard right-back or midfielder whom Tommy Docherty nicknamed 'The Quiet Assassin'. Opponents knew to take no liberties with Hay but he was fair as well as hard and was never once sent off. Celtic, Chelsea and Scotland were served with distinction before he retired prematurely because of injuries to his left knee and right eye. The vision in his eye had never been the same after he was hit by a toy arrow during a game of cowboys and Indians when he was eight years old. A subsequent detached retina accelerated the end of his playing career at Chelsea. Eventually he became blind in that eye.

Things came to Hay at the wrong time. By only 28 his distinguished playing career was over. Only seven years later, too young for a job of such scale, he was the manager of Celtic. Chelsea had given him a coaching role which he held until falling out with manager Geoff Hurst and returning to Scotland, un-employed and looking for work. Soon the first step into manage-ment was made as assistant to Ally MacLeod at Motherwell.

The pair of them were chalk and cheese: the gregarious show-man MacLeod and the laconic Hay, but they became teacher and student. When MacLeod left in the summer of 1981 Hay took over and won promotion as First Division champions in his first season. By then he had been seduced by the idea of living and working in America and resigned from Motherwell before he could enjoy their new Premier Division status. Within weeks visa problems had scuppered his emigration and he was out of work again. He opened a pub in Paisley, his home town, and there was a year when he came close to drifting away from football entirely. As a still inexperienced young manager, with one season under his belt, no football job but a pub to run in order to provide for his family, he received exactly the offer he craved above all. Celtic asked him to become their manager.

Hay was 35, excited and ferociously ambitious for 'his' club. He immediately promised to resign if he didn't win a trophy in his first season but thought better of it after finishing second in the league and both cups. A dramatic Scottish Cup final victory over Dundee United delivered silverware in his second campaign and the league title followed in his third. Hay's nerve showed as he refused to surrender the title to Hearts. The Edinburgh club had looked the likely champions for weeks but Celtic overtook them on the final, unforgettable day of the 1985–86 season. 'You know you read these things now about teams who cut things out of the paper that the opposition has said and use it as motivation? Well, the day before it had come to my notice that Hearts had printed T-shirts saying "Champions" or something. I remember saying "Right lads, let's make that an obsolete item, so nae bastard is buying it." That was a last-minute thing I threw in.'

Hay was a league-winning manager but the bigger picture was turning against him. Souness arrived at Rangers and was instantly indulged with millions to spend to deliver a revolution. The Celtic board never provided the transfer funds Hay or any other manager required to live with the new money being splashed around at Ibrox. There were grubby circumstances about the way Celtic directors decided to dismiss Hay in 1987 and offer Billy McNeill a second spell in charge. Hay took a long time to come to terms with how he had been treated by a board which had asked him to work with a hand tied behind his back.

'I just know that with a few more years under my belt I'd have been better equipped to do the job. I was better equipped to do the job when I was sacked than I was when I took it over in the first place. But you can't pick and choose your destiny or your timing in football. I'm pretty philosophical that it wasn't to be.

'When I lost the job at Celtic it hurt and it's easy for bitterness to creep in. But you just have to swallow the bitter pill, because if you don't it eats you up. I'm a great believer that when you take a job you take what comes with it. I don't offer sympathy and I don't look for it. You have to be hard enough to take what comes. You live and die by results. I didn't like it happening, but I could see why it happened.'

Hay had an unusual, mixed, nomadic career after leaving Celtic. There aren't many men who would turn down the Newcastle job to go to Lillestrom instead. Hay did exactly that when he felt Newcastle had not offered him the protection of a sufficiently long contract. He also felt the club was on a downer because Paul Gascoigne had just been sold. In his only season at Lillestrom he won the Norwegian League title.

There was a spell as an agent (he came close to taking on snooker's Alex Higgins as a client). He was assistant manager at Watford and Swindon and manager of St Mirren and Dunfermline, where he was unsuccessful, and Livingston, where he somehow pulled off the greatest feat of his management. Little Livingston had no right to win any of Scotland's major honours but Hay landed them the 2004 League Cup with a victory over overwhelming favourites Hibs. The club had never known a day like it, and almost certainly never will again.

By then the young pretender had become one of the country's managerial grandees, an elder statesman who was briefly touted as a potential Scotland international manager. 'I do sit and reflect on my career sometimes. I try not to be bumptious about it but I'm one of a group of people who has won everything in Scotland, every medal as a player and as a manager. I would have liked to have won more. It wasn't to be. But I can look back and claim to have been a successful Celtic manager.'

Gordon Strachan

'Maybe in England they saw me and thought "Aye,
that's what all Scottish guys look like".'

As he selected where he would sit Gordon Strachan made sure he
had his back to the wall and a clear view of all his surroundings, like
Mafia men supposedly do when they're in a public place and wary
of being whacked. This was Glasgow on a Saturday night. It
seemed like a lifetime ago since he was the manager of Celtic but
old habits die hard. Strachan, who was back in the city to attend a
function, always has his wits about him when he's out and about in
Old Firm territory. The offer of a beer was politely declined. A pot
of tea was the better option.

He has not always been able to avoid trouble – famously, he was
physically assaulted on a pitch and verbally abused off it – but in
more ways than one Strachan has always known how to look after
himself. The only small thing about him is his body, just 5ft 6in of
it. You could be forgiven for assuming most of his mass is taken up
by his tongue. This little man was a giant as a footballer and he has
been a big manager, and throughout it all he beamed brightly as a
huge personality. Some see him as the quintessential Scotsman:
wee, ginger-haired, quarrelsome, carrying a chip on his shoulder
and having plenty to say for himself. But he has always laughed a
lot, too, and even that description has made him smile: 'A big part
of my personality is about being Scottish. Maybe in England
they saw me and thought "Aye, that's what all Scottish guys look
like".'

There are plenty of his countrymen who bear a resemblance, but
only Billy Bremner and Jimmy Johnstone could also claim to have
made such a mark on football. Strachan has been a figure in the
British mainstream for years, a favourite on *Match of the Day*, a
columnist in the *Guardian*, and a popular subject for impressionists.
His managerial career has taken him to Coventry City, South-

ampton, Celtic – where he had great success – and Middlesbrough. Some of his acidic responses to journalists' questions are part of the lore of the Premiership era. There aren't just 'classic' Strachan quotes on the internet, there are entire pages and top tens of them.

That has been his defence mechanism. As a skilful, intelligent, goalscoring midfielder he was capable of embarrassing defenders. As a sharp-witted and cutting manager he could embarrass any of his own errant players or journalists who asked a silly question. Or, to be accurate, what he regarded as a silly question. He has always kept people on their toes. On occasion his sarcasm has been dangerously close to sounding cruel.

There was plenty for him to cope with himself. He does not wear the hardship of his upbringing as a badge of honour, but he had it tougher than most. He was raised in Muirhouse, an area of Edinburgh which has had more than its share of problems with high unemployment and drug-related crime. He refers to it as 'Trainspotting country', not least because author Irvine Welsh's family home was near his own.

His father, Jim, was a scaffolder and his mother, Catherine, worked in a whisky bond in nearby Leith. Inevitably his character was at least partly shaped by all of this. As a player he was always the talented wee ginger guy up against bigger, often unscrupulous opponents. He couldn't even see properly. He was left half-blind in his right eye by a childhood accident during an impromptu kickabout. Perhaps this was why he became distrustful of some reporters: the injury was caused by a pen. He was carrying one when he was tackled to the ground by a pal and it pierced his eye socket and damaged the optic nerve. For two and a half weeks the eye was covered by a hospital dressing and he worried about whether he had lost his sight in it altogether.

With smart feet and a smart mouth, he survived. It was an upbringing which seemed unremarkable to him at the time, yet there were lessons from it which hardened and equipped him for a life in football. 'I never felt Muirhouse was rough, I never thought it was living on the borderline or whatever, because everybody did it. It was only when I moved away that I sat and thought "That was quite hard".'

'What we don't like, as Scottish managers, is anybody bullying us. I hate getting bullied. I hate cheap shots. If I feel I'm being backed into a corner my instinct is to bite back. I didn't cultivate that when I became a manager. I had it as a kid, all the time. If I was going to get into a fight I would talk my way out of it, or run quicker than anybody else. I would never do anyone a bad turn by trying to hurt them, it would only be verbal.

'I was never a cheat as a football player and I was never a coward. I wouldn't kick anybody and I wouldn't go over the top. The only thing I did to get people back was talk. I would sort them out with my tongue. Whether you like it or not, I think the verbal thing has been a self-preservation mechanism for me. I've never hit anybody, I've never done anybody any harm, but there are times when I've had to defend myself and I've done it verbally. Jock [Stein] was like that, [Sir Alex] Ferguson's still like that. Verbally we can come back and hit you with something.

'Jock maybe had the physical presence to say "I'll knock your head off". I never had that presence so I had to be "yap, yap, yap, yap". [Bill] Shankly was a bit like that too. That's what we're good at, the Scots. If you start any verbal jousting you'll find that we're no' bad at that.'

An entire encyclopaedia of football wisdom has been poured into his ears over the years. He played under Ferguson for eight and a half years at Aberdeen and Manchester United and under Stein thirty-two times for Scotland. There was plenty of Shankly, too. 'I used to listen to Shankly on tape every time I got into Ferguson's car. We used to go to games together because when I was a young man he knew I loved football so he'd say "Hey Curly, do you want to go to a game the day?" So I used to listen to these tapes when we were going to Forfar or Arbroath or wherever. They're fantastic but it's just common sense mixed with sports psychology, and that's what Alex's good at.'

Strachan can quickly get into full flow on the subject of sports psychology. He regards it as the essence of what made so many Scottish managers great: an innate ability to motivate and communicate with players. The full, withering Strachan contempt comes down on many of those who attach themselves to clubs and claim to be the secret of a manager's success in this aspect of the job.

'Scottish football managers as sports psychologists is a huge concept. I think our best managers have been the best in the world at that. Sports psychology is what Jock Stein did. Alex Ferguson is the best sports psychologist in the world, by a million miles. You won't find his teachings in any university and the Geneva Convention might come down hard on him, but it works. That's what I do. I like coaching. I like to make these guys feel good about themselves, make them feel better, and give them the feeling that they can believe in themselves. Scots are great at that. That's what Shankly had. There was nothing cosmic about the way he played football, it was down to sports psychology.

'That doesn't mean the people who go about calling themselves "sports psychologists". These guys annoy me, the ones who come along and tag on to a Ferguson for a while and the next thing they're putting on their CV "Oh I was a sports psychologist at Manchester United". Fergie's been there for 25 years! It's got nothing to do with anyone else!

'You get these soothsayer types, but Scottish football managers are real psychologists, we deal with nitty-gritty psychology. Whether that's down to Jock Stein being down the pits or Alex Ferguson in the shipyards or people like myself coming from Muirhouse and having to deal with a problem or a crisis, all of it maybe played a role.

'We all have different ways of dealing with things but we all have that durability that you can go back and take another hit and another hit and you can roll with it. We're all different. Fergie's thing was anger. He works on anger. You look at the season where he decided to pack it in at the end of the year. There wasn't a fire in that team because there was a bit of magic missing from the man at the top, that real drive and determination was missing for a while.

'I remember Stein for being an imposing figure physically. His personality was imposing too. You knew to step well back because he had that aura about him. I think we missed the best of him when he was with Scotland. That had come earlier. But people talk about zonal marking these days. Do you know who was the first man ever to mention zonal marking to me? Jock Stein. Years ago. Big Alex McLeish was at a Scotland–England game and he told him where to be to head the ball. Big Alex said "But guys might come in over there" and big Jock said "If the ball comes in your area you heid it, what are you complaining about?" Simple as that. So he was the first one to talk to me about zonal marking and that was over 25 years ago.'

Strachan has his place in a tier of successful modern Scottish managers along with Kenny Dalglish, George Graham, Walter Smith, Alex McLeish and David Moyes. In 1996 he began almost five years in charge of Coventry City, a spell scarred by their relegation after 34 years in the top flight and his eventual dismissal. That was followed by two and a half satisfying years at Southampton in which he took them to an eighth place in the Premiership and to the 2003 FA Cup final.

When he resigned there he was voluntarily out of football for 16 months, a period he spent travelling with his wife, Lesley. They married in 1977 and she has been his constant companion ever since. There were times in his next job when coming home to his soul-mate was invaluable. Celtic transformed his managerial career from unremarkable to enormously fulfilling, although not without a few bumps along the way.

While he was out of work he was short-listed for the Liverpool and Scotland jobs but missed out on both of them. Instead he was destined to succeed Martin O'Neill at Parkhead, taking over in 2005 and staying for four successful, challenging, intense, turbulent years. The highs were intoxicating. He won the league title in his first three seasons, becoming the first Celtic manager since Stein to land three successive championships. There was a Scottish Cup and two League Cups as well. He delivered at least one trophy every season. The hugely popular and successful O'Neill had never taken the club to the last 16 of the Champions League. Strachan did so twice, recording stirring victories over Manchester United, AC Milan and others along the way. Artur Boruc, Scott McDonald and Shunsuke Nakamura were cheap signings who became hugely valuable. The glory was all the more impressive given that Celtic's debt and wage bill both fell dramatically while he was in charge.

The lows were draining. Surely no manager of a huge club will ever start as catastrophically as he did, with a 5–0 Champions League qualifier defeat to Artmedia Bratislava in his first competitive match in charge? It was a result which scrambled the senses. There were even whispers that he might not survive it. A little over five months later there was an aftershock when Celtic crashed out of the Scottish Cup to little Clyde. Thomas Gravesen was an expensive acquisition who offered little and Bobo Balde was stubbornly left in the reserves because of his attitude despite pocketing £28,000 per week. In his final season his team looked jaded and limped in behind Rangers in the league. More affecting than any of that was the death of his first team coach, Tommy Burns. A different public face emerged when Strachan struggled to hold back tears at the loss of his close friend. Many supporters viewed him differently after that.

He found elements of life in Glasgow claustrophobic. The intensity of the scrutiny, the culture of encouraging aggrieved supporters to spout off on newspaper hotlines or radio phone-ins, the shadows cast by ignorance and bigotry: he found all of it wearying. He responded to respect and good manners but witnessed too much of what he called 'yob culture'.

Acceptance from a section of Celtic supporters was grudging. He had a history with the club. As a young Aberdeen player he had twice been targeted by Celtic supporters who had invaded the pitch to get at him. As Celtic manager he agreed to have his picture taken with one fan on a stadium tour only to hear him say: 'You'd better be quick. He'll probably get the sack next week.' The comment irritated him so much he manhandled the fan out of the front door. The bloke thought it was a joke until he realised he wasn't being allowed back into the ground.

Strachan did not arrive at the club as a Celtic supporter and nor did he naturally identify with either the Irish or Catholic aspects of the club's heritage. Those elements of Celtic did not interest him. He was there to deliver success as a football manager. If it seemed like he never engaged with the club on a profound emotional level he was nevertheless respectful and grew genuinely affectionate about Celtic. For many supporters the feeling was quietly mutual. He acknowledged he had stayed long enough and tendered his resignation in May 2009.

By then it was being said that his squad had stagnated and that he had too many personality clashes with his players. The Italian midfielder, Massimo Donati, claimed Strachan had ostracised him to the extent that he felt 'dead'. In the final months of his management there was a bitter verbal exchange with Republic of Ireland winger Aiden McGeady in front of other players. McGeady was fined and suspended for a fortnight, although he returned to play regularly in Strachan's final months.

'Of all the guys I've worked with there's only been one or two that I've had an issue with. There's really only been one that I really never got through to. And I spent more time on that kid than on any of them. He's an unusual kid.' McGeady is a short, opinionated, talented right-sided midfielder, like Strachan himself. Neither of them would welcome the comparison.

'When I look back on it I haven't really had players coming out and being negative about me as a manager. Well maybe Massimo Donati did, but Massimo's problem was he had a heart the size of a pea. If he made one mistake in a game he'd go on to make ten that day.

'When I went to Aberdeen I was crap for the first year when Billy McNeill was the manager. I was horrendous. But I didn't blame Billy McNeill for it. It was my fault. I wasn't playing well. Some players blame the manager in that situation but it's not the manager who keeps giving the ball away.

'When I was captain at Leeds United I felt people were listening to me. All these players who I played with, when they phone me up now they still call me "Skip", not Gordon, because they saw me as the captain. I'll have had arguments with most of them but we're still mates. Whenever they phone me for advice I think I must have done something right if they're phoning me.

'A couple of years ago big Gary Breen came up to me.' Breen, a Republic of Ireland international defender, had played for him at Coventry. 'He'd always had plenty to say when he was a young player, Gary. But he came up to me and said "I have to apologise to you". I didn't know what he was on about. He said "Listen, I was a pest when I was a kid playing under you. I only realise that now. I realise what you were trying to do for me. I've worked with some arseholes since then." I thought that was big of him, to come up to me and apologise in front of my wife. Wee things like that keep me going for months.

'If you ask me what's the essence of great Scottish managers I'd say it's that we have that ability to get a good rapport going. We've got common sense and we're good at dealing with people. The best Scots are good at dealing with people. You can take it further. Look at English television: how many Scots are on it? Loads and loads of them. I've said this to people at the BBC: there's even something about the accent that sounds authoritative. We have this ability to communicate with people and get our message across. And there's the hunger. We feel that once we've worked so hard to get to the level we're at we're not going to let it go.

'We know how to organise, we know how to motivate, and we know how to get on with people. I think we're streetwise, we're clever, we're humorous. When I walked in the door of a club I had to make the secretaries happy, the women that I met in the canteen happy, all the workmen behind the scenes happy, so that the atmosphere at the club was good. So I come into work at 8 a.m.

and I have to generate that for a couple of hours before the players even come in, no matter how I feel.'

By now his cup of tea was empty and the pot cold. He had been talking for two hours. The only disturbances had been from a couple of Celtic supporters who spotted him and approached to ask for autographs and a photograph. They asked politely, so Strachan rose from that chair, with its back against the wall, and did that one last thing for them.

The Great Rangers Managers

William Wilton

'William Wilton laid the foundations for future success at Rangers Football Club. He guided the club through the introduction of the first Scottish Football League championship and helped them cope with professionalism. And also, let us not forget, he won 38 trophies in total when he was in charge.'
— Rangers historian Robert McElroy

There are managers nowadays who justifiably moan and groan about their workload. The stresses and strains they face are nothing compared to those faced by William Wilton, the first manager of Rangers. He wasn't only the man who was responsible for the first team. He was the public face of Rangers Football Club, and a man who worked tirelessly for them, first as a player, then as an administrator and then as manager for a total of 37 years.

If leading his team to eight Scottish League championships and one Scottish Cup was not enough, he was also the driving force behind the early and significant redevelopment of Ibrox Stadium. Wilton also fronted with great dignity the club's campaign to raise thousands of pounds for the 25 spectators who died and 587 who were injured in the Scotland versus England game that was played at Ibrox in 1902.

Wilton was also a man who pushed for early change within the Scottish Football Association. He convinced the governing body to introduce ideas the game takes for granted today, such as pitch inspections, because he did not want fans inconvenienced by travelling to games that were called off at the last minute. He was also well versed in public relations: it was his idea for Rangers to send footballs to troops on the front line during the First World War so that they could have a kick-about to raise morale.

Wilton was not just the first manager of Rangers but also arguably its greatest in terms of what he did for the club. He helped guide them through the changes taking place in the game as a whole during the introduction of professionalism, and also attempted to lift spirits within Ibrox during the 1914–18 war. A little later he earmarked his successor as Bill Struth, which proved to be an inspired appointment.

Wilton officially became the manager of Rangers only after an annual general meeting in the Trades Hall in Glasgow in May 1899, the same meeting at which a vote was passed to make the club a limited liability company. But he had already been involved at Ibrox for many years as honorary match secretary. He had been a promising but not top-class footballer in his youth. Although he signed for Rangers at the age of 17, he made it only into 'The Swifts', who were to all intents and purposes the Rangers second team.

What Wilton lacked in natural football ability on a field he more than made up for in terms of his drive and personality in other areas. He was organised, precise and, having realised he would be no more than a journeyman footballer, knew he should move into the administrative side of the game, so he became secretary of the Swifts.

He did such an impressive job that he was proposed, at the

tender age of just 23, for the prestigious position of honorary match secretary of Rangers Football Club. And he was elected for the position ahead of James Gossland, who was already in the job and had much more experience than the young Wilton. It seemed the old football adage 'If they are good enough, they are old enough' resonated among the committee men at Rangers. They put great faith and responsibility in Wilton, whose energy and enthusiasm impressed them.

During the 1890s, before he officially become the first Rangers manager, he immersed himself in every aspect of running the club. You may think a match secretary would have been up in the stands in the directors' box on match days, but that was not the case. Wilton was expected – as were people in his position at other clubs – to 'run the line' like a modern referee's assistant.

Wilton also knew a football club needed money to survive and grow, so the more events held at Ibrox the better. In 1889 he set up the Ibrox Sports Day, including athletics, a five-a-side tournament and cycling. That became both popular and profitable and remained part of the Scottish sports summer calendar until 1962.

Wilton was also one of the architects of the Scottish Football League, which was constituted at a meeting in March 1890. So impressed with the articulate Wilton were the representatives of the 10 other leading clubs in Scotland that they made him secretary of the new league organisation. Inevitably, he was delighted when Rangers shared the first-ever Scottish League championship with Dumbarton in 1891. Two years later he helped convince the SFA to sanction professionalism in an attempt to ensure that all of the leading Scottish players did not leave the country to play in England.

Wilton had become one of the most powerful figures – if not the most powerful – in Scottish football at the time and his influence grew in May 1899 when he was named as the first official manager of Rangers. That was the year the Ibrox club made history by winning every one of its 18 league matches, setting a world record.

He took over team affairs and also tried to put in place the funds for a new-look 80,000-capacity Ibrox.

The famous architect, Archibald Leitch, who went on to build stands for Arsenal and Hearts among others, was brought in to oversee the work and, remarkably, by 30 December 1899, a redeveloped Ibrox was officially opened.

With Wilton at the helm Rangers won four championships in a row up until 1902 but tragedy struck on the afternoon of 5 April of that year. Rangers had campaigned successfully to have a Scotland versus England match played at their new top-class stadium. But too many people packed the east terracing on the day of the game, which meant that the timber and iron lattice structure collapsed, killing 25 people and injuring 587. Incredibly, the disaster occurred during the first half yet the match was still allowed to continue after only a short, 18-minute delay.

The incident was a hammer-blow to the all-powerful Rangers Football Club. The fall-out for the club and Wilton, the identifiable face of Rangers, put him under real pressure. An inquiry into the incident put the blame on the style of terracing and from that moment clubs moved towards creating banks of earth for fans to stand on.

The SFA set up a fund for dependants of the dead and injured and so did Rangers, with Wilton as the principal trustee. He helped raise over £4000 but in the wake of the disaster it was clear that general improvements were still required at Ibrox, and they would not be cheap. Reluctantly, but realising the necessity of the move, he was forced to put all 22 first team players up for sale to pay for fresh ground redevelopment, which did not make his 'other' job as manager any easier. By the end of 1904 Rangers had spent £42,000 on upgrading Ibrox – a big rise on the £12,000 that had been spent on creating the ground in the first place back in 1899. It was another seven years before Rangers were strong enough to become league champions again but they then won it three times in a row up until 1913.

Wilton was not called up during the First World War because the Home Office ruled that he was in gainful employment at Ibrox. In addition, he was helping out at Bellahouston Hospital. He also sorted out Ibrox's 'Aircraft Insurance' in case the stadium was bombed by the Germans. He secured such a good deal on premiums from an insurance firm that in 1917 the club accounts show he was awarded a £50 increase on his salary, taking it up to £350 a year.

After the war Wilton concentrated on working with the Rangers players and quickly put together a top-class side. Sandy Archibald, who had joined from Raith Rovers for £250 in 1917, turned out to be one of his best signings. The little winger played for the Ibrox club for 17 years, turning out in 580 games. He was part of a side that included the likes of James Bowie, Tommy Cairns and Jimmy Gordon, who all came to the club when Wilton was manager. He also showed he had an eye for talent when he brought the legendary Davie Meiklejohn to the club in 1919. Meiklejohn went on to win twelve league championships and five Scottish Cup winner's medals.

Although a strict disciplinarian, Wilton had a close affinity to some of his players and was liked and respected to the extent that he was best man at the wedding of John McPherson, the most versatile player in the history of Rangers, who played in every position, including goalkeeper, between 1890 and 1902.

'William Wilton laid the foundations for future success at Rangers Football Club,' said Robert McElroy, a club historian, 'He guided the club through the introduction of the first Scottish Football League championship and helped them cope with professionalism. He also helped facilitate the move to the present Ibrox stadium site. And also, let us not forget, he won 38 trophies in total when he was in charge.'

The first proper, non-regional Scottish League championship after the war was held in 1919–20 and Wilton's Rangers team romped away with the title. They scored 106 goals and lost just 25. He had put together a team that looked like it could dominate

Scottish football for a long time. But then an extraordinary tragedy struck.

On Sunday, 2 May 1920, Wilton went boating on the River Clyde at Gourock. He was a passenger on a boat called the *Caltha*, which was owned by former Rangers committee man James Marr. The boat was torn from its moorings in a terrible storm and battered into the wall of Caledonian Pier. Marr and J.P. Buchanan, another Rangers committee man, managed to clamber out of the boat and onto the pier to safety but Wilton was not so lucky.

He fell into the water, and although Marr bravely dived in to try and save his friend the rescue attempt was unsuccessful. Such was his standing in the community that many laid flowers where the accident happened and there were tributes to him from all over Scotland. It was a sudden and tragic end to the life of a man who had given his heart and soul to Rangers. He died, far too young, at the age of only 54.

Bill Struth

'No man is bigger than the club.'

Bill Struth's background gave no indication that he would go on to become one of the most successful managers Scottish football has ever seen. His first love was athletics, and even when he became involved with his country's national game it did not take a complete grip of him. Glasgow Rangers found its way into his heart. Football in general never did.

Between 1920 and 1954 – the beginning and end of his astonishing reign – he won eighteen official Scottish League titles, ten Scottish Cups and two Scottish League Cups. Add a further seven unofficial Scottish championships spread over the war years, nineteen Glasgow Cups, twenty Glasgow Merchants' Charity Cups and other lesser competitions and it is clear that the Ibrox trophy haul was swollen enormously by his management. He won more than 80 trophies. He was a formidable and stern character who tended not to accept either criticism or advice, but he protected his players fiercely and allowed the trusted senior ones to dictate tactics on the pitch. Above all, he insisted that Rangers should be seen as the biggest and best club in the land. He set standards and established 'the Rangers way' of doing things. His approach was hugely successful.

It was quite a trophy haul for a man who had hardly played football at any level before becoming involved in the coaching and managerial side of the game. He was the exception to the rule that a man has to have the game 'in his blood' in order to be a successful coach or manager. What Struth had in his blood was athletics, his abiding passion when he was growing up in Milnathort in Kinross-shire.

Struth's love of athletics was directly to Rangers' advantage in later years as he brought top runners to the 'Ibrox Sports Day', including legendary figures such as Eric Liddell and Harold Abrahams, whose rivalry featured in the film *Chariots of Fire*.

Also taking part were runners of the calibre of Paavo Nurmi, the Finn who won nine Olympic Gold medals, as well as Sydney Wooderson, the Englishman who held the world record for the mile and dominated the distance in the late 1930s and early 1940s. Struth, although a decent runner, had never come close to matching such figures. Struth was a stonemason who had spent every weekend travelling up and down Britain taking part in professional athletics meetings as a teenager. He was good — especially at the half mile — but not good enough to make a living out of it.

He had to supplement his income, and with his experience of rigorous athletic training regimes he became a respected coach of Scottish runners. With physical fitness a prerequisite for footballers before the First World War he was in great demand. When Hearts heard about his work they brought in Struth to train their players. It was an unlikely introduction to senior football for a man who would go on to become a legendary Scottish figure.

After leaving Hearts he had a short period at part-time Clyde, where his potential was spotted by Rangers manager William Wilton, who made him the trainer at Ibrox. After being in that role for six years he was promoted to manager at the age of 45 after Wilton died in a tragic boating accident in May of 1920. The huge significance of physical fitness within football at the time and Struth's expertise in that respect meant his promotion to manager was predictable. If injured players required an operation, Struth would often accompany them to the operating theatre.

Struth wanted to give his all to his new job, to the extent he bought a flat at 193 Copland Road near the stadium so he could spend most of his waking hours at the ground. Just what his wife, Kate, who died in 1941, thought about that was never recorded. Luckily for him, managers in Struth's day were given much more respect. Even when Rangers had the odd bad result there were no angry fans banging at his door after the match.

When he took over at Ibrox his goal was to continue the good work started by Wilton and make sure the standing of Rangers remained high in Scotland. Image mattered to Struth in more ways than one. He was a well-dressed dandy who ordered his players to have the same sartorial elegance and attention to detail as he had himself. He was so keen on looking good that he had several suits in his office at the club, sometimes wearing one in the morning and a different one for the afternoon. He even occasionally used sun lamps, which were used in the rehabilitation of injured players, to top up his tan.

He insisted that his players were always well turned out. Woe betide anyone who arrived at Ibrox without his tie straightened, his shoes shining and his bowler hat on at the right angle. Or, for that matter, anyone who showed up with his hands in his pockets. One player, Adam Little, was pulled up for knotting his cravat the wrong way.

Above all it was a bowler hat that Struth was most strict about and he insisted all his players wore one on match days when they were on club duty, or at any other time if they were anywhere within the vicinity of Ibrox. Today the stadium's dressing rooms still have hooks for bowler hats.

Some of them did attempt to stage their own half-hearted rebellion by taking their hats to Ibrox in brown paper bags rather than putting them on their heads. Sometimes it was only when they turned into Copland Road, and walked past Struth's flat, that they put their hat on, just in case the boss was watching. The fact that this was their only available form of protest showed exactly how much power Struth had over his players, and for that matter over everybody else at Ibrox. Even the Rangers directors were under his control. One of them was once told to take a cigarette out of his mouth when he was speaking to him.

Struth always put his players first. He made sure they had their lunch before the club directors in the Ibrox dining room. He made them feel valued, and they responded by being loyal and helping him to take the club to great success. He was a mentor to many of the young men who walked through the doors of Ibrox, most of whom had no idea what to do with their signing-on fee and weekly wage. He saw himself as a form of social worker to the young, often naive players who came to him as nervous teenagers. Without Struth's advice about saving their cash – for special occasions or for when they retired from playing – it is unlikely some of them would ever have done so.

When one of his players, winger Torrance 'Torry' Gillick, wanted to become engaged, Struth knew he would never save enough money for the ring because, quite simply, he was not very good with cash. With the player's best interests at heart Struth took money out of Gillick's weekly wage packet and kept it in a separate account for him. When Gillick wanted to buy the engagement ring he went to Struth, who gave him a lump sum and even told him the name of a good jeweller. Being involved in the players' personal lives, knowing everything about them, helped Struth gain control. And they respected him for it.

Although he was Rangers manager for 34 years and even became the club's major shareholder, he never lost sight of the fact he was just a small part in a bigger machine. During all his time as manager he had a sign on the table in his office which read: 'No man is bigger than the club.'

The sentiment was very true, but when Struth was in charge at Ibrox it was a close-run thing. As a coach and manager at Rangers, he was ahead of his time in terms of fitness work, and would tailor sessions and running drills to suit each individual footballer. A player lacking stamina would be given more long runs to do; wingers would be told to embark on a series of sprint races. He always started training with a one-mile walk around the track so that his expert athletic eye could check for faults in their step or gait.

It quickly became clear that although he was essentially a top-class physical trainer he did have an eye for footballing talent. He brought players of the calibre of Alan Morton – who went on to become one of the Wembley Wizards – to the club as well as Billy McCandless and Willie Robb. In his first official season, 1920–21, Struth's team won the league title and went on to win the championship a further eight times in the following decade.

Although they dominated the league, they struggled to the point of embarrassment in the Scottish Cup. That was not unusual for Rangers back then. His predecessor, Wilton, had also found success hard to come by in the tournament. When Struth's Rangers made the Scottish Cup final in 1928 that particular trophy had not been won by the club since 1903, when Wilton was in charge. The fact they won that final 4–0 against Celtic in front of 118,115 supporters at Hampden enhanced Struth's reputation among the fans.

For a man in charge of a club for more than 30 years it was clear that he knew how to rebuild teams. He did so often and effectively, although it is a matter of record that the directors also had an influence on who was signed. When players like even the great Morton were past their best Struth replaced them and brought in a new generation of high-quality replacements such as Gillick and Alex Venters, who helped Rangers to a sweep of trophies in the

1933–34 season when they won the league title, the Scottish Cup, the Glasgow Cup and the Charity Shield.

He strengthened further right up until the outbreak of the Second World War in 1939 and was able to do so mainly due to the quality of a scouting structure he put in place which covered the whole of Britain. During the war the free movement of players saw stars like Stanley Matthews playing for Rangers. He won a Charity Cup medal with them in 1941. Although the Scottish League had been disbanded during the war years there were regional leagues, and Rangers dominated. Out of 30 major competitions they entered during the war years they won 25. An indication of Struth's dominance during the war years came in the fact that they won every single championship – seven in a row. Although titles won through the war years are often excluded from official records, it was a record of which Struth was always proud.

He was equally proud of being the Rangers coach when they took on the touring Moscow Dynamo team in 1945. In the first all-ticket match held at Ibrox around 90,000 people packed the stadium to watch a 2–2 draw. The huge attendance was an indication in the level of interest in all things Rangers under Struth. They played attractive football and averaged around 28,000 for every home game, impressive for a time just after the war when money was tight although the appetite for football was huge. The 1947 league title was Rangers' ninth in a row if the war championships were included. Struth justifiably thought the Rangers fans and club's board of directors were firmly behind him.

The only negative against him by that point was his age. Some on the Rangers board thought that in 1947, at the age of 71, he should step down for a younger man. Some of them also felt Struth had too much power at Ibrox and felt he wasn't showing other members of the board enough respect. It was true that Struth had huge control at Ibrox, not least because of having built up a major shareholding in the club. He had always fancied some more power by becoming a club director. At that point though he could not legally become one as the Rangers constitution stated that no director could hold another office and he was already manager. In other words if he wanted to be a Rangers director he had to step down as manager, which he had no intention of doing.

Struth's solution? Stage a palace coup against chairman Jimmy Bowie and change the rules! He managed to do this and after meetings of shareholders and an historic annual general meeting he became the first man to be both manager and director of Rangers.

Things did not unfold smoothly at the beginning of his dual role. Hibs won the 1947–48 league championship and although Rangers beat Morton in the Scottish Cup final it felt like small beer for a team that wanted to win title after title. That blip was quickly shrugged off by Struth. In 1948–49 Rangers won the country's first national treble, picking up the Scottish League title, the Scottish Cup and the League Cup.

In the late 1940s, when he was in his 70s, the years started to catch up with Struth and his health deteriorated. He had various stomach complaints and in 1952, after gangrene set in, he lost his left leg below the knee. Many thought the disability would stop him turning up at his office inside Ibrox but not even the famous marble staircase proved to be too much of a problem. On the days when he couldn't manage to get up it himself, members of the Ibrox backroom staff such as Joe Craven and Jimmy Smith used to carry him up. As Struth got even older Rangers had a dip in success. Although they won the double in 1952–53, it was the beginning of the end for his time in charge.

After a fall within the stadium after a game against Stirling Albion on 2 January 1954, he was rushed to hospital. It was clear that the time had come for a new man to take over. He may have had the respect of fans who were concerned for his health but like supporters of any generation, when the results faltered they began to complain. His team was ageing, there was talk that he had lost the dressing room and it was clear – most of all to Struth – that he had to resign. He did so on 30 April 1954. He had been manager of Rangers to the age of 79.

He was succeeded by Scot Symon, the former Rangers player

who was manager of East Fife at the time and who had been recommended for the job by Struth himself. In retirement he continued to attend Rangers games and any divisions between himself and supporters in his final seasons were quickly healed. The level of respect in which he was held by the whole of Scottish football was evident by the extent of the grieving when he died two years later, on 21 September 1956.

His final hours were not spent in his beloved flat in Copland Road but in his new house at 27 Dalkeith Avenue, Dumbreck, Glasgow, where he had moved when it became too difficult for him to climb the stairs to his flat. His death at the age of 81 came just a day before an Old Firm game at Parkhead. It was the fixture he loved more than any other and an indication of his standing in the game came when fans on both sides bowed their heads for an impeccably observed minute's silence. Struth had long before picked out the spot for his grave at Craigton Cemetery. Standing at the side of his headstone, which has the Rangers crest at the top, anyone paying their respects can see Struth's beloved Ibrox Stadium in the distance. It was his perfect final resting place.

Rangers honoured his memory in fine style. The main stand at Ibrox was renamed as 'The Bill Struth Main Stand' and there is a bronze bust of him within the ground. Those were dignified tributes to a man who won more silverware than any other Rangers manager. Bill Struth *was* Rangers.

Ralph Brand was in the Rangers team from 1954 to 1965. The former Scotland forward was a teenager when he signed for Struth, who was in the twilight of his extraordinary Ibrox reign. 'The first time I saw Mr Struth was in 1952 when I was a 15-year-old boy from Edinburgh and he was a 77-year-old football legend. From the first minute to the last time we met he kept talking to me about the Rangers tradition. He used to say: "Once you put that Rangers jersey over your head you will grow a few inches, son. Wear it with pride." And that's exactly what I did. He was such a huge character you just felt the need to do well for him as you didn't want to let him down. That, for me, is a sign of a great manager. A man you looked up to. Someone who is firm but fair, and who had your automatic respect.

'What he taught me as a teenager influenced me a lot in my life. He taught me how to behave, how to dress smartly, how to treat people. It all goes back to him. He was a great man with very high principles. When I signed on schoolboy forms I had been on Rangers' radar for a while and Bobby McAulay, their east coast scout and former player, recommended Mr Struth get my signature quickly as he knew Hearts were also interested. What swung it for Mr Struth was not Bobby's views but my performance for Scotland against England in a schoolboy international at the Empire Stadium in April 1952.

'It was one of the few football games televised live back then, albeit it was just the second half they showed. I remember it was such a big deal that reporters from the *Scotsman* newspaper took my mum and dad into their offices to watch the game on their television so they could interview them as it was going on.

'Apparently Mr Struth also saw the game – which we lost 1–0 – and was so impressed with my performance that he wanted to sign me. I remember the match well because one of my opponents was Duncan Edwards, who was the England captain and who went on to play for Manchester United and tragically died in the Munich air disaster. A few days afterwards I came home from London to my house in Edinburgh and a telegram arrived from Mr Struth inviting me and my father to go through to Ibrox to talk about signing. I remember the telegram said I had to telephone Mr Struth personally to arrange a time. I was shaking when I went up to the phone box at the top of my road to phone him. He had a booming voice. To a 15-year-old kid it was a difficult call to make. I couldn't get off the phone quick enough, I was so scared.

'I can't remember how much money was mentioned. Whatever it was, it wasn't too much or very important to me or my family. They wanted a manager who would look after their son and Mr Struth fitted the bill. They weren't disappointed, as he turned out to be like a grandfather to me. As I was only 15 I used to go through to train at Ibrox with the reserve players every Tuesday and Thursday evening from my home in Edinburgh. It was Willie Findlay, Jimmy Duncanson and Bob McPhail who took the reserves. Mr Struth made sure they were very good to me.

'That was the beginning of my Ibrox days, which proved to be very successful. I signed full professional forms for Rangers when I was just 16 and I learned a lesson from Mr Struth straight away that I should never to get too big for my boots. He used to say "No player is bigger than Glasgow Rangers Football Club" and he personally made sure that was the case.

'For example, when I was getting a bit of money it was about the time of the Teddy Boys. It was the era of drape suits, very tight trousers and all that. I remember going to a shop at the top of Leith Walk in Edinburgh where the St James Hotel is now. It was a top-quality tailor shop and I spent a lot of money on royal blue drainpipe trousers and a beautiful blue and grey striped jacket with four pockets. I didn't have what they called a DA haircut but I did have a crew-cut. A few days after buying my new outfit I wore it to Ibrox and felt a million dollars. I walked up Edmiston Drive and through the swing doors into the stadium. Within seconds I was ordered to go up to Mr Struth's office. There was a small button you had to press on his door to tell him you were there. There was a sign that told you either to enter or wait. Nobody ever got "enter" straight away.

'I pressed the button and waited ten minutes before I was called to see him by his secretary, Mrs Alison Dallas. He had just had the latest in a number of operations as his health was failing. He'd had a leg amputated and used a walking stick. Despite his illnesses he was still on top of things and Rangers was very much still his life. His desk was a big, beautiful mahogany one with a glass top. Every-thing on it was immaculate and in place. His telephone was just right, his papers straight and his walking stick was lying across the top of the table.

' "Yes, Ralph," he said.

' "You sent for me, Mr Struth."

'I sat down and there were a few moments of silence. Then he took up his stick and he whacked it down on top of this glass table. Christ, I got a right bloody fright. He didn't crack the glass or anything but he scared the life out of me. "You are now a Rangers player," he said at the top of his voice. "Everywhere you go you represent Rangers Football Club. I am going to tell you to go back to Edinburgh, get yourself changed into a proper, respectable suit and come back again later today."

'He sat down, didn't say anything else and I left. In those days I didn't get the train from Edinburgh to Glasgow as I was just a young lad and didn't know how. I used to get the bus because it used to leave from outside my door in Calder Road on the west side of Edinburgh and go through Harthill all the way to Ibrox. So less than half an hour after arriving at Ibrox, proud as punch, I was on the bus back through to Edinburgh where I got changed out of my flashy suit and put on a more sedate one before arriving back at Ibrox just after lunchtime. When Mr Struth saw me again he said that I was better dressed, but he was still not satisfied. He ordered me to go down to a bespoke tailor opposite Central Station in Glasgow and get myself measured up for a blue Rangers club suit.

'Now, Rangers were going on a tour to Canada that summer and the fact he told me to go and get a royal blue blazer with red edging, white braiding and with the club badge on it made me think I was going to North America. I went back to see Mr Struth thinking he would tell me I was going to be part of the first team travelling party that was going on tour.

' "Ralph, my boy," he said. "You have to dress properly, like a Rangers player. No more suits for you that young people wear. You wear the club colours."

'Unfortunately for me, going on the club tour of Canada was never mentioned. The suit was simply to make me look more respectable. Still, I had learned a lesson early in my career about how important it was to have standards when you are representing a great Scottish institution like Glasgow Rangers Football Club. It's a shame that some players from the new generation seem to forget that far too quickly. I always wore the Rangers club suit in

Glasgow when I knew he would be watching me. I must admit, though, once or twice I wore my Teddy Boy outfit to the dancing in Edinburgh. But I never got caught, thank goodness.

'Although he was tough on dress sense and discipline he always made me feel special. Although I was just a teenager he told me to go to the best restaurants, to get the best seats at the pictures and to do everything first class. All because I was a Rangers player and they should feel special. It was quite funny for him to ask me to maintain a high-quality lifestyle because at the time I got £20 as a signing-on fee and hardly anything as a monthly wage. That didn't matter to me, though, as I was part of Rangers Football Club. If I had to live beyond my means to keep standards up, then so be it.

'I had two years under Mr Struth's management and would have liked more. When I broke through to the first team aged 17 I saw less of him than when he signed me. Mr Struth never went anywhere near training and didn't come into the dressing room very much. A lot of his orders to the players came through his secretary, Mrs Dallas, and Rangers captain George Young.

'I will never forget Mr Struth. He launched my career and did so much for Rangers. I made my debut in 1954 as a 17-year-old when they had an injury crisis. I scored twice against Kilmarnock that day and dedicated both goals to Mr Struth. It was the least I could do for the man.'

Scot Symon

'We don't have to tell our players what we expect at Rangers. The new boys at once sense the club's traditions and follow the example, without being coerced.'

One of Scot Symon's greatest results as a player got lost in the mists of time, while one of his worst as a manager will never be forgotten. Ordinarily if Rangers routed Celtic 8–1 it would be a time of great rejoicing and endless bragging rights for the Ibrox club's supporters. But because the victory fell on New Year's Day, 1943, when the Second World War was raging, it received little prominence at the time or since. Symon played in the match.

By the same token, when his Rangers team lost 1–0 to part-time Berwick Rangers at Shielfield Park it instantly became a permanent scar on his reputation as a manager. That Scottish Cup first round tie on 28 January 1967 will never be forgotten. 'This is the worst result in the club's history. There will be hell to pay for this,' remarked Symon after the defeat. He was absolutely right.

Through the years, whenever Symon's name is mentioned the defeat to Berwick Rangers often pops into the head of any supporter who knows their football history. That is unjust. A look at his record as a manager – at East Fife, Preston North End and especially Rangers – quite clearly suggests it was a freak result in an otherwise extremely successful and impressive career.

At his peak in the early 1960s he was in charge of a highly effective and stylish Rangers team that played entertaining football and included Jim Baxter, Jimmy Millar, Ian McMillan and Ralph Brand. He was in charge from 1954 to 1967 and won six league championships, five Scottish Cups, four League Cups and the treble in 1963–64, as well as a runners-up placing in the 1961 and 1967 European Cup Winners' Cup finals.

Symon was a Rangers man through and through. He was signed by Bill Struth – the man he would succeed as manager – from Portsmouth in August, 1938, and became part of a team that included top players of the generation like Bob McPhail and Willie Thornton. Although football did continue during the Second World War the leagues were regionalised and the importance of picking up trophies greatly diminished because of the sacrifice many young men were making for the war effort.

Symon played through the war but retired in 1947 aged 35. He immediately took over as manager of East Fife and led them to promotion to the Scottish First Division at the first attempt. He managed to consolidate them in the top league and remarkably helped win them the Scottish League Cup in 1947–48 and again in

1949–50. Not surprisingly, these incredible achievements by a young manager at an unfashionable team resulted in larger English clubs knocking on his door.

He chose to take over at Preston North End in 1953 and took them to the English FA Cup final the following year where his highly-talented team, including the legendary Tom Finney and Tommy Docherty, narrowly lost 3–2 to West Bromwich Albion in front of 100,000 fans. On the back of his relative initial success with Preston he was expected to stay south of the border for years to come. It was only the persuasive power of the Rangers board – and especially departing manager Struth – that tempted him back to Ibrox in 1954 just 13 months at Preston.

Although Struth had done a peerless job over the years his power had waned as he aged and his health deteriorated, and he left Symon with a major rebuilding job on his hands although there was a young and promising side to build upon. Symon made it clear from day one that he would have no favourites. Nobody was allowed into his office at the top of the marble staircase at Ibrox unless it was to get a dressing-down for stepping out of line. 'We don't have to tell our players what we expect at Rangers,' he said, 'The new boys at once sense the club's traditions and follow the example, without being coerced.' He was not a regular on the training pitch and never took the sessions. When he did go trackside he stood on the sidelines watching every move, occasionally shouting orders, but that is where his input began and ended.

In 1954 Symon had to cope immediately with the loss of defender Willie Woodburn when he was banned from professional football for life by the SFA after repeated ordering-off offences. Still, the Rangers defence was pretty strong as it included the talented Eric Caldow and Bobby Shearer with the powerful George Young at centre-half. Symon also bought well, with one of his best acquisitions being Don Kichenbrand, a rumbustious centre forward the fans nicknamed 'The Rhino'.

Symon led Rangers to the championship in his second season

and also took them into the European Cup for the first time, when they lost at the first hurdle against Nice. Perhaps he had a crystal ball and sensed he would have much more success, but he brought together all of the trophies Rangers had ever won and created a big, special trophy room at Ibrox to display them.

His first Scottish Cup win came with a 2–0 final victory over Kilmarnock in 1960, which was the same year his team lost in the European Cup semi-final to Eintracht Frankfurt (the Germans themselves were famously beaten 7–3 by Real Madrid in one of the greatest finals ever played at Hampden). One of the main reasons for Rangers' growing success was Symon's inspired signing of Jim Baxter from Raith Rovers for £17,500.

Many believe Baxter was the most skilful player ever to wear a Rangers jersey. Certainly he shone in a team that dominated the early years of the 1960s.

In 1961 they won the championship and the League Cup. They reached the final of the European Cup Winners' Cup where they lost to Fiorentina. Although Baxter was the star, others like John Greig and Willie Henderson came into a team that was constantly praised for its fluent and attractive football.

In the 1963–64 season they won the treble. That was Symon's team at its peak. After that the trophies did not come quite so thick and fast as Symon had hoped. In 1965 Kilmarnock under Willie Waddell – who would later manage Rangers himself – won the title and although the Scottish League Cup was retained by Symon it was scant consolation.

The following year the figure of Jock Stein started to fully emerge in Scottish football and Symon suffered in his shadow. Stein was a young manager who had been a huge success at Dunfermline Athletic and Hibernian and was just starting to make his mark at Celtic. He was a strong character and a 'tracksuit manager', in stark comparison to Symon. To emphasise their differences Stein was a great communicator with the fans and the press, and used the media to his advantage. Symon was the polar opposite: an introvert who did not court the media. That made him an easy target when things went wrong at Ibrox, as the newspapermen had no great affinity with him.

An example of how poor a relationship he had with the press came when he was asked on the phone by a sportswriter about the weather conditions at Ibrox, the writer having been told by colleagues that parts of Glasgow were fog-bound and the game might be in doubt. 'No comment,' said Symon.

Maybe if he had courted the newspapermen in the way Stein did he would have won himself more time as Rangers manager. But with Celtic in the ascendancy the defeat to Berwick Rangers – and the way Symon handled it – meant it was the beginning of the end for him at Ibrox. He was criticised for claiming the only reason his team lost to Berwick was because they did not have any decent strikers. His decision to make his front men, George McLean and Jim Forrest, the scapegoats did him no favours. Forrest was just 22 years old and a great talent but he was shipped out to Preston while McLean left for Dundee. The only positive to come out of the Berwick Rangers defeat for Rangers was that because he had dropped so many players Symon was forced to give Sandy Jardine, who went on to be one of the most loyal and distinguished Ibrox servants, his debut a week after the Scottish Cup debacle.

What was largely forgotten in the years since the Berwick Rangers defeat was the fact that Symon and his team had a great chance to make amends by winning the European Cup Winners' Cup a little over four months later. Celtic had made their way to the final of the European Cup in 1967 and because of that Rangers' push to the final against Bayern Munich was overshadowed.

When Celtic beat Inter Milan 2–1 to be the first British side to lift the European Cup there was huge pressure on Rangers to complete a European double. With Bayern Munich's captain, Franz Beckenbauer, in top form the match finished 0–0 at the end of 90 minutes. Rangers could have won it but with strikers McLean and Forrest out of the picture Symon had not had the time to buy a new front man. He had to play defender Roger Hynd in attack, with little success. In extra time the game was finely poised until Franz Roth – the man Symon had singled out as the main Bayern danger man – burst into the penalty area to score. It was the end of Symon's last full season.

He took Rangers into the start of the 1967–68 campaign and on 28 October 1967, they were top of the table after six wins and two draws in their opening eight games. However, the Rangers board was nervous about Celtic and Stein. After a 0–0 draw with Dunfermline, Symon was sacked. His assistant Bobby Seith, who was highly regarded at the time as one of the best training field coaches in the business resigned in protest.

Rangers' decision was seen as harsh and undignified, and even the news of the dismissal was poorly handled. Symon was greatly hurt by his treatment by the board and rarely returned to Ibrox apart from on the occasions when he had no option during a brief subsequent spell as manager of Partick Thistle. Symon deserved far better treatment from a club he had served with distinction.

Harold Davis was an 'Iron Man' defender for Rangers from 1956 to 1964, serving under Scot Symon there as he had in an earlier spell at East Fife. Davis nearly lost his life in a jungle firefight during the Korean War and was told by medics he would never play again, but after two years in hospital he defied them by making a remarkable comeback under Symon.

'I first signed for Scot Symon when he was manager at East Fife in 1949 but my time working under him was disrupted two years later when I went to do my National Service with the Black Watch in the Korean War. I might have avoided the fighting if I had chosen to become a PE instructor, but I didn't want to hide. I told the army if there were other Scots boys going out there to risk their lives then I wanted to join them.

'I was involved in pretty fierce stuff and it was sheer hell out there. The Yanks and the Commonwealth troops were against the North Koreans at the 38th Parallel where it was trench warfare, with everybody just trying to blast each other to death. In one firefight I took some bullets from a high-calibre machine gun that tore into my abdomen and sliced away part of the instep on my right foot. I was in such a bad state that I drifted in and out of consciousness and had to be airlifted to safety in one of those helicopters you used to see in the American television series *M.A.S.H.* Ten days later I came round in a hospital in Japan and was transferred back to Britain. The surgeon suggested I'd better start looking for another job as I would never play football again.

'As part of my convalescence I was taken to the Bridge of Earn Hospital where Davie Kinnear, who was the hospital physio, recognised me. He was also the physio at Rangers, where Mr Symon had become manager in 1954. Although I had been told I was not going to play football again, with Scot Symon's encouragement and Davie pushing me hard I started to think I could get into the game. A lot of the other patients were older, content to simply get fit enough to stay alive. I wasn't. I was determined to get extra-special fit to be a footballer again.

'Because of the seriousness of my injuries I knew I had to show I was fitter than the rest of my team-mates. Mr Symon gave me great encouragement and after I played a few games for East Fife during my comeback he signed me for Rangers in 1956. Moving to such a big club made me become even more obsessed with my fitness. I knew a team like Rangers could not possibly have survived with a passenger in the side, which is why I worked hard in training and did extra sessions.

'I became one of the fastest over 100 yards at Ibrox and never mentioned what happened to me in the Korean War, or the extent of my injuries. I'd like to think Mr Symon signed me because he thought I was a good player rather than through sympathy. I never knew him well enough to think it was an old pals' act because he was always a bit aloof, which, to be honest, contributed to his downfall. He didn't want to be anybody's pal. He wanted to show you who was the boss. He was a quiet man who had his own ideas and stuck to them rigidly. Looking back, probably too rigidly.

'The only time I think he did deviate from the norm was when I was turned from a wing-half into a centre-half alongside Bill Paterson, which was quite an unusual tactic back then. It worked pretty well but maybe that was because our full-backs Bobby Shearer and Eric Caldow were fantastic players who could cover in behind us.

'I wasn't happy with the way he handled Jim Baxter. Jim had a superb gift but seemed determined to waste it. You could smell the drink off him at training and sometimes on match days. Don't get me wrong, he was an absolute genius. But for every two good games he had one bad one. The boss should have taken him aside and brought him into line because of his drinking.

'The manager lost a lot of respect among the senior players, including myself, because he didn't do that and he pandered to Jim. Maybe he had an impossible task, but he should have at least tried to make a stand and tried to keep Jim in line. Of course I accept that when Jim was on his game he was brilliant, but being treated differently did little for team morale. In fact I think the manager lost the dressing room at key moments because there was a split in it over the way Jim was treated.

'One of the biggest disappointments I had in a Rangers jersey was when we lost the 1961 European Cup Winners' Cup final to Fiorentina, but the good times outweighed the bad. I played 261 times for the club from 1956 to 1964 and won four Scottish league titles, two League Cups and a Scottish Cup.

'I left Rangers to join Partick Thistle at the end of the 1964 season and being along the road at Firhill meant I was still close enough to things at Ibrox to understand why his time at the club came to an end. His inability to change tactics was a problem, as was his reserved personality, especially when results like the defeat to Berwick Rangers in the Scottish Cup went against him and the press was asking questions. Being quiet and reserved at the same time as Jock Stein arrived on the scene at Celtic was a problem. Mr Stein had an overpowering personality and was younger and more vibrant than Mr Symon.

'If you were a newspaperman who spoke to Scot Symon you would get a one-sentence answer. If you spoke to Jock Stein you would get a paragraph. Football was changing in the 60s but Mr Symon never really acknowledged that. He kept working on the same tried and trusted formula that had served him so well. But you could understand why he kept to his usual team formations because it won him six league championships, five Scottish Cups and four League Cups. I have a lot to thank Scot Symon for because he signed me for the great Glasgow Rangers Football Club. And I like to think I repaid him in full by the way I played for him.'

Willie Waddell

'You are playing for Rangers. Never forget how important that is.'

Willie Waddell's time as manager of Rangers was short and sweet, and ended with him masterminding the greatest victory in the history of the club. It is true to say that overall Waddell never entirely electrified the club during his two and a half years in charge at Ibrox, but he was manager when the club won the European Cup Winners' Cup. In addition to what he had previously achieved in charge of Kilmarnock, his managerial career hit great peaks.

Affectionately nicknamed 'The Deedle', an abbreviation of 'Deedle Dawdle', rhyming slang for his surname, Waddell was a former Rangers player who played 558 matches over a 17-year period from 1938 to 1955 and also won 17 caps for Scotland before he retired. After two years he took over as manager of Kilmarnock. His achievements at the Rugby Park club now look remarkable: they were league runners up in 1959–60, 1960–61, 1962–63 and 1963–64 before, gloriously, winning the championship in 1964–65. At no other time in their history have they finished in the top two. They also reached a Scottish Cup final and two League

Cup finals. All of these were fabulous achievements for a man whose managerial career was on the rise. And then Waddell walked away from football. Or, at least, from management.

Having a young family, he wanted time away from the sharp end of the game and instead took a job as a newspaper reporter with the *Scottish Daily Express,* covering matches. A championship-winning manager going from the dugout to the press box, and writing match reports and comments about the teams he had beaten, seems unthinkable nowadays. Yet it proved to be an easy transition for him to make.

He was so perceptive and biting in his comments in the *Express* – particularly about Rangers under Davie White – that when White was sacked in 1969 there was a huge well of opinion among the Ibrox faithful that Waddell should be considered for the job. Rangers chairman John Lawrence felt he had the passion, insight and experience to take over the club. He had talked the talk in his newspaper column about how he could revitalise Rangers. Now could he walk the walk?

On Monday, 8 December 1969, Waddell was given his chance when he was installed as the new Rangers manager. He went about his rebuilding plans with gusto and decisiveness, bringing in goalkeeper Peter McCloy and allowing Rangers legend Jim Baxter to leave the club. Others who were given a chance included Alex MacDonald and Colin Jackson, both of whom went on to become mainstays at Ibrox for many years. A new signing would be told: 'You are playing for Rangers. Never forget how important that is.'

Waddell went out of his way to ensure Rangers had no prima donnas. Although his team was full of characters, like wee Willie Henderson, he made it clear all the players would be treated, and paid, the same. The wage structure meant the young players at Ibrox could expect the same wages as established stars from the moment they broke into the first team. In keeping with Rangers tradition, he was a man who liked his squad to be well turned out. In an era where facial hair was *de rigueur* he had his work cut out to get players to get rid of their moustaches and beards. His message did finally get through and even Henderson, who used to sport a Mexican bandit moustache, bowed to the wishes of his manager and shaved it off. There was a distinct lack of revolt in the Rangers dressing room when Waddell was at the helm, not least because he had brought Jock Wallace in from Hearts as his chief trainer and coach. The pair of them took no nonsense. They were tough guys who clobbered any indiscipline or back-chat.

Waddell was also a manager who took risks. Early in his time as manager he was unafraid of throwing young players in at the deep end. One example was Derek Johnstone, who at the age of 16 was given a start against Celtic in the Scottish League Cup final in front of 106,000 fans on 24 October 1970. It was a decision for which Waddell was hugely rewarded. The big, enthusiastic teenager gave the Celtic defence a torrid time, especially in the air. Billy McNeill may have had great experience compared to Johnstone, but he struggled to cope with his power. Five minutes before half-time Johnstone outjumped the Celtic captain to score a magnificent headed goal that won Rangers the League Cup. Johnstone became an instant club hero. There was recognition, too, of Waddell's boldness in picking him, not least because it gave Rangers their first prize after four trophyless seasons.

Within weeks it would be overshadowed by dreadful tragedy. On 2 January 1971, 66 people died and over 140 were injured when supporters were crushed on a stairway at the end of an Old Firm derby. In the aftermath, mainly because Rangers chairman Lawrence had been struck by illness, Waddell had to deal with most of the worldwide press attention. Although he had been a journalist it was still stressful and demanding. Waddell also made it clear he wanted his players to attend the funerals of the dead and to go to the hospital bedsides of the injured. He handled a terrible situation with great sensitivity.

The Ibrox disaster left a huge cloud of despair over everybody at Rangers. Such a dreadful event could have broken many men and left many lesser clubs struggling to cope in the aftermath. Domestic form the following season was predictably poor: Rangers finished third in the championship, did not get out of their qualifying section in the League Cup, and reached only the Scottish Cup semi-finals. In the European Cup Winners' Cup, though, something extraordinary happened.

The road to victory was a difficult one, especially in the second round. First the French club Rennes were polished off but Rangers then faced the powerful Sporting Lisbon. In the first leg at Ibrox Rangers raced to a 3–0 half-time lead but two second half goals from the Portuguese brought them firmly back into the tie. In the return leg more than 60,000 fans expected Sporting to triumph and, due to an error by the referee, many thought that they had. After 90 minutes the result was 3–2 to Sporting Lisbon which forced the match into extra time. During the additional 30 minutes Henderson scored for Rangers with the home side scoring again to make the result on the night 4–3 to Sporting Lisbon. Away goals scored in extra time counted double in the event of an aggregate draw, but the referee was unaware. He ordered a penalty shoot-out, which Sporting Lisbon won.

The Portuguese fans celebrated wildly but a furious Waddell knew the rules and immediately headed to the UEFA observer to lodge a protest. It took the observer only a few minutes to realise that the referee had made a major error and that the Henderson goal was indeed decisive. It was 6–6 on aggregate and Rangers were through on away goals. After such a let-off people began to murmur that maybe Waddell's team had its name on the trophy. An excellent 1–1 draw against Torino in Italy, and a 1–0 victory at Ibrox eased Rangers into the semi-finals.

They faced a formidable Bayern Munich side including Franz Beckenbauer and Gerd Müller. Still, Rangers came away from Munich with a 1–1 draw. Although club captain John Greig missed the return leg through injury it still turned out to be a glorious night for Waddell. Sandy Jardine scored in the first minute and another from Derek Parlane – playing only his third game for the club – put them into the final.

Getting to Barcelona for 24 May 1972 was an achievement in

itself. Waddell would make sure that preparations for the game against Moscow Dynamo in the Nou Camp would be as close to perfection as he could manage. He personally selected the team hotel, which was well outside the main city centre and would allow him time to prepare the players away from the tens of thousands of Rangers fans who descended on the Spanish city. Compare that to the poor, unfortunate Moscow Dynamo players who had to endure being stuck in a city-centre hotel on a street with nearly 20 guest-houses full of Rangers supporters. Waddell also decided to bring the Rangers party's food with them from Scotland to ensure there was no risk of food poisoning.

Waddell was thorough. He banned his players from sunbathing in case they got sunstroke. He ordered them to wear tracksuits every time they went outside. While other hotel guests were lounging by the pool the Rangers players would be sitting in the shade in their tracksuits. Because the players were well away from the hustle and bustle of downtown Barcelona they had no idea how many thousands of their own fans had taken over the city. It was only when the bus left for the Nou Camp that they realised the extent of the numbers.

Waddell decided to make those fans the subject of his pre-match team-talk and made it clear to his players they could not let these people down. His words fired up the Rangers players. Goals from Colin Stein and two more from Willie Johnston put them in control. Two late goals from the Russians made it a nervous last few minutes, but Waddell's team held on to win. At the end there was a celebratory pitch invasion that turned sour. There were fights between the Rangers fans and the Spanish police that took the shine off an otherwise great night for the Ibrox club. Rangers captain Greig was not allowed back on the pitch to receive the trophy and instead it was handed to him in a back room in the bowels of the stadium.

It was a sad end to a great European run for Rangers under Waddell. It was also the end of his management. He told the club directors he could not think of a better time to resign. Only two weeks after their European victory it was announced he was moving 'upstairs' voluntarily to be general manager and that his right-hand man, Jock Wallace, would take over as manager.

In the aftermath of the Ibrox disaster Waddell began to work tirelessly on the redevelopment of the Rangers ground until 1981. When the new-look £10 million stadium opened there was, fittingly, a Waddell Suite: a room full of memorabilia in honour of a visionary and distinguished Rangers man who was a player, manager, general manager, managing director and vice-chairman of the club. He died in 1992, aged 71. He will not be forgotten at Ibrox.

Peter McCloy was Willie Waddell's first signing and became a fixture in his team for the three years of his management. The tall goalkeeper nicknamed 'The Girvan Lighthouse' went on to play 535 matches for the Ibrox club over a 16-year period.

'Willie Waddell signed me for Rangers on a Friday the 13th. He kept reminding me there was nothing unlucky about that. I was surprised that he came in for me because I had hit a form slump and was playing for Motherwell reserves. Keith MacRae was keeping me out of the team and I hadn't played first-team football for a while. I can only assume Willie remembered me when I was at the top of my game and felt he could help me get back there. I signed in March 1970, and was in at the start of what I can only describe as a fantastic time for Rangers under him.

'When Davie White was sacked Willie brought in his own people including Jock Wallace as his assistant, who proved to be a godsend to me. Back then there was no such thing as specialised goalkeeping training. I ran round the track with the outfield players and did all the exercises. The only time I went in goals was when the strikers needed some shooting practice. Because Jock had been a goalkeeper with Berwick Rangers he used to stay behind after training sessions and we used to work on crosses, shot-stopping and other things. Nowadays it is unthinkable for a goalkeeper at a big club not to have a specialist coach to train him. Back then, me working with Jock – at the behest of Willie – was groundbreaking.

'Willie was a very eloquent manager who could really inspire you with his motivational team talks. He pressed the right buttons time and time again, mainly because he knew our minds. He could read us all and get under our skin. If he felt someone had not been pulling his weight he would tear a strip off them. Not in private, but in front of their team-mates in the dressing room so he got his point across and embarrassed the player into upping his game. Guys who needed a confidence boost would be told they were a million miles better than the player they were due to face on a Saturday.

'I was with him for the full three years he was at Ibrox and saw all his tricks. He was a man you could never, ever win an argument with, especially when it came to the time for your contract to be renewed. In those days managers could be more brusque with players than nowadays because there was no freedom of contract. The club always had the upper hand and could virtually dictate terms. When my deal was up I got a letter from Willie setting out his terms for my new contract. He called me into his office to ask if I had got the letter and when I would be signing it. When I said I wouldn't be because I wanted a pay rise all he said was "Remember to shut the door behind you." He never spoke to me again for a month! I still got picked but it was only when my deal was nearly up that he called me back in, probably knowing that I'd had no other offers. So I signed for the money he had put on the table.

'Willie was tactically astute and always open to new ideas. For instance we didn't do man-for-man marking in domestic games but we always did in Europe, with great success. He could change tactics when required. That worked particularly well against Bayern Munich in the European Cup Winners' Cup semi-final first leg when we had Dave Smith at the back as the extra man. Dave had been brilliant for us after Ronnie McKinnon broke his leg in the second round. We came away with a 1–1 draw from West Germany. What happened in the dressing room before the second leg against Bayern Munich summed up Willie Waddell for me. He gave a really motivational team talk and everybody knew exactly what their role was going to be. I was last out of the dressing room and just before I left he pinned me up against a wall and said "I did you the best favour of your life when I signed you for Rangers. Go out there tonight and repay me with a shut-out."

'As it turned out that's exactly what I did. We won 2–0 and went on to win the final against Moscow Dynamo. After the final I went up to him and said "I did you the best favour of your life by making some good saves and helping Rangers win the European Cup Winners' Cup. Repay me tonight by giving me a rise." He smiled and said "No chance." You could never get the better of Willie Waddell.'

Jock Wallace

'When Jock Wallace was manager of Leicester City he pinned me against the dressing room wall at half-time and called me a lazy English this and that. We were 2–0 up and I'd scored both goals! I didn't score in the second half as I was still shaking.'
Gary Lineker

Mention the name Jock Wallace to those who played under him and they will probably still feel like straightening up and checking that they look smart. The above quote, from Gary Lineker, captured Wallace's ability to make his players' knees tremble. Wallace was a hard-as-nails disciplinarian. He was also a manager who wanted his men to be as physically fit as possible, and would stop at nothing to get them there.

Wallace had served with the King's Own Scottish Borderers, spending part of his service in the jungle of Malaysia fighting Communist guerrillas. In an attempt to bring a level of discipline to football which had been evident in the army, when he became a coach and manager he used to shout out orders on the training field like a sergeant major on the parade ground.

He also practised what he preached. He kept himself in good physical condition and used to do press-ups with the players and take part in weight-training sessions. Famously, he led his players to Gullane Sands in East Lothian and made them run up and down the dunes. The most notorious dune, and one that featured in every Rangers pre-season training session under Wallace, was nicknamed 'Hell Hill'. It was straight up and down. Tough to walk up, let alone run. Wallace forced his Rangers players to race each other up and down Hell Hill several times during every training session until some were physically sick. It was a ferocious training regime.

'We lived in fear of whatever torture Jock and Tom Paterson, who was a fitness expert, would have in store for us anytime we went down to Gullane,' remembered former Rangers striker Derek Johnstone, who rated Wallace as one of the greatest ever Scottish managers. 'I always remember trying to run uphill in sinking sand with big Jock at the top of the hill with his stop watch in hand, growling down at me. It was tough as hell, but by God, it got us all fit.'

Wallace knew Gullane Sands well as that was where he had gone on day trips from the small mining community of Wallyford where he was brought up. He was as tough as the miners who used to work in the collieries. His dad, Jock senior, was a professional goalkeeper with Raith Rovers, Blackpool and Derby County, and Wallace followed in his footsteps to keep goal for Airdrie and West Bromwich Albion among others. Wallace had the unique distinction of being the only player ever to play in the English, Welsh and Scottish Cups in the same season. This odd record was set during the 1966–67 campaign when he played in the Welsh Cup and FA Cup for Hereford United and, unforgettably, in the Scottish Cup for Berwick Rangers. It was as player/manager of little Second Division Berwick that he made his name by overseeing one of the most incredible shocks in Scottish football history: Berwick Rangers 1, Rangers 0. Wallace saved every shot that came his way and Sammy Reid scored the only goal.

Hearts took him to Tynecastle as assistant coach to John Harvey but it was not long before Willie Waddell brought him to Ibrox as his first team coach. Wallace was therefore Waddell's right hand man when Rangers won the European Cup Winners' Cup in 1972. When Waddell then moved upstairs to be general manager, Wallace took over. Celtic won the title in Wallace's first season as Rangers manager but he was not afraid to shed Ibrox heroes such as Colin Stein and Willie Johnston in an attempt to reconstruct his side and break the Parkhead club's domination under Jock Stein. Wallace got the better of Stein in the Scottish Cup final of 1973. It was the SFA's Centenary Cup final and with the game level at 2–2 a header from Johnstone came back off the inside of one post, ran along the goal line, hit the other post and fell for a very grateful Tom Forsyth to poke the ball over the line from a few inches out.

It was not the classiest of goals but it was vital for Wallace, who had his first piece of silverware. The 1973–74 season promised much but delivered nothing. Celtic won their ninth successful league title. One trophy out of six from his first two seasons was not the sort of record of which any Old Firm manager could be proud. Wallace needed and wanted much more. He took the risk of allowing Dave Smith, one of the mainstays of the Ibrox side, to leave to join Arbroath while Alfie Conn moved to Tottenham Hotspur.

Although Aberdeen put them out of the Scottish Cup it was clear that stopping Celtic from winning ten in a row was the Holy Grail for Wallace. Winning both Old Firm fixtures – the second a comprehensive 3–0 victory on 3 January – set them on their way to doing just that. Ten consecutive championships were beyond Celtic and instead it was Hibs, under Eddie Turnbull, who exerted the most pressure on Wallace's team. It was a 1–1 draw at Easter Road that finally won Rangers the title and broke Celtic's domination of Scottish football. Wallace had delivered Rangers' first league title in 11 years.

Wallace's side went further in the following season, 1975–76.

An Alex MacDonald goal secured the Scottish League Cup with a final win over Celtic and Hearts were beaten 3–1 in the Scottish Cup final to give Wallace the treble. It was one of the proudest moments of his life.

The following season they were never in contention for the league title; crashed out in the first round of the European Cup to FC Zurich; beaten 5–1 by Aberdeen in the League Cup semi-final and lost the Scottish Cup final to Celtic. From being the manager of a treble-winning side Wallace was suddenly under pressure. The response was emphatic: another treble.

Playing a 4–2–4 system with Tommy McLean and Davie Cooper on the wings, the Rangers fans were treated to some vintage football. Rangers beat Celtic in the 1977–78 League Cup final with a goal from Gordon Smith, who years later would become chief executive of the Scottish Football Association. A win over Motherwell in the final league match at Ibrox won Rangers the championship, and Aberdeen were defeated in the Scottish Cup final.

Wallace had delivered two trebles in three seasons; six trophies out of nine. Just when it looked like he would take Rangers to new heights and his team might dominate Scottish football in the way that Celtic did under Stein, everything fell apart. It was believed at the time that Wallace was angry at his own pay level and that of his players. Wallace was understood to be on around £12,000 a year, a lot less than managers at English clubs. His reasoning was that Rangers were one of the top clubs in Britain – not just Scotland – and he deserved more than he was on. Stein was on £15,000 a year at Celtic while Liverpool manager Bob Paisley was on around £25,000 at Anfield. Surely he was worth at least the same as Stein, argued Wallace. After all, he had won two trebles and stopped Celtic pulling away into the distance ahead of Rangers.

The plea fell on deaf ears and Wallace left the club in 1978, feeling undervalued and angry. Within weeks he resurfaced at Leicester City on a salary of £25,000. He won them promotion to the top flight in 1979–80, reached the FA Cup semi-finals in 1982, and was remembered as the man who brought Lineker into the first team. On top of that he nearly succeeded in making the most high-profile signing in Leicester City's history. Wallace, never shy of approaching the best in the game, tried to get three-time European Footballer of the Year Johan Cruyff to the club in 1981.

There were three weeks of secret talks between Wallace and Cruyff, who was then 33 and playing for Spanish side Levante. Leicester had beaten Manchester United and Liverpool but were still deep in relegation territory with Wallace believing, not unreasonably, that the Dutchman could get them out of it. Unfortunately the move broke down at the eleventh hour when the compensation package due to be paid to Levante proved to be too much.

Back at Rangers his successor, John Greig, was struggling in the manager's chair. Greig may have been a playing legend but he had been given the job too soon. He had little coaching experience and his five years in charge were not a success. Greig led Rangers to two Scottish Cups and two League Cups but the league title was never won.

When Wallace left Leicester in 1982 he had one season at Motherwell before returning to Ibrox as Greig's successor. Even in his short time away, only four years, Scottish football had been transformed. Wallace's return was not universally acclaimed. Rangers wanted Sir Alex Ferguson, who was at Aberdeen, and then tried for Jim McLean of Dundee United. Both rejected the overtures, which meant the Ibrox board turned again to the talismanic Wallace. He had ignored the traditional football advice to never return to a club after previous success there.

Wallace did begin well when an Ally McCoist hat-trick delivered a League Cup final win over Celtic in 1983–84. Relatively speaking he had money to spend on new players and forked out £500,000 in his first seven months in charge. Bobby Williamson arrived from Clydebank for £100,000 and Cammy Fraser and Iain Ferguson joined from Dundee for a total of £365,000. It was Ferguson who retained Rangers' Scottish League Cup with a winner against Dundee United in 1984–85, but it was to be Wallace's final trophy. Rangers were nowhere in the league. In the following season, with his team going from bad to worse and attendances crashing, he was sacked in April, 1986.

Wallace may have been forced to leave his beloved Rangers but his managerial career continued. He was still only 50 and had an unlikely spell at Sevilla in Spain during 1987–88 before finishing with Colchester United. Wallace became a victim of Parkinson's Disease. He fought the illness with dignity and the strength of character for which he will always be remembered and revered at Rangers. He died on July 24, 1996, aged only 60.

Tom Forsyth was one of Jock Wallace's first signings and remained at the club for the whole of his first spell as manager. The defender nicknamed 'Jaws' was cut from the same cloth as Wallace, and he remembered a hard task master who pushed for perfection.

'It took me years to realise it but Jock Wallace's bark was a lot worse than his bite. He was a man who loved Rangers and who looked on the club as one big family. He was a huge guy, physically very fit, who didn't know his own strength. I remember soon after I signed for Rangers from Motherwell for £40,000 he was getting really wound up in the dressing room before a game. He turned his attention to me and to make his point he thought he would hit me in the stomach. To big Jock it probably felt like a playful slap. To me it was a real hard punch in the guts and I doubled up in pain. He was really surprised I had nearly gone down but just turned around and started talking to the next player. He assumed I would be okay and looked on me as if I was some kind of softy. Luckily I recovered but felt a bit dodgy as I ran out onto the pitch. Not being able to play because my own manager had punched me in the stomach before kick-off would have made a headline or two.

'When I first arrived at Ibrox I was as intimidated by Jock as everyone else was. He had managed a Scottish League team that I played for against the English League a year before he signed me and I assume that was when he first thought I could do a job at

Ibrox. One of the big problems I had when I played for that Scottish League team was understanding what the hell big Jock was saying. He was from Wallyford in East Lothian which isn't that far away from where I grew up, in Stonehouse in Lanarkshire, but he could have been from a different planet. He talked so fast that I used to go up to other members of his coaching staff to ask them what he had actually said. It took me a few weeks of working with him on the training ground on a regular basis at Ibrox to come to terms with the way he spoke.

'What is less well known about big Jock is that he could take a joke and laugh at himself when the situation arose. For instance, we were coming back from a game up north and Jock thought it would be okay for us to stay the Saturday night in a hotel on the road back home to Glasgow and have a team night out. When I say "team night out" Jock kept out of the way, as he always kept his distance to show us who was boss. That night we thought we would try and play a trick on him and send some of the players back to the team hotel early to tell Jock that our centre forward, Martin Henderson, had been lifted by the police for being drunk and disorderly. Now Jock didn't like any of his players stepping out of line and being told Martin had been arrested meant there was steam coming out of his ears. The fact that he knew an offence like that would bring shame to his beloved Rangers made him absolutely mad.

'When big Jock was going daft we got the police to bundle Martin into the back of a Panda car and deliver him into the lobby of our hotel. The officers would inform Jock that Martin had to appear in court on the Monday and to look after him until then. By the time the police car arrived with Martin in the back Jock was as furious as I had ever seen him. The minute the police brought Martin into the hotel lobby big Jock ignored the coppers and went for him for "bringing shame to Rangers". You had the hilarious situation of the policemen trying to keep the Rangers manager off one of his players. He was really going to belt him.

'Back in the bar we were laughing our heads off and the

policemen cracked up too and gave the game away. It was at that moment Jock twigged what was going on and let out one of those great belly laughs of his. He had been had big time and laughed as loud as the rest of us. Not many managers would have taken that wind-up so well but that was Jock for you.

'He could also admit he was wrong and did so after I got sent off early on in a league game against St Mirren. At half-time in the dressing room he laid into me, claiming I had let the team down and I was a disgrace. I protested my innocence but he was having none of it. He went mad and didn't speak to me in the bus back from the match. On the Monday morning I got a call to go upstairs to see Jock in his office at Ibrox. I feared the worst and expected another barracking. Instead he sat me down, said he had seen the sending-off incident on television, and felt the referee had got it wrong. He apologised and sent me on my way. That showed me that Jock Wallace was a fair man, a man who was big enough to admit his mistakes.

'When I was at Rangers I was at my physical peak because of him. He used to take us down to Gullane Sands and make us run up and down that bloody Hell Hill. It was murder. He was big on body strength and being a former goalie he had a strong upper body himself. He wasn't big on tactics but he was huge on motivation. He was a great example to us all.

'Jock always had the fans at heart and made every member of the Rangers first-team squad attend as many functions as possible. He was very inclusive. I remember once, halfway through the season, the Ardrossan Rangers Supporters' Club was having a function and Jock ordered us all to go. Not just the players but also the tea ladies and all the staff. He saw Rangers as a family – including the supporters – and wanted them to be together as often as possible. We all went to that function, had a great time and stayed in the Seamill Hydro Hotel where Jock Stein used to always take Celtic. That gesture was typical of Jock. He was a man who knew the value of Rangers fans.

'He left me in no doubt of how privileged I was to play at Ibrox.

When I moved from Motherwell – and no disrespect to Motherwell, who are a great club – it was like moving from a job in the local corner shop to ASDA. The club and big Jock treated me well, for which I will be eternally grateful.

'I guess the one moment that I will always remember, and the one I get asked about more than any other, is my goal from six inches out that won Rangers the Scottish Cup against Celtic in May 1973. To score the winning goal in the centenary year made it even more special. It was a great moment for me. Jock was the first to congratulate me at the end. I could see by the look on his face what winning the cup meant to him. He was a true Rangers man through and through.'

Graeme Souness

' "Would you sign a Catholic?" was something that every new Rangers manager was asked at his first press conference and I was no different. I was married to a Catholic so I could go back and live with my wife but I could not sign a Catholic for my football club? Ridiculous. I knew, if the right Catholic player came along, exactly what I was going to do." '

As a player Graeme Souness was tough. As a manager he was even tougher. He had to be, from the moment he decided to become the first Rangers manager to sign a high-profile Catholic. Only a few footballers from that faith had played for the Ibrox club before Souness took over in 1986 and those who did – like Don Kichenbrand and John Spencer – were never encouraged to broadcast details of their religion. An unspoken policy not to sign Catholics was swept aside when Souness signed Maurice 'Mo' Johnston from under the noses of Celtic on 10 July 1989 – three years after he took over as Rangers player/manager.

Johnston was not the first Catholic targeted by Souness. He had approached the Glasgow-born Oxford United player Ray Houghton and Hibs' John Collins, who turned him down. When Johnston did sign – the deal agreed in a Paris café, far away from prying eyes – it infuriated Celtic manager Billy McNeill, who believed he had bought him from Nantes for £1.2 million. Johnston had been recently paraded at Celtic Park before he signed for Rangers, but the publicity stunt was premature. Johnston had not actually signed on the dotted line. When Souness heard that from Bill McMurdo, who was Johnston's agent, he made his decisive, controversial move. Glasgow was shaken.

Souness offered Johnston much more cash than Celtic and promised he would protect him as best he could from the media firestorm that would inevitably surround his signing. The decision led to some fans burning their Rangers scarves outside Ibrox. Souness became a hate figure to some of them. It was worth it for him. Ending sectarian bias was something Souness wanted to take on from the minute he walked into Ibrox on 7 April 1986, even if it took him three years to find the right man. Souness had grown up in the east of Scotland, where sectarianism was much less of an issue than in the west. His wife at the time was a Catholic, his children had grown up in the faith, and Souness had no time for the insidious 'What school did you go to?' culture often evident in Glasgow.

For years Rangers had ignored Catholic footballing talent. Struth, Symon, Waddell, Wallace and others either supported the club's stance or were prepared to put up with it. Skilled Catholic players ended up elsewhere and, if they were particularly good, that tended to mean Celtic. That troubled Souness from the moment Jock Stein discussed it with him when they were manager and player together on Scotland international trips. Stein told him Celtic used to go all-out to secure the signature of talented young Protestant players much sooner than they ever would Catholics. According to Stein, Celtic knew they had more time to deliberate over Catholics as there was no way Rangers would sign them. When Souness arrived at Rangers – supported first by owner

Lawrence Marlborough and club chairman David Holmes and later by new owner Sir David Murray – he made it clear that those self-erected barriers would be obliterated. ' "Would you sign a Catholic?" was something that every new Rangers manager was asked at his first press conference and I was no different,' said Souness. 'I was married to a Catholic so I could go back and live with my wife but I could not sign a Catholic for my football club? Ridiculous. I knew, if the right Catholic player came along, exactly what I was going to do.

'When I said I was going to sign a Catholic, I meant it. But what's sometimes forgotten is that I wasn't just going to sign any Catholic player just to prove a point. It was always going to be first and foremost a football decision. We were looking for a striker and for me Mo was the best around at the time. He was playing well for Nantes and had scored eight goals for Scotland in a single season. The fact that Celtic tried to sign him too showed he was a player in demand. The fact I had signed a Catholic made the headlines, but I had also signed a top-quality striker for Glasgow Rangers. For me that was the important thing, regardless of his religion.'

Six weeks after the signing Rangers played Celtic at Parkhead. Johnston looked ill at ease in a 1–1 draw. He was never going to appease all Rangers fans but the fact he scored the winning goal in the last minute against Celtic at Ibrox just ten weeks later changed how he was perceived by many of them. A further indication of how his religion dwindled as a factor came from the fact that he was named Rangers' Player of the Year by 14 different supporters' clubs at the end of that 1989–90 season.

Signing Johnston alone would have earned Souness a place in the history books, but in fact he transformed Rangers Football Club – and indirectly the entire Scottish football scene – during his five years in charge. It became 'The Souness Revolution'. He was signed as player/manager from Sampdoria for £300,000 and was the first man to be appointed to the top job without having any previous involvement with the Ibrox outfit. It was a big, bold declaration of what Rangers wanted to become after several seasons of mediocrity and dwindling attendances. There was huge pressure on Souness to hit the ground running. He did not disappoint.

'I was the right man at the right time for Rangers,' he said, 'It was, and remains, a great club. But in the 1980s it was stuck in its ways a bit. It needed a rocket up the backside and I like to think I helped give it that from day one. We had success on the field, which was great. On top of that we bought top players from England with a resale value so the balance sheet was looking good as well, which nowadays everybody knows is very important.'

Ally McCoist, who had a few run-ins with Souness during their time together at Ibrox, remembered his initial impact on both the dressing room and the club in general. 'My first impression was the presence he had,' said McCoist, 'He was dressed immaculately, looked very fit and had a tan from his time in Italy. He didn't say much when he first met the players but he told us all we would all have a chance to show him what we could do. He got straight to the point that day and he was like that for all the years he was at Ibrox. He didn't beat about the bush with his opinions.'

Souness was given an unprecedented level of money to spend and also benefited from the fact that for five years from 1985, because of the Heysel tragedy, English clubs were not allowed to compete in European competitions. Because of that Souness managed to lure top players north of the border immediately, including leading internationalists like Terry Butcher, Chris Woods and later Ray Wilkins, Trevor Francis, Gary Stevens, Mark Hateley and Trevor Steven. England's leading players were leaving en masse to sign for a Scottish club: it had never happened before in British football history. Rangers were rich and massive, and Souness was the charismatic figurehead.

His hugely upgraded team made an immediate impact in terms of vastly increased attendances and lucrative shirt sponsorship deals. Rangers even cashed in on the high number of well-heeled fans who wanted to catch the action by offering corporate hospitality packages to games, something which had not happened on a major scale before Souness arrived.

In his first full season, 1986–87, he won the Scottish championship – Rangers' first for nine years – and the League Cup. His impact was dramatic and controversial from the start. In his league debut against Hibs at Easter Road in Edinburgh, not far from where he was brought up, he was sent off after picking up two yellow cards in the first 34 minutes. The second yellow came after a dreadful tackle on George McCluskey that saw the Hibs player being carried off the pitch. With Souness's father watching from the main stand he said later that it was one of the lowest points of his football career. On top of that his expensive Rangers team were beaten in the Scottish Cup by Hamilton Academical at Ibrox, much to Souness's embarrassment.

Although Souness was known as a player who liked a good night out he came down hard on any Rangers players who stepped out of line. McCoist once went to Cheltenham Races without his permission. The striker was forced by Souness to hold a press conference to publicly apologise to supporters for his behaviour. Souness banned players from playing too much golf. Several ignored that ban although the younger ones were not so bold. One, Gus MacPherson, even withdrew from the final of his golf club's junior championship in case Souness found out.

Rangers were dominant. The Scottish title was won again in successive seasons, 1988–89 and 1989–90, and two more League Cups were secured for the Ibrox trophy cabinet. Success had the sponsors pouring money into Rangers, who had a £4m deal with Admiral sportswear and a multi-million pound long-term contract to carry the McEwan's Lager name on their shirts. Rangers chief executive Alan Montgomery revealed that two-thirds of the club's income would come from sources other than gate money.

During Souness's five years in charge the only domestic trophy he never won was the Scottish Cup. Progress in Europe – undermined by UEFA's only-three-foreigners-rule – was limited to reaching the last eight of the 1988 European Cup. But he broadened and redrew Rangers, signed major English 'names' and won three titles and four League Cups. It seemed that the sky was the limit. Then, suddenly, with as much drama as there had been at his arrival, it was announced that he was leaving.

Souness resigned four games from the end of the 1990–91 season with a third consecutive championship close. Kenny Dalglish had resigned at Liverpool and Souness could not resist the lure of Anfield. The decision rocked Rangers. 'The Souness Revolution' was not over – the chain of events he began was unstoppable – but the man who ignited it was gone.

Souness had few regrets about getting out of Scottish football, mainly because of his frequent run-ins with the Scottish Football Association. His outspoken after-match comments led to him being fined many times by the governing body. He was also banned from the touchline on numerous occasions but sometimes got around those penalties by naming himself as a substitute, which entitled him to have access to the dugout.

Memorably he met his match in his final season, not from among players or officials but from a tea lady. Rangers players had allegedly left St Johnstone's away dressing room in a dreadful mess and Aggie Moffat took the manager to task over it. Used to winning arguments, he had no chance this time. Moffat rounded on the famous footballer. 'Would you leave your home like that?' she demanded of Souness. He had no response.

Souness's chairman and friend, David Murray, felt let down by his decision. He made it clear that he felt Souness would live to regret the decision and that he was walking away from a club where he could win many more trophies. The fact that he won just three more trophies in his entire managerial career – the 1992 FA Cup with Liverpool, the 1996 Turkish Cup with Galatasaray, and the 2002 League Cup with Blackburn Rovers – vindicated Murray's opinion that he would experience much less glory after Rangers.

Souness can now admit that he would do things differently if he had his time again. 'I was a new, young manager who had just stepped out of the dressing room into the manager's chair and I wanted success yesterday,' he said, 'I was ambitious and was maybe a bit too aggressive in my approach, but really that was my personality back then. I was a bit of a bull in a china shop. I would take a more measured approach if I had my time again. The game has changed a lot as well and I'm not sure I could get away with an aggressive, dynamic managerial approach any more.'

Much was expected of Souness when he arrived in Liverpool, but he spent three unfulfilling years at the club, where he had been an iconic figure as a player. He only won that FA Cup in 1992 after a 2–0 victory over Sunderland. He was struck down by ill health, too. He needed emergency heart surgery that led to him missing the FA Cup semi–final win over Portsmouth, which was only secured after a penalty shoot-out at the end of a replay. The morning after the win he gave an ill-advised interview to the *Sun* newspaper in which he toasted the Liverpool win and his successful surgery. The story ran on 15 April 1992 – the third anniversary of the Hillsborough disaster. Many people on Merseyside had boycotted the *Sun* because of its coverage of the tragedy. Souness admitted it had been a bad lapse of judgement, and many Liverpool fans never forgave him. After mediocre form and no further trophies he left Anfield in January 1994, after an FA Cup defeat to Bristol City.

His managerial career then became nomadic and unpredictable. He joined Galatasaray in Turkey. He guided the team to a Turkish Cup final win over Fenerbahce on their deadly rivals' own ground in 1996. At the end of the game Souness ran half the length of the pitch to plant a huge Galatasaray flag into the centre-circle, much to the wrath of the home supporters. There was nearly a riot as he put it into the ground and because of that he became a cult hero for Galatasaray. The act may have made him popular but it could not save his job. He was fired after just one season, mainly because he had failed to win the Turkish championship.

There were spells at Southampton, Torino and Benfica before he took over at Blackburn Rovers in 2000. It was at Ewood Park that he restored his reputation, signing players such as Tugay, Brad

Friedel, Damien Duff and Dwight Yorke. He secured promotion back to the Premiership in his first full season in charge and goals from Andy Cole and Matt Jansen earned them a 2–1 League Cup final victory over Tottenham.

Budgetary restrictions at Blackburn persuaded him to accept an offer to join Newcastle United in 2004, but once again his strong personality managed to alienate some established figures. Craig Bellamy was loaned out to Celtic after a fall-out. Newcastle fans never entirely took to Souness as their manager. He may have made the quarter-finals of the UEFA Cup and an FA Cup semi-final but that wasn't good enough. Even the signing of Michael Owen from Real Madrid for a club record fee of around £17 million did not help his fortunes, even if it meant the side had a formidable Owen–Alan Shearer partnership in attack.

Souness continued to splash out the money but expensive signings like Jean-Alain Boumsong from Rangers failed to make an impact. Poor results and unhappy supporters led to him being dismissed in February, 2006. He then spent much of his time working as a television pundit although he was behind a plan to buy Wolves in 2007 which was rejected after the Molineux board claimed his consortium had under-valued the club.

'I have been out of management for a while now but still have a huge love of a game that gave me so many happy memories. To any new manager taking over a club nowadays I would tell them to trust their instinct and make sure they get good people around them. When I first went to Ibrox I had Walter Smith as my number two. He was the perfect sounding board. Having a man like Walter around made my job easier. But never forget it is your head on the chopping block. Try never to leave a job in management thinking "If only". I never did. Make sure you do things your way.'

Alex McLeish

*'I grew up with pals who were absolutely mad, mental
Rangers fans. They wouldn't wear anything green or
eat anything green.'*

Alex McLeish had a taste of a different life, a life of briefcases, books, spreadsheets, calculations and figures. He could have been an accountant. Today the idea seems a bit of a giggle. 'Big Eck', scarred and grizzled Scotland centre-half, highly-decorated Aberdeen legend, hardened and successful Rangers manager, streetwise English Premier League boss: imagine this great sportsman and character poring over numbers in a ledger, imprisoned in the office of an accountancy firm. That's exactly what he did during the first year of his career as an emerging Aberdeen player. While his head raced with the prospect of making it as a professional footballer, he worked part-time on a day-release scheme in an Aberdeen accountancy office. Why? Because his father told him to.

In the late 1970s the elder McLeish, also Alex, demonstrated the grounded, pragmatic elements of his own personality by recognising the great uncertainty – and the high casualty rate – attached to young men trying to make it as football players. He needn't have worried. He had already armed his son with more than the potential safety net of a career in money if the football didn't work out. Alex McLeish always had the pedigree DNA to be a thoroughbred Scottish football manager. His father worked in the Glasgow shipyards.

Throughout his childhood McLeish had only to sit at his father's knee to quietly absorb lessons from a hard, intelligent, charismatic, natural leader. 'My da'? Yeah, he shaped me more than anyone. He had leadership traits in him in terms of being a gaffer, a shop steward in the yards. He was a fighter and that meant being a fighter for his pals. As a shop steward he was always fighting for the men. That side of him must have rubbed off on me. He was a big, big influence. I'd go as far as to say he drove me to where I am now.

Sir Matt Busby revolutionised football. He redefined the balance of power between managers and directors and was the first to introduce a professional approach to scouting and youth development. Busby's image was benign and statesmanlike but he was streetwise and shrewd. *Getty Images*.

Right. In some respects Willie Maley's upbringing and beliefs did not make him a typical Celtic man, but over a 52-year association with Parkhead it's debatable whether anyone did more to turn the club into an enormous success story. But, strictly speaking, was he a Scottish manager?

Below left. John Madden was a multiple league winner during 25 years with Slavia Prague, and in 1930 he took them to the final of a prototype version of the Champions League.

Below right. Iraq, Iran, Libya: the adventurous Danny McLennan managed them all as well as seven other overseas countries. In Libya his team was once banned from playing matches because of the Lockerbie bombing.

Above. Bill Struth shaped the image of what it meant to represent Rangers. Discipline and a strict dress code mattered enormously during his 34-year reign as manager. Players were sent home to change if they turned up in the wrong suit. His record 18 Scottish league titles is unlikely to be beaten. *www.scran.ac.uk*

Left. Scot Symon is in the top five when it comes to the number of trophies won in Scottish football, with 17. He once refused to comment when a reporter telephoned to ask what the weather was like around Ibrox. *SNSPix*

Right. Tommy Walker's 15 years in charge of Hearts yielded seven major trophies and made him by far the most successful manager the club has ever had. *SNSPix*

Below. No-one messed with Eddie Turnbull. A trophy winner with Aberdeen and then Hibs, Turnbull was strong, outspoken, and second-to-none when it came to reading a football match. *SNSPix*

A giant towering over football: Bill Shankly at home. Liverpool matter in world football because of what the electrifying 'Shanks' built them into during the 1960s. His quotes were legendary. He was asked his size for a golden boot to honour his contribution to football: 'If it's in gold, I'm a 28.'
Getty Images

Willie Waddell pulled off two remarkable achievements. He made Kilmarnock the champions of Scotland and then went on to win the European Cup Winners' Cup for Rangers in Barcelona. *SNSPix*

When Rangers appointed Jock Wallace they finally had the man who could end Jock Stein's domination with Celtic. Here he holds aloft the Scottish Cup at Hampden as Gordon Smith and Peter McCloy follow. *SNSPix*

Out of the darkness, the man who lit up Scottish football. Jock Stein spent years in the inky blackness of Lanarkshire coal mines before emerging as a managerial genius. He was a deep and sometimes melancholic figure yet his brilliant players and philosophy won the European Cup during a decade of Celtic domination. *SNSPix*

Right. Dundee United players endured 22 years of Jim McLean's angry, vein-bulging perfectionism on the touchline. His dictatorial genius took United to a league title, a couple of League Cups, and a Uefa Cup final, but he came to regret how much he gave to the club. *SNSPix*

Below. Manchester United players Steve Coppell and Gordon Hill aim rifles at manager Tommy Docherty's head. 'The Doc' preferred to shoot from the lip. *Getty Images*

Left. When he was in full flow Ally MacLeod was a charming, magnetic personality. He promised Scotland the world ahead of Argentina '78 but a chaotic campaign broke his reputation. *Getty Images*

Below. Billy McNeill never liked what this picture seemed to show. On the day he became Celtic manager he shook hands with chairman Desmond White as Jock Stein mournfully watched the end of his own reign. But the appointment had Stein's blessing and there was a strange explanation for the awkward handshake.

Kenny Dalglish's glittering career continued seamlessly from playing into management, although unthinkable tragedies took their toll. Here Blackburn Rovers coaches Tony Parkes and Ray Harford help him with the English Premier League trophy. *Getty Images*

The body language may look uncomfortable between Graeme Souness and Mo Johnston, but the Rangers manager knew exactly what he was doing by signing such a high profile Catholic player. It was the most dramatic and significant act of the turbulent 'Souness Revolution'. *SNSPix*

The master. Sir Alex Ferguson has been an epic managerial figure, the most successful of them all. The perception is of furious, angry, raging Fergie putting the fear of God into his players. There's far more to him than that. He is an extraordinary individual who just happens to be a football boss. *Getty Images*

Andy Roxburgh wanted to make a gesture to show his solidarity with fans at the 1990 World Cup finals. He found a red tartan scarf and wrapped it around his neck before leading Scotland out to beat Sweden in Genoa. He kept the scarf as a souvenir. *Getty Images*

Craig Brown remains the last Scotland manager to qualify for both the World Cup and European Championship finals. 'Wee Broon' was still going strong in club management into his seventies. *SNSPix*

Overseeing another celebration. As a young Rangers manager Walter Smith had money to help him dominate the 1990s. When he returned to an impoverished club in 2007 he had to rely on wisdom and exceptional man-management. But having 'The Stare' helped. *SNSPix*

Right. Alex McLeish won the treble for Rangers despite the challenge from a formidable Celtic team. His reputation grew in a thrilling year in charge of Scotland. More than 50 men who played under Sir Alex Ferguson have gone into management and McLeish is the most successful of them all. *SNSPix*

Below. In his playing days the nickname was 'Stroller', as a manager it became 'Gaddafi'. George Graham won trophies for Arsenal and Tottenham, either side of the biggest mistake of his career. *Getty Images*

An edgy, complex and charismatic figure who has divided opinion throughout his football career, Gordon Strachan has been highly successful both as a player and manager. *Getty Images*

Davie Hay won all the Scottish honours as a player and then did so again as a manager of Celtic and Livingston. Here he leads Celtic out against Aberdeen and a young Alex Ferguson. *SNSPix*

The heir to the throne? David Moyes has the toughness and intensity of past greats and the willingness to embrace new ideas required to be a modern managerial heavyweight. A Glasgow upbringing hardened him: 'You're taught that you don't show weakness.' *Getty Images*

'I remember how he used to take his work home with him. He was very conscientious about the shipyards and about the way the industry was going. I remember him coming home and saying "They don't care any more, the young ones". It was the new generation of apprentices. He would say "There's no' the same passion that we had for the industry and for the yards". Maybe he saw the writing on the wall for it.'

His father died in December 1981 aged only 43. Even the nature of his death said something of the type of man he was. He had had a serious heart attack in the August and was told to stay off work until January. There are working–class men who see time spent 'on the sick' as a personal affront. They feel they should be back out there, earning their wage, doing their share of the graft with the others. McLeish's father hated being cooped up in the house, sitting around all day doing nothing. The doctors' orders were ignored and he returned to work a few weeks early to go back on the night shift. One morning a colleague dropped him off a mile from the house. He was walking home when he collapsed on the street, the victim of a second, massive heart attack.

McLeish was an established Aberdeen player by then but he was just 22 and too young to be robbed of a father figure. A guardian of sorts stepped forward in the shape of another shipyard worker's son, just a couple of years younger than McLeish's father and also called Alex. A deep, lasting bond was formed when his manager at Aberdeen at the time, Alex Ferguson, promised to do what he could to take his father's place and be a protective influence. McLeish was glad of it at the time. He has been glad of it ever since.

Ferguson had a compassionate instinct to make himself available to a vulnerable young man who had gone through a harrowing personal ordeal. The shared geography of the shipyards only made it more natural to offer a permanent arm around the shoulder. Neither of them could have had an inkling of it at the time, but Ferguson would go on to become a giant figure in management. And of more than 50 of his players who went on to manage in their own right, McLeish would win more trophies than any of them.

The pair of them shared a sense of time and place in terms of Scotland's industrial past and how it forged remarkable men. 'The shipyard connection among a lot of people in football is quite astonishing,' says McLeish, 'I remember Stuart Kennedy – the great Aberdeen full-back, I'm still pals with him – saying that when Alex Ferguson went to [part-time] Falkirk he asked Stuart what he did for a living. Stuart said, "I work in the shipyards". Straight away Fergie took him under his wing. That's where Fergie's da' had been, so he loved that. He'd talk about "people with character". Single-minded. Determined.

'It was the same in mining. That was the great Jock Stein quote to Fergie, wasn't it? That "You might not know the guy beside you but he could save your life." To see the backgrounds these men came from, and see how successful they went on to be as football managers, it was obviously no coincidence. It made them. It made their character and it made them the type of leaders that they were.

'My da' was a very competitive guy. I think undoubtedly that's where I got it from. When I was young and playing in games I used to fall out with him all the time and then get up the road and realise on reflection that he was probably right. He made me think about my game just by having those wee fall-outs. After an hour or two of my mother, Jean, moaning at him for shouting at her boy I'd say "Ach, leave it ma, he's right". But you absorb all these things from your parents without knowing it, the traits and the enthusiasm and the never-say-die attitude and the decency.

'When I was five we moved to Barrhead and I spent the next twelve years there. It was a wee, working-class Scottish town. Your childhood would be full of trials and tribulations but you had respect for the police. When you saw the police walking down the street everyone would straighten up a bit and say "There's the polis" even though you'd done nothing wrong. We don't have that kind of society any more.'

There is another significant similarity between the backgrounds of Ferguson and McLeish. Both were the sons of a Protestant father and a Catholic mother. Being products of inter-faith marriages ought not to matter but in the west of Scotland it did. A balanced household meant that both had it drummed into them that in their families there would be no tolerance of intolerance. Both men were much the better for it, and thankful in later years. The insidious lure of sectarianism which is so widespread in that part of the world did not claim them.

'I think it helped me. I didn't have "Rangersitis",' said McLeish, referring to the club he supported in childhood (as Ferguson had). 'I'm not at all interested in the religious bigotry between the clubs and the fans. I grew up with pals who were absolutely mad, mental Rangers fans. They wouldn't wear anything green or eat anything green, things like that. I grew up with these boys, went to school with them, I'm still pals with them. But I was brought up not to be a hater of Celtic. My da' was a bam when he was a young Rangers fan. My mother's a Catholic and my mother's family are all Celtic people. I think my ma got a hard time verbally when she was younger and he was coming in through that door after Rangers had got beaten and he was all boozed up and things like that. But when he mellowed, when the kids came along – myself, my sister and my brother – there was respect. He said if Celtic beat Rangers, don't hate them. That can happen sometimes. I grew up with no hatred of Celtic.'

McLeish was even-handed about dishing out beatings to both Glasgow clubs in a glorious, 16-year playing career with Aberdeen. He was relentlessly successful, winning three league championships, five Scottish Cups, two League Cups, the European Cup Winners' Cup and the European Super Cup. He was there for the duration of Ferguson's transformation from sacked St Mirren manager in 1978 to the man Manchester United wanted as their boss in 1986.

Another figure also loomed large: 38 of his eventual 77 international caps came when Stein was the Scotland manager. 'Jock was a big influence on me. He's another of those types of managers who were kinda awesome and commanded respect just by walking in a room. He had that presence. I had seen in my Aberdeen days that Fergie was very much in contact with Jock. He came to Gothenburg as the guest of Aberdeen [when they won the 1983 European Cup Winners' Cup in Sweden]. You knew that he was a mentor for the boss.

'Managers always want to learn. But let's face it, a lot of us have tried to copy big Jock and Fergie and might think it's about making up fancy words and bamboozling our players with tactical stuff and making long-winded speeches. But then you hear them and you realise that they made it really simple. They have common sense, they're streetwise, and there's great intelligence there. Fergie has always been very keen to improve and advance. He is a big reader. He's read books on all the leaders. He told me he was reading one on Lenin and Stalin and it reminded him of a couple of players he used to have!' That he meant McLeish and Willie Miller, the twin towers of Aberdeen's great side, was left unspoken.

McLeish tore himself away from Aberdeen to become player/ manager of Motherwell in 1994, admirably finishing second behind Rangers in his first season. In 1998 he resigned to take over at a bigger club, Hibs. They were heading for relegation at the time and he was unable to prevent it, but he took them back up as First Division champions the next season and to consolidation and a Scottish Cup final appearance in the following campaigns.

People talked about Hibs. They liked their style and liked their charismatic young boss. Among the admirers was Dick Advocaat, the Rangers manager who intended to step down and told club owner Sir David Murray that McLeish was the man who should replace him. It seemed unlikely – Rangers fans expected a major, proven name in the dugout to equal those on the field and McLeish had yet to win a major trophy – but at the end of 2001 he became only the 11th manager in Rangers' history.

The move was a step up for McLeish and redefined him as a major managerial figure in Scotland. There was no question he would take the job but he was still entitled to swallow hard when he looked at the circumstances. Advocaat had not coped with the success of Celtic under Martin O'Neill. Rangers were already effectively lost in the league when McLeish took over. Worse, the tide was turning. The millions available to Advocaat were suddenly absent for McLeish. He would have to downsize Rangers while taking on the most formidable Celtic side there had been since the Stein era.

'When I got the job I thought "Well, I've taken it, no one can ever say that I've never been the Rangers manager even if I get sacked next week. It was about stepping stones, setting little targets. The first target was beating Celtic. I thought I couldn't get sacked as the Rangers manager without having ever beaten Celtic. The second target was to win a trophy: I couldn't leave the Rangers job without having won a trophy; that would have been absolutely terrible. The next target became winning the league and then, ultimately, some kind of push in Europe as well.

'Celtic were as strong as they'd been since Jock. It was a huge challenge. We knew we had to beat that really strong Celtic team because we were getting licked by them at that time. Dick said he'd had enough, couldn't do it any more, couldn't motivate them any more, so we needed a different approach to management. We got a smile on their faces. I would like to think that my character was ready-made for that type of job. The one thing about being a manager is that, when you do go through the mill, you are able to bounce back. That's a trait that is evident when you talk about leaders and leadership.'

McLeish proved to be a match for the Rangers job. He won both cups in his opening few months in the job and remarkably claimed a treble in 2002–03, his first full season in charge. The summer of 2003 was his high watermark. Financial restrictions were tightening at Ibrox. When good players left the replacements were cheaper and inferior. They finished behind Celtic the following season but then won another League Cup and in an impossibly dramatic climax to the 2004–05 championship they snatched the title in the closing minutes, giving McLeish his second SPL title and, as it turned out, his final honour at the club.

Although the following season brought the pleasure of reaching the last 16 in the Champions League it was unsatisfying domestically and Rangers announced, in February, 2006, that McLeish would leave at the end of the season.

'I am really proud of my time at Rangers. When I look back I can say "Phew, four and a half years, seven trophies, the last sixteen in Europe". It was quite significant, and against difficult financial circumstances. It is difficult to leave clubs like that. In 2003 we had won a treble and I thought it might be a good time to walk out and try to get down to England or something. But it's hard to leave clubs like Rangers or Celtic, especially when you've just achieved something. Inevitably you stay for another year. So when you do actually leave you've not achieved what is expected in your final season.

'I was tired at the end. It drains you. It was a draining final season. So you think "Well, it's time for a little break". But we are so masochistic that if I'd been asked the very next week to go and manage a Premiership club I'd probably have said aye. I did have a break but you're not out of it for long before you start to get itchy feet again.'

Sitting idle has never suited a McLeish, father or son. Having left one of the three truly prominent managerial posts in Scotland he resurfaced eight months later in one of the others, swapping Rangers for Scotland, one shade of blue for another. There was a neat, self-contained, uplifting feel to his time in international football: he took the job at the start of 2007, left at the end of it, had ten games in charge and won seven of them. At 70 per cent his win ratio is easily the best of any Scotland manager who has spent a decent spell of time in the job. In the course of taking the country agonisingly close to qualifying for Euro 2008 he delivered one of its most magnificent results, a 1–0 away win against the mighty France. He will always have Paris.

There were moments when the enormity of being in charge of his country scrambled his senses. 'I was standing on the track at times, looking around Hampden and thinking "God, this is some journey you've had, big yin". I was thinking I'd played in this stadium, I'd scored in this stadium, I'd played for Scotland there, and here I was managing my country. That was a real spine-tingling feeling. Before a game you're looking around asking yourself "Is this real, is this really happening?"

'I did think back to being a wee kid. I relived my Hampden memories: going to games as a fan, going to cup finals, going to home internationals. All those years had passed and here I was being in charge of the nation. I think those kind of feelings and thoughts go back to what you were taught when you are young: respect, humility, and always keeping your feet on the ground. And then I'd think "There's a game here, I'd better get on with it . . ."'

McLeish resigned from the Scotland job to become manager of Birmingham City. The move upset some supporters but came as no surprise either to those who acknowledged the economic pull of English club football or who recognised McLeish's eagerness to test and broaden himself. At almost 50 he had spent his entire playing and managerial career in Scotland. Birmingham became another Hibs: he arrived, could not save them from relegation, but secured immediate promotion after only one season out of the top flight. In October 2009, as a Premier League outfit again, the team began a 15–game unbeaten run which became the longest in the club's history.

He had his place among a group of prominent, modern Scottish managers. Respected and admired, he has been touted for larger jobs including Liverpool's and, inevitably, Manchester United's. It was an honour for him to be a part of this gang. 'As Scottish managers there is a certain pride in it for all of us. It's great to see the boys doing well. Owen Coyle, Davie Moyes, Gordon [Strachan]. Obviously Sir Alex is the leader. He comes into the highest possible calibre. We have a brilliant tradition of managers. Maybe that work ethic, I don't know, determination, the kinda chip on the shoulder attitude of the Scots. The "We'll show you" kinda thing. I think all of these traits are evident in us.'

He has said that he will not manage again at club level in Scotland but, one day, a return for a second spell in charge of his country might be an attractive proposition. 'The family will always have a base up the road. Always. The Scotland job is a question that's difficult to answer until you get asked it. But I couldn't rule that out if there was an opportunity again in the future. I don't think any of us can switch off. It's so tough to do that. I think that's why Fergie delayed his initial retirement plans in 2002. Because it just dawned on him "What am I gonnae do?" Jock died in the dugout. As a manager you can identify with that. It's such a huge part of your life. You hear of people taking early retirement and their body goes into malfunction because they are so used to working.

'Hopefully retirement's a long way off for me. But I think that's what we as managers are probably scared of, not knowing how to fill the void when the football's over.'

Accountancy never had a hope of landing him.

Walter Smith

'Jim McLean was interested in what I had to say.
Well, apart from one time. I happened to be reading a
book on tactics by Sir Alf Ramsey just before one of
Jim's team meetings. I brought up something that Sir
Alf had said in the book. That was the only time I
saw Jim angry at my input.'

Walter Smith placed nine framed pictures on the walls of his office at Murray Park, the Rangers training ground. There was one of Ibrox Stadium which took pride of place behind his desk. Down the right-hand side were four pictures of former players: Eric Caldow, Jimmy Millar, Willie Henderson and George Young, all of whom Smith used to idolise in his youth. On the left-hand side were images from another era: Brian Laudrup, Paul Gascoigne, Ian

Durrant and Richard Gough, four of 'his' players that he managed with great success.

Smith is steeped in Rangers tradition. If ever there was a Scottish manager who found his spiritual home it was Walter Smith at 150 Edmiston Drive, Ibrox. When he was a schoolboy Smith used to go along to Rangers home games with his grandfather. He was such an avid fan that at the age of 14, when he broke his leg playing football, his father wrote to the club asking for special dispensation to allow him to sit at the front of the stand, near the touchline, so he could stretch his leg out. The correspondence is now in the Rangers trophy room, a little piece of Smith family history in among all the silverware.

'My sister, Liz, found the letter when she was having a clear-out at the house in Carmyle where we were brought up,' said Smith, 'I remember my dad asking the manager, Scot Symon, if I could sit on the touchline. We got a nice letter back from him, basically saying "No".'

That reply from Symon, dated 28 August 1962, actually reads: 'I regret that I cannot grant permission to your boy to sit on the track. Such a position would be frowned upon by the police and at the same time expose him to the risk of being struck by the ball. Trusting you appreciate our position, please extend to your son our sincere sympathy in his misfortune and our hopes that he will make a speedy recovery.'

Good job for Rangers that Smith has never been the type to take the huff or bear a grudge. That rejection never deflected him from following his team. He was born in Lanark in 1948 and can talk long into the night, and with great affection, about the Rangers teams of the late 1950s and even more so of Symon's side of the early 1960s which included Millar, Jim Baxter and Davie Wilson.

There are parallels between Symon and Smith's spells in charge of Rangers in terms of them both having to deal with wayward personalities. Symon had to cope with the legendary Baxter and made allowances for him to the extent that he alienated some of the other players in his squad. Through the years Smith had to deal with similar maverick individuals – most notably Gascoigne, but also the less talented but equally newsworthy, for the Scottish tabloid press at least, Allan McGregor. Smith was always of the view that a manager should treat every player the same, but he also found that was often easier said than done.

'I don't know first-hand the situation between Scot Symon and Jim Baxter because obviously I was not in the dressing room, but dealing with so called "star" players, men who can turn a game for you, is difficult. As with many geniuses, they have their flaws. One of the great American football coaches said if an ordinary line-backer fell asleep during one of his lengthy meetings then he would sack him. If it had been the great quarterback Dan Marino then he would wake him up politely and ask him how he was.'

Smith's own memorable demonstration of something similar came when he invited Gascoigne to spend Christmas in his house, knowing that the likeable but troubled Geordie might become lonely and morose if left by himself in a hotel. That was man-management, but there was compassion and decency in the gesture too.

'There is a difference between the top players – who can win matches for you on their own – and the rest of a team. The vast majority of managers are conscious of that and try their best not to make distinctions. But sometimes if you have an outstanding player then you have to bend a wee bit. Some guys have personal problems. Footballers are no different from anybody else. From my point of view I was never an outstanding player so it never occurred to any of my own managers to treat me specially.'

Only in management did Smith become outstanding and special. When Rangers won nine consecutive titles between 1989 and 1997 he took over for the final games of number three and went on to win four, five, six, seven, eight and nine. There were three Scottish Cup and three League Cup wins as well. In 1992–93 Rangers won the treble and almost reached the Champions League final. That was his greatest side. They played sixty-four times that season and lost only four.

They often struggled in Europe but domestically Rangers were dominant. Smith was the silver-haired, cardigan-wearing gaffer no one could topple, Sir David Murray the chairman with the resources to outbid any domestic rival. Ibrox was the place to be. Together they brought outstanding players to Rangers: Brian Laudrup, Gascoigne, Andy Goram, Stuart McCall, Alexei Mikhailichenko, Duncan Ferguson, Gordon Durie, Basile Boli, Alan McLaren, Jorg Albertz. The signings were endless. And stalwarts like McCoist, Gough, Durrant, Mark Hateley, Ian Ferguson and John Brown were still there. For season after season the club lived high on the hog. And there was barely a murmur of discontent or insubordination towards Smith from any of them over all those years. They liked him, simple as that.

Still, every empire falls eventually and Smith and Rangers seemed to have run their course when at last the club finished trophyless despite more heavy investment in 1997–98. Smith's departure was announced midway through that season and he left after losing the Scottish Cup final. Few, then, imagined he would return nine years later and start winning silverware for Rangers again. By the end of 2009–10 his major trophy count stood at 19, behind only Willie Maley, Bill Struth and Jock Stein.

The highlight of his second spell in charge was winning consecutive league championships against a background of savage budget cuts and financial downsizing at Rangers. Cynics thought he would damage his own legacy at the club, that he didn't know what he was letting himself in for, that this wasn't the same Rangers he had known in the 1990s. Smith was a match for every obstacle. 'Winning the league title in 2009–10 was a wee bit special for me,' he said, 'I always feel grateful to have been in a position to win trophies but that year was a little bit different because of the circumstances and difficulties we faced.' At the end of that season Smith had not been allowed to buy a single player for 21 months. His own contract had run out during the season and the club was not in a position to offer new terms. He agreed to stay on and work without one.

'I didn't take any pleasure from what was happening at the club because of its financial problems. We had a good group of players, we just didn't have a lot of them. We certainly didn't have a squad of the size needed for a club like Rangers. That is what separated that title from the others I have been fortunate enough to win. We did it with a smaller group, and a little bit against the odds.'

While heavy debt and uncertainty over ownership crippled Rangers' ambitions at that time, all they could hope for was an unflappable, experienced manager who had a profound emotional connection to the club. They needed Walter Smith. He had been a part of the Scottish football furniture for decades.

He was Scotland assistant manager under Sir Alex Ferguson from the end of 1985 and through the 1986 World Cup, and served Ferguson again for three and a half months at club level with Manchester United in 2004. When he was Scotland under-21 coach in the early 1980s Smith worked, albeit for a short time, with Jock Stein. At club level he first came to prominence at Dundee United in the 1980s as number two to the charismatic and autocratic Jim McLean. Enormous mutual respect grew between Ferguson, Stein, McLean and Smith.

He served a long apprenticeship as an assistant manager, having identified early in his moderate playing career that his long-term future lay in coaching. He was a United player from 1966 to 1980 apart from a couple of seasons spent at Dumbarton. He was only 24 when he took his first SFA coaching course at Largs and was put through his paces by Craig Brown.

'Walter was a natural. You could tell even back then that he was destined to make an impact,' said Brown, 'He had an under-standing of tactics and of man-management, and he knew how to deal with players. He was a thinker and a scholar of the game who always wanted to learn.'

With his coaching badges secured Smith was appointed player/coach at United under McLean, who had himself introduced some modern coaching techniques to the club after the 12-and-a-half-year reign of previous manager Jerry Kerr ended in 1971.

'I played under both Jerry and Jim,' said Smith, 'Funnily enough, the older I get the more I can appreciate Jerry Kerr's way of working. He was much more rigid than Jim in terms of tactics. For instance, he got experienced players, put them into positions and let them get on with the game, whereas Jim was sharp and could change tactics. The older I get I appreciate that sometimes the simple approach works better. They say football is a simple game, and Jerry kept it that way. You have to remember he put together a team that beat Barcelona home and away in the 1966 Fairs Cup, so he knew what he was doing.

'At the time I maybe didn't appreciate his ways that much as I was wrapped up in learning all I could about new coaching methods. I had a real interest in the way the game was played, and in things like the shape of teams. I went for the coaching early in my career, maybe because I knew I wasn't going to be a footballer of any note and I knew this was the way for me to stay in the game. At 25, after I got my full coaching badges, Jim asked some of the players if they wanted to help take the schoolboys. I started taking them for training on a Monday evening. When I got a pelvic injury that ended my own career Jim said to me, in his own inimitable fashion, that I was better at coaching than I was as a player and should stick in at it.'

The advice might have been brusque, but Smith knew it made sense. By the time he made his final first-team appearance for United, in 1980, he was already making in impression on the club's coaching staff. 'I learned a lot from Jim McLean. Everybody knows he managed in his own very individual way. I couldn't follow him in terms of his personality. That would have been totally wrong because as a manager you always have to find your own way of doing things. What I learned from Jim was how to set out your team and how to adapt to situations.'

Despite McLean's reputation as an unyielding dictator, Smith noted that he did encourage questions and feedback from his players. 'I would not volunteer an opinion when I was a player under Jim unless he asked. But, when he did, he really listened and liked his players to be involved. He didn't like them all sitting in the dressing room saying nothing and agreeing with him all the time. He maybe thought they weren't thinking enough. And if they weren't thinking they would not be sharp out on the pitch.

'I talked with Jim a lot and read a lot of books about coaching. He was interested in what I had to say. Well, apart from one time. I happened to be reading a book on tactics by Sir Alf Ramsey just before one of Jim's team meetings. I brought up something that Sir Alf had said in the book and that was the only time I saw Jim angry at my input. He was okay when I had my own thoughts but he didn't want me stealing somebody else's. He was an independent thinker and he wanted his players to be a bit like that too.'

United won the Scottish title in 1982–83 and there were two League Cup triumphs and a run to the European Cup semi-finals. It was a period of astonishing success under McLean, but the contribution of his assistant had not gone unnoticed. In 1986 Graeme Souness arrived to revolutionise Rangers and asked Smith to be his assistant. Smith was 38 when he joined the Ibrox payroll for the first time.

According to McLean it was 'a huge blow to Dundee United', a view he still held a quarter of a century later. 'I remember I said at the time that Walter had all the attributes required to be an outstanding coach and losing him was worse than losing any player,' said McLean, 'I stand by that statement. What he has achieved during his managerial career since he left as my assistant at Dundee United has proved me right.'

Choosing the correct assistant and the right team captain are two of the most important decisions any manager must make. 'You have to trust your assistants and get them involved,' said Smith, 'I have no problems in delegating. If you have assistants – or 'colleagues' as we are now being told to call them – and don't show them the respect of giving them responsibility, then players and other people who work for you get to know that and won't take them seriously. You can't simply appoint an assistant and ignore his opinions.

'It's the same on the pitch with the man you appoint captain. He has to be, if you like, part of your management team. He takes your points of view out onto the pitch. He has to be a leader who can unite the dressing room and take the club forward. He also has to be respected by everybody. He represents the players. He is the man supporters relate to.' Gough was Smith's iconic captain first time around and David Weir on his second tour of duty.

Smith was Rangers' assistant manager from 1986 to 1991. When Souness dramatically resigned to take the Liverpool job it was generally assumed that ambitious, free-spending Rangers would go for another big-name manager. Smith was widely respected but relatively low-profile. Club chairman Sir David Murray saw him as a figure of real substance, though. Smith became the first manager appointed by Murray. He was 43.

'Looking back I maybe worked for too long as an assistant but you can't change circumstances and I have to say I had learned a lot and was ready to be a manager when my time came. At Dundee United Jim was not ready to retire when I was there and that would have led to frustration on my part as I knew I would never be manager at United. I then had five great years working under Graeme at Ibrox. When he left and I took over in 1991 I was confident in my own ability. I knew what pressures came with being a manager.'

Over the following two decades Smith become one of Scotland's managerial heavyweights. A sense of humility dictated that he could never refer to himself as the equal of Stein, Ferguson or McLean, but they were leaders cut from the same cloth. 'These men were absolute managerial greats. I have done okay but these guys were incredible and I learned a lot from them all. For instance when I took the Scotland under-21 team I sat down and met Mr Stein, who was coaching the full squad. Not for a minute would I say that I knew him very well, but he was one of those people whose strength of personality was there for everybody to see. He had an aura about him. I don't mind admitting I was a bit in awe of him. Anybody of that era who had witnessed the work he had carried out with Celtic must have felt like that. If you had thoughts of being a coach or a manager he was the person you aspired to be. Sir Alex and Jim McLean were up and coming, but he was the man. When we sat down to pick those players for the Scotland under-21 team he would have his thoughts and input on players and he was so knowledgeable. He knew all about them and had done his homework on them all. He worked hard.

'That is something that all three of those great managers did. They never stopped. When I worked with Sir Alex at Manchester United he was still as hungry for success and as driven as I remember him being at Aberdeen. My time at Manchester United let me see what it was like to be at the top club in what was probably the best football league in Europe.'

It was a joy for Smith to experience the English Premier League as an employee at a wealthy club. That contrasted vividly with his four years at Everton. After leaving Rangers he moved to the blue half of Merseyside in the summer of 1998, remaining there until he was sacked in March 2002. It was a beleaguered spell for Everton and there were few resources for Smith. He had been tempted there with the promise of transfer funds but those never materialised and senior players like Duncan Ferguson had to be sold to balance the books. Smith was always battling to keep the club above water, always in the wrong end of the table. He was dismissed and replaced by another Scot, David Moyes.

'It was a tough time for me but Everton are a great club and managing in the Premiership was a great experience. I knew when I went there I would never have the same level of success I had had in my first stint at Rangers because so many teams are capable of competing near the top of the table in England. Even so, it was a time when I took a lot in. Working at such a big club when budgets were tight was good experience, I suppose, for working under similar circumstances with Rangers.'

Other than the short spell at Manchester United, Smith was out of the game for almost three years between leaving Everton and taking over as manager of Scotland in December 2004. The SFA chose Smith ahead of Gordon Strachan. It was to be an inspired appointment. Smith brought stability and restored pride after the previous Berti Vogts regime. Scotland drew with Italy and won in Norway. They won the Kirin Cup tournament in Japan. Scotland's qualifying group for Euro 2008 was formidable – Italy, France and Ukraine were in it – but Smith began with three consecutive victories, including an astonishing Hampden win over the French. And then, one game later, he resigned.

Given his age and previous sense of fulfilment at Rangers, the Scotland job seemed like a good fit for him, but few had envisaged Murray offering him the Ibrox job again at the start of 2007. Smith found it impossible to refuse. Some Scotland supporters thought it a betrayal; others appreciated that Smith was a man for whom club came before country. It was briefly messy between the SFA and Rangers, but the decision was irreversible.

'Rangers had always been in my blood. That is why I went back. I brought back Ally McCoist, who had worked with me with Scotland. He was young and ambitious and another who had Rangers in his blood. I also had Kenny McDowall with me so I had young guys out to make their mark and who I knew would be good for the club. I was excited by the challenge of going back to Rangers.'

It was a second spell at *his* club, but this was a different Rangers. Years of extravagant spending had caught up with owner Murray. Smith had returned to a club which was relentlessly downsizing. He made some relatively expensive initial signings but then the money dried up altogether. A talented but slim, pared-down squad won him the championship in 2009 and again in 2010. There were two more Scottish Cups and two more League Cups too. Although European results were generally as disappointing as they had been in his first spell in the 1990s – with the dramatic exception of an unexpected run to the 2008 UEFA Cup final, which was lost to Zenit St Petersburg – Smith proved that in Scotland he could win with vast resources and also without them.

His teams were pragmatic, organised, hard to break down, hard

to beat. Detractors thought his style too cautious; admirers ap-
plauded his ability to build relationships with players and to send
out sensible, effective football teams. A stern manner and a famous
ability to deliver a withering stare gave the impression of a strict
disciplinarian, although Smith's sociability, intelligence and dry wit
are well known. He has been one of Scotland's many tough,
successful managers, and throughout it all he retained a thorough
sense of decency.

'There have been many great football managers and great leaders
in industry and politics who have been Scottish. Part of the reason
for their success is a strong work ethic that is drummed into most
Scots of a working-class background early on. In Scotland you are
brought up with a real love of football. I was trained as an
electrician but never wanted to go back to being one once I
started playing professional football as I loved the game so much.
To get paid to be part of a sport you love is a fortunate thing to
happen. I never took that for granted. It made me just try harder to
remain good enough to be involved.'

Eventually that would mean having the awareness and instincts
to react as football and management themselves evolved. 'When I
started Jim McLean was involved in every aspect of Dundee
United. He used to be hands-on with everything. Back then it
used to be him and the chairman who made the decisions. Now it
is the chairman, the chief executive, the manager and also some
other folk taking the decisions at clubs. I feel I have a better focus
now than I used to have when I started out as a manager. When
you first begin there is drive and determination but you tend,
possibly through inexperience, to dive headlong into every aspect
of trying to run the football club. The older you get, the more you
realise what is important and what is not.

'For instance if you are doing media interviews and somebody
writes something bad about you, sometimes you react badly to
that. As time goes by you shrug it off more easily. You don't take it
that seriously. I have come to realise that if your team is winning
the media will praise you. If your team is being beaten they will

criticise you. Simple as that. If you had told me that simple fact, say 20 years ago, I would have argued with you. Nowadays I just concentrate on trying to make Rangers a better team and ignore what is written and said. I hope that my decision-making as a manager is a bit clearer and is not as clouded as it used to be when there were lots of other things going on that I had to deal with.

'The other change is that a lot of managers are having to handle a financial situation at a club which has not been of their own making. You don't get to operate in the manner you feel would bring success to the club as your hands are tied at times. That's frustrating but it's just the way things are nowadays. You have to work with the cards that are dealt to you, which I found at Rangers when things got tough off the park. You just keep going, have faith in yourself and the people around you, and draw on your experience to try and get things right.

'One bad result and the pressure is on at Rangers. It has always been like that and you have to deal with it. I don't think there is a secret for the successes I have had. Of course you need that wee bit of luck but that has always been the case. The big difference is that I have had to adapt to try and bring instant success to the club. Maybe, say 20-odd years ago, you could create a team over time. Now, like everything else in life, success has to be instant. Patience isn't a word you hear much in football.'

Smith got there in the end, though. And just think: if he was a different type of character, and much less of a supporter, he might have taken one look at that boyhood rejection letter and ended his relationship with Rangers there and then.

Chapter Six

Who are 'the Largs Mafia'?

Largs: a popular seaside resort with a pier in the Firth of Clyde. The birthplace of actress Daniela Nardini and the golfer Sam Torrance. A location where many Glaswegians and other Scots used to go for their holidays. A home of good ice cream.

There are people who would come up with those distinguishing features if they were asked to name something synonymous with Largs, but not anyone given to caring about Scottish football. To those consumed by the national game it means something else altogether. In one corner there are those for whom 'Largs' evokes one of the most respected and productive football coaching systems in Europe, the venue for a conveyer belt of outstanding Scottish managers.

And then there are those who regard 'Largs' as meaning something else entirely for Scottish football. To them it is a byword for a chummy, jobs-for-the-boys culture in which a brotherhood of Scottish managers looks out for each other to the exclusion of outsiders or mavericks. It has even spawned an evocatively-named offshoot. Whenever there is something to complain about – and especially when some fresh calamity has befallen the Scotland team – it does not take long before someone pins the blame on 'the Largs Mafia'. To those who fiercely defend the contribution Largs has made to Scottish football, men like Andy Roxburgh, Craig Brown and David Moyes, it is depressing to hear disparaging references to a supposed coastal Cosa Nostra.

When Dundee were looking for a manager in 2000 their chairman, Peter Marr, was quoted saying: 'We won't be appointing anyone from Scotland because there's a Largs Mafia here. They jump from one club to another.' Instead the club went for a complete outsider, Ivano Bonetti, an unknown, charismatic Italian He lasted two seasons.

'I want to dispel this "Largs Mafia" myth,' said Craig Brown, who can sound immediately exasperated by the mention of it. 'When people use that phrase to me I say "That's a compliment". As far as I'm concerned the Largs Mafia is Sir Alex Ferguson. It's Jim McLean. It's Gordon Strachan, Walter Smith and David Moyes. It's Jose Mourinho.'

How did a quaint North Ayrshire town with a population of fewer than 12,000 become such a significant and divisive venue within Scottish football? How is it that Mourinho, Eusebio, Rinus Michels and Arrigo Sacchi can all be said to have 'passed through Largs'? Why does it seem to be revered and reviled in equal measure?

Largs and Scottish football became intertwined in the late 1950s. It wasn't the seaside, the weather or the ice cream which attracted the SFA 39 miles west of its Glasgow headquarters. The appeal was a sports facility which had been opened shortly before the Second World War. The Inverclyde National Sports Training Centre on a wooded hillside behind Largs had everything the SFA needed: training pitches, meeting rooms and accommodation facilities which would allow for residential courses. Coaches could stay on campus at the end of each day's lessons. The residential aspect was essential to Largs' emergence: coaches could work all day and play – hard – at night, with little more to worry about than stumbling back up the hill to their beds. The courses would take place over a couple of weeks in the summer, out of the football season.

In 1957 Hugh Brown, the Principal of Jordanhill College in Glasgow and the father of subsequent Scotland manager Craig, was approached by the SFA to establish its first coach education course at Largs. The SFA was ahead of its time. There was no input from UEFA and other countries' football associations had yet to reach the stage of joined-up thinking when it came to a national coaching structure.

In those days the emphasis was on physical conditioning, and that was Hugh Brown's speciality. He had been a physical training instructor for the RAF at Cosford (his assistant was Walter Winterbottom, who later managed England). One of the men who had impressed him there was Dave Russell, a Scot who was managing in England. Russell had been a member of the East Fife side which won the 1938 Scottish Cup and later managed Odense in Denmark, the 1948 Danish Olympic side, and then spent most of the 1950s in charge of Bury and the 1960s as manager of Tranmere. He might have become the first manager of Scotland. The SFA invited him to manage the national team at the 1958 World Cup finals but Bury refused to release him for it.

Russell was Scottish, a working manager and – crucially, in relation to Largs – had qualified during the war as a physical training instructor at Cosford. All of this made him attractive to Brown, and Russell accepted his invitation to contribute to the first SFA course. Soon he took over how they were organised and served as the part-time course director until 1967.

Like most managerial obsessives, Russell had to juggle football and family. During the annual two-week summer course he would take his two sons to Largs, where they occupied themselves on the sidelines as the prominent Scottish coaches of the day went through their lessons. 'I remember one day when my father spent a whole morning providing a lecture and practical presentation on the 4–2–4 system used by Brazil to win the 1958 and 1962 World Cups,' said his son, Robin Russell, 'This caused quite a stir as it appeared that few coaches knew the exact positional responsibilities of 4–2–4 at the time. I noticed one student making copious notes and then buttonholing Dad after the session, so much so that he didn't have time for lunch or much attention for his young son! I was somewhat put out that this student had monopolised my father's time just so he could get more notes and I asked Dad who it was. He told me it was a Sean Fallon. I am not sure what, if any, influence this presentation had on Mr Fallon but I like to think it may have played a small part in his thinking.' Fallon was Jock Stein's assistant when Celtic won the European Cup in 1967.

Gradually the SFA's annual occupation of Largs took shape. Young coaches would live in the rooms for two weeks every close season, listening to lectures and working on the training grounds during the day and going out for boisterous nights together when the work was over. Russell handed responsibility over to Roy Small, the head of physical education at Jordanhilll College. Small did not have a managerial background but he was liked and respected within the SFA and was allowed to take charge of Scotland's youth teams. At Largs he gave the courses extra credibility by inviting experienced senior managers, such as Willie Ormond and Eddie Turnbull, onto the staff to tutor the young coaches. That was important because until then there had been an impression that the work at Largs was largely about physical education.

In 1966 Sir Alex Ferguson came to Largs for his first coaching badge. 'I found the course inspiring,' Ferguson wrote in *Managing My Life*, his autobiography, 'My room-mate at Inverclyde was Jim McLean. We struck up a friendship that has survived to this day. I used to go back to Largs every summer for a refresher course. I'd have a fortnight's holiday with Cathy and then two weeks in Largs.' Ferguson defended Largs against the accusation that Jock Stein seemed to have managed perfectly well without it (Stein never sat any courses at Largs). 'Jock, having shown himself to be a manager of the highest calibre, had nothing to prove. Jock didn't need a badge. Jock emerged in a different era, so I don't think there is any substance in efforts to criticise him for not going to Largs.'

McLean described his experience at Largs as one of the building blocks of his highly successful career as manager of Dundee United. 'I was part of the Largs system, as coach and assessor, and while it was a vitally important stage of my development, it no more defined me as a manager than it made Alex Ferguson the best boss in the world. Largs helped us go a long, long way but football management, like so many careers, is a constant challenge between using the nuts and bolts of theory and practice with the tools of your own opinions, thoughts and beliefs.'

That made Ferguson and McLean bona fide Scottish members of 'the Largs Mafia', as were the likes of Roxburgh, Brown, Turnbull, Ormond, Moyes, Walter Smith, Strachan, Alex McLeish, Willie Miller, Alex Smith, Tommy Burns, Bobby Williamson, Archie Knox, Eric Black, Alex Miller, Jocky Scott, Billy Stark and many others.

Roxburgh took over from Small when he successfully applied to become the SFA's first full-time technical director in 1975. Roxburgh had big ideas. Stein had shown little interest in what was going on at Largs, but Roxburgh persuaded him of its merits. The man who won the European Cup was never a staff coach at Largs but he became an admirer of the set-up and began coming along to speak to young coaches. 'Andy gave the courses credibility by ensuring the best teachers were around,' said Craig Brown. Roxburgh also gave the courses an international dimension. He was friendly with the AC Milan coach, Arrigo Saachi and soon had the Italian along for a series of visits to the Ayrshire coast.

'Sir Alex Ferguson said that his experience at the SFA's coaching centre changed his views of football forever,' said Roxburgh. 'I was the same. Remember, we were trained by top managers at the time. Even outsiders held the programme in high regard. The Italian FA were regular attendees and Jose Mourinho and Carlos Queiroz of Portugal attended twice. The critics were usually people who had never attended and who were prejudiced against the training of coaches.

'Our aim was to prepare coaches who were practical, thoughtful and creative. There was no textbook, no regimental way of working, only the input of experienced, top-class staff sharing ideas and offering their guidance. Walter Smith, Craig Brown,

Alex Ferguson and many others. We taught students *how* to coach, more than *what* to coach.'

Other heavyweights followed as a result of Roxburgh's connections on the international coaching circuit: Michels, Eusebio, Queiroz, Mourinho. The self-styled 'Special One' was an unknown 25-year-old teacher who coached Vitoria Setubal's under-15s when he attended Largs in 1988 and soaked up its commitment to coaching excellence. In 2000 he returned to study for his A licence (there are courses for a B licence, then an A licence, and finally the UEFA pro-licence). Fabio Capello did not go to Largs but as part of the managerial student exchange between the SFA and the Italian FA headquarters at Coverciano, Capello flew to Scotland at the beginning of the 1980s and, among other things, watched Brown take a training session when he was manager of Clyde.

It also helped Largs' status that the leading Scottish players of the day were prepared to go there each summer and enrol on the coaching courses. Initially there had been some scepticism – notably from Celtic and Rangers – which was partly attributable to wariness about what there was to learn from coaches whose background was in education rather than management. 'The SFA spent a lot of time and energy developing Largs and for a long time it got nothing but abuse and criticism,' said Ernie Walker, the former secretary of the SFA. 'There was a sneering attitude towards "blackboard footballers". People would say "Matt Busby didn't need a bloody certificate to become a manager". The association had great difficulty getting credibility for its ideas for coaching. But that came eventually. Gradually the courses became popular.'

Leading Scottish players reaching the end of their careers realised there was plenty they could learn from the SFA's attempts to turn them into managers. 'When Howard Wilkinson was England's technical director he once told me that he was amazed we could always get the top players to come on our courses at Largs,' said Brown, 'In England the Glenn Hoddles, the Bryan Robsons, and the Kevin Keegans didn't think they had anything to learn from the coaches. We didn't have that problem in Scotland.

'Our coach, Frank Coulston, went round the clubs early each new year and asked each manager if he could speak to his players. Each manager knew Frank and liked him so they would agree. Frank was a good salesman. He'd tell the players their careers wouldn't go on forever and they should think about coaching and management. It worked. We had all the top players in that era.'

When Brown replaced Roxburgh as technical director (and also Scotland manager) in 1993 he invited respected managerial figures such as Gerard Houllier and Roy Hodgson to give lectures at Largs. Later Carlos Alberto Parreira and Marcello Lippi – a pair of World Cup-winning managers – were the SFA's guests and invited to speak to young coaches. In 2006 there was considerable media interest when Alan Shearer went through an SFA course. In 2009 Henrik Larsson announced that he 'had faith' in Largs rather than any comparable scheme in Sweden and intended to enrol.

One of Scotland's hottest managerial tickets, David Moyes, found the lessons he learned at Largs were second to none. 'Think of all those managers giving up their time to help other coaches. That's why I think the Scottish system is well-respected. I have done plenty of work with the SFA since then and I've also done the English FA coaching badges. Why did I do the English badge? Because I wanted to prove that I could do it in England as well. No disrespect to the English one – it was good, there were good people in it, I enjoyed it – but I have to say, the Scottish one was day and night . . .'

Moyes and any other famous names coming either to teach or learn on the Largs courses are eagerly embraced by those who bristle at the criticism it receives. Former Scotland internationals Davie Provan and Steve Archibald have publicly accused the SFA of fostering a chummy culture where those who attend Largs are looked after in the managerial jobs circuit.

'By inviting a certain clientele every year it became pretty closed,' conceded Jimmy Sinclair, Brown's successor as technical director in 2002. 'And the closed shop therefore became "the Largs Mafia". Suddenly club directors and chairmen needing to find a manager would ask "Who's done well on the Largs coaching courses?" and so some people perceived it as being a jobs-for-the-boys culture.'

The origin of the 'Largs Mafia' term is unknown but the phrase stuck. It is used by those who regard the likes of Brown, Alex Smith and Jocky Scott as part of this country's managerial establishment, popular men who can always call in a favour and find their next job somewhere as a result of their place in an intricate web of connections.

Critics also blame Largs for churning out an identikit idea of what makes a good coach, namely a structured, formulaic approach to teaching young players which can rob them of individualism. It is a hollow accusation. Coaches are at Largs for only two weeks in the summer; there is no way those handful of sessions can determine the way Scottish football is played in the remaining 50 weeks of the year. 'Two weeks at Largs doesn't standardise the way people take football teams for the rest of the year,' said Sinclair, 'It's like taking a driving test. You don't drive like that for the rest of your life.'

There was a different accusation which bothered Sinclair when he took over. He suspected that the social aspect of Largs was too prominent. Coaches were entitled to enjoy themselves at night, he reckoned, but some were overdoing it and the course work was in danger of being affected. Sinclair took some of the courses away from Largs and to Stirling University, St Andrews, Rangers' Murray Park complex and Peffermill in Edinburgh.

'When I took over there was a culture there,' Sinclair recalled, 'To my mind the football guys worked really hard all year and they invited them down and it was almost like a half-holiday, half-work situation. They blew off steam at night, to an enormous degree I thought. While a lot of them were fantastic managers and coaches I felt they weren't preparing properly given the money that had been paid for them to be there. I broke that up a wee bit and took a lot of the courses out of Largs.

'That's not to criticise Largs, not at all. Let me make it clear that I would never say a negative thing about it. Interestingly, a lot of the foreign coaches who came to it thought that the spirit, the culture of it, was the essence of its appeal. They felt that the coaches and managers socialising together and swapping tales in the pubs at night was hugely rewarding. A lot of the serious chat at night was football-related and they would get as much education then – maybe even more so – than they did during the day.

'I just felt the culture sometimes let Largs down. On balance I thought the whole essence of football management and coaching had become so professional that our courses had to make sure they matched that. Sometimes I felt the culture got a wee bit excessive. I didn't want to have that criticism levelled at the courses, that you go down to Largs, go on the courses and then get blitzed at night.'

For some, Brown included, breaking the link with Largs undermined what had made the marriage between location and the SFA so special for almost half a century. 'You would go to the pub at night and talk football. The humour and the camaraderie developed. My view was that it was a mistake to take the main courses elsewhere. We used to walk down to town have an ice cream in Nardini's with Turnbull and Ormond, a couple of pints in the Clachan Bar, on to the bingo, then a bag of chips on the way home. You'd be sitting there at the bingo listening to Turnbull and Ormond talking about football. What an education!'

Love it or loathe it, there was only one place where it could have happened.

Chapter Seven
The Great Club Men

Eddie Turnbull

'George Best is the greatest regret of my managerial career. He was the only player ever signed behind my back. At his peak he was up there with Pele, Maradona and Cruyff but he was on the way down and way past his peak when he played at Easter Road. All he did was disrupt the dressing room with his behaviour.'

The dining-car steward on the Aberdeen to Glasgow train has long since finished serving lunch but still a large group of men are hunched conspiratorially around a table in the otherwise empty compartment. Three are sitting down but the others have to either stand or kneel to see what is going on as they hang on every word of the man moving a tomato sauce bottle and a tea cup around the table.

The group has been given special dispensation to remain in the dining car by the head conductor, who has also agreed they can keep the salt and pepper shakers along with the sauce bottle and the dirty tea cups for as long as they like. As rail staff scurry around them clearing every other table, Aberdeen manager Eddie Turnbull moves the sauce bottle to the right edge of the table, a salt shaker to the left, and pushes the tea cup up the middle. Sitting next to his assistant, Jimmy Bonthrone, and across from club captain, Martin Buchan, he uses the cutlery and condiments to illustrate how he wants his three strikers to break forward against Celtic at Parkhead the next day.

His players listen intently to every word from the man who talks tactics with them whenever he can. Even if, at times, that meant turning his table in the dining car into an impromptu tactics board. It wasn't just before games he brought out the salt and pepper shakers, the sauce bottles and tea cups. In the aftermath of Saturday games, on the train back to Aberdeen, he would use the same items to explain to his players what they'd done right or wrong.

Turnbull clearly remembers the days back in the 1970s when he explained his tactics on a train, and can't see any manager nowadays resorting to such measures to get his point across. 'Can you imagine Sir Alex Ferguson getting the Manchester United players round a train table and representing Wayne Rooney as a tea cup, that Berbatov chap as a bottle of sauce and Ryan Giggs as a salt shaker?' asked Turnbull, 'It just wouldn't happen, would it? They all work out their tactics on laptop computers nowadays, don't they? In my day I used whatever I had in front of me to get my point across.'

Turnbull is an example of a great player who became a great manager, a man who was willing to learn from whoever he could. He read coaching manuals from abroad, studied the great Hungarian side of the 1950s in precise detail and went with his friend Tommy Docherty to watch Bayern Munich's training techniques. On top of that he maintains that he was the first Scottish coach to actually give players a ball to play with in training.

'I never saw a ball at training in all my years playing for Hibs in "The Famous Five" team. People got it into their heads back then if you kept the ball off players at training they would want it even more on a Saturday and be hungry for it, which was utter rubbish of course. Even the manager we had up until 1948, Mr Willie McCartney, was never on the training pitch. He just picked the team. Didn't even mention tactics. Before kick-off he would throw the ball at the captain, wish us luck and that was it. The rest was up to us.

'Mr McCartney, and a lot of managers in that era like Willie Maley at Celtic and Bill Struth at Rangers were more like figureheads. Very good figureheads, mind, as they were big characters and you need to be that as a manager. For instance, Mr McCartney was an impresario, a huge man, immaculately dressed and always with a carnation in his buttonhole. He cut a dash.'

Turnbull admits he didn't learn much about tactics from McCartney, whom he played under for two years, early in his Hibs career. What he did learn from him was a manager's need to get respect from players, to make them want to play for you, and to rule them with an iron fist.

'Mr McCartney came to every home game and 15 minutes before the end he would come down from the stand, walk down through the tunnel and stand at the entrance to the pitch, just within our sight. We all knew he did it, all knew it would happen, but whenever we saw him we ran that bit faster, tackled a bit stronger. Why? I can only assume that we were a bit scared of him. He kept us on our toes by doing that and when I became a manager I made sure my players weren't totally sure what my next move would be.'

As a would-be manager Turnbull was frustrated at some of the training techniques of the time, which he thought did little to improve players. 'You trained as an athlete not as a football player, and that was wrong,' he remembers, 'It was all running, nothing on the field. The Hibs team used to run up Arthur's Seat, or on Gullane Sands, up and down the main stand, round the pitch. You name it, we ran up and down it. We were an incredibly fit team, no question. As for tactics, though, we hadn't a clue. There weren't any.'

Even when Hugh Shaw took over as Hibs manager after McCartney died from a heart attack in 1948, nothing much changed. 'Hugh had been the trainer when Mr McCartney had been manager so sometimes, after he got promoted to manager, he would get into his tracksuit and rolled-up jersey and get us to run round the park. He would have us running and doing exercises and he would stand there looking on. He was hard as nails and I respected him, as did the rest of the players, but he didn't know much about tactics.

'He was big on motivation though and after telling us the team, he would, for some reason, always say "Right lads, give them 'The Reel of Tulloch' out there". That was an old Scottish Highland dance tune that he liked and I think he meant he wanted us to put the wind up them, although I was never too sure.'

Turnbull believes that in the years after the Second World War players held the upper hand and had more responsibility than they do today. 'People have asked me who should take credit for "The Famous Five" side winning trophies and I say it was the players that did the business. The manager or trainer encouraged us but it was us that won the games.'

When he was still playing for Hibs in the late 1950s Turnbull was hungry to learn all about coaching. He decided to travel abroad to try and pick up coaching ideas from clubs on the continent. Both he and his close pal Docherty went to see Bayern Munich train, but were less than impressed. That surprised them both, as this was an era when West Germany was a major world football power. It should have been an exciting learning experience.

'We had an interpreter each and while "The Doc" watched their training I took part as a player. We were due to compare notes at the end and put both of our experiences together. I thought they would be trying lots of new things but they didn't teach either of us anything we didn't know. They hardly used the ball either. It was hardly ground-breaking stuff they were doing.

'Maybe I was a wee bit biased against them as the German coaches obviously didn't think I was much of a player. They took one look at me and said, "You, get in goal." Even back then I felt the SFA coaching course at Largs was miles ahead of any others and I can say that because I had been to check out other clubs and other courses on the continent.'

Turnbull learned more from Docherty than he did from the Germans. When he visited him a few years later, when Docherty had become manager at Chelsea, he saw an innovation that he copied and continued to repeat throughout his career. 'I can't understand managers who stand on the touchline watching games,' said Turnbull, 'What do they see? You can't get an overall view of the game from down there. You can't watch the runs off the ball properly because you are on the same level as the players. "The Doc" knew that and he built a platform at Stamford Bridge, way up in the main stand. He could see everything from up there. That's where managers should be, not on the touchline.'

When Turnbull took the step up to management his main aim to begin with was to ensure his players knew who was boss. 'I was a big one for discipline as I knew how important it was and what it could achieve if you had a group of well-drilled young men on your side. They knew they couldn't mess with me as I knew what I was talking about when it came to football. I got that knowledge from playing the game and keeping my ears open. That is the key for me. As a manager you have to have more knowledge than your players. If they ask you a football question, you have to have the answer. That's why so many Scots became good managers. As a race we are always willing to learn. We aren't afraid to ask questions and improve ourselves.'

Turnbull first started to coach at Hibs under Hugh Shaw but left after a personality clash with Walter Galbraith, who took over from Shaw in 1961. Turnbull, never shy in coming forward, felt Galbraith was behind the times and claimed he didn't realise the role of a manager in the early 1960s was evolving and that he had to become much more pro-active.

'I didn't have too much respect for Galbraith, in fact I thought he was a nonentity in football terms. He knew nothing about world football. For instance, the Hungarians changed things tactically by fielding a team with a deep-lying centre-forward. They did that first when Nandor Hidegkuti played there for Hungary way back in 1953 when they beat England 6–3 at Wembley. A deep-lying centre-forward meant the central defenders were split, and poor ones got confused and didn't know who to mark. They had Ferenc Puskas as well. They were a joy to watch. It was as if the Hungarian way of playing football had never happened when you worked with Galbraith. I couldn't work with a man who knew nothing and went about with his head in the sand.

'I was very interested in the 4–4–2 system which was being introduced from Europe in, I would say, around 1962. It was a time European football was to the fore and had to be studied. Galbraith never bothered. I saw the Hungarians in particular as the nation that was changing football and I wanted to learn from them.

'The Italians were also breaking new ground but for me they did nothing for football because they were far too defensive. Remember, I had played for Hibs and was part of "The Famous Five". I was brought up on attractive football. As a manager, you always have to adapt and Galbraith never did. Only bad managers didn't adapt.'

Turnbull coached the Scottish youth team and then, from 1963, Queen's Park, where he did such a great job that Aberdeen came calling in 1965. It was a much bigger club but when he walked through the doors of Pittodrie he was less than impressed with what he found.

'When I arrived at Aberdeen there were a lot of players who were mediocre to say the least. They weren't up to the job and I knew I had to make changes. I knew the game, had coaching experience under my belt and wanted to play a 4–2–4 formation. As a manager it was up to me to buy the players to fit into the system and that's what I did. I knew if I could pass on my belief in myself to the players we would go places.'

The first day at any club is vital for any manager. Turnbull made sure his players and the staff he had inherited from the previous manager, Tommy Pearson, were left in no uncertain terms that they had to pull their weight or they would be heading out the exit door.

'You only get one chance to make a first impression as a manager and it's vital you go in to your new club and start as you mean to go on. Day one at Aberdeen I remember laying down the law and I got rid of Bobby Hume because I didn't like his attitude and I really got rattled into the rest of the players. I told them I wanted total commitment. I shouted and bawled, and then did an abrupt about turn and walked out of the dressing room and let my assistant, Jimmy Bonthrone, smooth things over. It was a good cop/bad cop approach. I think that is an important mix for any management team to have. Players need to find the manager a bit aloof, someone to be respected, but they also need someone in his backroom staff they can turn to and have a moan. Not a big moan, right enough, but just enough to make them think they are being listened to. That's what happened at Aberdeen. I picked the team, and the players who weren't playing moaned to Jimmy. And by God, there were lots of them. Jimmy would tell me who had been moaning about me. At least they had an outlet in Jimmy for their frustration but that is part and parcel of being a manager. You are never going to please everybody, all of the time, so don't try.'

The highlight of Turnbull's six years with Aberdeen was a famous 3–1 Scottish Cup final victory over Celtic at Hampden in 1970. It was a victory – secured by two goals from youngster Derek McKay and another from Joe Harper – he savoured more than any other win because nobody really gave his team a chance.

'What people forget is that we beat Celtic twice in 18 days. Once at Parkhead in the league and once at Hampden, and with two different teams. I made five changes between the first game and the second, which was unheard of because people would ask "Why change a winning team?" In the first game at Parkhead we knew that if Celtic won they would win the title and I was damn sure that wasn't going to happen. Not against my team. I ripped into my players before kick-off and I said there was no way that a team of mine would allow another to celebrate a league championship victory against us. I must have put the fear of death in them because they were magnificent and won 2–1.

'Then we had them again in the Scottish Cup final and I made five changes, one enforced. I had paid £40,000 for Steve Murray from Dundee and he was brilliant in the game at Parkhead but he was ineligible for the final and couldn't play. I think it is important that managers have the guts to trust their instinct, and although I hadn't played Joe Harper at Parkhead I put him in against Celtic in the Scottish Cup final as I felt the 4–2–4 system would work better with him in it. I was right. Jim Forrest and Harper were brilliant and Jim Brogan and Billy McNeill in the Celtic defence didn't know what to do. Brogan was tearing his hair out and McNeill looked lost. We were brilliant.

'Don't listen to a manager who says he is trying to protect his young players by not playing them much. If they are good enough, they are old enough to be thrown into any team. Martin Buchan was just 21 years old when he lifted the Scottish Cup as captain of Aberdeen. That victory made him grow up quicker than anything else that could have happened to him.'

Turnbull enjoyed his time at Aberdeen and narrowly finished behind Celtic in the 1970–71 league race. But his family, particularly his wife, never properly settled and when an offer came to return to Easter Road as manager of Hibs in the summer of 1971 it was obvious he would jump at the chance. 'It was the move I had wanted all my life but I felt I had let the Aberdeen boys down. I felt responsible for them. I sat them down and explained that sometime in their own careers they would have to make a similar decision to the one I had just made. They would only know if it was wrong or right afterwards.'

When he had been manager at Queen's Park and Aberdeen Turnbull laid down the law from day one. When he arrived at Easter Road he once again found things not to his liking and had an excuse to get angry. 'I still remember what happened to this day,' said Turnbull, 'On my first day there I was handed a tracksuit by the physio, Tom McNiven, with a hole in it. I was the new manager and I got a tracksuit with a hole in it. Not good enough. I went mad. From that day on, every Friday at Easter Road, the trainer would come round and hang the gear up properly for the game the next day. Every article of clothing would be pressed and looked over with a fine-tooth comb. Anything untoward and I would give the chap who laid it out absolute hell. There were no holes in any training gear or our strips from that day on.

'For me, proper match day preparation is vital. Everybody in my team had to wear suits on match days. They had to look smart. I can't believe what happens nowadays with players walking off the team coach in tracksuits, chewing gum with great big headphones on listening to music. That would never happen in my day. It's a disgrace. They are representing their clubs, not going down the pub. Even on the pitch the players get away with murder with the way they turn out. "Dress smart, play smart", I always said. Everybody in my teams had to be the same. No shirt outside the shorts. Tuck them all in. Look like a team and you play like a team.'

The highlight for Turnbull during his time at Hibs was yet another win over Celtic, this time in the 1972–73 League Cup final at Hampden which they won 2–1. His stylish team became known as 'Turnbull's Tornadoes' and finished second in the league in 1974 and 1975. For many Hibs fans the unforgettable result was a 7–0 win over Hearts on New Year's Day, 1973. It was a match that Turnbull believes was won because of pre-match research on the way Hearts played, not by him but by his assistant, John Fraser.

'Everything I did at Hibs I wrote down in a big ledger. After finishing training I would sit with John Fraser and we would write things down. How certain players had performed, who needed a boot up the bum, who was looking sluggish. I kept updating it and you could see which players were improving, which ones were getting worse. I also did lots of research before each game on the opposition. Before that famous game against Hearts it was John who studied them closely and found they were weak down the left-hand side. They didn't play with a left-winger and the midfield didn't push up much. John thought if I made Alex Edwards an attacking right-sided midfielder he could cause damage down that side, and by God he did. That idea came from John, not me, and showed that sometimes, if you have good people around you, people you can trust, it works for you.'

Turnbull's great time as manager of Hibs came to an end under circumstances he regrets to this day. It involved one of the greatest players in the world, the late George Best. The Hibs fans may have rejoiced when Best joined the club as they were fighting relegation in the 1979–80 season, but not Turnbull. He was furious when Best was brought in by chairman Tom Hart behind his back.

'He is the greatest regret of my managerial career. He was the only player ever signed behind my back. He was an alcoholic when he came to us. At his peak he was up there with Pele, Maradona and Cruyff but he was on the way down and way past his peak when he played at Easter Road. All he did was disrupt the dressing room with his behaviour.

'Tom Hart, who ran the club, was adamant that Best would be coming whether I liked it or not. We were going through a sticky spell and it's well known that directors do not like the crowd getting to them. They can't take it. They brought Best in without telling me and it was a huge mistake. They only brought him in to get the crowd off their backs. He added little to the team and was a waste of time.'

It was the beginning of the end for Turnbull. Feeling compromised by the decision to sign Best, and with results going from bad to worse, he knew his time at Hibs was up. He left the club at the end of the season and the curtain came down on his managerial career in 1980 at the age of 57.

Looking back, Turnbull admits that his players probably saw him as a barrack-room sergeant with no soft side, a man they could not really get close to. 'They were probably not far wrong. As a manager you have to take a step back. You have to remember I had to be tough as I was up against some great managers at the time. Jock Stein was a big rival of mine. We certainly weren't big pals, as we were different types of managers. I could take my players out on the training field and work out tactics with them. Stein was a blackboard man, noughts and crosses instead of real players. That was him. I listened to managers I admired like Tommy Docherty and Matt Busby. Matt took his football knowledge and gave it back to his players on the training field. Bill Shankly was a great man but more a man-manager than Busby. They are the best two I can think of.

'Nowadays Alex Ferguson is the best, but then again I taught him on the SFA coaching courses! He was in the training squad that Willie Ormond and I took when he was trying to get his badges. He learned a lot on that coaching course and has kept learning all the time. I bet he is still learning now.'

What advice would Turnbull give to those wanting to be a manager? 'My advice to young managers today would be to be positive and get the players believing in themselves. Talk to them, talk to them all the time, tell them how good they are, go out onto the training field and work with them. You also have to learn yourself, all the time. Remember, the more you know what you are talking about the more you will have the upper hand over your players. You are older than your players, more experienced. Play on that. Show them what they are doing right and what they are doing wrong. Let's face it, some of the young players you work with aren't the sharpest tools in the box.'

Turnbull was saying all of this at the age of 86. Still as sharp as ever.

Jim McLean

'I could never relax as a manager and I still struggle with it to this day. Even when I cut my grass I take it seriously. I get blazing mad if I don't cut it evenly. I want it done as perfect as it can be, just like I wanted my football.'

Jim McLean, to paraphrase the late, great Frank Sinatra, certainly did it his way when he was the manager of Dundee United. Like the famous crooner he has regrets, and more than a few.

To say he has been left with a few inner demons to deal with because of his time in football management is something of an understatement. He may have had great success but he keeps asking himself: at what personal cost? There are many football managers out there who ended up divorced and sadly had bad relationships with their children, all because football took over their lives. McLean is not one of them, and counts himself lucky that he has a happy marriage and a good relationship with his grown-up children.

But he accepts it could so easily have gone the other way because of the time he gave to the job. 'Football managers, in general, end up neglecting their family because the job just takes them over,' said McLean, 'If I had my time again I would have had a better balance in my life. I gave too much to football and too little to my family, and I regret that a lot.'

At least McLean can look back with a degree of satisfaction on the fact that his personal sacrifices turned out to be professionally worthwhile. For a golden period in the 1980s he and Alex Ferguson, who was manager at Aberdeen, created the 'New Firm' of Scottish football. Their ability to find and nurture top talent made both teams genuine challengers to Celtic and Rangers.

Although the haul of trophies won by Ferguson at Aberdeen far outweighed the number lifted by McLean's Dundee United, the competition was fierce between the two managers. Although for the most part good-natured, it did reach comical proportions at times. 'When "Fergie" was at Aberdeen he heard we had a good five-a-side team made up of the coaching staff at Dundee United, which included me and Walter Smith. He got a team together from Aberdeen with players like Archie Knox and Jim "Chalky" Whyte from his coaching staff and they came to Dundee and we gave them a real tanking.

'At the end of the game Fergie claimed the match was over two legs, obviously because he had been beaten, and we had to return to Aberdeen to play them the following week. We had no choice in the matter. We had to go. We quite fancied the challenge but when we got there Fergie had his under-18 goalkeeper between the sticks and had a youth player in his team. And do you know, we still beat them! He was so, so furious. He wanted to make it best of five games but we said no and that we were the five-a-side champs. Fergie was even more angry this time and that fury over a simple five-a-side game showed how competitive he was. He was running a professional football club but still got mad when he lost a couple of bounce games. It was attitude, the desire never to be beaten at anything, that made him a great manager.'

While Ferguson eventually decided to leave Aberdeen and join Manchester United – only after turning down others, including Rangers – McLean stayed at Dundee United for all of his career, making him the longest-serving manager of a Scottish League club in the post-war period. From 1971 to 1993 he was manager and got the best out of household names like Paul Sturrock, David Narey, Paul Hegarty, Davie Dodds, Hamish McAlpine and others in some great Dundee United teams.

He took the Tannadice side to the Scottish Premier League title in 1982–83 and the semi-finals of the European Cup the following season, where they lost narrowly to Roma. He won the League Cup in 1979–80 and 1980–81 and steered United to the final of the UEFA Cup in 1987, where they were beaten by Gothenburg. Before McLean arrived United had never won a major trophy. On the road to that UEFA final he masterminded a quarter-final victory over Barcelona, who were coached by Terry Venables, and a semi-final win over Borussia Monchengladbach, whose manager was Jupp Heynckes.

'The win over Barcelona was one of the sweetest of my career,' remembers McLean, 'Terry Venables was their manager and they had Gary Lineker and Mark Hughes on their books. The English press, and no doubt the Spanish press as well, gave us no chance. We won the first leg 1–0 at Tannadice and the second 2–1 at the Nou Camp. That result, more than any other, put Dundee United on the football map. After all, we were a club with attendances of around 10,000 at home that had just beaten the mighty Barcelona, who could get 100,000 people at some games.

It wasn't like-for-like, but us Scots like being underdogs. It makes us fight more.

'To lose the UEFA Cup final was a disappointment. I wanted to follow Jock Stein, Willie Waddell and Alex Ferguson in winning European trophies with Scottish clubs, but we'd had a long, hard season and the matches against Gothenburg were too much for us. We lost the first leg 1–0 away and drew 1–1 at home. Even now, that defeat to Gothenburg is my biggest regret in football. Professionally, it was a dark night for me.'

McLean had more than a few dark nights in football and always looked on edge whenever he was prowling a touchline. He was the sort of manager who provoked controversy wherever he went. A complex character, he received love and loathing from his players in equal measure and made no apology for his single-minded attitude during his time at Tannadice.

He was the man who fined his Dundee United team for not trying hard enough in a game they won 6–1 at Motherwell; who admitted to crying in frustration after matches and who claimed he felt he did not pull his weight when assistant manager of Scotland under Jock Stein, although Stein never at any stage criticised his work-rate. On top of that, he always worried he might die in a dugout just like Stein tragically did, such was the intensity he felt when he was on the touchline. McLean also had a quick temper, which cost him dearly when he punched a BBC reporter, John Barnes, who asked him an after-match question he didn't want to answer.

For a man who should have been praised to the heavens in his own land – especially in the Dundee area – he admitted that at times during his career he felt strangely alone, angry that he gave so much of his life to football. Even now he sounds bitter at what he perceives as the personal cost of his football career.

'Success is important for football clubs but not at any cost, which is something I lost sight of. I will always regret that I was a stranger to my kids when they were at school. I gave my all to Dundee United and everything else was pushed into the background.

Because of that I would never recommend football management as a way of life for anybody. For me it was a seven-day working week, morning and night. I'm not saying I was much different to most managers of my time but people don't realise the sacrifices I made. I was 22 years as manager and 29 years 10 months in total with Dundee United and I worked like a dog through it all. Nothing got pushed to the background at the club. I confronted everything and brought my problems home.'

McLean remains good friends with Sir Alex Ferguson but believes the single-minded attitudes they brought to their professional careers came with a heavy cost to their personal lives. 'It is a Scottish trait to work hard,' said McLean, 'Alex Ferguson has been a beacon to other managers, especially Scottish ones, and showed what can be achieved through putting the hours in. That all comes at a cost, though. Alex said his wife Cathy brought up their kids because he was so busy all the time with football. That is both embarrassing and sickening to think about and 100 per cent true in my case as well.

'My wife, Doris, brought up our two kids as I hardly saw them because I was working all the time. I don't want to insult Alex Ferguson, as he is a great man, but I just hope he was in contact with his kids more often than I was with mine. I wasn't around enough and felt constantly guilty because of it. You never get that time with your kids back. Also, let's face it, what long term thanks did I, or any other manager, get for putting his club before his family? None.'

McLean claimed he was never close to having a mental breakdown during his time as a manager but admitted that he felt a bit depressed on a number of occasions. Being away from his family and the constant pressure of keeping up the high standards he set with United became too much at times.

'I went to Denmark where Morten Wieghorst, who used to play for Celtic and Dundee, was playing for a team we were due to face in Europe. I found myself walking up to the stadium, which also had a swimming pool and a tennis court for kids. Out of the corner of my eye I saw a dad walking towards me hand in hand with his two kids and I nearly started crying. It made me think of how little I saw my children. My youngest son played ice hockey at ten o'clock on a Friday night as that was the only time we could get ice for practice so Doris took him because I had a game on a Saturday and that I would be in bed. That day in Denmark just reminded me that I didn't have time to do things with my kids and what I had been missing out on. These feelings came and went during my career and near the end, when I was chairman and manager of United, I got really down at times and was on anti-depressants.'

McLean sometimes looks back in anger at his time in football, which is a shame considering the pleasure and enjoyment he gave to United fans and the success he brought to the club and to Scottish football. He still asks himself just why he did it. When he left the club there was a period when some United fans ignored him or, at the very worst, turned against him. It was only in the summer of 2009 that he made his peace with them, receiving a standing ovation as guest of honour at a Dundee United Centenary dinner.

He can talk with emotion about the amount of effort he put into his managerial career, the endless hours he spent away from home. Such are the traces of bitterness left in McLean you get the feeling he doesn't really care too much what people think about him nowadays or about what his legacy will be. 'My time at Dundee United was not 99 per cent, it was 100 per cent. It started on a Sunday morning and went straight on to the following Saturday night. I never went to church on Sunday morning because I was out all over the public parks of Dundee with Doug Cowie and Davie Small, the local scouts, looking for talent. Doris took my youngest son, Gary, to football on the Sunday.

'Monday I was at Tannadice at nine o'clock in the morning, took training and went home for my tea at five o'clock. I then went back up to Tannadice to watch the part-timers train and the schoolboys and although I didn't take the Monday sessions I felt it was my duty to be there. Tuesday I was at the club all day then had a Jim McLean Coaching School at Gussie Park to attend in the evening and on Wednesday, if we didn't have an evening game, I would be at the club till late at night. Thursday I was there all day and had another coaching school in the evening. Friday night should have been the only night I had free to be with my family. But most times I liked to play reserve games on a Friday night so I could see the fringe players before the first-team game on a Saturday, and of course Saturday I was away with the first team. Then the whole thing started again on the Sunday. It was just too much, and for what?

'There is no way anybody should commit themselves the way I and other football managers did. Bill Shankly was wrong to say football was more important than life or death. Rubbish. Football is not more important than life and I would never live that way again. People might think I am bitter because of what happened at Dundee United and the way we fell out for a while, but that's not the case. I'm bitter because of what I missed out on in ordinary life, things that other people took for granted.'

McLean remains a mercurial character and there are stories from players who portray him as a bully who kept them on long-term contracts and would never let them leave the club until the price was right. He was aloof, with a quick-fire temper towards them, and many never warmed to him. Born in Larkhall and raised in nearby Ashgill, Lanarkshire, McLean emerged as a powerful and single-minded personality. Some interviewed for this book refused to go on record about McLean, but talking to them it was clear that he may have been respected but he was also disliked by some of them for the way he ran the club with an iron fist. That complexity of character seemed to be linked to a lack of confidence that dogged him throughout his life. He freely admitted he lacked self-esteem, and without the support of men like Dundee manager John Prentice, who took him to Dens Park in 1970 as his assistant, he would never have made it as a manager.

He also holds in high regard men like Eddie Turnbull, who he believes was the best coach of his generation. According to McLean the Hearts boss Bobby Seith, who also worked with Rangers, never got the recognition he deserved as one of Scotland's top coaches. 'Managers like Turnbull and Seith made you want to play for them, made you feel wanted. When a player is insecure in his own ability, like I was, a quiet word in his ear before kick-off makes all the difference. Seith was one of the best coaches in Scottish football and Turnbull was the absolute best in the business. I went down to get my SFA coaching badges at Largs and wasn't sure I would be good enough to get through. Eddie was in charge of my class and explained things superbly and helped me get through it.

'Also I remember I had to room with Alex Ferguson on that course, who I hadn't met beforehand. He told me he'd got married the day before the course started and I said to him "You're not having your honeymoon with me!" I like to think he was joking, but the way Fergie and folk like me gave our lives to football, you can never be sure.'

As a manager McLean's philosophy was a simple one, which he maintains gained him success. He suspects that nowadays maybe too much information is given to players.

'Possession, possession. I used to try and drum into my players the importance of keeping the ball. Get possession and keep possession and you should win games provided you have penetration in front of goal, which we always had at United. Square balls and balls back to defenders never hurt the opposition. Get forward. Be positive. Also get a hard-tackling ball winner in midfield. As a player I couldn't tackle a fish supper but I always knew it was important to get a guy with dig in the middle of the park.'

McLean was offered 11 other jobs while at Dundee United – the most high-profile being the chance to move to Rangers in 1983 after John Greig resigned. The Ibrox club put together a lucrative package that included a £100,000 house for McLean in the west of Scotland, doubling his basic salary and guaranteeing him the same pension and bonus rights he enjoyed at Tannadice.

'When I was offered the Rangers job the United chairman Johnston Grant was on the phone crying down the line, pleading with me not to go. Later he brought flowers for Doris and sweeties for me. It was a Saturday night and we had just lost to Dundee. Because the players hadn't tried a bloody leg they were probably in raptures at the thought of getting rid of me before I got stuck into them at training on the Monday morning. I thought long and hard about joining Rangers but felt because I had put some players on long-term contracts, had a real affection for the club and wanted Dundee United to be successful, I didn't have it in my heart to walk away. I would have been a real hypocrite to turn my back on Tannadice.

'What made my mind up finally was when I thought about my time as a joiner before I was a footballer, when I built a few houses. To me a football club is like a house – much easier to knock down than to build in the first place. I felt I had laid the foundations at United, the roof was about finished and I didn't want to knock everything down by moving to Rangers.

'Looking back, in football terms I was a fool not to take the Rangers job, and my loyalty was misplaced. I was very much against being under pressure not to sign Catholics for Rangers if I took the job – although I was told I could if I wanted to – but I should have still taken the job anyway and tested their resolve.

'The resources at Ibrox would have been great and it would have been a tremendous challenge for me to take over such a big club. I got other offers from Hibs, Hearts, Chelsea and West Ham to manage them but I also turned them all down through the years. I stayed with Dundee United out of loyalty. I wouldn't say, for a time, that loyalty was recognised properly by all the supporters.'

Looking over his career McLean felt that maybe he was not best suited to being a manager. That self-doubt, his inability to accept he was ever doing a good-enough job, drove him on to a professional life that at times was full of torment. 'I enjoyed being a coach more than a manager. I loved taking training sessions but didn't particularly like speaking to the press. I maybe did get a bit too uptight about what they wrote. I was very superstitious and I had to wear the same underpants, socks, shirts, shoes if we won. I never came close to cracking up. I was depressed a lot but never worse than that. In saying that, I was on anti-depression pills late in my career, more when I was chairman. I found taking the job as chairman of Dundee United was one of the biggest mistakes I made. It was stupid. The pressure was huge and it was stupid of me to stay on.'

McLean stepped down as manager in the summer of 1993, remained as chairman until 2000, and severed his formal connection by selling his shareholding in 2002. He remains a keen watcher of football and football managers, and in the modern game the two things that bother him more than anything are the amount of diving and the financial demands from players. 'The British game has always been a physical one and I felt it was one of the most honest in the world. Back in my day players didn't dive the way they do now. That sort of nonsense has been brought into the Scottish and British game by the foreign players. Some of the worst offenders a few years ago were the Hearts players like that Lithuanian chap Saulius Mikoliunas who dived to get a penalty for his country against Scotland. That was a disgrace.

'Also the money the players are asking for is ridiculous. I cringe nowadays when I hear people say they need a house, a car, their phone bill paid before they will even put pen to paper. I was 27 before I got into full-time football. We did not have a phone in our house and I drove a second-hand Vauxhall Viva which cost £40. I paid for that with my own money and it was the first car I ever had.'

McLean has always been able to spot whether or not players had the right attitude to the game, and felt that managers should look for the extent of their competitive edge before they buy. 'Managers are spending millions on players nowadays and I would tell them to learn as much as they can about their signings beforehand. I always called in character references before I signed anybody. I wanted players with the right attitude. Everybody who succeeds in the game hates losing. Show me a good loser and I will show you a loser. As a manager you have to keep one step ahead of the players. Always remember that when a team wins the players see themselves in the dressing-room mirror. If they lose they see everybody else and want to blame their manager rather than themselves. I could never relax as a manager and I still struggle with it to this day. Even when I cut my grass I take it seriously. I get blazing mad if I don't cut it evenly. I want it done as perfect as it can be, just like I wanted my football.'

McLean believes that any manager wanting to be successful in the game should not be afraid to ask for advice and listen closely to the more experienced men, in the same way he learned from Turnbull. 'My advice to young managers would be listen closely and choose whose coaching techniques and managerial style you want to copy. I used to go to Hibs games in the early 1970s when Turnbull was manager because he was the best in Scotland at the time. I used to go to Perth, Greenock, anywhere to watch Hibs. It didn't matter who they were playing. I went all over the place because there was always something new to learn, maybe from the way he set his team out or the way he changed tactics at half-time.

'Watching Eddie's teams made me realise that one of the most stupid statements in the world is that your job as a manager finishes when the players cross the line and the match starts. Absolute and total rubbish. When the players are out on the pitch you are watching, taking notes, working out what to say to them at half-time. Who to substitute, who to put on. Games can be won and lost by managerial decisions made over the 90 minutes.'

The basic fundamentals of football management remain unchanged. 'One thing I think never changes in management is how you should deal with the players. You have to have a single-minded approach. If a manager is liked by the players then you can look at him being out of a job very quickly. If players get it easy in training then they'll take it easy in games. Players won't give their best unless they are pushed. Golfers or tennis players, sportsmen in individual sports, don't have the same attitude as footballers. In our game players want to blame others. Individual sportsmen accept responsibility. Some footballers don't. I always did and I have lain in bed after bad results and cried. I can't imagine many players have done that.'

Tommy Walker

'Walker may have had a gentle personality but, being born of a West Lothian shale-mining family, he was no soft touch.'

Heart of Midlothian's honours list exposes one of life's great myths. Conventional wisdom has it that nice guys finish second. They say you can't be a good manager without being ruthless, without taking decisions which are painful and hurt people. Supposedly a man has to make all sorts of concessions in his personal integrity if he wants to make it in the dugout. When Liam Brady took over at Celtic he said: 'I've heard it said that you can't be a football manager and tell the truth. Well, I'm going to have a go at it.'

Brady didn't last at Parkhead, not that the Irishman can claim that it was his honesty which had anything to do with that. In fact, because of what happened at Hearts between 1951 and 1966 no manager in Scotland can ever allege that they had to compromise their beliefs and personal morals to succeed. In those fifteen years Hearts claimed seven major Scottish trophies, by far the most successful period in their history. The manager who won them was one of the most decent men ever to grace Scottish football. Tommy Walker was the nice guy who finished first.

Walker tended to receive a description which is rarely applied in football these days. Almost everyone thought him 'a gentleman'. He had a warm, kind face and a demeanour which exuded inner and outer calm. Throughout his life he was active in the service of

St George's West Church in Edinburgh, and in 1937 he embarked on a course of theological studies. After a wartime spell in India he returned in philosophical mood and seriously considered studying for the Ministry of the Church of Scotland. In the end the Church lost out to Hearts, but it was a close contest.

As a skilled and elegant inside-forward he was one of the finest players Hearts and Scotland produced. Arsenal wanted to pay a world record £12,500 for him in 1934 but Hearts were fearful of how supporters would react to his sale and successfully kept hold of him. They had him all the way until he joined Chelsea for less than half that amount at the end of the Second World War. For Scotland there were nine goals in twenty appearances, including a couple that made him a hero.

Walker may have had a gentle personality but, being born of a West Lothian shale-mining family, he was no soft touch. In John Rafferty's book, *One Hundred Years of Scottish Football*, he recounts the famous penalty Walker took against England at Wembley in 1936: 'It was a windy day. He placed the ball on the spot and stepped back. It was blown off. He replaced it and as he moved to take the kick it was blown off again. The crowd were silent, guessing that one so young must be at breaking point . . . Again the ball was placed, firmly driven into the ground, and it stayed. Tommy Walker shot the equalising goal as if it were a practice match.'

Scotland were a goal down at Wembley with only 13 minutes left when Walker nervelessly stuck away that penalty. He was just 20 years old. Two years later he went back to Wembley and scored the only goal in a 1–0 Scotland win. As a player he made 354 appearances for Hearts, scored 190 goals, and won nothing.

More revealing of the man than his admirable ability with a football were the exceptional levels of sportsmanship and fair play he brought to the game. Walker did not trouble match officials. Whenever he appeared to have hurt an opponent – it goes without saying that he only ever did so by accident – he was immediately and genuinely apologetic. He would shake his opponent's hand if he had committed a foul and he sought no advantage from bending the rules or questioning decisions. Once, when Hearts put the ball in the net only for the 'goal' to be disallowed for an infringement, only one of their players did not crowd the referee in an attempt to reverse the decision. Walker stood aside. Needless to say, he did not swear. There is usually a suspicion that players with such angelic reputations are too nice for their own good, certainly too weak to be serious candidates for management. Not this one. Albeit that he worked in more innocent times, when there were no agents and a less aggressive media to deal with, Walker would show himself to be a man of substance.

London could not keep him away from Tynecastle for long. He left Chelsea to return as Hearts' player/assistant manager to Davie McLean at the end of 1948 and took over as manager on 18 February 1951 after McLean's sudden death. The circumstances were sad but in a football sense it was a highly promising time to take charge. In 1949–50 Hearts had begun a sequence of 11 consecutive top-four finishes in the league. Walker inherited 'The Terrible Trio' of Willie Bauld, Alfie Conn and Jimmy Wardhaugh, three club legends to whom he would add a fourth of his own: Dave Mackay.

Hibs had scheduled an interview with the teenage Mackay (who was on Hearts' books as a schoolboy at the time and was a fan of the club) but Walker got wind of it and was cute. He arranged an interview as well, to take place 30 minutes earlier than Hibs's one. The outcome was a formality. When his distinguished career was over Mackay wrote in his autobiography, *The Real Mackay*: 'I was never sent off in 30 years of playing football and neither Bill Nicholson nor Tommy Walker were managers who would entertain having a dirty and cynical player in their teams. It was not their style. Never did Tommy Walker, Bill Nicholson or Brian Clough tell us to waste time or adopt defensive tactics.'

Walker encouraged his players to express themselves, to show their individuality and to play with freedom. His captain, Bobby

Parker, said of his trophy-winning years: 'It was certainly Tommy Walker's team. My recollection is of Mr Walker's tremendous influence on me and the other young players.' When possible he would promote young talent. Typical was his decision to play 17-year-old Alan Gordon in the 1961–62 League Cup final against Rangers rather than the ageing club legend Willie Bauld.

There were early signs that Walker would be innovative in his efforts to make Hearts a force. When the club made a pre-season tour of Germany he was impressed by the fitness of players at Kickers Offenbach and invited their coach, Paul Osswald, to Scotland to help with the conditioning of his own players before the 1951–52 season.

Walker always acknowledged the solid foundations he inherited from his predecessor, and although there was the sense of things slowly coming together for Hearts his labours would not bear fruit until victory in the League Cup final of October 1954. That was Hearts' first trophy since 1906. More than that, it opened the floodgates. The club began the greatest era in its history. In the following campaign, 1955–56, he steered Hearts to Scottish Cup victory for the first time in 50 years. 'We knew each other and our respective strengths and weaknesses inside out,' wrote Mackay, 'Tommy Walker's personality and ethos had been stamped on us. Without overtly saying it, he had taught us to believe in ourselves without slipping into arrogance or complacency.'

After a trophyless season there were then three in a row which yielded silverware: the championship in 1957–58, another League Cup in 1958–59, and a championship and League Cup double in 1959–60. The last trophy won under Walker – his seventh – was the 1962–63 League Cup. The title-winning side of 1957–58 was phenomenal. Hearts scored a Scottish top-flight record of 132 goals in that campaign and over 34 matches they claimed 62 points from a possible 68. They lost only once. They played the Old Firm four times that season and won the lot.

It was the club's greatest side. Mackay left early in 1959 and 'The Terrible Trio' disbanded months later, but for 1959–60 Walker rebuilt a second great team and set Hearts on the way to their second league title in three seasons. He was thorough: he would send scouts to watch future opponents and pore over their findings. A commitment to professional training methods included using weights to work on specific muscle groups, which helped make Hearts perhaps the most physically impressive team in the country. His thinking could be innovative, if not always rewarded. In 1960–61 he was ahead of other managers by setting his team out in a 4–2–4 formation, but Hearts sold stars Alex Young and George Thomson and scored only 51 goals to finished seventh in a poor defence of their championship.

There were another five full seasons under Walker, who had by then been awarded an OBE, but it was to be a period of slow decline, in which the club won another League Cup but challenged for the title only once. In 1964–65 they should have been champions again and had only to avoid a two-goal defeat against Kilmarnock at Tynecastle to win the league on the final day. They lost by a dreaded 2–0 and surrendered the championship by 0.04 of a goal under the old goal average system. They scored 90 league goals to Kilmarnock's 62 that season, but that counted for nothing.

People looked for a scapegoat and Walker was an obvious target. The writing was on the wall for an increasingly divided club and dressing room. In the book *Hearts Great Tynecastle Tales*, Bobby Kirk, who served as full-back from 1955 to 1963, gives an unflattering account of Walker's man-management. 'I read in an early edition of the *Evening News* that I was being released. I expected to be shown a bit more respect after spending eight years at the club but that seemed to be the way they worked in those days. That was Hearts' style at the time, and I blame Tommy Walker.

'He had a great reputation as a player but he wasn't respected as a manager, certainly not by me anyway. I ended up back at Tynecastle coaching the youngsters in 1967, but the only reason I went back there was that Tommy Walker had left. I couldn't have faced him again, that's for sure.' Others were critical towards the end, too, but that was a minority view. Most of the players who served him regarded Walker as an outstanding manager and an exceptional man.

Hearts finished seventh in Walker's last full season. In September 1966, in the aftermath of eight players having submitted transfer requests and general suggestions that he had 'lost' the dressing room, the Hearts board put pressure on Walker to resign. His nature dictated that he would do as they asked rather than challenge the directors who wanted him out, even though by agreeing to resign he forfeited much of the severance payment to which he was entitled. It need hardly be said that he made no public complaints to the press about his treatment. The club's 'reward' for dealing with one of their legendary figures in such a merciless fashion was a long period of bleak decline and eventual relegation.

After being Hearts manager for 15 years he was not lost to football for long. There were spells at Dunfermline and Raith Rovers and work as a scout for Sheffield United. His personality was also reflected in the period he spent working in social services, concerning himself in the care of children with special needs.

When Lord Wheatley was asked to compile a government report on crowd control after the 1971 Ibrox Disaster he consulted widely and praised the shrewd, charitable contributions made by Walker. For the most part he had a low profile after leaving Hearts.

People moved on from Tynecastle and in October 1974 Walker accepted an invitation to return and become a Hearts director. He remained on the board until May 1980. It was where he belonged. When this softly-spoken, compassionate man passed away in Edinburgh at the age of 77 on 11 January 1993, Hearts lost the most successful manager the club has ever had.

Such is Walker's legendary status down Tynecastle way that in 1998, when Hearts won the Scottish Cup, manager Jim Jefferies stood in Edinburgh City Chambers at a civic reception and said how proud he was to follow in the steps of the late, great Tommy Walker in lifting the trophy. The whole Hearts first team broke into spontaneous applause. It was a fitting tribute to a true Tynecastle great.

Willie McCartney and Hugh Shaw

'He never once gave us the ball to play with. He was one of those who thought that if we were starved of it through the week we would be desperate to get it on the Saturday.' – Lawrie Reilly

Between them, Willie McCartney and Hugh Shaw assembled the most successful and famous team in the history of Hibernian Football Club. The key area of their most exciting side was a forward line that would be known forever as 'The Famous Five'. They had a quarter of a century of Easter Road management: McCartney was in charge for 12 years and then Shaw stepped up to replace him for the next 13.

McCartney, a former referee who had previously been in charge of Hearts for 16 trophyless years from 1919, became the manager and Shaw the first-team trainer at Easter Road in 1936. They worked together successfully for 12 years, during which Hibs steadily improved to the point that they were league and Scottish Cup runners-up in 1947. Just when they were on the point of a breakthrough the formidable partnership was brought to a premature end when McCartney died of a heart attack after a Scottish Cup tie against Albion Rovers on 24 January 1948.

With Hibs top of the league at the time, just ahead of Bill Struth's Rangers, the Hibs board of directors moved quickly to minimise disruption within the club. While they grieved for McCartney, Shaw was appointed as his successor within a week. It was a speedy decision that paid off handsomely. Hibs held their nerve to pip the Ibrox club to the 1947–48 league title by just two points and bring the championship flag to Easter Road for the first time since 1903.

It had been Shaw who'd seen them over the finishing line, but the groundwork for that 1948 success was laid by McCartney. He signed all of 'The Famous Five': Gordon Smith, Bobby Johnstone, Lawrie Reilly, Eddie Turnbull and Willie Ormond. Only Johnstone, who was brought into the first team by Shaw, did not emerge under McCartney.

Hibs were the finest side in the land. After the 1948 title win they finished second in 1949–50 before becoming champions again in 1950–51 and 1951–52. There would have been a third consecutive league triumph in 1953 if Rangers had not denied them on goal average, having finished level on points. They were runners-up in the 1950–51 League Cup. In 1955 Shaw's Hibs became the first British side to play in European competition (they were invited to represent Scotland despite having finished fifth in the league). They defeated German and Swedish opposition to reach the semi-finals of the inaugural European Cup before being eliminated by the French club Stade Rheims, who narrowly lost the final to Real Madrid.

Shaw had five good years at Easter Road before the sparkle started to fade. A pivotal moment came in 1955 when Johnstone left for Manchester City and 'The Famous Five' were fractured. Shaw could find no major new talent, apart from Joe Baker, to maintain Hibs' status and prolong the glory era at Easter Road. The side deteriorated and slipped to mid-table mediocrity. By November 1961, when he resigned after almost 14 years in charge, the great days of the late 1940s and early 1950s were a distant memory.

Reilly played under both men, signing for McCartney in 1946 at the age of 16 and then playing for Shaw for a decade. 'They were a good double act when McCartney was manager and Shaw the trainer, but they were very different people,' he said, 'Willie McCartney was a formidable figure and despite the fact he had been Hearts manager before joining Hibs he was very popular with the fans. The fact he had moved across the city really captured their imagination. I'm told more than 25,000 turned up to watch his first game in charge. Hibs had been pretty poor before he arrived but he transformed them. When he came to sign me he cut a real dash with his bow tie, Homburg hat and big overcoat. That was his usual garb, even on match days. You could see him coming a mile off.

'He was a larger-than-life character who was a father figure to me in the two years before he died. He was an impresario, a real showman, but to be honest I'm not sure he loved football that much despite his years in the game. He was a referee before he became a manager, which you have to say is an unusual route. He never took the training, never gave a team talk, never really got involved too much in team affairs. He would just tell us to go out there and enjoy ourselves. But he was a shrewd businessman on behalf of the club. I got £20 as a signing-on fee and Gordon Smith got a tenner. He was always tight with the club money. He must have been pretty good with his own money too as he had a big house in the Barnton area of Edinburgh, just off the Corstorphine Road.

'He was very much his own man who didn't like interference. For example Harry Swan, who was the Hibs chairman, used to come into the dressing room at half-time in most games, something which most managers would go mad at nowadays. McCartney would let him speak but then when he left used to say to us "Just forget everything that little bastard just said." And we always did.

'Hugh Shaw was more of a football man than McCartney as he had been a player with Hibs in the 1920s and played in two losing Scottish Cup finals. He was our trainer for a long time under McCartney. There were no problems when he made the step up to manager. When he was trainer he used to have us running up and down Arthur's Seat, up the steps of the stand, anywhere he could think of. He never once gave us the ball to play with. He was one of those who thought that if we were starved of it through the week we would be desperate to get it on the Saturday. Like McCartney, he was never one for big pre-match team talks. In the late 1940s and early 1950s it must have been easy for Shaw as the team very nearly picked itself. We had a great group of players who were a credit to the club and it's just a shame there wasn't more success because we came close to winning the league on two other occasions. I'll always look back fondly on both McCartney and Shaw. They laid down some very good foundations for Hibs.'

Bob Shankly – the quieter brother

'Look, listen, learn and keep your tongue to yourself.
Respect and listen to the older players. Bring any
problems straight to me. Do anything I say if you
want to get to the top.'

Bob Shankly had something of his famous younger brother's way with words, it was just that he chose to play to smaller audiences. Bill Shankly had a love affair with the cameras and microphones which was almost as strong as his infatuation with Liverpool Football Club. Bob was cut from a different cloth. When the veteran sports broadcaster, Arthur Montford, reflected on his career he noted that Bob Shankly had been the only Scottish manager who had turned him down for an interview in 32 years. Shankly wasn't rude, just private.

He was an Ayrshire miner: robust, hard, down-to-earth, no-nonsense, short-back-and-sides haircut. He was a man of few words – his wee brother seemed to have taken the family's entire share – but streetwise and in full possession of the trademark Shankly wit. Craig Brown, the popular but peripheral Dundee player who later became a successful Scotland manager, remembers that when the official squad photograph was taken at the start of each season Shankly would tell him to position himself at the side because 'It would be easier to cut you out with the scissors.' When journalists asked him for team news he would tell them next to nothing, explaining that the matter was out of his hands because of his wife: 'Oor Greta hasnae picked the team yet.' As a Shankly, she probably could have.

Although Shankly was a chain-smoker, he believed in a high level of fitness for his players. Hard-work, organisation, simplicity and aggressive, attacking football were his other ideals. Players knew where they stood with him. He kept his football uncomplicated but was ahead of his time in terms of understanding tactics and placing an emphasis on what the opposition would do and how good they could be. Ingenuity was not beyond him. Late one winter night he clambered over the wall of Inverness Caledonian's ground in order to check the state of their pitch before Dundee played a Scottish Cup tie on it the following day.

He once explained the instructions he gave to any new player, especially a young one. 'You could call them the Shankly commandments,' he said, 'Pay attention to what you're told. Look, listen, learn and keep your tongue to yourself. Respect and listen to the older players. Bring any problems straight to me. Do anything I say if you want to get to the top. Above all behave away from the ground so you can command the respect of the public. Oh, it's quite a wee pep talk!'

Like Liverpool's famous 'Shanks', Bob emerged from their home in the tiny mining village of Glenbuck and served his time down the pits, working there long into a playing career which continued until he was 37 and included spells at Alloa and Falkirk. He began coaching at Stenhousemuir before taking over as manager of Falkirk and then Third Lanark. In October, 1959, a few months short of his 50th birthday, he took over at Dundee, being appointed on the day his brother submitted a late application for the job.

Bob Shankly and Dundee scaled the heights together. He inherited a highly promising team and added the inspired finishing touches which turned them into one of the finest sides in Europe. Dundee finished tenth in his first full season but in his second,

1961–62, they were the best in the land. They had outstanding players like Ian Ure, Alex Hamilton, Bobby Cox, Gordon Smith and Alan Gilzean, and they had Shankly to channel and drive them. They went 19 games unbeaten in the league, during which they shocked the country with a 5–1 win against Rangers at Ibrox.

Shankly knew what they were capable of. 'We have a great chance to create some history here,' he said midway through that campaign. They won the championship on the final day of the season, beating St Johnstone 3–0 in front of over 26,000 fans in Perth. Dundee had never been Scottish champions before (or since) and much of the city celebrated long into the night. Shankly? He was seen out mowing his lawn before 9 a.m. the next day.

Dundee mounted a poor defence of their title the following season, finishing ninth in 1963, but Shankly almost won them the European Cup. Dundee eliminated Cologne (beating the German champions 8–1 at Dens Park), Sporting Lisbon and Anderlecht en route to a semi-final meeting with AC Milan. Dundee had finally met their match, losing 5–1 in Italy before the consolation of a 1–0 win in the second leg.

His wonderful team began to break up a couple of years later and Shankly became disillusioned by the club's willingness to sell. When the brightest star of all, Gilzean, joined Tottenham Hotspur at the end of 1964 it was the final straw and he resigned as manager in February 1965. Jock Stein helped him get the Hibs job that had just become vacant because of his own departure for Celtic. Stein was one of Shankly's closest friends. He was an unhurt passenger in the back seat when Stein was seriously injured in a car crash in 1975.

The odd aspect to Shankly's career is why he did not achieve more. He was a strong character with a shrewd football brain. He took Hibs to third in 1968 but they were a long way behind the Old Firm. In the 1967–68 Fairs Cup they eliminated Porto and then produced an astonishing 5–0 Easter Road win over Napoli after losing the first leg 4–1 in Italy. Hibs lost, narrowly, to the great Leeds United side in the next round.

When his attempted team-building was again undermined by losing his best players to bigger clubs, notably Colin Stein to Rangers, he decided to resign. Hibs talked him out of it but when he handed in his notice for a second time in 1969 his mind was made up and he retired from management altogether. In 1971 little Stirling Albion sensed he was unfulfilled and tempted him back into a dugout. He spent two years in charge before becoming the club's general manager and then a director. There was the novelty of Bob being in charge at Stirling's former Annfield ground at the same time that Bill was manager at Anfield.

Another Shankly brother, John, had suffered a fatal heart attack at Hampden while attending the 1960 European Cup final between Real Madrid and Eintracht Frankfurt. Bob would also be taken in a football context. He was representing Stirling Albion at an SFA meeting in 1982 when he, too, suffered a fatal heart attack. He was 72. Almost two decades later Dundee supporters showed he would never be forgotten by voting to name 'The Bob Shankly Stand' in his honour at Dens Park.

There is barely any footage of Bob Shankly and little in the way of his archived quotes. But Liverpool isn't the only city where a 'Shanks' is celebrated.

The 'Sailor' and the Babes

For virtually half a century the Old Firm had it sewn up. In all the years between 1905 and 1947 there was only a single season when neither Rangers nor Celtic finished as the best team in the country. In only one campaign did another club, and another manager, prove to be too good for them.

John Hunter earned his nickname because of the way he walked. He had such a rolling gait that he was said to look like a seaman struggling to cope with dry land, hence he became known to everyone as 'Sailor'. He was a large character, well-liked and respected. His career lasted forever, from playing for Abercorn as an 18-year-old to finally leaving Motherwell aged 80. The highlights as a player were appearing for Liverpool, where he won the First Division, and Arsenal, and scoring a Scottish Cup final winner for Dundee. He was a strong, forceful centre-forward.

But he's not remembered for any of that. The club 'Sailor' is inextricably linked with is Motherwell. When he took over as manager in 1911 it was an era in Scottish football when men could be in charge of a club for decades, and 'Sailor' duly led Motherwell for 35 years. For a spell they consistently finished in the top three and also reached three Scottish Cup finals. Taking the club on tours to South Africa and South America showed his vision and ambition. They were winners, too. A visit to Spain in 1927 saw his team return with both the King of Spain Cup and the Barcelona Cup after beating Real Madrid 3–1 and drawing 2–2 with Barcelona.

'Sailor' was Motherwell's first manager, is still their longest-serving, and is the only one ever to make them champions of Scotland. No-one could live with them in 1931–32. They scored 119 goals in only 38 league games and finished five points clear of Rangers and 18 ahead of Celtic.

He became their manager at 32 and when he finally handed the reins over to someone else he was 67. Not that he was finished working for his club. He put in another 13 years as secretary before failing health nudged him towards retirement aged 80. The great old man of Motherwell passed away seven years later, in 1966.

By then he had enjoyed being a witness to two fine managers who succeeded him. George Stevenson, an inside left who played almost 600 games under 'Sailor' and was a member of the title-winning side, took over as boss in 1946. He outscored his mentor in terms of trophies: the 1950–51 League Cup was won under Stevenson and the 1952 Scottish Cup quickly followed.

Motherwell were a declining force in the league, though, and after nine years Stevenson resigned, creating a vacancy for Bobby Ancell. He was to become one of the evocative names of Scottish football. Early in his reign there came a bold declaration that he would develop exciting young local talent rather than sign older, experienced players. At one point Ancell went almost six years without buying anyone in the transfer market.

Motherwell won nothing under his decade in charge from 1955 to 1965 but for supporters of a certain age the teams known as 'The Ancell Babes' were cherished for their youth and vibrant, attacking football. The nickname was born during the 1958–59 season as Motherwell scored 83 goals in 34 league games and finished third. In 1961 they pulled off a stunning 5–2 Scottish Cup victory against Rangers at Ibrox, although they failed to go on and win the trophy.

Inevitably their play attracted predators as well as admirers. When their star, Ian St John, was plucked away by Liverpool in 1961 Motherwell never successfully replaced him. Others also left, the Babes began to fade, and Ancell resigned, to take over at Dundee early in 1965.

Chapter Eight
The Giants in England

Tommy Docherty

*'Remember, lads, if football directors are too old to do
it to their wives, they'll do it to their managers.'*

Tommy Docherty had all the qualities required to have his name
up in lights. The quick, waspish sense of humour, the irreverence,
the appreciation of how to perform, the willingness to please and
few fears about saying the unsayable: Docherty genuinely could
have made a living as a stand-up comedian. Take this crack from his
after-dinner routine: 'Everybody in Liverpool is getting into this
"City of Culture" thing. I spoke at a dinner there and when I came
out my car was up on four encyclopaedias.'

It wasn't to be. Destiny dictated that he would become one of
the finest football managers of his generation and among the first to
recognise the value of courting the media. He was a showman long
before he was a manager. When he was 11 he would gather other
children to take part in impromptu variety shows for his neighbours in the rough Gorbals area of Glasgow. Songs or jokes, he
would turn his hand to either. Listening to Sid Field, Flanagan and
Allen and George Formby on the family wireless gave him an
appreciation for comedy and entertainment which was still with
him seven decades later. It was the background of a man ideally
suited to a job where people gather round with notebooks and

microphones hoping for a good quote. Few delivered more than Docherty. For reporters, he gave more gifts than Santa.

'I like a laugh. Always have. I have a terrific sense of humour. That's one thing I can claim on my own behalf. Some of the one-liners just come instantly to you and sometimes they're better that way. I enjoy comedy and there are some comedians I really like. I liked Bernard Manning. Having said that, I can swear with the best of them but I don't like the comedians who eff and blind all the time.'

Docherty's best lines entered football folklore: 'I've had more clubs than Jack Nicklaus.' 'I promised Rotherham I'd take them out of the Second Division and I did . . . into the Third.' 'In football when one door shuts, another will slam in your face.' They were so good they were repeated too often and became tired, although that was hardly his fault. An active post-football career as a radio pundit and after-dinner speaker gave him the time and motivation to generate new material, some of it a match for those on the professional stand-up circuit.

'John Barnes' *Football Night* is billed as "The programme that has the whole nation talking". What we're saying is "When is this going to end?"'

'When I watch that antiques programme on TV and see David Dickinson, he strikes me as being living proof the stuff does exactly what it says on the tin.'

'Ron Atkinson couldn't be here. His hairdresser died. In 1946.'

'I can't watch Wimbledon, Watford or Sheffield Wednesday. Football wasn't meant to be run by two linesmen and air traffic control.'

'To the Scots, football is a lovely, incurable disease.'

There has been a price to pay for all the laughs and it is captured in the line about having more clubs than Nicklaus. The jokes have altered and cheapened Docherty's reputation. For many the first things which come to mind about him are the one-liners, the controversial punditry, and the image of a nomadic, hired-and-fired manager. A rent-a-quote who would keep making wisecracks between P45s.

There was much, much more to Docherty than that. Not for nothing had he managed Manchester United, Chelsea, Aston Villa and Scotland by the time he was 49. He was a focused, hungry, driven manager with a fastidious attention to detail. He was years ahead of his time in embracing sports psychology and media manipulation, in checking the bloodline of players who might be eligible for Scotland caps, and in bringing African players to the English League. He was still serving as a player when the SFA asked him to compile reports on the opposition at the 1958 World Cup finals. These aren't the acts of someone who was nothing more than a tabloid windbag. Docherty was a manager of substantial talent and vision.

'My reputation has maybe overshadowed whatever ability I had. That doesn't really bother me. I think I was a good manager, although I think you also have to be a lucky manager. I got to five semi-finals in the FA Cup and reached two finals. So with a wee bit of luck I could have won the cup five times. I never looked on myself as being a big personality but maybe other people did. I looked upon it that I was getting paid for something I loved. If people take the piss out of me, I don't mind. If you give it out to them you have to expect to take it back.'

So what did Docherty have beyond the gags and the big opinions? It was during his years in the army that he began to acquire man-management skills and be seen as a potential leader of men. He did his national service from 1946–48, witnessing 'unimaginable carnage' when he was guarding the King David Hotel in Jerusalem as a bomb went off which killed 91 people, including many of his fellow soldiers and friends. The incident hardened Docherty. Nothing that football and life could throw at him – and there was plenty to come – could hurt him after that.

He had shown enough to rise to the rank of sergeant and be offered a position in Officers' School and a career in the military, but football called him. He played nine times for Celtic in 1948–49 without properly establishing himself and left for the defining period of his playing career, the nine seasons he spent as an attacking wing-half for Preston North End. He helped them to the Division Two championship in 1951 and to a (losing) FA Cup final appearance in 1954. Those two medals were all he won as a player. Scotland picked him 25 times. In 1958 he left for three rewarding seasons with Arsenal, then appeared briefly for Chelsea before moving into coaching.

Several years earlier he had decided management would be his way of staying in football. He studied it, took notes, spoke to opponents and coaches, and began to formulate ideas and strategies of his own. His enthusiasm was infectious and his knowledge respected. He was just 30, still a player, when caretaker Scotland manager Sir Matt Busby asked him to watch England play Wales and compile a tactical report. All of this was a far cry from the way Docherty tends to be perceived today.

For a while he was the king of the King's Road, the manager of Chelsea from 1962 to 1967. At his job interview some of the directors thought him 'cocky' but they sensed he was what Chelsea needed. It was all about London, Carnaby Street and the swinging '60s. Docherty was the tough, gobby wee Scotsman who would put them on the map. He was brimful of ideas. He changed the colours of their strip, held open days for fans, and embraced the press to secure national coverage for a club which had previously been easy to ignore. Not any more, not with Docherty getting them promoted, finishing fifth in his first season in Division One, winning the 1965 League Cup and reaching the FA Cup final two years later.

'I was always a winner. Second best was never good enough for me. I always wanted to do it my way. In my early days as a manager I was a bit too much of a disciplinarian. I was too much of a sergeant-major, as if it was a throwback to my army days.' Some said his hard line cost Chelsea the English title in 1965. Eight players broke his 10.30 p.m. hotel curfew during a stay in Blackpool with two games left in the season. He was furious, took a stand on a point of principle and sent them all packing back to London. Replacements were called up from the reserves but

Chelsea lost both their remaining games and finished third. It was the closest he ever came to making a team the champions of England. Things were never the same again for him and Chelsea. By October 1967 he had had enough and resigned.

For the record, the complete Docherty managerial roll call is as follows: Chelsea (resigned), Rotherham (resigned), QPR (resigned), Aston Villa (sacked), Porto (fulfilled contract), Scotland (resigned), Manchester United (sacked), Derby County (resigned), QPR (sacked), Sydney Olympic (resigned), Preston (sacked), South Melbourne (fulfilled contract), Sydney Olympic (fulfilled contract), Wolves (sacked), Altrincham (resigned).

Fifteen jobs at twelve clubs. Had he moved around like that in today's market he would have made a mint in pay-offs and compensation. 'Oh aye. One sacking would've been enough today, not half a dozen. Managers today can become millionaires by being failures.'

In assessing Docherty only two clubs matter: Chelsea and Manchester United. Physically he looked different by the time he arrived at Old Trafford at the end of 1972. Lean and sharp-suited in his Chelsea days, he was rounder and fuller-faced at United but still the charismatic, livewire manager who had consistently impressed Busby. Docherty was in charge of Scotland, and watching a match at Crystal Palace's Selhurst Park, when Busby approached and tapped him up. If he wanted the job, United would double the money he was on from the SFA.

There was a lingering feeling that Docherty 'did the dirty' on Scotland by leaving for Manchester United. That he 'walked out on his country'. The status of the national side was greater then and it was not inconceivable that he would turn down the Old Trafford club. Part of the resentment felt towards Docherty for leaving was down to frustration. Supporters felt the country was going somewhere under him. There was an outstanding squad of players – Denis Law, Billy Bremner, Kenny Dalglish, Jimmy Johnstone, Peter Lorimer, Davie Hay et al – and a young manager who was getting the best from them.

It turned out that he would be in charge for just 13 months. Scotland played twelve games, won seven and drew two. Qualifying for the 1972 European Championships was a lost cause by the time he took over but he sent the country hurtling towards the 1974 World Cup finals. His only two qualifying ties were home-and-away wins over Denmark: the 4–1 win in Copenhagen was among the country's finest performances of the 1970s. Only one more win was required to guarantee qualification, and by the time Scotland got it Docherty was gone.

It was a shame. His patriotism remained undimmed by decades spent in England and years later he could still get a lump in his throat at the thought of having managed Scotland. He immersed himself in the job. He checked the lineage of leading English players who had not been capped – no manager had previously done so – and discovered that Arsenal's Bob Wilson was eligible through his Scottish grandparents. Supporters lapped it up when he told them Scotland's pool of natural talent was second only to Brazil's. But the yawning periods of inactivity between matches did not suit Docherty's restless energy and there was always friction between his fiery temperament and the dusty, officious, House of Lords-style atmosphere of the SFA. In the end it came down to the money offered by United.

'I loved being Scotland manager. I only moved away from it for the money. The wages were too good to turn down. I didn't get a hard time when I left the Scotland job but I didn't get a lot of help from the managers when I was in charge, even from big Jock [Stein], God rest his soul. I remember saying to big Jock that I wanted to take Dalglish and wee Jinky to Brazil and he said "Naw, you're not taking them". In those days you had to get the okay from the club to take players for friendlies. That's what you were up against.

'I almost took us to the World Cup in '74. I was a point away when Willie Ormond took over from me and qualified. That's the thing that annoyed me, I was in the right place at the wrong time. I was dying to take Scotland to the World Cup. Ach, what players we had. I'd say the '74 squad was the strongest one we've ever had. I remember the SFA secretary, Willie Allan, said to me "Are you going to watch Dalglish on Saturday?" I said "What do I want to watch him for? I know he's world class, why waste my time watching him again?"'

Manchester United was another Docherty riot. Another four and a half years of turbulence, drama, the extreme on-field lows and highs of his entire career, and, in the end, a bona fide tabloid scandal which changed his life. The Holy Trinity of Denis Law, George Best and Bobby Charlton all ended their United careers under him. Charlton took the decision to retire and so, at just 27, did Best after a familiar period of talks, promises and false dawns. Most controverisally Docherty gave Law, 33, a free transfer when there was still a year left on his contract. That decision showed his mental strength.

In 1973–74 United were relegated. Docherty was shamed but United showed a loyalty to him which would be absent three years later. He had quickly brought them back to the top flight and gone on to win the 1977 FA Cup – the biggest prize of his managerial career – when the story broke which finished him at the club. 'I don't go to games at Old Trafford now. A couple of years ago I asked for two tickets and they sent me a pair and invoiced me for £88. That was the message for me: "Come in number two, your time's up!"'

Docherty lived his life to the full, and not without hardship, pain, distress and huge controversy. Intentionally or otherwise, he inflicted plenty and was the recipient of just as much. When Docherty was nine his father died and he found his upbringing in the Gorbals one of such unremitting poverty that he talked of blessing the day he, his mother and sisters were 'liberated' from it by moving to Shettleston. He wasn't alone in that, but his later life brought problems which were uniquely the Doc's.

One of his former players, Willie Morgan, described him on television as the worst manager he had ever played for. Docherty was persuaded to launch a defamation case, lost it in court and was then charged himself with perjury. He was cleared at a second court case but the entire episode hung over him for nearly four years. While that was going on he was taken in for questioning – but never accused – in a transfer 'bungs' inquiry. 'I've been in more courts than Bjorn Borg,' said Docherty.

None of that affected him like the consequences of the relationship which cost him his United job, his first marriage and his children. Docherty was having an affair with Mary Brown, the wife of the United physiotherapist, and when that was revealed the club lost its nerve and sacked him on the vague charge of breaking the 'moral code' at Old Trafford. He thought that hypocritical but the personal and professional fall-out was massive. Through it all, and through all the subsequent years, he and Mary stayed together, married and started a new family.

He has had feuds and fall-outs with football figures such as Morgan, Paddy Crerand and Sir Alex Ferguson, who he claimed had not spoken civilly to him since a 1987 radio show in which Docherty said one of his signings, Ralph Milne, showed that 'If you pay peanuts, the likelihood is you get monkeys'. Making enemies is an occupational hazard of his successful turn as an acerbic, no-holds-barred after-dinner speaker.

'I call a spade a shovel. I call it as I see it. It's all about opinions, isn't it? Some people take the hump. If you say you think someone's crap they get on their high horse about it. I'm not claiming to be right or wrong, it's just an opinion. I've often felt I could have bitten my tongue but it's always too late for that.'

Impulsive, tempestuous, abrasive, unselfish – he took United to play a friendly at Newport County after learning that the Welsh club was in dire financial trouble – and engaging, Docherty has been one of football's great characters. One of its biggest mouths. One of its best managers. By the end of it all he was at peace with himself. Still talking football with anyone who would listen. Still cracking the jokes.

'I was a good judge of a player but maybe not a good judge of character. I think I could get the best out of players. One or two weren't good signings, but I got rid of them quickly. Despite my reputation I didn't think I had many battles with chairmen. I told them what I thought and if they didn't like it, well, cobblers. I never managed a club in Scotland. I was offered a job at St Johnstone when I was out of work, but after being the manager of Scotland I didn't think that would be right. I never had interest from Celtic or Rangers and that never bothered me. If they want you they know where you are. Maybe they were frightened of me! Aye, that could've been it.'

George Graham

'I learned that in football, as in life, 99 per cent of people want to be led. The other 1 per cent are leaders. There are a helluva lot of Scots in that 1 per cent.'

George Graham could have no comprehension of what it would mean to him, but one of the most profound moments of his life happened when he was only three weeks old. His father, Robert, died. His mother, Janet, was left with seven children to bring up on her own. 'People talk about footballers being heroes, which is all fine and well,' said Graham, 'But it's not a word I would use for them. I grew up with real heroes, like my mum. My mum, with help from my oldest brother, Andy, kept our family together.'

Graham had a predictably hard upbringing in the former mining village of Bargeddie on the outskirts of Glasgow. A desire to better himself, to make his mother proud after all the sacrifices she had made for the family, drove him on. Like all the other familiar managerial names from similar stock – Sir Matt Busby, Bill Shankly, Jock Stein and Sir Alex Ferguson – Graham was proud of his working-class roots. That did not extend to wanting to spend the rest of his life in the place where he grew up.

Like many Scottish teenagers of his generation (he was born in 1944) he sensed that football provided an escape route. Because of that he practised with a ball for hours in the local park. He stayed outdoors until it was dark. 'I wanted to make it as a footballer and my mum told me the only way I would make it was through hard work. I was proud of my upbringing and never looked down my nose at anyone. But I knew I wanted more and I knew it was football that could take me out of Bargeddie. I wasn't alone as all my mates wanted to be footballers. I guess I was one of the lucky ones to make it in the game. Coming from my background, and having no financial safety net, meant I also had the fear factor to drive me on.'

Another element of fear provided motivation. Graham had the insecurity of growing up in a household without a father. His dad had worked in the local steelworks until he died of tuberculosis and heart failure on Christmas Day, 1944. As Graham grew up, being part of a loving family in a supportive working-class community helped him come to terms with the absence of a father figure. It also hardened him against easy sentimentality.

For example, Graham always felt too much was made of the fact many of the greatest Scottish managers come from social backgrounds such as his own. 'I know people go on about how the poor, working-class upbringings of Scots like me spurred us all on and made us more ambitious, but I don't buy that completely. Of course guys like Stein, Shankly, Ferguson, Busby and myself came from similar backgrounds but when you live through it you know no different. I'm never sure why parts of Scotland are singled out more than, say, parts of England. There were just as many poor areas down south as there were up north. Scotland didn't have the monopoly on poor areas. Of course a working-class background is a common denominator but there must be more to it than that. In my case it was the fear factor, the fear of not being able to escape from Bargeddie, the fear of letting my mum and my brothers and sisters down. That drove me on.'

Whatever other disadvantages he had to overcome, Graham had something special going for him. His first steps out of Bargeddie came via his top-class midfield performances with the Scottish schoolboy team in 1959. Clubs were taking notice. He came close to signing for Rangers. What put him off was something that Scottish coaches of that generation felt was a good thing for young players, but with which the teenage Graham vehemently disagreed. He knew his own mind even then.

'I went to Ibrox and met Rangers manager Scot Symon when I was 15 but I didn't sign because, like all the Scottish clubs of that time, there was no youth policy. All they did was farm young players out to junior teams. They thought hardening them up that way helped their development. I didn't buy it then and I don't buy it now. Scot Symon wanted to farm me out to Muirkirk in the Ayrshire juniors, which were full of former professionals, really tough guys at the end of their careers. They gave young players a hard time. I would be playing against men, getting pulverised in tackles. It would be tough. Although there was always macho talk about how that made young players ready for professional football I felt that was rubbish. I still do.

'In English football there was a very good youth policy that didn't involving farming players out to junior teams where players would be kicked up and down the park and risk serious injury. Down south you started in the youth team, had a recognised youth coach, and played against players your own age. Taking on young guys who were coming through the ranks and being looked after properly in England was more tempting to a lot of young Scots. That's why so many of us in the 1960s left to go south. The English coaching set-up for young players was way ahead of Scotland. We had to go down south to get our real football education.' Graham never returned.

He signed for Aston Villa on his 17th birthday, made a handful of appearances over the next two-and-a-half years and then moved to Chelsea in 1964. He won a League Cup medal there but was one of a few players who had a strained relationship with his fellow Scot, manager Tommy Docherty, and that resulted in another move. It took him to the club with which his name is still synonymous. He made his Arsenal debut in October 1966.

Graham was always a cool customer, so much so that as a player he was nicknamed 'Stroller'. Under the laid-back exterior was a steely determination. Both qualities served him well in management. He won the Fairs Cup with Arsenal in 1970 but the finest achievement came when he was part of their double-winning side of 1970–71. It was a team of leaders.

'If you looked around that double-winning dressing room of 1971 and tried to work out who would be successful managers I would have been near the bottom of the list. In fact, if you had suggested to someone like Frank McLintock, Pat Rice or Bob McNab that I would be the one to make the transition from player to eventual manager of Arsenal they would have laughed out loud. That was because when I was playing I had no real interest in tactics. I just wanted to get the ball and get out there and play. When Frank, Pat and Bob would be talking tactics with our manager, Bertie Mee, and his assistant, Don Howe, I would be sitting in the corner winding them up, telling them they were over-analysing things. There were always players who were interested in coaching but I wasn't one of them. I just wanted to play football.'

So what changed? How did Graham end up as one of Arsenal's most successful managers, a boss who also won the League Cup with Tottenham and secured a promotion for Millwall? 'When I was about to retire Terry Venables asked me to get involved in youth coaching at Crystal Palace then Queens Park Rangers. Within a few weeks of working with Terry I had caught the coaching bug. He was my inspiration when it came to coaching. He made me realise that if you have that desire and drive to succeed, then anything is possible.'

He was plucked from a position with the youths at QPR to be head coach at Millwall after their chairman, Alan Thorne, saw his work. Millwall were bottom of the old Third Division in 1982 when Graham took over but he helped them avoid relegation. Two seasons later, in 1984–85, they were promoted to the Second Division. His managerial promise, and his status as a club favourite, meant Arsenal came calling in 1986.

Arsenal were a major club, but not the enormous commercial machine they are today. They had won nothing since the FA Cup in 1979. Graham refreshed the squad, brought in younger players and imposed stricter discipline, both in the dressing room and on the pitch. Guidelines were given to the players and he exerted his authority by keeping a distance from them to the point that behind his back they nicknamed him 'Gaddafi'. He was single-minded and sure of himself. 'When I went in to Arsenal they were under-achieving big time. The minute I got in there I sat everyone down and told them where I was coming from. Regardless of who you manage, those first few days as a manager, when you arrive at a club, are absolutely vital.

'It is absolute rubbish to suggest you get an open arms welcome by players when you arrive. Believe me, most of the players hardly say anything to you. You have to do the talking. They size you up, try and find out whether you are tough. Once they think they've worked you out they'll come up to you on the quiet with millions of questions, mostly about whether you're going to play them or not. It is a team game but the players care about themselves first and foremost. Don't try and let anyone kid you otherwise. Those most on edge are the previous manager's favourites. Those with a bounce in their step are the guys who he didn't use to play.

'Any good manager should make it clear in those first few days, like I did at Arsenal, that you are not going to stand for any nonsense. I wanted to show the players who was boss. The best managers, like Stein, Shankly and Ferguson, have to be very strong men to stand alone. You have to live or die by your own decisions. You can never let yourself be too influenced by other people. I didn't like interference. I told every club I was at to let me run the football side, and that's what they did.'

The bigger the club, the bigger the problems. Arsenal were no different. 'For me to keep track of what the players were up to after they left Highbury was very difficult. Everyone now knows that Tony Adams had an alcohol problem and Paul Merson a gambling one. Both were great for me at Arsenal but in London you can't keep track of them all the time. If you are in Manchester or Liverpool or Glasgow you kind of know the nightclubs your players will go to. They will be spotted and you'll find out. London is so massive it was difficult to keep an eye on them all.'

Some of his players went off the straight and narrow when they were out of Graham's sight but the minute he focused his steely stare on them it was a different story. 'Sometimes when I walked into a dressing room and heard highly-paid footballers talk about how hard life was I used to get a bit angry. They didn't know they were born. It made me even more determined that they would appreciate what they had and not blow the opportunities they had been given.'

Arsenal's form improved under Graham, so much so that the club was top of the league at Christmas 1986 for the first time in a decade. They went on to win the 1987 League Cup. The team was built around centre-half Adams, who Graham made his captain at only 21. He marshalled a top-class defence that included players like Lee Dixon, Nigel Winterburn and Steve Bould, who formed the basis of the club's back four for more than ten years. 'You need to keep your players very fit,' said Graham, 'If you look at guys like our defenders, most of them played on well into their 30s and that was down to the way they trained and looked after themselves.' Graham was so fixated with defensive organisation that in training he used to literally connect his back-four together with a long length of rope so that they could practice pushing up in a line to catch opponents offside. It was simple, unorthodox and clever.

In midfield Graham kept faith with the likes of Merson, Michael Thomas and David Rocastle, while up front Alan Smith was a proven goalscorer. At the end of Graham's third season, in 1988–89, the club won its first league title since 1971. The circumstances were impossibly dramatic: they overtook Liverpool at Anfield in the final minute of the final game of the season.

Arsenal needed to win by two goals on Merseyside to take the title. Smith scored early in the second half to make it 1–0, but as time ticked by Arsenal struggled to get a second, and with regulation time completed they still needed another goal. Liverpool were poised for the crown. With only seconds to go, a flick-on from Smith sent Thomas through to calmly lift the ball over Bruce Grobbelaar into the net. The league title had been won.

They didn't manage to win back-to-back titles in 1990 but Graham bought goalkeeper David Seaman and he became the final piece in his defensive jigsaw. Arsenal won a second title in 1990–91 and reached the FA Cup semi-finals, losing to Tottenham Hotspur. Graham always had an eye for talent and signed Ian Wright from Crystal Palace, who repaid him by going on to become the second highest scorer in the history of the club.

Arsenal became cup specialists and in the 1992–93 season became the first side to win the FA Cup and League Cup double, both times beating Sheffield Wednesday by the same scoreline of 2–1, although the League Cup final required a replay. The next season they won the European Cup Winners' Cup after they beat the favourites and holders Parma thanks to a tight defensive performance. The Italian club threw everything at Arsenal after Smith's 21st-minute goal but Adams was a colossus at the back as his team held out. The result was one which became synonymous with Graham to the extent it became a terrace chant: 'One–nil . . . to the Arsenal'. The other well-known chant of the day, which began as a taunt by rivals but was then adopted by their own supporters because of the consistency of their wins, was 'Boring, boring Arsenal'.

That famous victory was Graham's last trophy with Arsenal. In February 1995 he was sacked after nearly nine years in charge after it was discovered he had accepted an illegal £425,000 payment from Norwegian agent Rune Hauge while buying John Jensen, one of Hauge's clients, back in 1992. Graham was eventually banned for a year by the Football Association after he admitted he had received an 'unsolicited gift' from Hauge. He was the first high-profile manager to be caught and punished under football's fight against its 'bungs' culture. 'I made a mistake then and paid for it,' said Graham, 'It was a difficult time, but I was determined to return to football as I still had the desire to manage.' For a while Graham felt like a pariah, although there were moments of light relief. He once said: 'At least all the aggravation will keep me slim.'

After serving his ban Graham returned to football management with Leeds United in September 1996. He took over a team that was struggling against relegation but lifted them to a respectable 11th place in the Premiership table. For a man whom some fans accused of playing defensive football he nevertheless had an eye for a striker. At Leeds, Jimmy Floyd Hasselbaink was brought in, and with the Dutchman in their ranks Leeds finished fifth. In October, 1998, Graham's two years at Leeds ended when he was appointed manager of Arsenal's great rivals, Tottenham. This was north London's equivalent of Mo Johnston playing for Rangers after Celtic.

He was not welcomed by many Tottenham supporters. He converted many of them five months into his time in charge when he guided the club to victory over Leicester City in the 1999 League Cup final. Graham was streetwise. Having noticed that players seemed to spend an inordinate length of time on the club's injury list, he rescheduled their treatment times to coincide with the London rush-hour traffic. Hey presto, many began to become available again sooner rather than later.

Still, he was to be one of many managers who had false dawns at Spurs. Although they were competitive in cup competitions they never finished above tenth in the Premiership. Graham was sacked in March 2001, to the relief of those fans who had never wanted him in the first place. Graham famously kept lots of Arsenal memorabilia in his home and once said he would always have 'Arsenal-red blood' in his veins. His departure from White Hart Lane also satisfied those Arsenal 'Gooners' who thought it beneath him to be manager of Spurs in the first place.

Although he was linked with several leading jobs in subsequent years they never materialised and he became a television pundit with Sky. He remained a close analyst of the modern game. It had been a long managerial career with more success than failures. Graham never served a Scottish club and has lived in England since he was 17, yet he believes that Scotland will continue to produce talented managers because of a collective predisposition to leadership.

'I learned that in football, as in life, 99 per cent of people want to be led. The other 1 per cent are leaders and there are a helluva lot of Scots in that 1 per cent. A lot of them go on to be successful football managers and businessmen. The Scots as a race are well used to leaving the country they grew up in, so you have to be leaders to survive. They also like honesty and can't abide phoneys. You can't be a phoney if you are a football manager.

'The two things you want to achieve as a manager are firstly to win and then, secondly, do it by playing attractive football. To make that happen, whether you are running an amateur club or Barcelona, you have to remember three basic rules: maintain discipline, choose your assistant correctly and make sure you get the right captain. You don't have to walk around with a big stick to be a disciplinarian. Start with simple things like making sure everybody's time-keeping improves. If training is due to start at ten o'clock make sure all your players are ready for that time. If they aren't let them know about it, just like other people who turn up late for work in the real world get a row. I was strong on that. The favourite word at Arsenal was "standards". My players had to meet standards every day they were at the club.'

Graham did not manage again after leaving Spurs, in 2001, when he was only 56. Yet he is a content, relaxed figure now. The once-regular links with available jobs have largely finished. He is happy to have a comfortable life outside management. The young lad from Bargeddie is independently wealthy and enjoying a privileged lifestyle in London, a reward for hard work which began when 'Stroller' was young.

'Football management affects your personality. You sometimes can turn into a person you don't recognise. I loved the job but I had to make sacrifices and my family life suffered. You can't switch off at 5 p.m. when you are a football manager. It is a 12-months-a-year-job and even when I used to sit on the beach on my summer holiday I would be reading the newspapers, checking on what players were on the market and who I wanted to sign. I can see the same Scottish work ethic in managers like Sir Alex Ferguson, who remains the best of them all. Davie Moyes, Owen Coyle, Alex McLeish and Alan Irvine are others who are on the way up. My generation had its fair share of good Scottish-born managers. The current one looks potentially just as good.'

Kenny Dalglish

'Mibbes aye, mibbes naw.'

Bill Struth was 79 when he finished as a manager. Willie Maley was 71. Jock Stein died in the job aged 62. Sir Matt Busby picked a Manchester United side for the final time when he was only weeks short of his 62nd birthday. Bill Shankly quit Liverpool at 60. Walter Smith was still going strong for Rangers in his early sixties. Sir Alex Ferguson showed no sign of slowing up as he approached 70.

It is no coincidence that these exceptional managers performed to an age when they could be accurately described as distinguished elderly men, eligible for their pension in some cases. Longevity is a prerequisite for managerial greatness. A man has to be around for long enough, he has to put enough miles on the clock, before he can amass the collection of trophies and accomplishments which demand his inclusion among the best. Well, normally.

Kenny Dalglish has always been his own man. He was never the quickest as a footballer – a flaw obliterated by his array of extraordinary other gifts – but he made up for it when it came to management. He won the title three times with Liverpool and another once with Blackburn Rovers. He won two FA Cups. He was the first Liverpool manager to land the double and is one of only four men ever to have won the English title with different clubs. And he did all of that by the age of forty-four, only five years after he made his final competitive appearance as a player. He has not managed at all since he was 49. The man they called 'King Kenny' abdicated early.

The notion of Dalglish being some sort of lost figure in management, someone who had so much more to give but drifted to the periphery of football, is academic. No-one ever talked Dalglish into something he didn't want to do. If he didn't wish to manage any more then that was that. Even those he admired and respected more than most have tried and failed to get him to change his mind. Jock Stein attempted unsuccessfully to keep him as a Celtic player in 1977 and Liverpool chief executive Peter Robinson could not dissuade him from resigning as manager in 1991. Graeme Souness once described him as having the negotiating ability of a Govan shipyard shop steward. Even before Dalglish picked his last ever team for a competitive match – steering a poor Celtic side to a 2–0 win over Dundee United on 21 May 2000 – he had decided his time was up. 'I think Kenny had had enough of football management,' said the former Celtic chief executive, Allan MacDonald.

It was a sour, depressing end to a managerial career which began in far, far worse circumstances. No man in football history has taken charge of an enormous club at the age of 34 and, in his very first press conference, faced questions about how and why 39 people died at his team's match the previous night. Had he played a game of football knowing there had been deaths on the terraces around him? That was Dalglish's hellish baptism. He was one of a handful of men who knew he would take over from Joe Fagan to become player/manager of Liverpool after the 1985 European Cup final against Juventus, but none of them anticipated that being the aftermath of 'Heysel'. Italian supporters died at the Brussels final on the Wednesday night and by the Thursday Dalglish was flown back to Anfield to be shown off to the media as the new manager. Questions came at him that day about crushing, suffocation, death, hooliganism and a decrepit stadium. For what it was worth, Dalglish had not known there were deaths before he played in that black night in football history.

The story of Scottish football managers is one of gruff, uptight men being shaped by hard, unforgiving upbringings in the mean streets of Glasgow, around Lanarkshire coal mines or the Clydeside shipyards. Dalglish is as tough as they come but different in one respect: his suffering came as an adult. He has the unique and horrible distinction of having been present at three major football tragedies. As a young Celtic player he had a ticket for the other end of the stadium at the 1971 Ibrox disaster in which 66 supporters died. After a further 14 years he was a Liverpool player at Heysel. After just four more, he was the manager who witnessed the nightmare of Hillsborough.

No wonder Dalglish succumbed 22 months later and carried out the previously unthinkable act of resigning as Liverpool manager. He had the sense to acknowledge that his health was a mess and the courage to announce that stress had forced him to step down. That was a big thing to admit in football two decades ago. He had become unpleasant to live with at home, was shouting at his children, and started taking a drink to help unwind. Eventually his skin broke out in blotches. There had been headaches. On one occasion it was said he had arrived at the Anfield car park but been physically unable to get out of his car for some time, paralysed by stress. 'The pressure on match days is making my head explode,' he said, 'I can't go on. I could either keep my job or my sanity.'

Hard, streetwise, sarcastic Glaswegian football managers are supposed to sneer at stress, but not even Busby, who survived the Munich air disaster, had gone through multiple tragedies like Dalglish. Hillsborough had been unimaginably traumatic – at one point Dalglish feared his son, Paul, had been caught in the Leppings Lane crush – and he became the focus of a city's mourning with incredible strength and dignity. There were 96 fatalities; he lost count of how many funerals he attended. There were four in one day alone. There was a fortnight of burials. In one quiet moment inside an empty Anfield he took two of his children to the back of the Kop and the three of them sat and wept. He has called the sea of flowers, scarves and shirts which covered the pitch in tribute 'the saddest and most beautiful sight' he had ever seen. In an expression of great compassion it occurred to him that there had been a witness at Hillsborough who no one had thought about. He telephoned Ray Lewis, the referee at the match, to make sure he was okay.

That was a wonderful act of communication from a man renowned for being uncommunicative, dry and difficult. In happier circumstances there was similar class when Liverpool beat Crystal Palace 9–0 and he sent their manager, Steve Coppell, a letter to say the score had not reflected the play. Those are the small touches, the attention to detail, which are the hallmarks of an exceptional manager and Dalglish, for a decade, was exactly that.

He inherited a superb Liverpool team from Fagan in 1985 and improved it. Straight away he was decisive, strong and open-minded. A meeting was called with his former team-mates to decide how they should now refer to him. 'Boss' was agreed, but Phil Neal pointedly continued to call him 'Kenny'. Dalglish pulled him up about it. Before long Neal had lost the captaincy and then his place at the club altogether. They had been team-mates for eight years.

Dalglish's debut double in 1985–86 is sometimes belittled as having been won with his predecessor's team. It was nothing of the sort. He made changes. Steve Nicol replaced Neal, Jim Beglin came in for Alan Kennedy, and Craig Johnston, Jan Molby and Steve McMahon became a new midfield. Dalglish, a young, inexperienced manager in charge of one of Europe's biggest clubs, played thirty-one times himself, made three more appearances for Scotland, scored the goal which won the title at Chelsea on the final day of the season, and saw his men beat Everton in the first all-Merseyside FA Cup final. Bob Paisley had been a valued adviser to him throughout it all, but it was Dalglish's breathtaking triumph.

For his second season he wanted to sign John Barnes, Peter Beardsley, Ray Houghton and John Aldridge. It was impossible to get them all in time, although he made some brave changes to the backroom team. Liverpool were runners-up and the campaign finished trophyless. By 1987–88 he had all four of the men he wanted. Instantly, Liverpool's football was thrilling, more exciting than it had been even in Dalglish's own playing career. Sir Alex Ferguson wrote the foreword for his autobiography and included an awesome tribute: 'He signed Peter Beardsley and John Barnes and took Liverpool a stage further than they had been before.'

At his peak Dalglish was a formidable manager. It did not matter that journalists resented his reticent, defensive and sarcastic demeanour towards them, or that he was sensitive to criticism. The calculated vagueness of his answers became a running joke: 'Maybe yes, maybe no', or as it came out in Dalglish's unyielding Glasgow accent 'Mibbes aye, mibbes naw'. What mattered was the excellence of his man-management, the attention to detail, the encyclopaedic knowledge of players, and his sheer presence. In training he watched quietly, letting others do the shouting while he might whisper something in a player's ear. On match days he liked to stand beside the dugout because it made him feel slightly closer to the action.

And then came 1988–89, the season which ended lives and changed his. Molby was jailed for drink-driving during the campaign and the league title was snatched away from Liverpool at Anfield because of a goal from Arsenal's Michael Thomas in stoppage time of the last game of the season. It didn't hurt as much as it could have: Hillsborough had happened 41 days earlier. Winning another FA Cup final against Everton felt like a tiny but necessary tribute to the dead.

The following season the goals of Barnes, Beardsley and Ian Rush propelled Dalglish to his third championship as Liverpool manager. On 1 May 1990, aged 39, he made his first appearance of the season and his last ever one for Liverpool, as a substitute for the final 18 minutes against Derby County on the day the championship trophy was presented. It was a happy day for an increasingly unhappy man.

The trauma and stress of Hillsborough crept up on him. It

chilled him to return to that haunted ground for a league fixture against Sheffield Wednesday the following season, the Leppings Lane end closed and eerie. Resigning in 1990 crossed his mind (he was electrocuted in an accident with a faulty strimmer that summer) but he continued until 22 February 1991, the day after a 4–4 draw with Everton. Enough was enough. He felt too unwell to continue and sensed that his decision-making was being compromised. He told chief executive Peter Robinson and chairman Noel White he was tired and wanted to resign with immediate effect. In his opinion there was a need to go for the club's sake as well as his own. Much of that day was spent with ashen-faced directors trying to talk him out of it, but to no avail. It was Shankly 1974 all over again. Dalglish was gone. In his five full seasons in charge of Liverpool the lowest they finished was second.

A point had come when he needed a break. In general Dalglish's background and personality left him perfectly equipped for the routine psychological demands of representing enormous clubs like Celtic and Liverpool. He is as stubborn and unyielding as they come. His father, Bill, was a diesel engineer in a motor company and his mother, Cathy, a housewife. He was born on 4 March 1951, and brought up in Glasgow – first in Dalmarnock near Celtic Park, then in Milton, then in Govan near Ibrox Stadium – but has scoffed at the idea that his family was stereotypically poor. 'There was none of this running around with no shoes on', he wrote in his memoirs.

Instead, his childhood and youth was dominated by an uncomplicated obsession with football and his evolution through various school teams until signing provisional forms with Celtic in the month they won the 1967 European Cup. He had no problem with initially continuing to serve as an apprentice joiner, turning up for evening training in jeans and a donkey jacket sprinkled with wood shavings. He saw no contradiction in training as a young Celtic player and then boarding a Rangers supporters' bus to go to any of their games he could manage. When Celtic assistant manager Sean Fallon initially came to visit his house Dalglish had to rush to his bedroom and rip down the Rangers posters on his wall before Fallon could see them.

He would have preferred to join Rangers but the club never came for him. They must hold their heads in their hands about that blunder even now. Dalglish became a great Scottish manager only after an enormously distinguished career as a world-class forward. There were 167 goals in 321 appearances for Celtic, 172 in 515 games for Liverpool, and 30 in 102 caps for Scotland. He was a league champion ten times, won the same number of domestic cups, and lifted the European Cup three times. He was the finest player of his generation and the greatest his country had produced.

Dalglish's status made him attractive to club chairmen. He was not regarded as damaged goods through having left Liverpool because of psychological pressure. It was the city he had to get out of at that time, not football entirely. There was a general acknowledgement that he would be fair game to be connected with real or potential vacancies after his necessary rest. He was linked with Celtic and Rangers (effectively in a job swap with Souness, who had replaced him at Anfield) and with Aston Villa and Marseille. The months passed: March, April, May, June, July, August, September. Dalglish holidayed, he golfed, he spent time with his family. He recuperated. He began to angle for media work. He turned up at games again. He became restless to return.

Two years earlier a Lancashire businessman called Jack Walker had sold his steel business for around £350 million. Walker was a proud local figure in his 60s who loved his football club, Blackburn Rovers, although they were often hard to love. The club's best days seemed long gone. 1966 was a bad year for Blackburn and for Dalglish. The club was relegated from the old First Division (and had not been back since) and England won the World Cup (Dalglish is deeply patriotic and claims to have voted only once in his life, for the Scottish National Party when he was 18).

Walker had the resources, the will and the ambition to rebuild Blackburn and identified Dalglish as the man who would transform the way they were perceived and take them into the Premiership. Walker talked money. He talked money for Dalglish, who always knew how to stand up for himself when it came to negotiating terms. Bob Paisley once said of him: 'Kenny calls all his goals "tap-ins" until we come to end the end of the season and we're talking money. Suddenly he changes his mind.' Then Walker talked money for new players and money to improve Ewood Park. Dalglish was sceptical but intrigued. Eventually he accepted. On 12 October 1991, he returned to football as their manager. Dalglish moved down in the world and Blackburn up. He remembers having to take a spanner to screw in bolts and assemble the goals before some of his first training sessions on a school pitch. He loved it.

Blackburn Rovers became one of the great stories of the 1990s. Seven months after his arrival Dalglish led them back to the Premiership after that 26-year absence. They grew like ivy. Alan Shearer was signed for £3.3m. Colin Hendry, Graeme Le Saux, Stuart Ripley, David Batty and Tim Flowers gave him backbone. In 1992–93, Dalglish's first full season, they finished fourth. The year after that they rose again to finish second behind Manchester United. Somehow Blackburn were from a bygone age but nouveau riche at the same time. Either way, England had a major new force and Dalglish was back.

Blackburn were solid, organised, disciplined and hard-working. They had an entirely different style from that great Barnes/ Beardsley Liverpool side, but they were formidable. When Dalglish signed Chris Sutton, his 'SAS' (Sutton and Shearer) attack powered them towards the title. Alex Ferguson knew what his United side was up against and tried to load on the pressure, questioning Blackburn's 'bottle' and saying they would have to 'do a Devon Loch' to lose the championship. Dalglish affected not to understand the reference to the famous Grand National faller. He was too strong to buckle. Blackburn were the 1994–95 champions. Dalglish even clinched it on the final day of the season against Liverpool at Anfield, where the home support was delighted equally by his success and United's failure. The Kop forgave Dalglish for the fact their club had slipped into decline since he left (2010 marked 20 years without a league title for Liverpool since the last one he won for them).

Dalglish received a warm letter from Ferguson congratulating him and his Blackburn players on a great achievement. Five days after the title was won Dalglish stepped down as manager. There were echoes of his Liverpool departure, although this time he moved to become director of football with his previous assistant, Ray Harford, taking over as manager. Dalglish had again lost the appetite for day-to-day involvement and the responsibility of management. 'I did not crave another trophy after Blackburn won the championship,' he wrote in his memoir.

Under Harford Blackburn declined, finishing seventh the following season, 21 points behind champions United, and were bottom of their group in the Champions League. Dalglish grew frustrated at his lack of involvement. He was not consulted by Harford as often as he had wished or expected and he felt spare and marginalised. In August 1996 Blackburn sent a letter to his home saying the relationship had run its course. Dalglish felt the same way but thought the decision could have been handled better. His Blackburn side remains the only club outwith Manchester United, Chelsea and Arsenal to have won the English Premier League.

He was out of football again – more holidays, more golf, more time with the family – but made headlines by signing for Rangers. Technically it was Rangers chairman Sir David Murray who employed him, to promote a golf event at Loch Lomond and also do some scouting work for manager Walter Smith. The relationship was intriguing but short-lived. In January 1997 Kevin Keegan resigned as Newcastle manager and they turned to Dalglish.

It seemed contradictory of him to accept given that he seemed to have lost his appetite for front-line management at Blackburn, but not even the hothouse pressure of a demanding city obsessed with a single club could put him off. Newcastle appealed to him. The directors were ambitious, the infrastructure and fanbase were right, there was money to spend, and he was inheriting a squad containing Shearer, Batty, Beardsley, Les Ferdinand, Faustino Asprilla and David Ginola among others.

Newcastle finished second in his first half season. For 1997–98 there was talk of Dalglish becoming the first manager to win a title with three clubs. They came nowhere near. He sold Ginola and Ferdinand only to lose Shearer to a long-term injury. There was a famous home victory over Barcelona but they still did not progress from their Champions League group. Dalglish reinstated the reserve team that Keegan had disbanded, invested in youth development, and took to life in the north-east. It was not mutual. Supporters criticised his signings – Jon Dahl Tomasson, John Barnes, Ian Rush – and thought his tactics too cagey. Above all, he wasn't Keegan. They finished 13th in the league and lost the FA Cup final to Arsenal. Newcastle's board allowed him to spend £12m on seven players over the summer of 1998 and then sacked him in August.

Legendary status is as hard as granite. Even after 22 years it suffers no erosion. There were 2000 supporters outside Parkhead on 10 June 1999, when Dalglish stood beside Barnes as the 'dream team' which was taking over the management of Celtic. A few months earlier Dalglish had supported a consortium which wanted to buy out Celtic owner Fergus McCann. Now, with McCann having done a deal with others and on the way out, Dalglish was back without the need to pay his own wages. 'I was prepared to buy myself a job, but I didn't have to,' he said.

Dalglish was the director of football and Barnes the head coach. There was anxiety about the relationship from the start. Barnes's experience extended no further than taking some training sessions with Newcastle's reserves. Celtic were taking on Rangers, who had just won a treble, had Dick Advocaat as manager, and were flush with money. Surely Barnes was a gamble? 'Aye well, you take a risk getting up in the morning,' said Dalglish.

Barnes began well but his season unravelled through bad luck and his own poor judgement. Henrik Larsson suffered a broken leg in October and Barnes's tactics and some of his signings fractured the dressing room. When Celtic lost 3–1 at home to First Division Caledonian Thistle in the Scottish Cup his dismissal was announced within 48 hours and Dalglish was ordered to return immediately from a scouting trip to La Manga in Spain. He misjudged the mood in Glasgow when he was met by a scrum of reporters at the airport and tried to give them a withering response: 'Do ye no' think I've got a good tan?'

Tight-lipped and reluctant, Dalglish stepped in for the remaining 18 games of the season. The final trophy of his managerial career was the Scottish League Cup, lifted after a 2–0 final victory over Aberdeen. It did nothing to soften his entrenched attitude to a press pack he resented for its treatment of Barnes. Five days after that cup win Dalglish decided Celtic's weekly media conference would not be held at Parkhead but at a hardcore Celtic fans' watering hole, Baird's Bar on the city's rough-and-ready Gallowgate. The act seemed calculated to make journalists feel uncomfortable as they were eyed suspiciously by lunchtime regulars. The headline in one tabloid the following day said it all: 'Kenny's Driven us to Drink (and he didn't even get a round in)'. Some subsequent conferences were held at the equally inhospitable, for reporters, headquarters of the Celtic Supporters Association.

The Baird's Bar event became a signature moment in Dalglish's end at Celtic. Two days later Celtic lost 4–0 to Rangers, contributing to an eventual finish 21 points behind their bitter city rivals. Dalglish was sacked at the end of the season and was awarded £600,000 compensation later in 2000 after taking Celtic to court.

It was no way for him to remember the club, nor for the club to remember him. He withdrew from management over the following nine years, caring for his wife and soul-mate Marina when she was diagnosed with breast cancer and helping establish the Marina Dalglish Appeal, which raised £2m to build a new chemotherapy centre in Liverpool. As an ambassador for the fast food firm

McDonald's in Scotland he promoted youth football initiatives. He took a joke at his own expense by appearing in an amusing television advertisement alongside Graham Taylor and Terry Venables, being cared for by nurse Kelly Brook in a supposed 'retirement home' for managers.

In 2009 he returned to Liverpool Football Club to work in their academy and become a club ambassador. Earlier that year he broke a 20-year public silence on the Hillsborough disaster by discussing it for a television documentary. He handled it with sensitivity and dignity, just as he had in April 1989.

Titles and cups are all very well. But there are bereaved and grateful families in Liverpool who will always regard that period as the greatest act of management in Kenny Dalglish's extraordinary career.

Matt Gillies

'an intelligent, crinkly-haired Scot who might have become a doctor had professional football not held too many lures for him'

Spot the odd one out among this jumbled list of Scots who have plundered at least one of England's major trophies in the last half a century: Tommy Docherty, George Graham, Sir Matt Busby, Sir Alex Ferguson, Dave Mackay, Graeme Souness, Bill Shankly, Matt Gillies, Graeme Souness, Kenny Dalglish.

No need to worry: an involuntary urge to blurt out 'Matt who?' is understandable. Matt Gillies is an unheralded figure. As a manager of some substance he deserved wider recognition. Only in Leicester is he remembered as something of a visionary.

Gillies was an innovative thinker who began experimenting with the broad concept of 'total football' at unfashionable Leicester City a decade before it became synonymous with the cool sophistication of the Dutch. As a manager he had the sound judgement – and the nerve – to sell Gordon Banks just a year after he had helped England win the World Cup because he had a hunch that a 17-year-old coming through in the reserves might turn out to be just as good. The teenager was Peter Shilton.

Leicester City were 80 years old and had never won a major trophy when Gillies took over and embarked on a reign which lasted for most of the 1960s. He won them the League Cup, lost the final the following year, took them to two losing FA Cup finals in 1961 and 1963, and almost landed the league and cup double in 1962–63. In 1968 he broke the British transfer record to spend £150,000 on the then unproven Allan Clarke, later to become a star for Leeds United and England. Bill Shankly – not known for taking great notice of what anyone was doing beyond Liverpool and Liverpool reserves – said that in 1962–63 Gillies's Leicester City played the best football in England. Shanks had a ringside seat, given that his Liverpool team were beaten by them in the FA Cup semi-final.

Gillies, a clever, gentle man, was a contemporary of Busby and Shankly. In temperament he was closer to the stately, softly-spoken Manchester United legend than the vivacious Shankly, but the three of them were friends – he was also close to Jock Stein – and Gillies shared his illustrious pals' eye for a player. He had been the manager who had taken Banks to Leicester in the first place when he was young and barely known at Chesterfield.

The tactical innovation with which Gillies was synonymous sounds modest these days but it was imaginative and original for its time. Opponents would be wrong-footed when he switched his inside-right Graham Cross and the Scottish international right-half Frank McLintock. Shankly later started doing the same with Gordon Milne and Tommy Smith at Liverpool. Gillies's profes-sionalism extended to having his players work on set-pieces in training; few managers did at the time.

When Leicester reached the 1963 FA Cup final against Man-chester United the notes in the match programme gushed about Gillies' progressive approach: 'The man who leads Leicester out at

Wembley today is Matthew Muirhead Gillies, an intelligent, crinkly-haired Scot who might have become a doctor had professional football not held too many lures for him. Gillies is the first to admit that football is a simple game but it can be changed around. Why should the numbers on players' shirts shackle them to a fixed role? If eight men can attack, why cannot eight defend? Blend – everyone working for everyone else, rigid defence that sucks the opposition forward and then suddenly bowls them over with sudden, three-man raids – has taken Leicester far this season. They have been dubbed dull and defensive. Utter claptrap. When Europe and South America do it they are labelled scintillating perfectionists!'

The greatest moment of Gillies's career came at Leicester's own ground on 22 April 1964. The English League Cup final was played over two legs in those days and having drawn 1–1 away to Stoke City in the first leg they took them to Filbert Street and finished the job with a 3–2 win for a 4–3 victory on aggregate.

Gillies was born in Loganlea, the West Lothian village in what was once mining territory. His intelligence blessed him with the opportunity for further education and he was a medical student before serving for the RAF in the Second World War. As a player he served Motherwell as an amateur before a decade at Bolton and then four years at Leicester. He was one of their regular defenders as Leicester won the Second Division title in 1954. Two years later he contemplated a career in physiotherapy as his playing days wound to a close but instead went into coaching. He became caretaker manager of Leicester at the end of 1958, replacing fellow Scot Dave Halliday, and soon began to establish them as a real force in the land. Leicester previously had been a yo-yo club between the two divisions and had never known anything like the success Gillies brought

'Matt Gillies was incredibly successful for Leicester City. He was very gentlemanly and unassuming and he had the respect of the players,' said John Hutchinson, the club historian, 'He was known as being quite silver-tongued. I've got the Leicester minute books of the time and you get the impression that players were always going in to see Matt asking for more money and they came out convinced that they'd got a good deal when in fact they'd got nothing at all. He was obviously quite a smooth operator. Shankly thought very highly of him.

'He was a shrewd judge of raw talent and a canny operator in the transfer market. He was a very, very decisive manager. For him to be able to persuade the Leicester City board to break the British record transfer fee and spend £150,000 on Allan Clarke showed his strength of judgement and how persuasive he was at the club. He was a Justice of the Peace in Leicester and well considered in the community as a whole. He was loyal, too.'

Leicester made the mistake of underestimating that personal loyalty. By 1968 Gillies had been in charge almost a decade and the job had wearied him. He even succumbed to what would now be diagnosed as stress-related illness. Bert Johnson was his assistant and friend. They had been wartime team-mates at Bolton and Gillies took him to Leicester in 1959. He was the coach to whom Gillies would deflect all praise for Leicester's tactics. When the club said it was getting rid of Johnson in a cost-cutting measure, it lost the longest-serving manager it has ever had. In November 1968 Gillies resigned on a point of principle.

Many thought that would be it for Gillies and it was a surprise when he re-emerged the following year to take charge of one of Leicester's rivals, Nottingham Forest. In four years at the City Ground he could not rekindle the spark there had been at Leicester. The football was generally dour and when senior players left the club it lacked the resources or the will to adequately replace them. He briefly managed the fading Jim Baxter and wanted to become the first man to give Alex Ferguson a job in English football. Gillies asked Baxter why Ferguson was not in the Rangers first team at the time. Having received an encouraging explanation, a few days later Gillies submitted a £200,000 bid which was accepted by Rangers. Ferguson agreed to come before changing his mind and signing for Falkirk. Ferguson telephoned Gillies to apologise.

By the time he resigned from Forest in October 1972, a few months after they had been relegated, Gillies had become the manager who brought Martin O'Neill into English football, signing him from the Northern Irish club Distillery for £15,000. It was impossible for him to suspect that one day his name and O'Neill's would be bracketed for another reason. 'If you were to name Leicester City's top three managers there would be Peter Hodge, there would be Matt Gillies and there'd be Martin O'Neill,' said John Hutchinson.

Gillies wasn't often seen around the club after he left. He drifted out of football to work for an engineering firm. When he died in Nottingham on Christmas Eve 1998, aged 77, his old club was quick to pay its respects. Three days later Leicester played at home to Blackburn Rovers. The stadium fell effortlessly into a minute's silence for the gentleman who had given them the first taste of real glory.

Dave Mackay

'I felt vindicated and a great deal of personal satisfaction'

Dave Mackay straddled a gulf between two eras of domination by Scottish managers in England. What happened to Scotland's routine control south of the border between 1974 and 1985? In a dozen seasons the English title was claimed only once by a Scottish manager. By historical standards that amounted to an unimaginable drought.

It was down to Mackay to bridge the gap between the Sir Matt Busby/Bill Shankly generation and the modern reigns of Kenny Dalglish, George Graham and Sir Alex Ferguson. Mackay was the only Scot to lift the English title in that 11-year period. He did it with a club which has never won a major trophy since.

Mackay is remembered as the iconic, hard-as-nails left-half who inspired Hearts and Tottenham to league and cup victories in the 1950s and '60s. He is one of the legendary football figures of his time, a man whose name is used to illustrate an admirable combination of uncompromising toughness and a sense of fair play. The most famous image of him is when he held Billy Bremner at the throat when the Leeds man, no shrinking violet himself, had the temerity to foul him soon after a return from injury. Mackay's managerial career spanned more than two decades and is largely unremembered and overlooked in comparison to Scotland's other champion managers, but what he achieved at Derby County in 1975 was hugely creditable.

Derby had turned to him when 'God' left. With their supporters in uproar about the resignation of Brian Clough and Peter Taylor – they quit over boardroom interference – chairman Sam Longson knew there was only one man he could appoint who might appease them: Mackay, who had been signed as a player by Clough, performed there between 1968 and 1971 and captained them to the Second Division title and promotion. That was why Longson offered him the job, rather than because he had made a solid, unspectacular start to his managerial career with Swindon Town and Nottingham Forest.

The strength of feeling was so strong that Derby players, former team-mates of Mackay's, privately encouraged him not to come. It wouldn't be fair on him, they said. Clough was too popular and there was a chance he might be persuaded to return. The Clough story dominated the British news agenda. Newspapers reported that the team would not play for Mackay; that they intended to strike until Clough returned.

But Mackay had already accepted the job and his personal integrity meant there could be no changing his mind. He plunged into an enormously stressful environment. In 1973 he was a popular football man who had made himself unpopular by filling Clough's shoes. The town had taken to the streets with a 'BBC' campaign: Bring Back Clough. It took months for the anger to subside. In the meantime Mackay somehow overcame a dreadful

sequence of early results and led Derby to finish third in the old
First Division.

By signing Bruce Rioch and Francis Lee he showed keen
judgement of what his team required to take the final step. In
his second season, 1974–75, Derby County made it. The team
clicked, win followed win followed win, and ultimately Mackay
repeated Clough's achievement of three seasons earlier by making
Derby the champions of England. 'For the first time, I did not feel
the hand of Brian Clough on my shoulder,' he said years later.
'I felt vindicated and a great deal of personal satisfaction.'

It was by far the highlight of his managerial career. When the
team's results dipped the remnants of the 'BBC' mood was quickly
whipped up again and in 1976 Mackay was sacked. He managed
for a satisfying decade in Kuwait and Dubai, then later in Egypt and
Qatar. There were also spells at Walsall, Doncaster and Birmingham.

Sadly he never took over Hearts, his first football love. Scottish
football never quite got enough of the real Mackay.

Chapter Nine

The Odd Couple and the Voice of the Managers

'Unless you have a voice, the SFA will pick you off'

They might have seemed like the oddest couple since Oscar and Felix. One was the strutting, cocksure anti-hero who was in the process of implementing a football revolution in his own name. The other was a softly-spoken and approachable figure, familiar and respected as part of the Scottish football furniture. There didn't seem to be much in common between Graeme Souness and Alex Smith, but in the opening months of 1989 an issue emerged that irritated both of them to the point of action. They had a shared belief that the Scottish Football Association was taking liberties with managers.

If it would be an exaggeration to say Souness's run-ins with the SFA became legendary, then it would certainly be fair to describe them as a compelling soap opera of the time. The young Rangers manager had plenty to say and didn't give a damn who he upset along the way, including the grey and sober men in charge of the governing body.

The SFA saw Souness as jumped-up, a law unto himself and in need of having his gilded wings clipped. Their way of doing so was to bring the weight of their disciplinary procedures down on him. When his behaviour or language were controversial – which for a while came as naturally to Souness as breathing – they summoned him to their imposing old offices in Glasgow's Park Gardens to deliver punishments. He didn't take kindly to being treated like an errant schoolboy. One of Souness's many struggles at the time was to find a shred of respect for those who were disciplining him.

In February 1989 he was fined £1000 and banned from the touchline for the rest of the season for swearing at a linesman during a match at Tannadice. Another offence two months later earned a £2000 fine and a touchline ban until the end of the following season, a full 15 months later. It was during this ban that he was captured by STV cameras watching the action against Hearts from the mouth of the Ibrox tunnel (being so close to the pitch was a breach of his ban). The SFA rolled up its sleeves for the big one: Souness was hit with a £5000 fine and sent to the stands until the end of the 1991–92 season. When he left Rangers to take over at Liverpool in April 1991 he still had 13 months left on that SFA ban. He has never worked in Scottish football since.

Souness and the SFA were a collision waiting to happen, but surprisingly the placid and courteous Smith had been hit with a couple of £1000 fines and long touchline bans as well. His canny old chairman at Aberdeen, Dick Donald, took the news with a sense of amused detachment. 'Ah, I hope you'll be paying that yourself Alex . . .' he said, a gentle statement rather than a question. Smith did indeed pay the fines out of his own pocket but he felt managers such as himself and Souness were being excessively punished. £1000 fines? Season-long bans? It was time to find a voice and stand up to the SFA. Over a football dinner at the end of the 1988–89 season the bosses of those great rival clubs, Rangers and Aberdeen, discussed resurrecting something that had been unsuccessfully launched a few years earlier in Scotland: a trade union for managers.

The Scottish Managers' and Coaches' Association (SMCA) was born and Smith became its chairman and voice for two decades. Souness may have looked like a firebrand shop steward but in fact he was an Edinburgh Conservative. Smith was the one from Stirlingshire mining stock: natural union material. Whether he was in a managerial job or out of one, the association was to become the permanent fixture of Smith's career.

'The first attempt to set up a managers' association in Scotland came in 1979, a year after Argentina,' he recalled, 'A meeting was convened at the Dunblane Hydro. As I recall it was the idea of Fergie and one or two others. Of course Fergie was a bit of a union man.

'It started well, but after two or three years it just floated around in the wind until we started it seriously again in 1989. Graeme was getting into a lot of trouble with the authorities at the time, being fined and put to the stand. So at a football dinner I said to him it was madness that we didn't have an association looking after our interests. We were all individuals, we didn't even have someone going with us when we went up to Park Gardens to face the music. It was lambs to the slaughter.

'I thought we should get an association going. Graeme felt I had a point and a couple of days after the dinner he phoned me back to take it further. Looking back on it now there was great enthusiasm. We had a meeting of the managers in Bridge of Allan. Big Billy McNeill was there, Jim McLean, Tommy McLean, Walter Smith, Graeme. There were about eight altogether. We decided to fire ahead with it and I was appointed as the chairman.'

When a Scottish managers' union was first attempted in 1979 there was no structure behind it, no real organisation, and it withered. The rebirth under Smith was different. Tony Higgins, secretary of the Scottish Professional Footballers' Association (SPFA) at the time, helped get them up and running and attended their early meetings. 'Alex phoned me and invited me to a meeting,' said Higgins, 'The great and the good of management were there. I agreed with the need for an association. I told them "Unless you have a voice, the SFA will pick you off". Individually they were ending up in front of the SFA all the time and getting hammered. In time the association was able to change all that.'

Higgins helped them become formally adopted by the GMB Union, which brought legal and administrative expertise, advice and support. The lawyer and broadcaster, and subsequently Celtic chief executive, Jock Brown, helped draft a constitution. The Scottish union could never be mistaken for its counterpart south of the border. The League Managers Association (LMA) in England is three years younger but was successful in siphoning off some of the new broadcasting money flowing into the Premiership at the start of the 1990s. It told Sky if it didn't get an annual cut of income its managers would not agree to pre- and post-match interviews. With around £1 million a year coming in from the broadcasting deals, in 2009 the LMA had 12 people on staff. No such luxury for Scottish managers. Although there is administrative and legal support from the GMB, for 20 years the SMCA operation essentially amounted to Smith being endlessly giving with his time and taking calls on his mobile phone.

'I feel very passionately about it, I always have,' he said, 'It wasn't set up as a militant group, it wasn't out to change the world. But in our quiet way we got quite a lot done. Reducing the length of the bans managers could get was one of the things we were able to change. Those blanket one-year bans and £1000 fines were removed. We also had some influence on the committees within the SFA. We've helped find clubs for out-of-work managers and we've helped secure compensation deals for managers who have been sacked.' It was the SMCA that secured a £36,000 sportscotland grant for managers and their assistants to have heart checks and health MOTs because of the stress of the job.

After the early enthusiasm Smith and Souness inspired in 1989 the interest gradually dwindled as it had a decade earlier, but the association continued. This time it had the GMB and SPFA's support and it had Smith as the permanent figurehead holding it together. 'The managers kept changing – leaving or being sacked – and that meant it was hard to keep the association together, especially if it was a committee member who was sacked. So managers would leave for England, or go out of the game, and others might come in who didn't have the same enthusiasm for it. That was disruptive. We decided that if there was an issue and a football figure or a journalist needed a reaction on behalf of the Managers and Coaches Association they would come on to me and I would give an opinion on behalf of the rest of the managers.'

Smith won the Scottish Cup with St Mirren in 1987 and with Aberdeen in 1990, a few months after he had also taken the League Cup to Pittodrie. His managerial career began at Stenhousemuir in 1969 and also took in spells at Stirling Albion, Clyde, Dundee United, the Scottish under-21 team and Ross County in 2005. That meant 36 years in the dugout (except when the SFA banned him). The sheer longevity of his career, and the fact that for 20 years he was the man journalists would turn to for a quote on the managerial issues of the day, meant Smith became a father figure in the Scottish scene.

Any new manager in Scotland is eligible for SMCA membership and, should they join, they pay their modest subscriptions to the GMB, the same as any other union member. Among them, inevitably, someone will eventually emerge with the commitment to the aims and ideals that Smith has shown since day one. 'I have done it for years and I think it reached the stage where a younger man needed to come in and drive it on. It needed to be someone 20 years younger than me. Maybe a young manager who feels he's had a hard deal and needs to find a way back in. There will always be new blood coming in. I would hope that will safeguard the association's future.'

Someone has to carry on what the odd couple started.

Chapter Ten
The Scotland Managers

Andy Roxburgh

'You lose an opening World Cup game, you get
bombarded from every angle, we had pictures of players
supposedly out bevvying, we had calls for me getting
the sack.'

How does this sound for starters: one European Championship triumph, five European Cup wins, a couple of UEFA Cups, two English Premier League titles, two FA Cup successes and a place in the World Cup final? Not bad at all. In fact, quite a haul for teams led by schoolteachers.

Football has an odd relationship with the classroom. There is a suspicion of education and even more so of 'educators'. The game prefers to believe that its great managers must be hewn only from tough, masculine environments. In the past that would mean heavy industry or mining. More recently it simply meant coming through from an uninterrupted career in top-class football itself, a seamless transition from playing to coaching to management. Anyone who took a manager's job through any other route has always had a hard job selling himself as a 'true' football man.

Former teachers have found it particularly difficult to establish their credentials. There is something about the image of books and blackboards which seems to make many people in football uneasy.

Take this quote that the legendary Liverpool forward Ian St John gave in 2005 about the club's former manager, Gerard Houllier: 'You couldn't get anything less of a football man. Football men are the guys who have been at the coalface from the beginning. He wouldn't know anything about that. He's a fucking schoolteacher! That's his background. He worked his way up. He's a pen pusher! A paper shuffler!'

This inverted snobbery is based on the notion that giving lectures to children or students is all well and good, but it isn't going to get very far when dealing with hardened, cynical, seen-it-all footballers. Some managers can never quite shake off the stigma of having once been a teacher: after bad results the fact is cast up against them as if it were confirmation of a sort of softness. For others, the sheer magnitude of their achievements makes such criticisms utterly absurd. The list of honours in the opening sentence of this chapter was amassed by former school teachers whose names might sound familiar for what they did years after swapping the classroom for the dugout: Jose Mourinho, Ottmar Hitzfeld, Rinus Michels and – regardless of what St John thought of him – Houllier.

For 16 years the Scotland team was managed by two former teachers, Andy Roxburgh and then Craig Brown. Neither of them had exceptional careers as players; neither of them had many medals or any caps to lay on the table; neither of them had previously managed a big club or a team of top-class players. Some always held those facts against them. 'When people were on my back about the "schoolmaster" thing their comments were hopelessly out of date,' said Brown, 'I've not actually taught in a school since 1969. There's this inverted snobbery thing in Scotland. You're not allowed to be educated and in football.'

Roxburgh in particular was perceived as something of an outsider. He was seen as being a product of some sort of privileged, middle-class background and – perish the thought – a good education. From the beginning he had to swim against the tide when it came to securing the respect and credibility which should automatically be granted to the manager of Scotland. Roxburgh was intellectual, refined, studied and meticulous. He played part-time for Queen's Park, East Stirlingshire, Partick Thistle, Falkirk and Clydebank between 1961 and 1975. When he finished he gave up teaching to become the SFA's first Technical Director while working simultaneously as a youth coach and eventually as the full international manager. When he resigned in 1993 he relocated to Switzerland to work as Technical Director of UEFA – Europe's coach of coaches – beyond his 65th birthday. He spent his entire adult life in football, utterly immersed in the game, yet he never entirely shed the image of being a schoolteacher and a youth coach who had never proved himself in charge of a club. He guided a team including Paul McStay, Pat Nevin and Gary Mackay to the 1982 UEFA European Under-18 Football Championship, the only proper international tournament Scotland has ever won at any level. When he did take over as Scotland manager, a newspaper headline asked 'Andy who?'

In some quarters Roxburgh was already being hailed as a visionary. At the start of the 1980s he pioneered small-sided games for children rather than the prevailing culture of 11–a-side for all ages which meant kids could go through a game with barely a touch of the ball. It was a policy ahead of its time and resistance was entrenched. 'Fergie was doing it too,' Roxburgh recalled. 'You want to have seen the battle we had! We both got dog's abuse. In Italy or Holland or wherever, what we were doing would have been taken for granted. The problem we had was that attitude of "Ach, we've always just learnt to play football in the streets". But kids weren't playing in the streets anymore. We were just trying to replace street football in a more organised way.'

Jim Fleeting, the coach who became one of Roxburgh's successors as the SFA's director of coaching, felt those early ideas on small-sided games did not get the recognition they deserved. 'It became known as the Ajax [Amsterdam] system worldwide whereas it probably should have been called the Andy Roxburgh system. The Dutch listened to Andy. Unfortunately his own countrymen didn't.'

Roxburgh never regarded his background, his respect for education and his forensic appreciation of coaching as matters for which
there was any need to apologise. 'I came from the streets of Glasgow.
Maybe people misconstrued me as coming from some sort of
privileged background because I had an education. My education
came from my mother and father both going out to work so I could
be educated enough to survive. That 1950s, 1960s, early 1970s era: I
can't think of anyone who came from a really privileged background.
You get labels stuck against you. Jock Stein and Sir Alex Ferguson
would describe themselves as the manager of a football team. I would
say I was a coach of players who became a coach of coaches. I think
there is often a misconception. It's not a case of saying "Let me show
you how to kick a football" as if you are some sort of schoolteacher.
It's to do with organising and training teams to make them better.
Stimulating their imagination. It's too easy to pigeonhole people.
The main thing is, can you actually do it? Can you deliver? If I stick
you in front of a group of players, can you handle it?'

As Scotland manager, Roxburgh did handle it. Stein had first
given him the notion of taking the job and he became his
permanent successor after Ferguson's nine-month caretaker reign
ended at the 1986 World Cup finals. 'Big Jock asked if I'd ever
thought about it. I said not really and he said "Maybe you should".
That's really what triggered it. I remember it distinctly: the SFA
secretary, Ernie Walker, came to me one morning and said "The
international committee would like you to take over the international team". I was kinda taken aback by the idea. Then he
added "We've got a press conference scheduled for this afternoon,
so you have lunchtime to think about it . . ." No pressure there
then! But I didn't really need the whole hour. If you're asked to
take that job on then you accept straight away. It's an honour.
There is a sense of history and pride about it. But you then have to
get on with dealing with the practicalities. You can't get carried
away with the romance of it. People will find this peculiar, but I
said I'd agree to do it so long as I could keep my real job. By that I
meant the SFA Technical Director's role. So I took on both jobs.'

His remit was to take Scotland to the 1990 World Cup – it would be their fifth consecutive appearance at the finals – and he did so with the help of a magnificent Hampden victory over France in the qualifiers. The World Cup itself was typical Scotland: it began with the humiliation of losing their 'easiest' group game, the opener to Costa Rica. Criticism poured down on the management and the tabloids smelled blood. Mo Johnston and Jim Bett were accused of breaking a hotel curfew and an alcohol ban. The days between 11 June and 16 June 1990 – the dates of the Costa Rica match and the second fixture against Sweden – were the most stressful of Roxburgh's career. Years later he was giving lectures about it.

'Nowadays I talk to other coaches about "crisis management". I tell them that that particular week wasn't enjoyable for me but it was one of the most interesting and demanding weeks in a managerial sense that I ever experienced. You lose an opening World Cup game, you get bombarded from every angle, we had pictures of players supposedly out bevvying, we had calls for me getting the sack, then we had to play Sweden, who had lost only one game in two years. What do you do in that situation? How do you get everyone focused? There were people in the camp getting the faxes through of the newspaper coverage back in Scotland. I think I only saw two pages of what was written because in general I didn't read them. So stories about me getting the sack or whatever I could ignore. All that mattered was the cause, Scotland's cause, although I know that sounds very dramatic.

'I was sure we had a good chance of rebounding well after Costa Rica. The one thing that troubled me about the Sweden game was how the supporters would react. I remember before going to the game I was thinking "How can I let the supporters know that we are suffering as much as they are?" Just saying it in interviews wouldn't be convincing. So on the afternoon of the game I suddenly had this daft notion to put a tartan scarf round my neck. People said "What the hell are you wearing that for?" I just told them it was symbolic. I just felt I had to do something. At the end of the game, when we won, I just held the scarf aloft.' Scotland beat Sweden 2–1 in Genoa. They have never won a match at the World Cup finals since. Four days later they were eliminated when Brazil scored a late winner to send Roxburgh's team out.

Scotland had failed to qualify six times for the European Championships until Roxburgh became the first manager to succeed in 1992, although he could not end the sequence of never having progressed beyond the opening stage of any finals. A hat-trick of qualifications was beyond him and when the 1994 World Cup slipped out of sight he tendered his resignation. He was in charge for 62 matches, the shortest senior career of any manager in this book.

'The great tragedy was Jock not being there,' he recalled. Stein, of course, had died during the qualifying campaign for the 1986 World Cup. 'If he had been there he would have been the father figure. That sort of experience behind us would have been such an advantage, but sadly we didn't have that luxury. We just had to get on with it. We were thrown into the melting pot. There were times when the criticism was unbelievable and I hadn't been used to that. There is always criticism. You always get the disparaging comments. You lose a game and you are criticised; you win a game and you're a hero. It's always about extremes. In Germany or Spain or Italy you would never be criticised just because your forte, so to speak, was the coaching side of things.'

With Roxburgh it wasn't only the public and the press who felt they had carte blanche to criticise. Some players thought him fussy, dictatorial and unconvincing and they were prepared to twist the knife. 'I left school to get away from teachers bossing me around,' said Frank McAvennie in 1992, 'Andy Roxburgh is just a head-master.' That was mild compared to what Richard Gough un-loaded. It was Gough who claimed that Graeme Souness simply laughed every time Roxburgh's name was mentioned, and Gough who slapped the manager's hand away when he held it out to him at Glasgow Airport after the squad flew back from a World Cup

qualifier in Switzerland. The Rangers defender had travelled with
the squad but missed the match because of injury.

The loud argument over whether or not Gough had actually
been fit enough to play was witnessed by journalists and others, and
the relationship was irreparable. 'I don't think there is any working
relationship possible between the manager and myself,' said Gough
when he announced he would not play again under Roxburgh.
Theirs was an uncomfortable relationship almost from the start.
Gough felt they had never gelled and there was no chemistry
between them. He claimed Scotland's 5–0 defeat in Portugal came
after Roxburgh's assistant, Brown, had passed on gossip about the
Portuguese team which he had heard from a Lisbon taxi driver.
Brown's version was that he was in the cab with Sir Bobby Robson
and the driver was an official of the Portuguese Football Federa-
tion. It was a great story for the press: Scotland captain at war with
Scotland manager.

Years later, ensconced in his pristine, modern UEFA office, did
Roxburgh look back on Gough's comments as hurtful? 'I wouldn't
even give it the time of day. Everyone is entitled to their opinion.
It goes with the territory. If things go wrong some people go quiet
and other people start to say "It wisnae me, it was him". That sort
of thing was inevitable. I don't bear grudges. I understand players
being disappointed, supporters and the media too. If you don't
deliver, people won't be happy with you. What I can say is that all
the time I was there I tried the best I could to deliver.'

It all seemed like a lifetime ago for him. Roxburgh is well into
his second decade as a resident of Switzerland. His base is the
UEFA headquarters in Nyon. He lives a few miles away in a house
overlooking Lake Gevneva, and it is from there that he sets out on
endless international trips to spread the UEFA coaching mantra.
His coaching mantra. Roxburgh's office shelves groan under the
weight of folders and ring binders covering every aspect of
coaching. His approach to football is incredibly detailed, stripping
the game down to its structures, movements and patterns. He
compiles technical reports on the major club and international

fixtures, devises coaching strategies and attends endless courses, seminars and conferences. There is the odd football match too.

It is a world away from the coal face of frontline management which he inhabited with Scotland, and in truth it is a position which has suited him perfectly. As soon as he took root there Roxburgh was never likely to be levered out of his Nyon coaching bunker. 'I was never viewed as a club manager. One or two clubs have asked me about the possibility of becoming a technical director but I have never followed up on those approaches. I was seen as a national team manager, not a club manager. I think five or six times other national teams made an inquiry to me but it never went beyond that because I told them I couldn't take their team to play against Scotland. People have said to me "What kind of daft comment is that?" but everyone has their own style. For me, that was just one thing I would refuse to do. I just couldn't imagine taking a team to Hampden. Plotting Scotland's downfall? I couldn't handle that. If you've got tartan blood you can't change it. If I go to Moscow or Bucharest or wherever on UEFA business I don't go as someone from Switzerland. I go first and foremost as a Scottish coach. In a small way I feel like I'm carrying the flag for Scotland. I'm often at conferences with multiple interpreters and there's a standing joke where they say to me "We're sorry Mr Roxburgh, we don't have an interpreter for English into Scottish!" '

Roxburgh could never be described as eccentric or flamboyant, yet his career has been unusual. Without being a notable player or a club manager in Scotland he rose to rub shoulders and break bread with the coaching greats of European and world football, and found himself exactly the niche that was best suited to him. In fact, he was the first Technical Director the SFA, and then UEFA, ever had. It always seemed as though he was better appreciated, better understood, within the scholarly UEFA coaching circles than in the pubs, streets, terraces and maybe dressing rooms of Scotland.

Throughout it all there were two things of which he remained proud: his nationality and his background. Among his souvenirs at the house in Switzerland he still has that red tartan scarf he wrapped around his neck on that summer evening in Genoa against the Swedes.

As for his outlook, he once gave a quote which said it all: 'When they bury me I want one word only on my gravestone: teacher.'

Craig Brown

'Folk made fun of the age thing. Age means nothing if you have enthusiasm and energy, and I have plenty. You can teach an old dog new tricks.'

Craig Brown holds a distinguished record, one he would be perfectly happy to pass on to someone else. He was the last manager to take Scotland to the finals of a World Cup and a European Championship. It means he is arguably the most under-appreciated international manager the country has ever had. Others have qualified for major tournaments but only he and Andy Roxburgh have qualified from two consecutive campaigns. Even Jock Stein could not manage that.

Brown is unique in Scottish football in that as a coach he was directly involved in four successful qualification campaigns. The personal highlights, inevitably, were being manager at Euro '96 and then at the 1998 World Cup. He took a slow, unglamorous route to prominence. There was a long apprenticeship to serve before the expectations of the entire country were placed on his shoulders.

Brown was born in 1940 and raised in a tenement in Glasgow's Corkerhill. His father, Hugh – who was principal of the city's Jordanhill College and later established the SFA's first coaching courses at Largs – had encouraged Craig to complete his education in case things did not turn out well in his preferred choice of career, professional football. He did earn the qualifications necessary to subsequently work as a schoolteacher but his father need not have worried. Brown's ability as a young player exposed him to top-class coaching from an early age. He had an enjoyable playing career albeit one curtailed by injury, then became a successful coach and manager.

'As a boy I trained at Celtic Park with the likes of Billy McNeill,' said Brown, whose memory for detail has enhanced his skill as a storyteller and after-dinner speaker, 'The coach of the youth players back then was Jock Stein, who was in the early stages of his management and coaching career. Jock was something of a father figure even then. He took a personal interest in each one of us and coached us as individuals. He also had an amazing memory. Even from our very first meeting he remembered everything about me. If I hadn't seen him for ages he still remembered that our first encounter had been when I was a young hopeful visiting Celtic Park for the first time. It made me realise it was important as a manager to give young players confidence and to make them feel special. That's what Jock did with me and the rest of the Celtic youth team.'

Celtic did not offer Brown a contract but Rangers did and he joined them in 1958, at the age of 17. He never made a competitive appearance in their first team and moved to Dundee in 1961. There was the satisfaction of earning a league winner's medal there as part of their glorious 1961–62 squad, although he played infrequently. Subsequent spells at Falkirk and Stranraer were undermined by knee problems and after five operations he retired in 1967. It was to be as a manager, rather than a player, that Scotland would come to know 'Wee Broon'.

It was while working as a teacher two years later that Brown, always popular and well-connected, was invited to join the SFA set-up at Largs. His own first move into management came in 1974 as assistant manager to Willie McLean at Motherwell. Brown learned more about coaching, tactical awareness and man-management from McLean – the brother of Dundee United legend Jim – than anyone he subsequently worked with. 'I have to say Willie's management skills did not extend to directors, car park attendants, security men, ball-boys, tea ladies or any other person at the football club who he didn't think could influence matters on the pitch. He made it clear he didn't run the football club, just the team. Willie's efforts were focused exclusively on his players and the immediate coaching staff. I learned more from Willie than anybody, although I studied the methods of everybody who coached me. He was incredibly driven, very focused and very tough. The more managers I observed at work, the more characteristics I picked up, and that meant the more experience I could draw on when the time came to take my own turn in the driving seat. I would never presume to know all the answers, but I have certainly benefited from making a study of all the managers I have had the privilege of knowing.'

Brown moved to become part-time manager of Clyde in 1977 while continuing a parallel career in schoolteaching. It was to be a long relationship at Clyde, lasting until 1986. The highlight was winning the Second Division championship in 1981–82. In 1986 he left club football to take over as Scotland's under-21 coach and was a member of Sir Alex Ferguson's backroom staff at that year's World Cup finals in Mexico. Ferguson had agreed to become caretaker manager when Stein died in the autumn of 1985 but the agreement ended when Scotland were eliminated in a formidable opening group containing West Germany, Denmark and Uruguay. Ferguson returned to work for his club at the time, Aberdeen, while the SFA went about the task of identifying his permanent successor. As under-21 coach and a devotee of Largs, Brown was the coaching soul-mate of Andy Roxburgh, who was the SFA technical director.

When Roxburgh was approached to take over as Scotland coach in 1986 he asked Brown to be his assistant, as well as continuing in his role as under-21 manager. Brown accepted the offer but not before being seriously tempted to join the board of Rangers soon after Graeme Souness's arrival as manager. It may have seemed a rather unlikely appointment but the then Ibrox chairman, David Holmes, saw Brown as a man who could bring stability, common sense and expertise behind the scenes.

Brown decided he preferred being at the coalface of coaching with talented young Scotland players. In 1989 he took Scotland to a World Cup final. His youth team reached the final of the FIFA Under-16 World Championship. Their run caught the country's imagination that June and more than 50,000 fans were at Hampden to see them lose the final to Saudi Arabia on penalties. In 1992 he was in charge of the Scotland team which reached the semi-finals of the UEFA European Under-21 Championship.

'My first game in charge of Clyde was in the summer of 1977 against Preston North End who had just appointed Nobby Stiles, a great player from the England 1966 World Cup winning team, as their new manager,' said Brown, 'Apart from Jack Charlton not one of that famous England team did terribly well as a manager. Doesn't that tell you something? Just because a player reaches the top of the tree in international football it doesn't necessarily mean that he will make a great manager. When there is a clamour for a big name former player to be appointed as the new manager at some club somewhere, perhaps it might be a good idea to look at his coaching and management credentials instead. The qualities that are required to make a top player are not necessarily the same as those required to make a first-class team manager. There are exceptions of course like Kenny Dalglish, Johan Cruyff and Franz Beckenbauer, but you look elsewhere at guys like Arrigo Saachi, who never played professional football, and Jose Mourinho.

'I felt I improved my coaching by going on SFA coaching courses at Largs, where I kept up with the latest ideas and developments. In my view I would never have started at club management at Clyde if I hadn't gone on these courses. Also I feel strongly about people assessing club managers solely on match results and not looking at the other aspects of the operation, like keeping the balance sheet healthy. The best managers are not necessarily the ones with the big chequebooks at the prominent clubs. I have always said that men like Allan McGraw, who used to be at Morton, and Terry Christie, who was at Stenhousemuir and Meadowbank, were worth their weight in gold. They were managers of smaller clubs with limited budgets. They had to be jacks of all trades.'

Brown was to serve so long in coaching and management that he saw the value of experience above all other qualities. Composure, for example, was an asset which tended to come with age. 'When I was at Clyde I was always raving on the touchline and treating everyone else as a bitter enemy, but I'd calmed down a lot by the time I took over at Scotland. You become more focused if you don't rant and rave. Sven Goran Eriksson and Carlo Ancelotti are calm when everybody else around them is losing their heads. And they were successful.'

Although soft-spoken and affable, Brown was strong-willed. 'That doesn't come easy to begin with as you listen a lot to other people when you are a young manager. What comes through the years is an inner hardness and a determination to make your own decisions. If the axe is going to fall, make sure it is because you have done something wrong and not because you have allowed others to do wrong on your behalf. You have to be single-minded and autocratic. There seems to be a measure of democracy creeping into the dressing rooms, but I am of the old school. Whatever I say is the way it must be. And then I will face the consequences of my own actions.'

After being Roxburgh's assistant at the 1990 World Cup and Euro '92, when Scotland twice failed to qualify from their opening group, the Roxburgh–Brown double act went into action for the last time through the qualifying campaign to reach the 1994 World Cup. A series of poor qualification results, culminating in a 5–0 defeat against Portugal, meant the end for Roxburgh. Brown was appointed as caretaker manager.

In his first game Scotland lost 3–1 away to Italy in October 1993. There was no guarantee he would get the job full-time. Joe Jordan, Gordon Strachan, Kenny Dalglish and even Ferguson were mentioned as possible permanent replacements for Roxburgh. Brown was considered to be very much an outside bet.

'I thought I had become invisible,' he said, 'Everybody's name was mentioned but mine. Then, just before our game against Malta, which was our last World Cup qualifying match, I was called in to meet Yule Craig, who was chairman of the SFA international committee, and Jim Farry, who was chief executive of the SFA. They told me the job was mine, up to and including Euro '96 if we managed to qualify.' Although not the high-profile appointment some supporters had desired, Brown delivered a 2–0 win against Malta with goals from Billy McKinlay and Colin Hendry. A long reign as Scotland manager was off and running.

Brown's first proper campaign was huge. Scotland *had* to make it to England for the Euro '96 finals. He pulled it off. Scotland emerged from a group including Russia, Greece, Finland, the Faroe Islands and San Marino. At the tournament itself Scotland began with a 0–0 draw against Holland at Villa Park before the enormous fixture of the group against England at Wembley. It was to be heartbreaking for Brown. Alan Shearer opened the scoring before Gary McAllister saw a penalty saved by David Seaman. Within a minute England broke upfield and Paul Gascoigne lobbed the ball over the head of Hendry before slamming a volley past his Rangers team-mate, Andy Goram. Brown took no pleasure from witnessing one of the iconic goals of the decade.

Scotland still had a chance of qualifying from the group. For it to happen England had to defeat Holland by at least four goals and Scotland had to overcome Switzerland. At one stage England were beating Holland by 4–0 and Scotland were beating the Swiss through an Ally McCoist goal. The impossible dream seemed to be unfolding until Patrick Kluivert scored for Holland. That put the Dutch through, and Scotland out.

Still, Brown was respected and a decent campaign gave him encouragement going into the qualifiers for the 1998 World Cup against Sweden, Austria, Latvia, Belarus and Estonia. It was a comfortable qualification. 'I must admit, I went along to the World Cup draw in Marseille hoping we didn't get Brazil. So what happened? We got them. And in the opening game of the entire tournament. I wasn't scared of them but I didn't want to play them at the group stages. Later in the tournament, yes, but not straight away.'

It was to be an incredible experience for Brown, his players, the supporters and Scotland as a whole. Because it was the first game of the finals, and against the reigning world champions, the spotlight was firmly on Scotland in a way it had never been before. The entire planet was watching Brown's team. Tens of thousands of Tartan Army footsoldiers made the relatively short trip to Paris for the opening game in Group A. The match still burns brightly in Brown's memory. 'I remember going out onto the pitch with the players beforehand. It was an amazing experience for all of us. The Tartan Army was there en masse. The players were all up for the game. I knew we would do well.'

Brown prepared meticulously. Would the threat come from Ronaldo, Rivaldo or Bebeto? Instead, gallingly, Cesar Sampaio put Brazil ahead from a bread-and-butter set piece after only four minutes. Gloriously, Scotland equalised with a penalty from John Collins before half-time. With less than 20 minutes left they were holding the world champions. Then fate turned against them. Cafu saw one of his efforts saved but deflect off Tom Boyd and into the net. The look on Boyd's face when he put the ball into his own goal will live with Brown forever. 'It was a dreadfully unlucky moment, as I felt we were looking good to get at least a draw. We had matched the Brazilians man-for-man. We were unlucky to lose.'

Scotland then drew 1–1 with Norway in Bordeaux. Norway had taken the lead before Craig Burley equalised. Scotland's qualification chances rested on beating Morocco in the final group game in St Etienne. It was an awful night for Brown. Scotland fell apart, losing 3–0. Two goals down early in the second half, any chance of victory ended when Burley was sent off. Morocco added a late third. The date was 23 June 1998. Scotland have never been at the finals of a major tournament since.

Brown's third campaign was for Euro 2000. An away draw against the Faroe Islands was damaging and Scotland finished second behind the Czech Republic and were thrown into a two-leg play-off against England. The atmosphere for the first leg at Hampden was electric until Paul Scholes silenced the terraces

with both goals in a 2–0 English win. The tie seemed dead and
buried. At Wembley, on 17 November 1999, Brown had one of
the most bitter-sweet results of his career. Scotland won 1–0
through a Don Hutchison header but Seaman – who had kept
out that McAllister penalty at Euro '96 – defied them again by
pulling off an incredible close-range save to deny Christian Dailly a
goal which would have levelled the tie. Scotland won on the night,
but were eliminated.

Brown retained the backing of the SFA and got Scotland off to a
solid start in the quest to qualify for the 2002 World Cup being
held in Korea and Japan. Two wins and a draw were highly
promising, but then came the beginning of his international
downfall. A 2–0 Hampden lead against Belgium was squandered
and the match was drawn. The momentum was lost. A home draw
with Croatia and defeat in Belgium left Scotland finishing third.

Back-to-back qualification failures meant Brown and Scotland had
run their course. There was a mood for change which he acknowledged. He resigned after an academic 2–1 home win over Latvia in
the final qualifying tie in October 2001. He had been in charge of 70
games, winning 32, drawing 18 and losing 20. Of the victories, 26
came in competitive internationals. Scotland lost only nine competitive games under him. His teams were organised and pragmatic, and
there was quiet appreciation of his efforts from most quarters.

A year after leaving Scotland he joined Preston North End,
where he stayed for two unremarkable years before being replaced
by his assistant, friend and fellow Scot Billy Davies. For five years
Brown was then out of management but continued to work in
consultancy roles for Derby County and Fulham and as an engaging and perceptive radio and television pundit. He became seen as
a likeable old rascal when tabloid newspapers reported a series of
relationships with younger women. It seemed 'Wee Broon', even
in his 60s and limping because of that bad knee which troubled him
for most of his life, could still charm the ladies.

He was almost as surprised as everyone else to find himself coming
out of 'retirement' to become caretaker manager of Motherwell in

November 2009, at the age of 69. The caricature of him falling off his bath chair, choking on his false teeth and using his pension book as a fan to cool himself down when he was appointed to the Fir Park hot seat, as was depicted in a national tabloid newspaper, made him laugh uproariously. It seemed an unlikely extension to his managerial career late in life but Brown showed he could adapt by steadying the ship at Motherwell and quickly winning a couple of consecutive manager-of-the-month awards. Scottish football was delighted to have him back. Witty, likeable and respected, seemingly everyone's pal and without a bad word to say about virtually anyone in the game, 'Broon' was a welcome face back on the circuit. Besides, it gave everyone a chance to affectionately tease the old boy that he was knocking on a bit.

'I always had an emotional pull to Motherwell because that is where I got my first coaching job, but never in a million years did I expect to be back there as manager 35 years later. I like to think that me being appointed showed that experience counts and is still valued. Far too often managers are written off because of their age. Folk made fun of the age thing but Sir Alex Ferguson and Roy Hodgson were doing great jobs in their 60s. Age means nothing if you have enthusiasm and energy, and I have plenty. For all the pressures in football, being a manager keeps you young, gives you a buzz. I like to think my story shows it is wrong to write people off because of their age, regardless of what walk of life they are in. You *can* teach an old dog new tricks.'

Willie Ormond

'The next one to step out of line knows it's "Pack the bags and go home".'

Willie Ormond is the only Scotland manager to take his country to the World Cup finals and return undefeated. Brazil advanced from the opening group stage of the 1974 tournament at

Scotland's expense. Ormond's team had an inferior goal difference of one.

So near and yet so far. The nature of Scotland's retreat from West Germany that summer was cruel and hard for Ormond to bear. Arguably the greatest group of Scottish players ever assembled had been at his disposal, and he knew it.

'Wee Willie' had been appointed Scotland manager with just two games left in the qualification campaign for West Germany after Tommy Docherty suddenly resigned in 1972 to join Manchester United. Ormond certainly had solid credentials for the top job, but as a personality he was as far removed from Docherty as it was possible to be. 'The Doc' was a showman who had an exuberance that rubbed off on his players. Ormond was far quieter. He was a pleasant, likeable, gentle man, but he did not enjoy being in the spotlight.

The Scottish Football Association appointed him because he was regarded as a safe pair of hands who was expected to guide Scotland over the line to the World Cup finals after a 16-year absence from the tournament. Ormond had done a sterling job in six years with St Johnstone, having taken over at the Perth club in 1967. They reached their first national cup final under him, losing narrowly to Jock Stein's great Celtic side in the 1969–70 League Cup final. More remarkable was their third place finish – above Rangers – in the 1970–71 championship. That resulted in qualification for the following season's UEFA Cup.

In that 1971–72 campaign Ormond's team made headlines all over Europe when they beat the mighty Hamburg in the first round, overcoming a 2–1 away deficit to win the return leg 3–0 in Perth. The Saints went on to beat Vasas Budapest before going out to Zeljeznicar Sarajevo in the third round. Ormond's era is honoured by a stand named after him at McDiarmid Park.

Although a man of few words, Ormond commanded respect from the St Johnstone players because he had been a fine player and a member of 'The Famous Five' – the exciting Hibs forward line of the late 1940s and early 1950s. Ormond played for Scotland six times. Whether he commanded the same respect from powerful international players, once he took over the country, was always open to question. Ormond was regarded as a steady, sensible choice after Docherty. He made it clear he was at least partly motivated by a desire to exorcise some of the World Cup memories he had as a Scotland player at the 1954 finals in Switzerland. He had played in a 1–0 defeat to Austria but also the humiliating 7–0 loss to Uruguay in Basel, the low point of his career. He openly admitted that the chance to redeem himself from the dugout in West Germany was ideal.

Docherty had built up Scotland's World Cup hopes with back-to-back victories over Denmark in Copenhagen and Glasgow. When Czechoslovakia were held to a 1–1 draw by the Danes it meant a whole sequence of results had fallen kindly for the Scots. Ormond knew that all his team had to do to qualify was beat Czechoslovakia at Hampden on 26 September 1973. Easier said than done. The Czechs took the lead on the half-hour mark when Zdenek Nehoda hit a speculative shot towards goal that Ally Hunter let slip through his grasp. Rather than get on the back of their distraught goalkeeper, the Tartan Army started to chant his name in an attempt to restore his confidence.

There was constant Scottish pressure before Jim Holton scored with a powerful header to equalise. With 15 minutes left and the Tartan Army in full, desperate voice, one of the most famous goals in Scottish football history ignited bedlam on the terraces. A move down the right saw Willie Morgan put in a cross for Joe Jordan, who had come on as a substitute for Kenny Dalglish. The big centre-forward dived to head the ball into the net and send Scotland to the World Cup. The jubilant team paraded around the pitch. There was a great moment when the captain, Billy Bremner, brought Ormond, who had been watching the celebrations quietly from the touchline, onto the field. The Scotland players raised him shoulder high to the cheers of the crowd. The terraces rose as one to salute him.

In the 1974 Home Internationals prior to the World Cup

Scotland lost to Northern Ireland then beat Wales before Ormond took his team to Largs to prepare for the major fixture of the tournament against England. He cut his players a bit of slack when they arrived at the squad hotel and allowed them to go out for a few drinks. Those few drinks became more than a few. As they meandered home a group of players gathered by the seashore to watch Jimmy Johnstone commandeer a rowing boat and take it out onto the water. Johnstone was so drunk he had not realised he had chosen a rowing boat without any oars, and soon found himself drifting alarmingly out to sea. The rest of the squad – who had been serenading him with chorus of 'What will we do with the drunken sailor?' – suddenly realised the seriousness of the situation and quickly raised the alarm. Two men who had been out night-fishing in a small boat came to his rescue.

The incident went down in history as a bit of a jape, but not at the time. It was splashed across the front and back pages of all the newspapers and Ormond faced accusations of not being able to control his players. He was canny enough to realise that he did not want Johnstone to be banned so close to the World Cup finals, and so made major threats he knew he would never carry out.

'The next one to step out of line knows it's "Pack the bags and go home",' said Ormond at a press conference the day after the incident. 'By the same token it's better that it should happen here than a month later at the World Cup in West Germany.' When the England match came along, Johnstone's form was outstanding. He helped Scotland to a 2–0 win. As he celebrated at the end, the wee man ran towards the press box and gave a V-sign to the assorted hacks who had called on him to be banned for messing about on the water.

The following month Johnstone was discovered in the drink again after a friendly against Norway, only this time it was in the bar of the team hotel in Oslo. Once again it took a contrite Johnstone and a diplomatic Ormond to convince the SFA hierarchy not to send him, and his drinking buddy Bremner, home to Scotland on the next flight. When Scotland finally arrived in West Germany Ormond was delighted simply to have made it there without any further off-field incidents. But he didn't use Johnstone in any of the three games there.

The Scotland manager was in confident mood. The squad contained Bremner, Dalglish, Jordan, Denis Law, Danny McGrain, Martin Buchan, Sandy Jardine, Davie Hay and Peter Lorimer among others. Ormond knew his team had a good chance of qualifying from a group that included African minnows Zaire, the reigning World Cup champions Brazil and Yugoslavia. Zaire were beaten 2–0 in a game that saw the legendary Law play his one and only match at a World Cup. Unfortunately for Scotland, despite having a team full of great attacking players the fact that they scored only twice eventually proved to be costly.

After the Zaire win Scotland had a creditable 0–0 draw against Brazil. Ormond's team could have won. The best chance of the game fell to Bremner, whose close-range shot somehow squirmed wide of the post. The look of utter anguish on the face of the Scotland captain as he watched his effort narrowly miss was captured brilliantly on television and by Scottish press photographers at the game.

The goalless draw against Brazil was respectable but because Yugoslavia had beaten Zaire 9–0 it meant Scotland had to beat the Slavs in their final game to definitely qualify for the quarter-finals. It was beyond them. They only drew 1–1, and that through a last-minute Jordan equaliser. Still, the drama was not quite over: only a late Brazil goal to give them a 3–0 victory over Zaire in the other group fixture won them qualification ahead of Scotland. The final totals in Group 2 showed that Yugoslavia, Brazil and Scotland all had four points each. Yugoslavia finished top because they had a goal difference of plus nine. Brazil qualified in second place with a goal difference of plus three, one more than third-placed Scotland. The exploits of Ormond's men had galvanised the Scottish public and around 10,000 supporters gathered at Glasgow Airport to welcome them home and sympathise.

There was huge expectation on Ormond's shoulders after the near-miss of 1974. He did not carry it well into the 1976 European Championship qualification campaign. It was assumed Scotland would ease through to the finals but their campaign began with three winless games, from which they never recovered. Ormond's inability to control his players became an issue again after Scotland finally took full points from a 1–0 win in Denmark. Willie Young, Arthur Graham, Pat McCluskey, Joe Harper and Bremner were all suspended by the SFA after a row in a bar in Copenhagen. They became the infamous 'Copenhagen Five'.

That meant there had been three serious and very public breaches of discipline on Ormond's watch. While the other two misdemeanours were essentially tolerated, partly because his team had been winning at the time, the latest came in the middle of an unsuccessful European Championship qualification campaign. The poor results and his supposed inability to control his players meant Ormond caved in to pressure and resigned in May 1977.

He returned to club management almost immediately with Hearts, who had just been relegated for the first time in their history under John Hagart. Ormond's time at Tynecastle saw the club begin to yo-yo between divisions. He got them promoted at the first time of asking, took them straight back down again, and had them heading straight back up. Ormond was never really accepted by the Hearts fans because of his strong Hibs connections. The conspiracy theorists had a field day when, after he was sacked in 1980, he went straight across the city to be assistant to Eddie Turnbull at Easter Road. When Turnbull was sacked Ormond took over but it was clear his poor health made it impossible for him to continue. On 4 May 1984, Ormond passed away. He was only 57.

Chapter Eleven
The Mavericks

Ally MacLeod

'You can mark down 25 June 1978 as the day Scottish football conquers the world. For on that Sunday, I'm convinced the finest team this country has ever produced can play in the final of the World Cup in Buenos Aires . . . and win. I'm so sure we can do it that I give my permission here and now for the big celebration on 25 June to be made an annual festival . . . a national Ally-day! Over the next few days, I'm going to tell in depth and in detail, exclusively for Express *readers, the answer to that question the Scotland fans have been chanting so long: why are we so good?'*

Ally MacLeod was the chief cheerleader for Scotland in the run-up to the World Cup in Argentina in 1978. He really did think his team could lift the trophy, and he persuaded the nation that his optimism was not misplaced. He was in charge of the Scotland team for just 500 days but that was long enough for him to whip up the whole country into a frenzy before a ball was kicked. How else can you explain the fact that more than 30,000 expectant fans packed Hampden Park simply to wave the team off to South America? When a journalist asked MacLeod what he planned to do after the World Cup, he replied: 'Retain it.' A few hundred were at Prestwick Airport when MacLeod and his men returned. And it wasn't to welcome them home.

MacLeod will be defined forever by the World Cup in Argentina where it seemed that everything that could go wrong, did. There were rows over players' bonuses, allegations of drinking sessions, splits within the camp and the embarrassment of Willie Johnston being sent home for a failed drugs test.

And of course there were the results. An embarrassing defeat to Peru was followed by a humiliating draw to lowly Iran. Only a win over Holland by two clear goals would salvage the campaign and put Scotland into the quarter-finals. When Archie Gemmill scored one of the greatest goals in Scottish football history with 22 minutes left it looked like a miracle was on the cards. But two minutes later Johnny Rep was given space in midfield to fire a long-range effort into the Scottish net. The game finished 3–2 and Scotland were out of the World Cup. Peru topped the group with five points with Holland second on three, the same as Scotland who were eliminated on goal difference. 'We had had one of the best sides in our football history, but somehow we had blown the chance of a lifetime,' MacLeod said after the game.

MacLeod's reputation never recovered from the debacle in Argentina but such was his strength of character that, publicly at least, he never let his head go down for too long. Those who knew him well claimed the scars never really healed. Positive thinking was always the way for MacLeod, even when he started out in management as player/coach of Ayr United back in 1966. They were bottom of the Second Division when he took over but he set about transforming their fortunes on and off the park. As well as being player/coach he was also commercial manager. His breathless enthusiasm and need to talk things up got him into a habit of over-hyping things. It was a habit he never broke.

In his eyes nothing was impossible. So when Johnny Doyle, who went on to play for Celtic, challenged him to dive from the high board on a summer tour of Canada he took him up on his challenge. What Doyle and the rest of the Ayr United players didn't know was that MacLeod couldn't swim. They looked on as he flopped into the pool and it was only when he went under the water for the fourth time that they realised he was in trouble. Gerry Phillips, one of the Ayr players, dived in to save their boss from drowning.

MacLeod had something about him though, and it wasn't only a bucketload of charisma. He left Ayr to take over at Aberdeen in 1975 and one of his first acts was to take the captaincy from Bobby Clark and give it to a young Willie Miller. That showed MacLeod could spot a leader when he saw one, although the manner in which he broke the news to Miller was typically unorthodox. He called him into his office and told him he was going to give him a special wedding present. Miller was expecting some wine glasses or a fruit bowl but instead was told he was being made captain of Aberdeen. It was genuinely a great wedding gift for him, less so for his wife.

It was when MacLeod was at Aberdeen that he honed his skills at pushing forward his own name and that of his team. He built up a reputation in the newspaper industry as someone who was good for a quote. He could certainly talk the talk, and showed he could walk the walk by leading Aberdeen to a Scottish League Cup final win over Celtic in 1976, less than a year after he had arrived at the club.

MacLeod was a hot ticket. When Scotland came calling he could not resist and on a salary of £14,000 a year he took over in the middle of the 1978 World Cup qualifying campaign. Willie Ormond had been in charge when Scotland lost to Czechoslovakia in Prague and then beat Wales at Hampden. Wins in the return fixtures meant it was MacLeod who had all the glory of taking Scotland to the World Cup in Argentina. By then the country was in the grip of a MacLeod-inspired hysteria. 'Ally's Army' was on the march. Tens of thousands descended on Wembley on 4 June 1977, including those who invaded the pitch and broke the crossbars after a famous 2–1 win over England. The sense of mounting excitement was contagious. 'Ally MacLeod has a tremendous passion for fitba' and he is a natural optimist, so really there was no other attitude he could have taken when Scotland was building up to Argentina,' said Bill Shankly.

Optimism was putting it mildly. In the build-up to the tournament MacLeod agreed to write a column for the *Daily Express*. This was how he publicised the series in advance: 'You can mark down 25 June 1978 as the day Scottish football conquers the world. For on that Sunday, I'm convinced the finest team this country has ever produced can play in the final of the World Cup in Buenos Aires . . . and win. We have the talent. We have the temperament. And the ambition. And the courage. All that stands between us and the crown is the right kind of luck. I'm so sure we can do it that I give my permission here and now for the big celebration on 25 June to be made an annual festival . . . a national Ally-day! Over the next few days, I'm going to tell in depth and in detail, exclusively for *Express* readers, the answer to that question the Scotland fans have been chanting so long: why are we so good?'

MacLeod didn't bother going to watch Peru before Scotland met them in the opening game of the 1978 finals in Cordoba, despite the fact they were South American champions. He wanted to concentrate only on Scotland's tactics. His plan backfired as the Peruvians, spurred on by midfielder Teofilo Cubillas, controlled the game and ran out 3–1 winners. Matters deteriorated dramatically after the match when Willie Johnston, who had taken medicine for a cold, tested positive for the stimulant Fencamfamine, known as Reactivan in Britain. The story made headlines all over the world. The implosion continued with the 1–1 draw against Iran before the memorable 3–2 win over Holland brought the curtain down on Scotland's infamous World Cup campaign.

MacLeod was not immediately sacked by the SFA. He narrowly kept his job after the committee chairman Tom Lauchlan used his casting vote to keep him in employment. He was still Scotland manager for the start of the next European championships although when he named his squad for a fixture against Austria he refused to meet the press to discuss his selections because his relations with them had become glacial. He did not want to face more questions about Argentina, which would have have been inevitable.

Scotland lost their first match of the qualifying campaign in Vienna 3–2 in September 1978 and that turned out to be the straw that broke the camel's back for the SFA. They may have stood with him after Argentina, but enough was enough. It was goodnight Vienna for Scotland and for MacLeod. By then he was perceived as a sad, slightly broken figure, but he did not hide. Four months after his dismissal he returned to club football with Ayr United, but left to join Motherwell within a year. From there he went to Airdrie, back to Ayr for the third time in his managerial career, and finally to Queen of the South.

The Scottish public became rather forgiving to the likeable MacLeod over the years. The fact that he returned to club football after the Argentina debacle showed he was man enough to face up to the fans who he freely admitted had been let down by him in Argentina. By the time he died in 2004, aged 72 and after a long battle with Alzheimer's Disease, he had gone a long way to rehabilitating his professional reputation. He would never manage it completely as the hurt caused by the 1978 World Cup would never properly heal in his lifetime. Every Scotland team manager learned a salutary lesson after MacLeod. Since his reign, none has ever shouted from the rooftops that their team was destined for great things.

They all knew that making promises it is impossible to keep does not sit well with Scotland fans. MacLeod found that out to his cost and sadly his failure with Scotland, rather than his club success, will remain his legacy. Through it all he tried to keep smiling, though. Leading up to the summer of 1978 his smile was shared by a nation.

Alan Rough played 14 out of the 17 games in which Ally MacLeod was in charge of Scotland and was his goalkeeper at the 1978 World Cup. He remained a staunch defender of the extrovert, exuberant and sometimes outrageous MacLeod and did not blame him for the disaster in Argentina.

'I'm heartily sick of how Ally MacLeod has been demonised in some quarters as the biggest sinner in Scottish football history. Utter rubbish! He was a man who gave Scotland self-confidence and put a spring in the step of every man, woman and child in the run-up to the 1978 World Cup in Argentina. Nobody forced the Scottish public to agree with his confident predictions that we would "win a medal" at the World Cup. Nobody forced 30,000 of them to gather at Hampden to watch the team parade in an open-top bus before we left for Argentina. They all did that – including my family and friends – because it made them feel good.

'What Ally did was lift the spirits of a nation and put a smile on all our faces. He can't be constantly castigated for that. He didn't brainwash everybody. Scottish football was looking for a saviour at the time and he fitted the bill. Although it all ended in tears the blame for failure has to be aimed mainly at the players he selected. He had faith in us but we let him down. To all of us – especially me – Ally was always upbeat and positive. That may not be a national trait but it wasn't a bad thing. Of course he was rather unorthodox, but I loved that.

'I played for Scotland under Ally more than any other player and got to know him pretty well. He was like a father in the early days and I am eternally grateful for the way he helped boost my confidence when I first came into the team. Back then I was looked on as the weak link in the team because I was "only a part-time Partick Thistle goalkeeper" and not with a big club like one of the Old Firm or a top English side.

'Some people – particularly in the English media – used to look down their noses at me. Although I played well and had established myself in the team by the time we went to the World Cup in Argentina there were still stories in the press claiming that I could jeopardise Scotland's chances of winning the tournament. Ally stuck up for me, big time. He told the newspapers and the television people that I would emerge as the best goalkeeper in the World Cup. Granted, it didn't quite turn out like that, but it meant that when I arrived in South America for the tournament I was full of confidence and had no fear.

'I accept that Ally's strange ways may have got on the nerves of some players during his time in charge of Scotland. He was an acquired taste, but I could not get enough of him. For instance a lot of the Anglos in the squad – used to certain routines in training – could not get their heads round the way Ally prepared them for games. He used to have us playing "tig" or hopping about on one leg. Some of the Anglos, who maybe had a high opinion of themselves, used to dismiss that as kids' games and felt embarrassed to take part. They also felt the constant keepie-uppie competitions that Ally used to have were below them. I would love to say there was method in Ally's madness but in reality he was a big kid at heart and probably just enjoyed playing "tig". Also, he got bored easily and because of that kept changing his training methods.

'Because Scotland was the only Home Nations team that qualified for the 1978 World Cup the spotlight was on us even more. Ally loved that, as did all of us if the truth be told. We were stars and being swept away on the mood of national excitement.

'Clearly, to have so much media watching our every move was tough and there were a lot of negative stories, some of them untrue, that came out of our camp. The worst moment for us all was when Willie Johnston was sent home for drug-taking. To this day I'm sure Willie wouldn't know the difference between an illegal drug and a chocolate drop and I've always said it was a cock-up on his part, not an attempt to give himself an unfair advantage.

'I think the whole affair was handled badly by the SFA but to the end Ally tried to make a joke about it which, for once, was maybe not a good idea. I remember being with him when Trevor McDonald, the ITN presenter, asked him whether he thought Willie had taken drugs. Ally looked him in the eye and replied: "Willie would never have taken drugs. Certainly not on top of all the booze he had drunk the night before the Peru game." It was meant to be a joke but went down like a lead balloon when his answer was broadcast back home.

'For all Ally's bravado I knew what happened in Argentina changed him and nearly led to his emotional breakdown. Before the tournament he had been full of life. A few days before our final match against Holland, when the pressure on him was intolerable, I couldn't sleep as the heat kept me awake. I decided to go for a walk and at around half past five in the morning, as I was strolling round the hotel grounds, I turned the corner to find this man curled up in a ball, like a sleeping cat, on a park bench. I couldn't see his face to begin with but his body shape made me realise it was Ally. He was all alone, on the other side of the world, looking completely and utterly broken. I quietly said hello and immediately, as was his way, he tried to give the impression he was okay and had just fallen asleep. I knew better. I knew he had the weight of the world on his shoulders and wasn't coping very well.

'The game against Holland, which we won 3–2 but failed to qualify from our group on goal difference, remains very nearly one of the greatest moments in Scottish football history. I felt so sorry for Ally at the end. If we had scored one more goal against Holland we would have made the quarter-finals and we would be talking about him now as a Scottish football legend. Even finishing with a victory against the Dutch didn't help his public image. On the flight back from Buenos Aires the English-based players got off in London along with some of the guys who were going straight on holiday and some other smart guys in the squad who decided to get off there rather than go back with the official party to Scotland, where a hot reception was anticipated.

'I wish I had followed their lead. There was Ally, Joe Harper, Derek Johnstone and me and a lot of SFA types who flew into Prestwick Airport, hoping for the best but expecting the worst. Ally, fortified by a few drinks, was first off the plane and to be fair to him he took most of the flak in what was a poisonous atmosphere. Even some of the aircraft staff were swearing at us in broad daylight.

'Ally was never the same man after the World Cup. Then again, who would be? I met him occasionally through the years and he threw me a lifeline late in my career, for which I will be eternally grateful. I was living in a reasonably big house at the time, didn't have a job and was struggling to keep up the repayments. Ally had a young guy at Ayr called David Purdie as his first-choice goalkeeper and he took me to Somerset Park as his goalkeeping coach at the age of 35. I even ended up playing one first-team game against St Johnstone when David was injured. It was a joy to work with Ally again. He had regained a bit, but not all, of his old swagger. It was great fun. Ally was the king of comedy, a man who put the fun into football. And through it all, the highs and lows, Ally remained a really decent human being.'

Jim Leishman

'Oh lord, Oh lord, you know the dangers/Every time you go and play the Rangers/Dunfermline 2, Rangers 1/What a thrill to best the Souness man.'

His verses may be closer to William McGonagall than Robert Burns, but the rhyming couplets of Jim Leishman kept a generation of football fans entertained. Not surprisingly Muhammad Ali – another who could recite a verse or two – was one of Leishman's boyhood heroes. Both would use word power to get themselves noticed. Ali – or Cassius Clay as he was known when Leishman was growing up in Lochgelly, Fife – played a big part in his early love of sporting poetry. 'You know the first poem I wrote at school was about the rivalry between Cassius Clay and Sonny Liston? It won me an award, that did, mainly because it rhymed. Well, sort of.'

He never thought that decades later he would be known throughout Britain as the football manager who had a poem for every occasion. He may have won Dunfermline two promotions, saved them from relegation and taken them to a League Cup final but it was the wild grey hair, the trademark moustache, and above all, his way with words that made him one of Scotland's best known and most entertaining managers.

It all began on *The Saint and Greavsie Show*, a popular lunchtime football preview programme in the late 1980s, as Dunfermline were about to take on Rangers, revitalised under player/manager Graeme Souness, in a Scottish Cup fourth round tie. 'I was up at the Old Course Hotel in St Andrews in 1988 when ITV sent a crew up to get my prediction for the game and I thought I would give them my reply in verse. I read out my poem to Ian St John and Jimmy Greaves which had the payoff line: "Oh lord, Oh lord, you know the dangers/Every time you go and play the Rangers/Dunfermline 2, Rangers 1/What a thrill to best the Souness man." They loved it and asked me back again later on in the season to give some more poetry predictions. It took off from there. It was good they liked my poems, and my predictions weren't too bad either. We beat Rangers 2–0 at East End Park. Okay, I was just one goal out, but I was close enough.'

Looking back, does Leishman regret all his word play? After all, it eventually detracted from his success as a manager. He was the youngest ever coach of Dunfermline at the age of just 29 and had a great reputation as a motivator, yet first and foremost he is remembered as the man with the rhymes. 'Yeah I think I kept it going for too long. I felt I lost a bit of respect for keeping doing it. I'm not a poet. I'm a bloke who writes silly lines. Actually, make that a football bloke who writes silly lines.'

As a boy growing up in Lochgelly he used to walk the eight miles to watch his beloved Dunfermline in action. 'When I was walking along the road with my mates to the game I used to dream of playing for them. To go on and manage them? Never thought about it. I would never have believed that would happen.'

They say the best managers have had an unfulfilled playing career which left them hungry to succeed in the game. Leishman fitted that mould. He was a young full-back with great potential who made his debut for Dunfermline as a 17-year-old against Ayr United. By the time he was 20 things were going even better. He had consolidated his position in the Dunfermline team, Celtic and Birmingham were interested in signing him and Don Revie at the mighty Leeds United had considered a bid. Then, one cold Saturday afternoon in 1974, just inside the half way line at East End Park during a League Cup tie against Hearts, he went for a fifty-fifty ball with Jim Jefferies, who went on to be the manager of Hearts and Kilmarnock, and his world turned on its head.

'I knew the second the pair of us went in for the tackle that something was very wrong,' said Leishman, 'I remember hearing a crack and I was in absolute agony. My leg went one way, my foot the other.' He was stretchered off with what turned out to be a severely broken leg. It took him 17 months to get fit enough to play a first-team game but the injury never properly healed. He spent a period in the junior ranks but his professional career was over. 'I had to start again and at 25 took over as manager of the nearby junior club Kelty Hearts, and I loved it. Training Tuesday and Thursday evenings and playing on a Saturday. My wages were £5 worth of scratch cards. If I won anything I got to keep the money. It wasn't exactly high finance.'

He made such a big impression with the Fife team that he attracted the attention of Cowdenbeath who took him on as an assistant to Andy Rolland, but when Rolland resigned Leishman also left and ended up back at Kelty Hearts. He was back at square one. Or so he thought. Less than a month into his second spell there he received a surprise call from Dunfermline. 'I assume they liked the work I had done at Kelty Hearts and the way I could motivate young players. Pat Stanton was their manager at the time and he took me on as youth team coach and then I was moved up to reserve coach. Pat left then so did his successor, Tom Forsyth, which left me in temporary charge of the club for a month at the age of 29, their youngest manager ever. I was aware at the time that when I was kept on as manager some fans saw me as a cheap option. I wanted to prove them wrong.

'We were part-time in the Second Division and I got paid £50 a week plus petrol money. When I took over we were fourth-bottom in the bottom division in Scotland. In my first team-talk I said to them not to use the words fourth-bottom. In my eyes we were 34th top out of 38 in Scottish football. Even then, I never really prepared my team-talks too much. I had general themes I had thought about beforehand, maybe on the Thursday or the Friday before a game, but when the words started they just kept on coming. That was my style, my strength. When I was on a roll in the dressing room beforehand I was really on a roll. I didn't do my poems back then, that only came in the Premier Division, but I did talk to the players a hell of a lot. At the end of that first season, where we had average crowds of just 650, I had taken the team from 34th top in the Scottish leagues to 33rd top. I said to myself "Aye, Jim, the speeches must be working!"'

Still, what it meant to him to be manager of Dunfermline was immediately clear. 'It was a dream, an incredible feeling. My first thought when I was made full-time manager in 1983 was that I would be included in the Dunfermline centenary yearbook in 1985. In other words, I would be part of their history for all time alongside the greats like Mr Jock Stein and Mr George Farm. I was going to go into the history books whether I lasted one week, one month or one year. That was my genuine feeling. I remember thinking to myself "Ya beauty! I'm part of Dunfermline history."'

Leishman had an instant rapport with the fans, who recognised him as a true Dunfermline supporter, someone who had stood on the terraces and shouted on their heroes. 'I still think the first strength in management is to realise your weaknesses and admit to them. You also have to get all the coaching staff and obviously the players on your side, wanting to play for you and the football club. Every time I was successful I had good people around me who made up for my failings.

'I was a motivator and needed good young coaches around me so that's what I set out to get. To be honest I was not too fussed about coaching. Yes, I was there to supervise the coaching and wasn't completely absent from the training pitch but there were better men than me at it. Guys like Gregor Abel and John

Robertson loved coaching and were brilliant. I let them do the job. I didn't take that as a weakness from my point of view. I saw it as a strength that I was confident enough to admit there were better people than me.'

Leishman was so in love with Dunfermline Football Club it came as a huge shock when they moved to replace him as manager with his assistant, Iain Munro, in 1990. It was a pivotal moment in his managerial career. 'I don't think the club handled the situation well at all. They wanted me to be chief executive and replace me as manager but I told them I wasn't qualified to be chief executive. Maybe they knew I would turn the job down. I was only 46 years old. I was much too young to move "upstairs". As it turned out I had no choice. I could be chief executive or leave the club. I decided to leave, but it broke my heart.'

He wasn't the only one. More than 3000 people took to the streets of Dunfermline to protest at what was effectively his sacking. It was an incredible show of support for Leishman and to this day he hasn't forgotten their backing, which sadly for him came to nothing. Leishman was down, but not out, and had spells at Inverness Thistle, Montrose and even went back to junior football with Rosyth Recreation before being appointed at what was then Meadowbank Thistle. Even he couldn't believe the roller-coaster ride he would have with that club, which would undergo a metamorphosis into Livingston.

'In 1995 we moved from Meadowbank to Livingston and started a great run. We won the Third Division championship and the following year we were second in the Second Division. The Livingston board wanted a new man to take over and for me to move "upstairs". Unlike when I was at Dunfermline, I felt I was ready for such a move. We got Ray Stewart in and he won the Second Division championship when I was director of football. Ray left and I returned as manager. We won the First Division and the next year we finished third in the SPL. The table read: Celtic, Rangers, Livingston. Unbelievable. We got into the 2002–03 UEFA Cup and played Vaduz of Liechtenstein and then Sturm

Graz of Austria. What a game that was. They put us out 8–6 on aggregate. I remember Boris Becker was in the crowd at Livingston. Incredible.'

He spent nine years at Livingston. He left in 2003 and was dispirited when they first went into administration in 2004, just before winning the Scottish League Cup. He briefly thought of retirement, only to receive an offer to return to Dunfermline as general manager in 2005. With financial problems growing Dunfermline went into freefall and with three games of the 2004–05 season left, and relegation looming, manager Davie Hay was sacked and the club yet again turned to Leishman. He was back in a dugout in desperate circumstances. 'I won promotions for Dunfermline and took them to the League Cup final, but keeping them in the SPL when I was brought back with only three games left was the biggest achievement of my managerial career. Absolutely no question. We had Dundee, Dundee United and Kilmarnock to play and had to beat the two Dundee clubs back-to-back to stay up.

Dunfermline's penultimate game was against Dundee United at Tannadice. 'That was a pressure cooker of a match. They were queuing for hours to get into the Dunfermline end. With a minute to go we were drawing 0–0, which was no good to us. Then up popped Gary Mason to score in the last minute. That last 60 seconds felt like an hour to me. I kept shouting at the ref to blow the whistle and, when he did, ya beauty! I went down the Dunfermline end and put my arms out like an aeroplane on a bombing mission and celebrated like I had never celebrated before. The highlight of my managerial career, by a mile. It was more than winning a football match. I had saved at least 30 jobs by keeping Dunfermline up. What a feeling. Some people even approached the club after the game asking if they could build a statue of me doing the aeroplane impression. Unbelievable.' The following season he moved upstairs yet again, this time to be chief executive.

Leishman suspects his days as a manager are behind him. The pressure and financial rewards of management can change people, but he believes himself to have been unaffected over the years.

'There was only one time I let things get to my head and that was when I went back to Dunfermline the second time and the players were on good contracts. There was a lot of money in the game and for some reason I started to buy big cigars and fancy cars. I bought a Jaguar then woke up one morning and thought to myself "What the hell is this about? Why am I doing this? I'm a laddie from Lochgelly, my dad was a coal miner." Who was I trying to be? I didn't know. I went back to being myself and was much happier.'

There was terrible sadness in 2009 when his wife, Mary, died from cancer on their 30th wedding anniversary. Typically, Leishman threw himself into fundraising work. How will football remember him? For the poems? 'No, I hope not. I don't think so. The history books will spell out the success I had with Dunfermline and Livingston. Me? I would like to be remembered for bringing the smile back to football. Nothing more, nothing less.'

John Lambie

'I didn't let my players drink milk before games but that was my only rule. Milk is for babies. I used to allow them to get pished occasionally but not drink milk. Curdles the stomach, it does. As for food, Christ almighty. I don't believe in all this pasta shite. What if somebody doesn't like pasta?'

There has never been anyone in the history of Scottish football management quite like John Lambie. A cigar-smoking, pigeon-fancying, greyhound-owning, gambling manager who was nearly run off the road by a furious fan. He had his own unique way of running a football club.

For him it was not unusual to allow his players a glass of champagne in the dressing room before big games, to calm their nerves. He even took his players to a brothel to celebrate a win, albeit unintentionally. Unlike other managers Lambie didn't mind letting in club directors to see the players before kick-off. 'But if they said anything other than "Good luck today, boys", I used to kick their arses out of there.'

To say his managerial techniques were a bit unorthodox is an understatement. He had no problem with encouraging a scrap or two between his own players on the training pitch, he always let them eat what they liked, and he encouraged them to have the odd drinking session.

'I never minded the players having the odd punch-up on the training ground as it meant they were fired up, which is what I liked. To be honest I walked into the dressing room a few times, ready to have a good go at them, then found myself walking straight back out as they were at each others' throats without me. I would have a cigarette outside and they would be rattling into each other. That's healthy. It's a man's game after all.'

Lambie always tried to coach with a smile on his face and can claim to be the man behind one of the greatest quotes in football management. When striker Colin McGlashan was left concussed during a game and the physiotherapist told Lambie he no longer knew who he was, Lambie replied: 'That's great. Tell him he's Pele and get him back on.'

Although a deeply religious man, he once swore 56 times during a rant about a referee and on another occasion a fly-on-the-wall BBC documentary had to bleep him out 168 times for his profane language. Gruff and uncompromising, Lambie became a legendary managerial figure at Partick Thistle. He was born in 1940 and brought up in the West Lothian mining village of Whitburn. Such was the amount of talent in the mining areas of working-class Scotland in those days that Lambie's street alone produced five men who went on to become professional footballers.

'In Jubilee Road we had myself, my brother Duncan – who went on to play for Hibs – Jim Irvine who went on to play for Hearts and Middlesbrough, Wilson Wood, who played for Rangers, and Jimmy Ferguson, who was with Dumbarton. We played all the time apart from Sunday morning, as my dad was very religious and made me go to church and the Boys' Brigade.

'There is so much rubbish spoken about managers and coaches being able to turn players into superstars. In our day we would put two jumpers down and play. Nobody coached us to trap a ball or shoot properly. You picked it up yourself. If you are going to make the grade you will. It's bred in. I fell out with many a chairman who said practice made perfection. I don't believe that. If you could practice and become top notch everybody would be doing it and making millions.'

Lambie worked down a pit for six months before signing for Falkirk from Whitburn juniors. He was a decent player who, by his own admission, wasn't completely focused on football. That was partly because he had set himself up as a successful bookmaker. 'I used to be an expert at sliding down fire escapes after curfew before games. I knew all the tricks, which served me well when I became a manager as nobody could get the better of me.'

Lambie played until he was 33 but decided to hang up his boots because the SFA was on his case after several sending-offs. 'I thought they were going to ban me *sine die*. I was 33, I was naturally fit, but I got sent off a few times. I was harum scarum and when John Prentice came to Falkirk as manager he didn't like me that much so I chucked it.'

For all the press coverage of Lambie as a manager – pictured with a glass of alcohol in his hand and a cigar in his mouth – he never had either vice as a player. 'Apart from being a heavy gambler, I didn't smoke or drink when I played. That didn't happen until I became a coach. I suppose I made up for lost time. I started out coaching at St Johnstone and then Falkirk but I also had bookies' shops and worked the tracks. I even worked the Epsom Derby and was an ever-present at the greyhound tracks.

'All my betting took a back seat when I became a coach. Up until then I would bet on two fleas going up a wall. Coaching stopped me gambling as it was a big enough gamble every week just trying to put together a team to win on the park. In saying that,

I may have stopped gambling but I started smoking and drinking. I used to have Canadian Club and coke but never beer as I am a coeliac and can't take that.'

His coaching career really took over when Eddie Turnbull, who had put him through his SFA coaching badges at Largs, asked him to take the reserves at Hibs in the early 1970s. Turnbull had put together a top side that won the Scottish League Cup in 1972 and were defeated by Celtic in a Scottish Cup final. 'Eddie made it clear the only thing I had to learn was to "keep the heid". He said I was a natural coach and he liked the fact I stood up to him. If you want to sook backsides that's fine, but the best managers are usually the most confident, so they don't mind people challenging their opinion. Sadly, a lot of former players get into management not because of *what* they know, but *who* they know. A lot of top players walk into top jobs without any experience, which is wrong. They don't have to start with the shitty ones like I did.'

Lambie managed at Hamilton, Falkirk – a job he regretted taking, and where he was so unpopular one supporter tried to run him off the motorway – and at Partick, where he made his name during a career mostly spent below the Scottish Premier League. Despite that, it was widely accepted that he did a sterling job with the resources made available to him. During his time at Firhill he dealt with some strong characters, like the maverick midfielder Chic Charnley, who he helped polish as a player to the extent he went on to play for Hibs and was even briefly touted for a Scotland call-up.

'As long as you have the respect of your players you'll do okay as a manager. Ask Chic. I fined him for stepping out of line more than anybody, had more shouting matches with him than anybody. But I treated him like a man and he respected that and we never fell out. Even today Chic is always on the phone to me asking how I'm getting on. You have to treat players like they are part of your family. If a player got into money trouble I was always the first one there. As long as he needed extra money for his family – and not for gambling – I would give him it.

'You have to walk a fine line as a manager as some of your players will be quiet guys, especially the younger ones, who need their confidence built up. It's no good slagging these players off because, like a teenage son, he will go quiet, not work for you, then leave the house. You have to realise that everybody needs a pat on the back. Some managers couldn't do that.'

As a gambler it went without saying that Lambie loved working in the transfer market and quickly realised the value of money to lower-league clubs. He never had a contract as a manager and was always happier to take his chances on a day-to-day basis. His father got £9 a week at the pit compared to the £30 a week Lambie himself received when he started as a part-time manager with Hamilton in 1984.

'I always tried to buy sensibly and sell at a profit. I just loved all that wheeling and dealing. My best moment was when I was at Hamilton, and not doing too well, and asked Eddie Turnbull to come and watch my team play to try and identify what was missing. He was there for five minutes and said we needed a midfield player to make runs from deep, so I bought Albert Craig for £11,000 from Dumbarton and sold him to Newcastle United for £110,000. A right good piece of business.'

As Honorary Vice President of Partick Thistle he can watch as much football as he wants, but accepts that his rather unorthodox ways would not stand up to scrutiny nowadays. 'I remember our chairman, Jim Oliver, thought I was crazy when I sent three bottles of champagne to the players before we played Rangers at Ibrox. They were uptight. I thought "If the great Brian Clough could occasionally give his players drink before a big game, why shouldn't I do it?". And you know something? It worked. We got a draw.

'They go on nowadays about managers introducing great new training methods and strict eating habits. What a lot of crap. I didn't let my players drink milk before games but that was my only rule. Milk is for babies. I used to allow them to get pished occasionally but not drink milk. Curdles the stomach, it does. As for food,

Christ almighty! I don't believe in all this pasta shite. What if somebody doesn't like pasta?

'All I would ever ask of my players is to be honest with me, which might be hard to achieve nowadays. I would rather take six of the belt than tell a lie. My father brought me up that way. To any new managers out there I would say have fun with the players but don't take any of their bullshit. Also find out everything about them. Know their wives' names, anniversaries, all their kids' names. I always thought if you are trying to sign someone if you get to the wife, you get to the player. And don't take yourself too seriously. It's only a game after all. Have a laugh. You'll be deid soon . . .'

Chapter Twelve

The Scot who Invented the Dugout

Every football stadium in the world has a couple of them. Every manager for nearly a century has stood in them. Every supporter has hurled praise and abuse towards them. A few have even thumped on their roofs. They come in all shapes, sizes and colours and in 2006 there was even a book published which contained nothing but pictures of them. They are part of the fabric of football: the dugout. And it was a Scot who invented them.

Donald Colman was an intriguing character. He was born Donald Cunningham in Renton in 1878 but changed his surname to Colman so that his deeply religious father, who was opposed to professional football, would not be aware that his son was defying him. His playing career was unremarkable. He was a late developer and it was only after eight years with Maryhill Juniors that, aged 27, he entered the senior scene as a full-back for Motherwell and then Aberdeen. He was considered too old, and too small, yet at the age of 33 he won his first full Scotland cap and continued to play for Aberdeen until the age of 42 and then Dumbarton until 47. By then he was also coaching.

Colman was years, perhaps decades, ahead of his time as a football thinker. He lectured on the benefits of keeping possession, of running off the ball, of finding open space. Remember, this was in the 1930s. He designed football boots, gave them to players one boot at a time to encourage them to play using their weaker foot, and tried to create protective headgear for goalkeepers after

Celtic's John Thomson died in a collision during a 1931 Old Firm game.

While he was at Dumbarton he spent his summers coaching in Norway, where he saw Scandinavian managers huddling for shelter while trying to get near to the pitch to shout instructions to their teams. Colman had an idea. Why couldn't a covered area be built so that managers were close enough to be heard by their players without sacrificing the shelter of a grandstand?

When Colman became trainer-coach at Aberdeen under manager Paddy Travers in 1931 it followed that Pittodrie had the first dugouts in the history of football. It was from that innovative position that their next manager, Dave Halliday, improved Aberdeen to the point they won their first Scottish Cup in 1947 and their first Scottish title in 1955.

After Everton travelled north to play a friendly in 1938 they copied the idea and Goodison had the first dugouts in England. From there, Colman's simple, brilliant idea spread around the world.

Chapter Thirteen

'And That's Off The Record' . . . Managers and the Press

Jonathan Northcroft
Football Correspondent, *The Sunday Times*

'When you cover Manchester United you expect, at some point, "the hairdryer". My rite of passage came very early on. I was at the start of my career, working for *Scotland on Sunday* as the junior member of its sports team, and at United the "Golden Generation" of David Beckham, Paul Scholes and company were breaking through. Our editor, Kevin McKenna, was very forward-looking and decided a feature would interest a Scottish audience – providing we could get some words from Fergie.

'I sent United a fax begging for an interview, detailing that I was from Aberdeen, had played youth football against Fergie's sons, and that Fergie was a bit of a personal hero etc. I got no response. Three days into my trip to Manchester the best I'd come up with was a quote from a bloke who worked behind the counter at Lou Macari's Fish and Chip Bar round the corner from Old Trafford. Beckham and the others were playing in a reserve match at Gigg Lane, Bury, so I went along and couldn't believe my luck when I found my press seat was a few rows from the directors' box, where Fergie was sitting next to Ray Wilkins. This was it, my big chance.

'I went up. Fergie was telling Wilkins some anecdote. Unwisely

I interrupted. "Er, Mr Ferguson, I'm from *Scotland on Sunday* doing a story about your young players," I stammered, "Could I have a word?" You've heard of cars that do 0–60 in under five seconds? Fergie's face can go from normal to Ribena-coloured with its own turbo speed. "Who the fuck . . .?" his tirade began. I've blotted out the rest of it but the gist was that I had no right to just approach him and should have followed proper channels.

'When Fergie stopped shouting, and I was finally certain I wasn't going to cry, I blurted, "But I sent you a fax. . . ." This annoyed him further. "I've seen your fucking fax, I was going to give you an interview but no chance now!" he yelled. There was nothing left but to apologise. "Look, I'm really sorry," I said, "I can see I've gone about things the wrong way. I know you don't know me but if you ask Glenn Gibbons he'll tell you I'm all right." Glenn, a long-time friend and confidant of Fergie's, who was then Scottish correspondent for the *Guardian* and *Observer*, had kindly told me to use his name if I needed to. A slight change spread over Fergie's face, but only a slight one. "Neeauch. Call me tomorrow," he said, turning his back.

'Now I was confused. Did he mean he'd give me the interview after all? After a fairly sleepless night, I was up early. I knew Fergie got to United's training ground very early and reckoned I should get this over with. I called at 8 a.m. and got straight through to Fergie's cheerful secretary, Lyn, and she said "Yes, he's expecting you. I'm putting you through now." I heard him pick up. I began "I'm really sorry about yesterday . . ." only to be cut off by the beginnings of a fresh bollocking. It seemed he hadn't finished telling me what an impolite young idiot I was. I sat on the edge of my bed, in my cheap hotel room in Piccadilly, with the phone held away from my ear wondering what the course fees would be for me to retrain as an accountant.

'Finally the shouting stopped. "Anyway, Jonathan, I've spoken to Glenn and he says you're a good lad," he said suddenly, in a normal voice. "What do you want to know?" For the next 15 minutes he was sharp, insightful, generous and charming on the subject of his footballing philosophy and the Beckham crop of players. Pure interview gold.

'I've had the odd minor run-in with Fergie since and the odd press conference ban, and who on the United beat hasn't? But for the vast majority of the time I've covered United he has been helpful, trusting, even kind. And never anything other than utterly compelling whenever he's opened his mouth. No reporter could wish for better.'

James Traynor
Executive Sports Editor, *Daily Record*

'Graeme Souness was widely regarded as one of the game's hard men, one of those players who could put the boot in when it was required. Often, even when it wasn't. You didn't mess with his kind, especially when the teeth were clenched and the eyes narrowed.

'I must have missed that class while studying journalism because I wrote a fairly scathing piece in *The Herald* about Souness's tactics after Rangers had been beaten by Steaua Bucharest in the quarter-finals of the 1988 European Cup. Then there was a press conference at Ibrox on the Friday ahead of the Saturday league match. When Souness saw me standing there in the foyer with the rest of the scribblers he came bounding down the marble stairs.

' "You!" he boomed, "Get out. Consider yourself banned from Ibrox."

' "No problem, I've been thrown out of better places than this," I said, thinking back to the time the late Tommy Fagan, who owned Albion Rovers, ordered me out of Cliftonhill.

'Souness's pace quickened suddenly. His rage was boiling and his face was now so red I thought his head might explode. Of course, my fellow hacks were right at my back – darting and diving for cover behind the potted plants and chairs. "My daughter knows more about tactics than you!" he screamed.

' "In that case, maybe you should get her in to help you before you play in Europe again," I replied. Yes, I know, it was reckless. Then, remembering what my sports editor had always told me – "Never lift your hands, you'll only leave your groin exposed" – I wondered if it was too late for an apology.

"Out!" he bellowed, "You're nothing but a . . . nothing but a wee . . . a wee socialist shite! Get out!"

'I left but David Murray made Souness lift the ban and socialism returned to Ibrox. And during some dismal seasons since, so did the shite.'

Andy McInnes

Sports Editor in Chief, *Scottish Express* Newspapers

'It's not every day you're kicked up the arse by a legend, especially one with a renowned bad leg. It happened to me when Jock Stein caught me acquiring an exclusive story from Charlie Nicholas when he was part of the Scotland squad based in a Harpenden hotel ahead of an international with England at Wembley. Charlie had just met the then Manchester United manager, Ron Atkinson, "in secret" away from the team HQ. This was before his eventual move to Arsenal. I was hiding in bushes near his annexe bedroom waiting for his return. Unknown to me, Stein, who had banned all sports writers from the grounds, was on the prowl and spotted me chatting to Charlie.

'Despite his limp he was on us in seconds to grab me by the arm before kicking me – with power and precision – off the premises. Charlie ran away. To make matters worse the rest of the squad, who were having lunch in the hotel, had witnessed the scene. They were doubling up with laughter at my humiliation.'

Kevin McCarra
Chief Football Correspondent, *The Guardian*

'It would have been a blot on my record if I had not had an argument with Tommy Burns. He was famous for his temper. After he had managed Celtic to victory in the 1995 Scottish Cup final I wrote in *Scotland on Sunday* that he had better not try and use his popularity with the fans in an effort to wring transfer funds out of the then owner of the club, Fergus McCann.

'The cup final led straight into the close season so I did not see Tommy for a while. Once pre-season training was underway I knew I would have to go out and face him. I was standing outside the ground as the squad returned from the morning workout at Barrowfield. "You! My office!" he said. That office was very small. It was even more claustrophobic when Tommy's terrible temper was crammed into the room. His face was contorted, veins stood out and fists were clenched. "I ought to punch you," he said. The word "ought" came as a relief, with its hint that I might avoid a black eye after all.

'There was a small connection between us. Tommy had gone to school at St Mary's, beside the church where Celtic were founded. My dad had taught him there. I can only guess that criticism from me felt like some sort of betrayal. Then again, anger came easily to Tommy on many occasions and it also left him suddenly. We were soon chatting amicably. He clapped me on the back and said I had only to knock on his door if I ever wanted a word. There was a lot to admire about such a warm-hearted, funny individual. I wish he was still around so we could enjoy his humour and humanity, even if the potential fury would also be in the vicinity.'

Kenny MacDonald
Chief Sports Reporter, *News of the World*

'One of the more forthright managers of recent times was Bobby Williamson. Many's the Sunday morning I've been interrupted by the phone ringing and a conversation starting, without introduction, with some variation of "What's this pish I'm reading in the *News of the World* . . .?" However, there was one occasion when the self-styled reporter's nemesis showed his other side. Rangers had played Kilmarnock in an end-of-season game in May 2001. Ally McCoist was one of the Killie subs and with the game effectively over (Rangers eventually won 5–1) the home crowd spent the second half hoping for a last glimpse of their former favourite in what would be his final game at Ibrox. Williamson didn't put him on and was booed loudly by the Rangers support. I wrote that Williamson, frankly, had no obligation to give the Rangers supporters something else to cheer about while his own team was being gubbed. The next day he rang and said I was the only person who'd noted that point and that he appreciated me writing it. He gave me the distinct impression it stuck in his throat to say it, mind. From memory, I think his exact phrase was "Nice to see ye writing something correct for once . . .".'

Hugh MacDonald
Chief Sports Writer, *The Herald*

'The dynamic of the press and managers is driven by the headline. The old days of a quiet chat, an injury update and eight tight paragraphs for the back page are long gone. Sports journalists want "a line". Managers generally do not want to give them "a line". This produces a tension where managers try to deflect even the most innocuous of questions. Walter Smith is very good at spotting leading questions and avoiding them. Other managers go into a shell which means you tend not to extract anything of great note from a press conference. This changes if the managers themselves want something in the press.

'Managers do take you to task at times over what you write. I am perfectly okay with that. We, as journalists, are making judgements on managers and players and sometimes the criticism can be severe. For example, I once accused Gordon Strachan of incompetence over a team selection and he came back and made severe criticism of my judgement on him. I can handle that. If you dish it out, you have to take it.'

Glenn Gibbons
Observer Football Correspondent in Scotland

'Jock Stein was exceptional. He was intimidating, but it was an inverted thing because he could flatter you. Alex Ferguson once said to me "When I was a player and big Jock spoke to me I felt a million dollars." If Jock spoke to you, you just felt terrific. Before my first foreign trip as a reporter covering Celtic I said to him "Mr Stein, I'm going with the team on Monday" and he said "I know" – as if he wouldn't! I said "Do you mind if I call you Jock?" He said that was fine. I was so pleased I went away kicking my heels. He was a huge figure. I've never been affected by anyone else like that, at all. He was something different.

'It was true that you could walk into a room and know he was there without seeing him. It wasn't difficult to understand how he could influence the press. Some of the fights were legendary. Fierce. The same with Ferguson. Ferocious. It could be over anything. Something you'd written, a line of questioning, even a bad result. Going to see managers used to be a totally different experience from the way it is now. In the early days you didn't get inside the stadium foyer to sit and wait for someone. At Hampden we used to stand out on the steps. Scotland-England games, you'd stand there waiting for them to come out. So if it was raining you were wet.

'For the daily newspaper men the Sunday visit was the best of all when the two Jocks, Wallace and Stein, were in charge at Rangers and Celtic. You didn't see them at all on the Saturday after a game; you went out to see them on the Sunday, about 11 o'clock on the Sunday morning the day after a game. Big Stein was especially priceless because if Celtic had a bad result he would deliberately think something up for the newspapers to take the attention away. You were almost pleased if Celtic got a bad result because you'd get a better story from the manager. Especially if Rangers won that weekend. If Rangers didn't win he would be normal. But if Celtic lost and Rangers won he would come out with a line, and sometimes they were humdingers. Half a dozen of us would go out. Blether, blether, blether. Laugh. Joke. That relationship isn't there between managers and the press now.'

Roger Hannah
Chief Football Writer, *The Scottish Sun*

'There have been greater Scotland managers than Ally MacLeod. There have been greater club bosses than Ally MacLeod. But there can never have been a gaffer with the larger-than-life personality or all-consuming passion of the original "Super Ally". When he took over at Ayr United again in the late 1980s I was a cub reporter at the *Carrick Gazette* who would go on to work for the *Ayr Advertiser*.

'To us young reporters some of the stories about Ally circulating in the local Ayrshire newsrooms at the time were journalistic gold. For instance he'd welcome his players into his Ayr home on a Sunday afternoon to watch "The Big Match" on Ulster TV. It was the only way to watch England's big, live game in those days and he'd open beers while his wife, Faye, made the sandwiches. One Sunday, as George Graham's all-conquering Arsenal side strolled to a one-sided win he told his Ayr players: "We'd beat them, y'know."

'As fate would have it, the Gunners were the first pre-season opponents to appear at Somerset Park the following season. Result: Ayr United 0 Arsenal 6. Ally was furious. His shrill tones threatened to strip the paint from the dressing room walls afterwards. When one bold player suggested the manager was over-reacting, his reply was short and to the point. "I'm not angry with you boys. I'm just raging with whoever organised this game so early. With another week's training, we'd have beaten them!"'

Mike Aitken
Former Chief Football Writer and Chief Sports
Writer, *The Scotsman*

'When Sir Alex Ferguson was in charge at Aberdeen he used to have two rooms at Pittodrie where he used to meet the press after matches. There was an "on the record" room and an "off the record" room. In the "on the record" room you got a cup of tea as Alex gave you run-of-the-mill of quotes as well as some follow-up stuff for the day after that. Then you moved into the next room and he would be pouring the alcoholic drinks and you would have a blether. Nothing that was ever said in that room ever appeared in any newspaper, anywhere. It was in that room that he told you what he really thought about, say, the referee or anything else that was bothering him.

'Sadly the element of trust that existed between football writers and managers has diminished through the years. When I started out at the age of 22 there was mutual respect, at least in 90 per cent of cases. Part of the reason for that was that we flew on the same flights as the managers and the players, stayed in the same hotels and sometimes drank at the same bars. The managers knew all of the travelling press pack, which was much smaller than it is nowadays, and could put faces to the by-lines. That meant they could take us to task personally if they didn't agree with something we wrote. People may say that sportswriters back then were a bit too cosy with players and managers and, yes, I accept that may have been the case. We would turn a blind eye to most events that happened off the pitch or training field.

'Nowadays news reporters are all over stories involving the antics of players, with the "Boozegate" saga being a prime example. That led to the suspension of Barry Ferguson and Allan McGregor from playing for Scotland after an early morning drinking session. I am not convinced that story would have seen the light of day 30 or 40 years ago, at least it would have been unlikely to have been broken by football writers.

'Television has also not been blameless. A lot of managers think television will use a pretty girl to ask an awkward question which, if it had been asked by a man, would have led to a flurry of abuse both on and off camera. The managers I know feel they cannot respond in such a way to a young woman on air and feel some television channels are being manipulative and cynical by using this ploy.

'As for the characters I dealt with as a press man through the years, three managers stand far above everybody else. Sir Alex Ferguson, Jock Stein and Jim McLean – three of the greatest Scottish managers of all time – were all working in Scotland during my career, which was great for me as they all provided great copy. What all three of them had in common was that they were clever men. In the case of Sir Alex and big Jock they wanted to be in control of the press as best they could and were masters of using their press conferences to get their points across. Wee Jim couldn't care less and kept falling out with sports writers.'

Rhona McLeod
BBC Scotland sports presenter

'Ian McCall and myself still laugh when we remember the time he asked me out on air, and I knocked him back. He was manager of Clydebank and I was a young reporter covering his team's match against Alloa. He was in a good mood because Clydebank had won and as we were winding up the interview he asked me on air what I was doing that night. I said: "It's okay Ian, I'm busy."

'That's the only time being a woman reporting on football put me in an embarrassing situation. When I started out there was really only me, Hazel Irvine and Alison Walker involved in the football scene in Scotland, but that has changed a lot in recent years with more women working in all aspects of the football media, which is good. Certainly the fact I started out subbing football stories on a Saturday night for the *Sunday Mail* and then went on to cover Second Division games and worked my way up meant I maybe paid my dues and gained great experience before I started covering big press conferences and dealing with the top managers.

'Hanging about outside men's changing rooms may seem a little strange for a woman but I never used to bat an eyelid. I did a bit of work in the USA and while I was covering American Football matches it was the norm for all the reporters to be invited in to the changing rooms after games, whether they be men or women. Can I imagine the media being allowed into the dressing room after football matches here? Absolutely not, which is fine by me. I'm perfectly happy to be kept waiting outside the door.'

Mark Guidi
Chief Football Writer, *Sunday Mail*

'Hibs are the only club to threaten to take me to court over a story. I claimed Jim Duffy had Jackie McNamara Snr foisted upon him by the Hibs board when he took over at Easter Road in 1996. Duffy and McNamara weren't happy about the story. Fast forward six months to the 1997 Scottish Football Writers' Association Player of the Year dinner. It's about midnight and a few drinks have been taken by one and all. I'm in the lift ready to go down to the bar in the foyer and can see Jackie coming towards it. Now, I know him but he's never met me. But someone had tipped him the wink that I'm standing three yards in front of him. The doors are about to close and I think there won't be an incident. Then I see Jackie hit the button for the lift and the doors start to open again.

'"Are you Mark Guidi?"

'"Aye."

'"I want a word. Step outside."

'The only words that were exchanged came from him: "What about that fucking story you wrote?" The next thing, we're rolling around the floor of the Glasgow Hilton hotel. We had to be pulled apart. It was heading for a great scrap! We laugh about it now and meet up every year at the SFWA dinner and go through the motions of 1997. One thing makes me glad I wrote the story. I'd never have had the pleasure of Jackie McNamara's company for all these years if I hadn't written it.'

Roddy Forsyth
Daily Telegraph and BBC 'Radio 5 Live'

'Pittodrie under the pre-knighthood Alex Ferguson was incredibly lively. Other than the unexpected, you never knew what you would find there. I was walking along a corridor one lunchtime when the door of a storeroom opened very hesitantly and an old man peered out, with his finger up to his lips to indicate silence. Turned out he was hiding from Fergie and Archie Knox who had been press-ganging all available bodies into one or other of their sides for a game of headie tennis, which was an extremely competitive affair at Aberdeen at the time.

'One interview in his office was interrupted by a call from the chairman of Forfar who got Fergie's complete attention over the seemingly trivial matter of a reserve team lad he was offering to take on loan from Station Park. When the call was over, the future master of European football disclosed that he had been buttering up the chairman because the man was also on the local police committee and Fergie had been done twice for speeding in the previous week.

'At least he kept his clothes on, unlike Graeme Souness, who once suggested we record a radio interview while he took a shower in the ref's room at Ibrox. He meant it, too. A chat with Davie Hay in his office at Celtic came to a stop when he took a call then said he had to leave urgently. "I've got to go home right away – a bird's got into the house and my wife's going mental," he said. It says something about the nature of Scottish football that I automatically assumed that quiet man Davie had been enjoying a bit on the side and that the other woman had gone too far. It was only a few weeks later that I discovered the bird in question was actually a sparrow.'

Graham Spiers
Scottish Football Correspondent, *The Times*

'Apart from Jim McLean's brilliance as a coach, I was always struck by a touch of ego and vanity about him. For one thing, McLean always had the shiniest shoes I ever saw on a Scottish football manager. And then there was the comb-over hair – ludicrous as it was – patiently, even painstakingly, arranged to the last strand. And, for all his apparent contempt for the press, Wee Jim always had time for what were called "set-piece interviews" – and these usually involved a photographer attending along with the writer. Why, a photograph, too? Well, Jim never really minded that.

'My favourite-ever Jim McLean moment was one such interview. "Och, look, I'm really pressed for time", he told me grumpily when I turned up at Tannadice. A full hour of conversation later I nervously said to him, "Jim, the photographer here wonders if we could drive over to Broughty Ferry beach to take your picture there . . ."

"Och . . . I mean, how long will that take?"

"Maybe an hour in all," I replied with impressive frankness.

"Och, aye, okay, let's go."

'We were on that beach for an hour and a half, getting a brilliant image of McLean. He had given his whole afternoon to us. The following Sunday, when I saw the full-page treatment my newspaper gave him in words and pictures, I realised that he had known that this would be his reward.'

Tom English
Chief Sports Writer, *Scotland on Sunday*

'I met a Celtic fan in a pub once. Actually, it was more than one Celtic fan in more than one pub, but the question they asked was the same. "How come when you lot are talking about the Celtic manager it's Strachan or Mowbray, never Gordon or Tony, but when you talk about Smith, it's always Walter, Walter and more Walter?" I said I took the point and accepted that, from the outside looking in, the relationship between the media and the Rangers manager might look a bit cosy. But before we debated it any further I had to clear up one thing. "It's 'Sir Walter' to you."

'They didn't get it. Not surprising really, because it's a bit of an in-joke. Celtic people give us flak for talking about Him in such reverential tones, but we're not slow in mocking ourselves on that front. We ham up the praise. We lay on the Watty hyperbole with a trowel. Some might think this is an example of a pro-Rangers media at work, a sign that we're all pom-pom wielding Bears, but that's not it. If it was about Rangers fans with typewriters then Paul le Guen wouldn't have come in for such a severe shellacking in the press while he was at Ibrox. The Sir Walter thing is born out of respect for a great football man, but also for the very human and likeable bloke that he is. That explain it? Now, if you don't mind, I'm busy. It's my turn to rearrange the candles at his shrine.'

Brian Scott
Former Chief Football Writer, *Scottish Daily Mail*

'You crossed Jock Stein at your peril. This I discovered one Sunday when, having been critical of him in an article a few weeks before, I needed his help to preview the announcement of an international squad. It was in the autumn of 1983. I remember that because a group of us newspaper men were due to fly out that afternoon to Malta to cover midweek European ties involving both Dundee United and Rangers. Jock was quite cordial when I telephoned him at home, answering all my questions about who he might – or might not – name the following day. I duly thanked him for his assistance, knocked out my story, and hurried to the airport. Long past edition time that night, sitting at the bar of our hotel in Malta, a colleague asked: "Did you speak to Big Jock before we left?" I told him I had done.

' "And did he give you the Jim Bett story?" the colleague enquired.

' "What Jim Bett story?" I asked.

'Apparently Jock was leaving out Bett, an important player at the time, because of some injury or other. He'd told every one of his enquirers but me. "Touché", I thought. This had to have been his subtle way of getting back for the critical line I'd adopted those few weeks earlier. Moral to the story? Anyone who messed with Big Jock – even the "mellow" Big Jock of later years – had to be wary of the repercussions.

'If Jim McLean ever mellowed, it must have been when he quit football completely. For the most part I got on fine with him. But I can't forget two of our encounters: the first and the last. The first took place in the narrow dressing-room corridor of Tannadice where, in his early days of managing Dundee United, he was wont to meet the press after matches. Celtic had been their opponents this time and I'd asked him something which either he didn't like or may have misunderstood. Don't ask me now precisely what the question was but it may have implied that his side had been, well, you know, slightly defensive in their approach.

'"Shite, shite, shite!" he roared over the shoulders of a line of people squeezing between us at the time. Then he enquired in the same fraternal tone: "And, by the way, who the fuck are you?"

'As for our last encounter, it came in the latter days of his chairmanship when United were on a downward spiral. Incorporated in a report I'd done on them was a line suggesting it might be for the best if he severed his ties with the club. When I called him about something or other a couple of days later he greeted me with the line: "You fucking hypocrite!" Jim seemed to think that, somehow, I'd betrayed him after all the years of co-operation he'd given me. And here's the irony, in the newspaper column which he began doing some time later he admitted, more than once, it would have been better for United, and him, had he stepped aside earlier.'

Ron Scott
Chief Football Writer, *The Sunday Post*

'When I started out in the 1960s there were no organised press conferences after games and no mobile phones. So getting a word with the manager or any of the players wasn't straightforward. The *Post* had its Aberdeen edition, so I used to have to get their manager, Eddie Turnbull, for a quote on a Saturday night. Now, in the 1960s and '70s Aberdeen travelled to every away game by train and fortunately every train came through Dundee, where I lived. So I'd go and stand at the right platform and wait for them arriving. I'd jump on the train when it stopped, grab a minute or two with Turnbull, and jump off again. Thankfully "Ned" Turnbull was always quick and to the point. He'd say "We were shite and nobody was injured". Then I had to make sure I quickly got off that bloody train! The good thing was that it got me out of the office and I'd manage a pint on the way to the station. And another on the way back.'

Chapter Fourteen
The Future

David Moyes

'Jose Mourinho, he can carry it off. I think if you come fae Glasgow you don't get away with talking like that. I don't think you could be brought up in those streets and start saying "Hey, by the way, I'm The One". People would say "Are you kidding yourself on, who do you think you are?" '

The Glasgow suburb of Bearsden comes highly recommended. It is a prim, leafy, genteel place where most of the residents do very nicely for themselves, thank you. The houses are detached, the cars in the driveways expensive, the lawns neat and tidy. It is a place to have a skinny latte in the morning, a leisurely round of golf in the afternoon, and a nice glass of wine before dinner. No place, surely, for a fearsome Scottish football manager to be brought up? But seemingly it happened. Biographies and profiles of David Moyes – the latest quintessentially hard, intense, disciplinarian Scottish manager – usually describe him as being from Bearsden. There was nothing else for it, as he sat in his plush office at Everton's training ground – he had to be told that this simply wouldn't do. There was a stereotype to live up to. Where was the hardship, David? Where was the time spent on the mean streets? A laugh. 'Aye, I know. But my background is much, much tougher than that . . .'

And it was. The Moyes family did move to live in Bearsden but David was ten years old by then and those distinctive piercing eyes had already been opened by an early childhood in conditions which – gratifyingly – were difficult, demanding and ideally suited to sculpting yet another character who would emerge as a figure of managerial excellence. Moyes's story wasn't shaped in Bearsden at all, but in the more predictable and challenging environment of a tenement in Thornwood, in the north of Glasgow, in the late 1960s and early 1970s. No skinny lattes or golf back then. Moyes was too young to register on the radar of the local hard men but as he ducked and dived around the neighbourhood streets and alleys, always with a football, he developed an awareness of menace and threat which has remained with him ever since.

'We lived in a close in Thornwood. I remember that close. Unless you come from Glasgow you don't really know what a "close" means. A close was somewhere where you sometimes felt frightened going up it. It could be dim going up a close, it could be dark. Who was hiding in the back yards? So you would run up the stairs because of a little bit of that Glasgow fear in the close. You had to be tough. Not physically tough, mentally tough. I see it a lot in Liverpool too. There's a toughness to the people here and there's a toughness to the people in Glasgow. In those days, early 1970s, Glasgow was beginning to thrive. It was beginning to get better. But it was still a really tough, tough city, with a real working-class background for most people. You had to be able to go and do things by yourself, play and get on with it and be in and around the men and be able to handle it, know what they were talking about and know what it was all about.'

Moyes's background has another element found in all of Scotland's great managerial figures: a direct family connection to heavy industry. His father, also David, worked in the Clydeside shipyards as a pattern maker. 'Every day I could look down from Thornwood and see the ships getting built. I could see the shipbuilding area.' The "flit" which took them to Bearsden came when his father moved out of shipbuilding into education and became a school assistant principal. The change of location did nothing to soften Moyes. In fact, as a teenager his ability as a footballer meant he began to be genuinely exposed to the danger-ous aspects of Glasgow life which he had previously only sensed as a younger child.

His talent and height meant he had been identified as a promising centre-half and he responded positively when invited to sign by Celtic Boys Club. Twice a week he had to make his way, alone, from one side of Glasgow to the other to represent the club at Barrowfield in the East End. Barrowfield is no part of town for a teenager to be around on his own at night, especially one from elsewhere in the city. Carrying Celtic gear offered no protection against those looking for vulnerable prey.

'I'd get home to Bearsden after school and I'd have to walk to the train station, which was a good bit from where we were, and I'd get the train into the town centre. Then I'd get the number 64 out to Barrowfield. The amount of nights we got chased after the training outside Barrowfield! It happened all the time. Sometimes we'd get off at Bridgeton [a nearby but predominantly "Rangers" part of the city] and we were desperate for no one to see our green Celtic bags. So you were edgy *all* the time. You had to have your wits about you. You were taught that you had to be able to run, you had to be sure that nobody caught you. Glasgow was keeping you alert, keeping you alive to what you were doing when you were being brought up there as a boy. I wouldn't change any of it.

'You'd hear all the stories before going to a game somewhere. You'd be going up there in cars and you'd be thinking: "Aw, shit, they're going to be waiting for us up here. Bloody hell, will the gear be all right in the changing rooms?" So you were going there hardened for something happening. In the main it never did.'

His father was originally from Glasgow's Springburn and his mother, Joan, was from Northern Ireland. Together they instilled in their son an appreciation of hard graft and sacrifice. Because they both worked David often spent mealtimes at his grandmother's.

Today Moyes is wealthy but his instincts and sympathies remain unchanged. He has talked of being 'dead against' private schools and sent his own children to local comprehensives so they could become more 'balanced' as people.

'Not for a minute would I say we were skint when I was young but nor were we from a real wealthy background, especially in the early days. We are all conscientious about work. We know we have to do a hard day's work. And I don't know if it's a Glasgow thing, but you don't overpay for things. If you can go for a drink and it's two for one you'll do it. I saw my dad working really hard and giving up a lot of hours to amateur football where you get no reward. My mum had to sit back and accept my dad putting in those hours.'

His father ran the Anniesland College football team and then the well-known Glasgow club Drumchapel Amateurs. To the father it meant endless spare time and energy devoted to a labour of love. To the son it was a priceless education. Here were teenage lads from Drumchapel, Easterhouse, Springburn, Govan, Knightswood – some rough-around-the-edges boys from tough areas – being brought together, united and responding for a common cause.

'I was involved in that environment from a young age because I would go with my da' when he took the team. There were boys from backgrounds all over Glasgow. I had a chance to see it all, the good, the bad and what it was like. I was pretty privileged. Later we moved to Bearsden but in truth most of my early stuff was brought up with the boys from my da's teams. From him running the boys at Drumchapel I picked up the leadership, the organisation, the planning. I picked up how things should be done. These boys were turning up with shirt and tie, in a blazer, disciplined. They all came together to play football, looking smart and taking pride in the team and in what they did. I think that's where I got a little of my understanding of leadership from.

'My mum even washed the strips for the whole team. The strips would be on the whirly. I had to fold them and set them all out number by number, and the shorts as well, so that they'd be ready for the next game. I did all that. I think subconsciously all of that stuck with me. I had also been captain of just about every team I'd played for up until then. Why? Was it because I was a big, tall, ginger centre-half? Or was it because I shouted and encouraged and clapped? I think it was probably a bit more to do with that. I'd seen my father doing it and I think it was in me as well.'

Moyes became fascinated by coaching and management in childhood. Even during an honourable but modest playing career with Celtic, Cambridge United, Bristol City, Shrewsbury Town, Dunfermline, Hamilton and Preston he saw matches from a coach's perspective as well as a footballer's. He was a qualified SFA coach by the time he was 22. Every year the SFA ran two-week coaching courses at Largs, in Ayrshire, where the managers of the day went through a high-intensity residential programme involving training drills, lectures and examinations before coaches become formally qualified and 'got their badges'. The SFA asked some clubs to send younger players along to serve as 'runners' – effectively movable mannequins who were positioned on the pitch to act out the formations and tactical moves being explained and taught to the coaches.

As a young Celtic player Moyes was sent along as a runner. He also turned out to be a sponge. He absorbed everything. 'You were on the pitch for a whole day, every day. I loved it. I could have done the coaches' moves myself because I was so involved and I was so keen. I was only supposed to be a runner out on the pitch, but I think I could have done every move at that age because of the way they were teaching it. I wanted to know it all. After a year or two of playing I realised I was missing that. So that's when I actually put myself through the course and started to get myself qualified very early. I think it was just the love of being around the football people. Alex Ferguson, Jim McLean: they were SFA staff coaches at that time. Walter Smith. In my memory I can see them beside the pitch at Largs. Andy Roxburgh in control at the time, Craig Brown was around. These were people whose knowledge was unsurpassable. Andy Roxburgh was probably the biggest influence on me as a coach. I don't think people in Scotland realise that Andy Roxburgh was a really, really important member of the whole set-up. He was ahead of his time. He was talking about things and people were saying "Ach, are you joking?", but now you look at where football is and you realise he was right.

'And then at night in Largs it used to be great because everyone went down into the town itself. I was a young boy learning. I was nearly drooling, listening to them all talking about football. I just wanted to be around all of that. Obviously it's not just about being a good coach, it's not just about doing your badges. It's about having steel, about being able to handle the pressure when it's needed. It's about having leadership. It's about being disciplined. You've also got to marry all of that and be a decent guy at the same time. Now they try to address all that on the courses too. It has changed. At Largs you used to do role-playing in the lecture theatre. I remember one time I watched role-playing between two of the coaches that went like this:

' "Right, sit down, son. What do you want?"

' "What've you dropped me for gaffer?"

' "Well, you've not been doing this, son, you've not been doing that . . ."

' "Naw, you've left me out because I'm a Catholic!"

'The whole place was in uproar! How do you deal with that? So there was a lot of that role-playing. Now you have people dealing with the media side, people doing this and that, there's much more technology, it's about whether it all looks right. So it has moved on.'

Moyes was 15 and a half when he signed for Celtic under Billy McNeill. There would be only 34 appearances, albeit enough to earn a 1981–82 championship winner's medal, before he was moved on by Davie Hay five years later. He joined his seventh and final club, Preston, in 1993 and progressed from player to coach to assistant manager before taking over entirely in January, 1998. He was 34 years old.

He kept a struggling side in Division Two in that remaining

half-season, took them to the play-off semi-finals in his first full campaign and won the title in his second. With essentially the same squad he reached the Championship play-offs the season after that. It was the sort of uninterrupted improvement which guaranteed that Preston had no hope of containing him. There were links with Southampton, Middlesbrough, Sheffield Wednesday, Birmingham City and West Ham but the interest that was firmed up, and felt right, came in March 2002. He took over from Walter Smith at Everton, becoming a Premier League manager at the age of 38. Publicly Moyes is a little too serious and guarded for soundbites, but he came out with a memorable one when he arrived on Merseyside and it instantly stirred up the city. He said Everton was 'The People's Club'.

It was also a club which had gone through six permanent managers, with only one FA Cup victory to show for it, since the glory of Howard Kendall's reign in the mid-1980s. They were one point clear of the relegation zone with only nine games left when Moyes took over and they had an unenviable reputation as a downtrodden, dour club, very much the poor relation in its own city. They still had big names on the payroll, though. If Moyes was to succeed he would have to show that a journeyman footballer who had done well at modest Preston could handle himself. He can still recall how it felt to walk into a dressing room containing Paul Gascoigne, David Ginola, Duncan Ferguson and Thomas Gravesen, and he can remember how he responded.

'They don't teach you that on the courses. Until you get a job I don't think you're ever aware of what it feels like. I was relatively young when I came to Everton. So it was the Glasgow upbringing thing again. I'm looking around. I'm thinking: "I need to have my wits about me here. Is someone going to jump out of the close at me again?" That's how you go into a dressing room. But an old friend once said to me "You can't go on stage unless you've got an act." You have to be able to go out there and do the act. Earn that respect. You have to win and find a way of winning and getting people on your side.'

Everton pulled away from relegation in his first, tail end of a season and rose remarkably to finish seventh in his first full campaign. Consecutive placings of 17th, 4th (higher than Liverpool) and 11th hinted at inconsistency in his first four seasons, but then came three consecutive places in the top six and, in 2009, a run to the FA Cup final. In terms of the company he has kept, just below the traditional top four – challenging with Tottenham Hotspur, Aston Villa and Manchester City – he has rebuilt and stabilised Everton on the cheap. His net spend has been only £5 million per year and players like Tim Cahill, Joleon Lescott and Phil Jagielka revealed a sound eye for a player in a manager renowned for racking up endless road and air miles to watch matches and potential signings. The work ethic has not diminished.

He has embraced sports science, diet, nutritional expertise, psychology and all the other modern innovations. His Preston players were once shown soundless footage of the final three minutes of the 1999 Champions League final, when Manchester United incredibly came from behind to beat Bayern Munich. Moyes is open to everything. 'You need to do all of that these days. You can't just bark at players, they will realise that you only have one string to your bow. You need to multi-task.'

A recognition that he 'couldn't quite get there' as a footballer has contributed to his ferocious level of commitment, drive and ambition, but there are other aspects. There has always been a gladiatorial enjoyment in challenging other managers, including the many he has admired. Inevitably that list has included Sir Alex Ferguson, a man he once described as Scotland's second-greatest export after whisky. Early in 1999, when he was still at Preston, Ferguson invited him to come and discuss becoming assistant manager at Manchester United. 'I didn't get offered Fergie's number two job but we did meet. It was either me or Steve McClaren and he asked Steve to join him. I think one of the things that counted against me was my intensity. I *was* intense, only a couple of years into it. But maybe Alex was able to spot emerging talent in coaching. That tells me something about him as well.

There were never any hard feelings. To have been on his radar at all was probably important for me. It helped me at the time. And he went on to win the European Cup that year with Steve.'

More than a decade later Moyes has still to enhance his enormously impressive curriculum vitae with a trophy. His talent is not disputed. Peers in the League Managers Association voted him Manager of the Year in 2003, 2005 and 2009. He is seen as having the presence, toughness, awareness, intelligence and coaching nous to potentially end up at Manchester United as Ferguson's successor rather than his assistant.

Whoever replaces Ferguson will need balls of steel. A point will come when Moyes needs to find himself at a club which can satisfy his desire to win the championship and cups, and make an impression in Europe, season after season. He has been ready for that for some time, emboldened by an attitude which is both confident and grounded. 'I think we all carry self-doubt. But my self-doubt isn't about "Can I manage?" or "Can I do this or that?". I think I can, because that's what my life is, that's what I'm brought into. But you always doubt if you're doing a good enough job. If you have six defeats could you be out the window without having done too much wrong? So I think you carry that around.

'I don't know if you could be just supremely confident. There are one or two people. Jose Mourinho, for example, he can carry it off. I think if you come fae Glasgow you don't get away with talking like that. I don't think you could be brought up in those streets and start saying "Hey, by the way, I'm The One". You know what I mean? People would say "Are you kidding yourself on, who do you think you are?" I think you are quite quickly put back in your place. If you come from Glasgow you are knocked down quite a lot, it's a place like that. But it makes you stronger, you fight back, you stick at it. I hope I don't ever regret saying this, but I think you're taught never to give in. You're taught that you don't show weakness, you don't give in and you keep going.'

It wasn't difficult to identify the Scotsman when Moyes and Roberto Mancini had a memorable physical altercation early in

2010. Everton were beating Manchester City in the closing minutes when Moyes grabbed and held the ball at the touchline. Mancini, the City manager who suspected him of time-wasting, barged into him to get it back. Moyes reared up, chest out, his entire body language aggressive and uncompromising. Those eyes blazed with anger. Very Scottish. Very Glasgow. 'Aye. I don't know if that's a good thing or not. I've got quite a lot of Scottish staff here and we talk about it. Even if someone pulls out in front of you in the car, for a Scot it's like "What the hell are you doing, eh?" There's a real aggression. But I've heard people say "Davie Moyes might be a bit too intense". I think to myself: if you think I'm intense you should have seen Fergie and Jim McLean and some of the great Scottish managers in their earlier days. They make me look like a schoolteacher.'

No Pits, No Shipyards . . . when will we see their like again?

There isn't a Glenbuck any more – not in any meaningful sense. Sure, the name is still there on the map. Anyone driving through the remote backroads of East Ayrshire might come across a sign pointing off the A70 and showing the way to the village. But take the turn to travel along this minor road and it becomes impossible to detect where Glenbuck begins, or ends, or is, or ever was. The pot-holed, single-track road meanders through the countryside until it peters out into a dirt-black works track for lorries and other heavy machinery working a large opencast mine. This ugly scar on the landscape has swallowed up what used to be Glenbuck.

It is an ex-village. Where once there were pits and an iron works, a post-office, a school, a church and a railway station, nothing remains of the community which began to vanish when its last deep mine closed in 1933. There would be no obvious evidence of Bill Shankly or anyone else having lived there were it not for an elegant granite memorial erected by Liverpool supporters and others in 1997 to celebrate 'The Legend, The Genius, The Man'. The plaque lists his achievements with Liverpool and states simply: 'From Anfield, with love. Thanks, Shanks.'

When everything seems damp and silent and still, when there doesn't seem to be another soul for miles around and you get the feeling Glenbuck is a ghostly place that hasn't stirred for decades, it is hard to imagine a connection between this unpretentious little part of rural Scotland and the noise, bedlam, drama and sheer pulsating emotion of a life at the epicentre of European football. How could such an iconic figure in popular culture, still relevant and modern to the people of Merseyside and beyond, emerge from what seems such a small, forgotten backwater? Once Shankly had crossed between these two worlds there was no going back. When he died in 1981 he was cremated at Anfield Crematorium in Liverpool. Where else? Even if anyone had given a second's thought to the idea of having his remains scattered at Glenbuck it would have been pointless. The place as he knew and loved it had been erased.

So Shankly's Glenbuck no longer exists. Nor, at least in the way they knew them, do Busby's Orbiston or Stein's Burnbank or even Ferguson's Govan. Some of the street names remain but the actual communities and the social factors which shaped them have changed entirely. The environments which moulded the legendary Scottish managers are gone forever. Central Scotland's status as the workshop of the British Empire was surrendered decades ago as coal mining, shipbuilding, and finally steel manufacturing fell by the wayside. An entire way of life was wiped out. In numerous ways this social revolution was welcome and necessary given the poor pay, the dangerous work, the overcrowding, the often squalid housing, the inadequate sanitation and the infant mortality which came hand-in-hand with Scotland's heavy industry, especially in the first half of the 20th century. But to be blinkered, and look at this from a purely football perspective, it was that shared background which forged the values, the solidarity, the strength of character, the fearlessness and the burning desire for advancement which became the template for Scotland's truly great managers. Without the colossal influence of those lost communities in developing exceptional men, how can Scotland hope to produce more of them in the future?

'I would feel very proud of men like Busby, Shankly, Stein and Ferguson representing "us" beyond our border,' said author William McIlvanney, 'But in the shadow of that there would also be a wee chilly feeling and the question "Do we still produce people like that today?" I'm not implying that good managers can only come from that background. Naturally, good men and good managers will emerge who had nothing to do with that sort of background. But the people we're talking about do represent, as well as themselves, an interesting shared background which helped to create them as we came to know them.'

The managers of the present and the future will have to find other ways to develop the toughness, the cunning and the man-management skills which some of their predecessors seemed to absorb from their formative surroundings. 'Even if we allow for the transformation of Scottish society that has occurred in recent decades – not least because of the removal of heavy industry – the extent to which we've lost the capacity to produce great footballers is ultimately mystifying,' said Hugh McIlvanney, sharing his brother's concern. 'There are signs that we can continue to turn out remarkable managers but we must expect the flow to be drastically reduced. And whereas Ferguson was the natural heir to Busby, Shankly and Stein, it seems certain there will be no natural heir to Alex.'

Without the rough-and-tumble 'universities' of heavy industry, has Scotland lost the one thing it had going for it as a production line of great managers? After Ferguson, might Scotland be reduced to something it has never been since organised football began, namely an irrelevant little country, utterly barren as a producer of world-class players *or* managers? Alex Salmond, Scotland's First Minister, remains quite upbeat about there being managerial life after Ferguson. The sense of community and solidarity which shaped the greats of the past could still be found all over Scotland, he said, even if heavy industry was essentially over. 'Maybe that particular background was a breeding ground but I still think the small town identity, or any fierce local identity, can lead to amazing things.'

All is not necessarily lost. Perhaps the production line will not grind to an inevitable halt, but merely slow down or snake off to find future managers from other areas. The heavy industry is gone and so is the supply of world–class Scottish footballers who could command instant respect even when they took their first managerial jobs at huge clubs (as Graeme Souness and Kenny Dalglish did). Those are two substantial setbacks. There is no need to throw in the towel, though. Even if Scotland cannot hope to punch above its weight in this century to the extent that it did in the last, it still has things going for it. The collective national obsession with football continues. Perhaps not to the extent it once did, but then the same can be said of any country. Football's undisputed position as Scotland's national game is under no threat. Talented individuals always will be drawn to the sport and, for a chosen few, management will be the vehicle in which their ability fully blossoms.

If Salmond is correct, there is still an instinctive sense of solidarity to be found in communities, large and small, all over Scotland. That is the quality which helped give the great managers an ability to communicate and empathise with the reservoir of young, working-class men from which football continues to draws its playing talent. And there is another reason to hope that all is not lost. Managers are a different species now. The job is more sophisticated, more technical, more psychologically demanding, more focused on the intricacies of coaching. 'Get intae them!' won't cut it any more (not that the greats were ever so primitive as to rely on that old line). Today the leading managers have to think more than ever about sports science and diet and preparation and innovative motivational tools. They have to study.

'To be a top manager these days you need your coaching certificates,' said Archie Macpherson, 'None of these greats from the past had coaching certificates; in fact, Stein made a virtue of not wanting to ever have one. But the sport has become gentrified in that respect. It's become an area where men have to be more cerebral than in the past. Now that doesn't mean Stein, Shankly and Busby weren't intelligent people – they were – but now it's become so technical, and there is such a template laid on top of management that coaching certificates or coaching knowledge of some kind is essential. Consequently that kind of rougher individual, who came from the crowds of the working-class areas, is less likely to come through the system.'

In one sense the current crop of leading, younger Scottish managers have a new, shared background of their own. Not the pits nor the shipyards, but the classroom and the coaching courses. Men like David Moyes, Alex McLeish, Gordon Strachan, Craig Levein, Owen Coyle, Paul Lambert, Billy Davies and Sir Alex Ferguson's son Darren are all tough, substantial men who at times are reminiscent of their great predecessors. But each of them is armed to the teeth with coaching certificates. They could not progress in modern management without them, but in every case they embraced the opportunity to learn. Levein became manager of Scotland aged only 45 and Coyle was only 42 when he led Burnley back to the top flight of English football after a 33-year absence and then beat Ferguson's Manchester United in their first home game.

Moyes epitomises this sense of two managerial 'types' spanning different eras. He has the imposing intensity and presence of his illustrious predecessors. He is a quintessentially hard, 'Scottish' manager in style. Yet he was willing to bury his head in training manuals and textbooks in order to have harvested coaching certificates by the age of 22. He is an unashamed student of football, of its trends and innovations. And he subscribes to a view that is not especially fashionable among all of his peers: he believes there is much to be learned from the SFA's coaching courses at Largs.

'One of the things that I thought towards the end of my playing career was that with too many of the Scottish managers it was a little bit too "sergeant-major" in style,' he said, 'That was the one thing you could have levelled against the Scottish coaches. The toughness is still there. People have said it about me, and that's good because it's not about getting rid of it. It's not to go to the other extreme where you become everybody's pal. But I think society today wouldn't have you being just a sergeant-major type. I do feel part of a Scottish group down here in England. I came down here and I looked at the amount of Scots who have succeeded in England. Alex [McLeish] and Gordon [Strachan] were top international players. Alex Ferguson was a good player as well. I feel slightly different from them. I feel I maybe have to prove myself a little more than the others because of their level as players. I think the Scottish aspect of me is very much there. There's a bit of flying the flag. I'll speak with Scottish managers when they come down and I'll have them in. I like to give it back, because managers did that for me when I first came down.'

The ability to reflect the changing tide of management is one of the many aspects of Moyes's work which impresses Macpherson. 'We might be seeing the "Last of the Mohicans" in Davie Moyes because that race is beginning to virtually disappear,' he said, 'He is something of a traditionalist. He reminds me a bit of Stein. He gives the impression of having the stature of the great Scottish managers of the past.'

Others also recognise football management's general transformation from a platform for ex-miners and shipyard workers to one for coaching technicians and students. 'I wonder if we've reached a natural turning point,' said the broadcaster Stuart Cosgrove,

'I think management is so much more complex now. There is legislation. Managing in the workplace is more complicated, you can't shout, you can't swear, you can't threaten, you can't bully, you can't sack on the spot. That can't happen any more. A typical English Premier League manager now is articulate, multi-lingual and effective with the media. These are the new skills of management. Some Scots are likely to have those skills and some aren't. But Scotland won't be able to draw from an exclusive reservoir of great working-class managers any more, the reservoir that we had and hardly any others did.

'It will be impossible to be an outstanding Champions League-winning manager without having these coaching badges and if Scotland is to have a centre of excellence which trains and produces these people why shouldn't we boast about that? Why deny it? The things that happen at the SFA's centre at Largs mean that it is, in coaching terms, the St Andrews of Scottish football: a centre of excellence for coaching skills. In Scotland few are willing to admit that because it's much easier to have a go at "the blazers" and "the Largs Mafia" or whatever. But it may well be that we will start to measure Scots in management not in the sense of their gnarled industrial past, and their trade union roots and all the rest of it, but on the idea of being "trained in Scotland". Jose Mourinho and Moyes and Coyle and the rest share this background of having been through the coaching courses in Scotland. That could be what we're measured by in the future.'

Even if there are fewer of them, there surely will be great Scottish managers in the years to come. The supply of candidates continues. On the opening day of the decade, 1 January 2010, only two Scottish clubs didn't have a Scottish manager and there were a further ten in permanent or caretaker charge of English clubs including, of course, the greatest manager of them all at the biggest club of all. The exceptional ones will, first and foremost, be exceptional men. They will adapt to their circumstances as shrewdly as George Ramsay, Willie Maley, Bill Struth, Sir Matt Busby, Bill Shankly, Jock Stein, Ferguson and all the others did.

They will sound a little different to all of those great bosses, use different jargon, occupy themselves with new issues and technology and problems which never used to exist. But some will still break through.

They won't draw on the pits or the shipyards any more, those days are gone. But they will still have something special, something that has fuelled great managers since football began: Scottish DNA. It is a country where football and football management are in the blood.

Chapter Fifteen

The Roll of Honour

A complete record of Scottish managers' achievements

In Scotland

SEASON	LEAGUE (from 1891)	SCOTTISH CUP (from 1874)	LEAGUE CUP (from 1947)
1873–74		Committee (Queen's Park)	
1874–75		Committee (Queen's Park)	
1875–76		Committee (Queen's Park)	
1876–77		Committee (Vale of Leven)	
1877–78		Committee (Vale of Leven)	
1878–79		Committee (Vale of Leven)	
1879–80		Committee (Queen's Park)	
1880–81		Committee (Queen's Park)	
1881–82		Committee (Queen's Park)	
1882–83		Committee (Dumbarton)	
1883–84		Committee (Queen's Park)	
1884–85		Committee (Renton)	
1885–86		Committee (Queen's Park)	
1886–87		Committee (Hibs)	
1887–88		Committee (Renton)	
1888–89		Committee (Third Lanark)	
1889–90		Committee (Queen's Park)	
1890–91	Committees (Rangers and Dumbarton)	Committee (Hearts)	
1891–92	Committee (Dumbarton)	Committee (Celtic)	
1892–93	Committee (Celtic)	Committee (Queen's Park)	
1893–94	Committee (Celtic)	Committee (Rangers)	
1894–95	Committee (Hearts)	Committee (St Bernard's)	
1895–96	Committee (Celtic)	Committee (Hearts)	

In Scotland–*contd*

SEASON	LEAGUE	SCOTTISH CUP	LEAGUE CUP
1896–97	Committee (Hearts)	Committee (Rangers)	
1897–98	Willie Maley (Celtic)	Committee (Rangers)	
1898–99	Committee (Rangers)	Willie Maley (Celtic)	
1899–1900	William Wilton (Rangers)	Willie Maley (Celtic)	
1900–01	William Wilton (Rangers)	Peter Fairley (Hearts)	
1901–02	William Wilton (Rangers)	Dan McMichael (Hibs)	
1902–03	Dan McMichael (Hibs)	William Wilton (Rangers)	
1903–04	Frank Heaven (Third Lanark)	Willie Maley (Celtic)	
1904–05	Willie Maley (Celtic)	Frank Heaven (Third Lanark)	
1905–06	Willie Maley (Celtic)	William Waugh (Hearts)	
1906–07	Willie Maley (Celtic)	Willie Maley (Celtic)	
1907–08	Willie Maley (Celtic)	Willie Maley (Celtic)	
1908–09	Willie Maley (Celtic)	Cup withheld	
1909–10	Willie Maley (Celtic)	William Wallace (Dundee)	
1910–11	William Wilton (Rangers)	Willie Maley (Celtic)	
1911–12	William Wilton (Rangers)	Willie Maley (Celtic)	
1912–13	William Wilton (Rangers)	Willie Nicol (Falkirk)	
1913–14	Willie Maley (Celtic)	Willie Maley (Celtic)	
1914–15	Willie Maley (Celtic)		
1915–16	Willie Maley (Celtic)	(Scottish Cup not	
1916–17	Willie Maley (Celtic)	contested during the	
1917–18	William Wilton (Rangers)	First World War)	
1918–19	Willie Maley (Celtic)		
1919–20	William Wilton (Rangers)	Hugh Spence (Kilmarnock)	
1920–21	Bill Struth (Rangers)	George Easton (Partick Thistle)	
1921–22	Willie Maley (Celtic)	Bob Cochrane (Morton)	
1922–23	Bill Struth (Rangers)	Willie Maley (Celtic)	
1923–24	Bill Struth (Rangers)	Willie Orr (Airdrie)	
1924–25	Bill Struth (Rangers)	Willie Maley (Celtic)	
1925–26	Willie Maley (Celtic)	Johnny Cochrane (St Mirren)	
1926–27	Bill Struth (Rangers)	Willie Maley (Celtic)	
1927–28	Bill Struth (Rangers)	Bill Struth (Rangers)	
1928–29	Bill Struth (Rangers)	Hugh Spence (Kilmarnock)	
1929–30	Bill Struth (Rangers)	Bill Struth (Rangers)	
1930–31	Bill Struth (Rangers)	Willie Maley (Celtic)	
1931–32	John Hunter (Motherwell)	Bill Struth (Rangers)	
1932–33	Bill Struth (Rangers)	Willie Maley (Celtic)	
1933–34	Bill Struth (Rangers)	Bill Struth (Rangers)	
1934–35	Bill Struth (Rangers)	Bill Struth (Rangers)	
1935–36	Willie Maley (Celtic)	Bill Struth (Rangers)	

In Scotland–*contd*

SEASON	LEAGUE	SCOTTISH CUP	LEAGUE CUP
1936–37	Bill Struth (Rangers)	Willie Maley (Celtic)	
1937–38	Willie Maley (Celtic)	Dave McLean (East Fife)	
1938–39	Bill Struth (Rangers)	Paddy Travers (Clyde)	
———	(Competitions not contested during the Second World War)		
1946–47	Bill Struth (Rangers)	David Halliday (Aberdeen)	Bill Struth (Rangers)
1947–48	Willie McCartney/ Hugh Shaw (Hibs)	Bill Struth (Rangers)	Scot Symon (East Fife)
1948–49	Bill Struth (Rangers)	Bill Struth (Rangers)	Bill Struth (Rangers)
1949–50	Bill Struth (Rangers)	Bill Struth (Rangers)	Scot Symon (East Fife)
1950–51	Hugh Shaw (Hibs)	Jimmy McGrory (Celtic)	George Stevenson (Motherwell)
1951–52	Hugh Shaw (Hibs)	George Stevenson (Motherwell)	George Anderson (Dundee)
1952–53	Bill Struth (Rangers)	Bill Struth (Rangers)	George Anderson (Dundee)
1953–54	Jimmy McGrory (Celtic)	Jimmy McGrory (Celtic)	Jerry Dawson (East Fife)
1954–55	David Halliday (Aberdeen)	Paddy Travers (Clyde)	Tommy Walker (Hearts)
1955–56	Scot Symon (Rangers)	Tommy Walker (Hearts)	Davie Shaw (Aberdeen)
1956–57	Scot Symon (Rangers)	Reg Smith (Falkirk)	Jimmy McGrory (Celtic)
1957–58	Tommy Walker (Hearts)	Johnny Haddow (Clyde)	Jimmy McGrory (Celtic)
1958–59	Scot Symon (Rangers)	Willie Reid (St Mirren)	Tommy Walker (Hearts)
1959–60	Tommy Walker (Hearts)	Scot Symon (Rangers)	Tommy Walker (Hearts)
1960–61	Scot Symon (Rangers)	Jock Stein (Dunfermline)	Scot Symon (Rangers)
1961–62	Bob Shankly (Dundee)	Scot Symon (Rangers)	Scot Symon (Rangers)
1962–63	Scot Symon (Rangers)	Scot Symon (Rangers)	Tommy Walker (Hearts)
1963–64	Scot Symon (Rangers)	Scot Symon (Rangers)	Scot Symon (Rangers)
1964–65	Willie Waddell (Kilmarnock)	Jock Stein (Celtic)	Scot Symon (Rangers)
1965–66	Jock Stein (Celtic)	Scot Symon (Rangers)	Jock Stein (Celtic)
1966–67	Jock Stein (Celtic)	Jock Stein (Celtic)	Jock Stein (Celtic)
1967–68	Jock Stein (Celtic)	George Farm (Dunfermline)	Jock Stein (Celtic)
1968–69	Jock Stein (Celtic)	Jock Stein (Celtic)	Jock Stein (Celtic)
1969–70	Jock Stein (Celtic)	Eddie Turnbull (Aberdeen)	Jock Stein (Celtic)
1970–71	Jock Stein (Celtic)	Jock Stein (Celtic)	Willie Waddell (Rangers)
1971–72	Jock Stein (Celtic)	Jock Stein (Celtic)	Davie McParland (Partick Thistle)
1972–73	Jock Stein (Celtic)	Jock Wallace (Rangers)	Eddie Turnbull (Hibs)
1973–74	Jock Stein (Celtic)	Jock Stein (Celtic)	David White (Dundee)
1974–75	Jock Wallace (Rangers)	Jock Stein (Celtic)	Jock Stein (Celtic)
1975–76	Jock Wallace (Rangers)	Jock Wallace (Rangers)	Jock Wallace (Rangers)
1976–77	Jock Stein (Celtic)	Jock Stein (Celtic)	Ally MacLeod (Aberdeen)
1977–78	Jock Wallace (Rangers)	Jock Wallace (Rangers)	Jock Wallace (Rangers)
1978–79	Billy McNeill (Celtic)	John Greig (Rangers)	John Greig (Rangers)
1979–80	Alex Ferguson (Aberdeen)	Billy McNeill (Celtic)	Jim McLean (Dundee United)
1980–81	Billy McNeill (Celtic)	John Greig (Rangers)	Jim McLean (Dundee United)

In Scotland—*contd*

SEASON	LEAGUE	SCOTTISH CUP	LEAGUE CUP
1981–82	Billy McNeill (Celtic)	Alex Ferguson (Aberdeen)	John Greig (Rangers)
1982–83	Jim McLean (Dundee United)	Alex Ferguson (Aberdeen)	Billy McNeill (Celtic)
1983–84	Alex Ferguson (Aberdeen)	Alex Ferguson (Aberdeen)	Jock Wallace (Rangers)
1984–85	Alex Ferguson (Aberdeen)	David Hay (Celtic)	Jock Wallace (Rangers)
1985–86	David Hay (Celtic)	Alex Ferguson (Aberdeen)	Alex Ferguson (Aberdeen)
1986–87	Graeme Souness (Rangers)	Alex Smith (St Mirren)	Graeme Souness (Rangers)
1987–88	Billy McNeill (Celtic)	Billy McNeill (Celtic)	Graeme Souness (Rangers)
1988–89	Graeme Souness (Rangers)	Billy McNeill (Celtic)	Graeme Souness (Rangers)
1989–90	Graeme Souness (Rangers)	Alex Smith (Aberdeen)	Alex Smith (Aberdeen)
1990–91	G. Souness/W. Smith (Rangers)	Tommy McLean (Motherwell)	Graeme Souness (Rangers)
1991–92	Walter Smith (Rangers)	Walter Smith (Rangers)	Alex Miller (Hibs)
1992–93	Walter Smith (Rangers)	Walter Smith (Rangers)	Walter Smith (Rangers)
1993–94	Walter Smith (Rangers)	Ivan Golac (Dundee United)	Walter Smith (Rangers)
1994–95	Walter Smith (Rangers)	Tommy Burns (Celtic)	Jimmy Nicholl (Raith Rovers)
1995–96	Walter Smith (Rangers)	Walter Smith (Rangers)	Roy Aitken (Aberdeen)
1996–97	Walter Smith (Rangers)	Bobby Williamson (Kilmarnock)	Walter Smith (Rangers)
1997–98	Wim Jansen (Celtic)	Jim Jefferies (Hearts)	Wim Jansen (Celtic)
1998–99	Dick Advocaat (Rangers)	Dick Advocaat (Rangers)	Dick Advocaat (Rangers)
1999–2000	Dick Advocaat (Rangers)	Dick Advocaat (Rangers)	Kenny Dalglish (Celtic)
2000–01	Martin O'Neill (Celtic)	Martin O'Neill (Celtic)	Martin O'Neill (Celtic)
2001–02	Martin O'Neill (Celtic)	Alex McLeish (Rangers)	Alex McLeish (Rangers)
2002–03	Alex McLeish (Rangers)	Alex McLeish (Rangers)	Alex McLeish (Rangers)
2003–04	Martin O'Neill (Celtic)	Martin O'Neill (Celtic)	David Hay (Livingston)
2004–05	Alex McLeish (Rangers)	Martin O'Neill (Celtic)	Alex McLeish (Rangers)
2005–06	Gordon Strachan (Celtic)	Valdas Ivanauskas (Hearts)	Gordon Strachan (Celtic)
2006–07	Gordon Strachan (Celtic)	Gordon Strachan (Celtic)	John Collins (Hibs)
2007–08	Gordon Strachan (Celtic)	Walter Smith (Rangers)	Walter Smith (Rangers)
2008–09	Walter Smith (Rangers)	Walter Smith (Rangers)	Gordon Strachan (Celtic)
2009–10	Walter Smith (Rangers)	Peter Houston (Dundee United)	Walter Smith (Rangers)

Scottish Football Writers' Association Manager of the Year

1986–87	Jim McLean (Dundee United)
1987–88	Billy McNeill (Celtic)
1988–89	Graeme Souness (Rangers)
1989–90	Andy Roxburgh (Scotland)
1990–91	Alex Totten (St. Johnstone)
1991–92	Walter Smith (Rangers)
1992–93	Walter Smith (Rangers)
1993–94	Walter Smith (Rangers)
1994–95	Jimmy Nicholl (Raith Rovers)
1995–96	Walter Smith (Rangers)
1996–97	Walter Smith (Rangers)
1997–98	Wim Jansen (Celtic)
1998–99	Dick Advocaat (Rangers)
1999–2000	Dick Advocaat (Rangers)
2000–01	Martin O'Neill (Celtic)
2001–02	Martin O'Neill (Celtic)
2002–03	Alex McLeish (Rangers)
2003–04	Martin O'Neill (Celtic)
2004–05	Tony Mowbray (Hibs)
2005–06	Gordon Strachan (Celtic)
2006–07	Gordon Strachan (Celtic)
2007–08	Walter Smith (Rangers)
2008–09	Csaba Laszlo (Hearts)
2009–10	Walter Smith (Rangers)

Scottish Professional Footballers' Association Manager of the Year

2006–07	Gordon Strachan (Celtic)

PFA Scotland Manager of the Year

2007–08	Billy Reid (Hamilton)
2008–09	Gordon Strachan (Celtic)
2009–10	Walter Smith (Rangers)

Most domestic trophies in Scottish football

Willie Maley (16 leagues, 14 Scottish Cups) and
Bill Struth (18 leagues, 10 Scottish Cups, 2 League Cups): both 30 trophies
Jock Stein (10 leagues, 9 Scottish Cups, 6 League Cups): 25
Walter Smith (9 leagues, 5 Scottish Cups, 5 League Cups): 19*
Scot Symon (6 leagues, 5 Scottish Cups, 6 League Cups): 17
Jock Wallace (3 leagues, 3 Scottish Cups, 4 League Cups): 10
* as at 1 August 2010

Most domestic trophies with non-Old Firm clubs

Sir Alex Ferguson (3 leagues, 4 Scottish Cups, 1 League Cup): 8 trophies

Bosses who managed two different clubs to trophy success

Jock Stein (Dunfermline and Celtic)
Scot Symon (East Fife and Rangers)
David Hay (Celtic and Livingston)
Alex Smith (St Mirren and Aberdeen)
Willie Waddell (Kilmarnock and Rangers)
Eddie Turnbull (Aberdeen and Hibs)

Treble-winning managers
(League, Scottish Cup and League Cup in the same season)

Bill Struth (Rangers 1948–49)
Scot Symon (Rangers 1963–64)
Jock Stein (Celtic 1966–67)
Jock Stein (Celtic 1968–69)
Jock Wallace (Rangers 1975–76)
Jock Wallace (Rangers 1977–78)
Walter Smith (Rangers 1992–93)
Dick Advocaat (Rangers 1998–99)
Martin O'Neill (Celtic 2000–01)
Alex McLeish (Rangers 2002–03)

Non-Scottish trophy-winning managers in Scotland

Frank Heaven (England)
Reg Smith (England)
Ivan Golac (Yugoslavia)
Jimmy Nicholl (Northern Ireland)
Wim Jansen (Holland)
Dick Advocaat (Holland)
Martin O'Neill (Northern Ireland)
Valdas Ivanauskas (Lithuania)

East Fife's 1938 Scottish Cup victory under Dave McLean is the only time the trophy has been won by a team from outside Scotland's top division.

In England
What Scottish managers have won in English football

SEASON	LEAGUE (from 1889)	FA CUP (from 1872)	LEAGUE CUP (from 1961)
1871–72			
1872–73			
1873–74			
1874–75			
1875–76			
1070–77			
1877–78			
1878–79			
1879–80			
1880–81			
1881–82			
1882–83			
1883–84		Tom Mitchell (Blackburn)	
1884–85		Tom Mitchell (Blackburn)	
1885–86		Tom Mitchell (Blackburn)	
1886–87		George Ramsay (Aston Villa)	
1887–88			
1888–89			
1889–90		Tom Mitchell (Blackburn)	
1890–91		Tom Mitchell (Blackburn)	
1891–92			
1892–93			
1893–94	George Ramsay (Aston Villa)		
1894–95		George Ramsay (Aston Villa)	

In England–*contd*

SEASON	LEAGUE	FA CUP	LEAGUE CUP
1895–96	George Ramsay (Aston Villa)		
1896–97	George Ramsay (Aston Villa)	George Ramsay (Aston Villa)	
1897–98			
1898–99	George Ramsay (Aston Villa)		
1899–1900	George Ramsay (Aston Villa)		
1900–01		John Cameron (Tottenham)	
1901–02	Alex Mackie (Sunderland)		
1902–03			
1903–04		Tom Maley (Manchester City)	
1904–05	Frank Watt (Newcastle)	George Ramsay (Aston Villa)	
1905–06			
1906–07	Frank Watt (Newcastle)		
1907–08			
1908–09	Frank Watt (Newcastle)		
1909–10	George Ramsay (Aston Villa)	Frank Watt (Newcastle)	
1910–11		Peter O'Rourke (Bradford)	
1911–12			
1912–13		George Ramsay (Aston Villa)	
1913–14			
1914–15			

(Competitions not contested during the First World War)

SEASON	LEAGUE	FA CUP	LEAGUE CUP
1919–20		George Ramsay (Aston Villa)	
1920–21		Peter McWilliam (Tottenham)	
1921–22			
1922–23	Matt McQueen (Liverpool)		
1923–24		Frank Watt (Newcastle)	
1924–25			
1925–26			
1926–27	Frank Watt (Newcastle)		
1927–28			
1928–29			
1929–30			
1930–31			
1931–32		Andy Cunningham (Newcastle)	
1932–33			
1933–34			
1934–35			
1935–36	Johnny Cochrane (Sunderland)		
1936–37		Johnny Cochrane (Sunderland)	
1937–38			
1938–39			

In England–*contd*

SEASON	LEAGUE	FA CUP	LEAGUE CUP

(1939–46 competitions not contested during the Second World War)

SEASON	LEAGUE	FA CUP	LEAGUE CUP
1946–47			
1947–48		Sir Matt Busby (Man United)	
1948–49			
1949–50			
1950–51			
1951–52	Sir Matt Busby (Man United)		
1952 53			
1953–54			
1954–55		Doug Livingstone (Newcastle)	
1955–56	Sir Matt Busby (Man United)	Les McDowall (Man City)	
1956–57	Sir Matt Busby (Man United)		
1957–58			
1958–59			
1959–60			
1960–61			
1961–62			
1962–63		Sir Matt Busby (Man United)	
1963–64	Bill Shankly (Liverpool)		Matt Gillies (Leicester)
1964–65	Sir Matt Busby (Man United)	Bill Shankly (Liverpool)	Tommy Docherty (Chelsea)
1965–66	Bill Shankly (Liverpool)		
1966–67	Sir Matt Busby (Man United)		
1967–68			
1968–69			
1969–70			
1970–71			
1971–72			
1972–73	Bill Shankly (Liverpool)		
1973–74		Bill Shankly (Liverpool)	
1974–75	Dave Mackay (Derby County)		
1975–76			
1976–77		Tommy Docherty (Man United)	
1977–78			
1978–79			
1979–80			
1980–81			
1981–82			
1982–83			
1983–84			
1984–85			
1985–86	Kenny Dalglish (Liverpool)	Kenny Dalglish (Liverpool)	

In England—*contd*

SEASON	LEAGUE	FA CUP	LEAGUE CUP
1986–87			George Graham (Arsenal)
1987–88	Kenny Dalglish (Liverpool)		
1988–89	George Graham (Arsenal)	Kenny Dalglish (Liverpool)	
1989–90	Kenny Dalglish (Liverpool)	Sir Alex Ferguson (Man United)	
1990–91	George Graham (Arsenal)		
1991–92		Graeme Souness (Liverpool)	Sir Alex Ferguson (Man United)
1992–93	Sir Alex Ferguson (Man United)	George Graham (Arsenal)	George Graham (Arsenal)
1993–94	Sir Alex Ferguson (Man United)	Sir Alex Ferguson (Man United)	
1994–95	Kenny Dalglish (Blackburn Rovers)		
1995–96	Sir Alex Ferguson (Man United)	Sir Alex Ferguson (Man United)	
1996–97	Sir Alex Ferguson (Man United)		
1997–98			
1998–99	Sir Alex Ferguson (Man United)	Sir Alex Ferguson (Man United)	George Graham (Tottenham)
1999–2000	Sir Alex Ferguson (Man United)		
2000–01	Sir Alex Ferguson (Man United)		
2001–02			Graeme Souness (Blackburn Rovers)
2002–03	Sir Alex Ferguson (Man United)		
2003–04		Sir Alex Ferguson (Man United)	
2004–05			
2005–06			Sir Alex Ferguson (Man United)
2006–07	Sir Alex Ferguson (Man United)		
2007–08	Sir Alex Ferguson (Man United)		
2008–09	Sir Alex Ferguson (Man United)		Sir Alex Ferguson (Man United)
2009–10			Sir Alex Ferguson (Man United)

League titles: (out of 111) won by English managers 65, by Scottish 39, by overseas 7.

English title: Sir Alex Ferguson, with 11, has more wins than any other manager.

FA Cup: George Ramsay, with six, has more wins than any other manager.

League Cup: Sir Alex Ferguson and Brian Clough, both with four, have more wins than any other manager.

Bell's Manager of the Year

1965–66	Jock Stein
1966–67	Jock Stein
1967–68	Sir Matt Busby
1972–73	Bill Shankly
1985–86	Kenny Dalglish
1987–88	Kenny Dalglish
1988–89	George Graham
1989–90	Kenny Dalglish
1990–91	George Graham

FA Premier League Manager of the Year

1993–94	Sir Alex Ferguson
1994–95	Kenny Dalglish
1995–96	Sir Alex Ferguson
1996–97	Sir Alex Ferguson
1998–99	Sir Alex Ferguson
1999–00	Sir Alex Ferguson
2000–01	George Burley
2002–03	Sir Alex Ferguson
2006–07	Sir Alex Ferguson
2007–08	Sir Alex Ferguson
2008–09	Sir Alex Ferguson

League Managers Association Manager of the Year

1999	Sir Alex Ferguson
2001	George Burley
2003	David Moyes
2005	David Moyes
2008	Sir Alex Ferguson
2009	David Moyes

League Managers Association Manager of the Decade

1990s – Sir Alex Ferguson

European and International Club Football

European Cup/Champions League winners

Jock Stein (Celtic 1967)
Sir Matt Busby (Manchester United 1968)
Sir Alex Ferguson (Manchester United 1999, 2008)

European Cup Winners' Cup winners

Willie Waddell (Rangers 1972)
Sir Alex Ferguson (Aberdeen 1983, Manchester United 1991)
George Graham (Arsenal 1994)

UEFA Cup winners

Bill Shankly (Liverpool 1973)

UEFA Super Cup winners

Sir Alex Ferguson (Aberdeen 1983, Manchester United 1991)

Intercontinental Cup winners

Sir Alex Ferguson (Manchester United 1999)

FIFA Club World Cup winners

Sir Alex Ferguson (Manchester United 2008)

International Football

Home International Championships

Championship wins when team picked by a selection committee – 1884, 1885, 1887, 1889, 1894, 1896, 1897, 1900, 1902, 1910, 1921, 1922, 1923, 1925, 1926, 1929, 1936, 1949, 1951

Ian McColl – 1962, 1963
Bobby Brown – 1967
Willie Ormond – 1976
Ally MacLeod – 1977

1985 Rous Cup – Jock Stein

2006 Kirin Cup – Walter Smith

1982 UEFA European Under-18 Football Championship – Andy Roxburgh

Scotland's Managers

Manager	Reign	Pl	W	D	L	Win rate
Selection Committee	1872–1954 & 1954–57	254	148	48	58	58%
Andy Beattie (part-time)	1954	6	2	1	3	33%
Dawson Walker (interim)	1958	6	1	2	3	17%
Sir Matt Busby (part-time)	1958	2	1	1	0	50%
Andy Beattie (part-time)	1959–60	11	3	3	5	27%
Ian McColl	1960–65	28	17	3	8	60%
Jock Stein (part-time)	1965–66	7	3	1	3	43%
John Prentice	1966	4	0	1	3	0%
Malcolm MacDonald (interim)	1966–67	2	1	1	0	50%
Bobby Brown	1967–71	28	9	8	11	32%
Tommy Docherty	1971–72	12	7	2	3	58%
Willie Ormond	1973–77	38	18	8	12	47%
Ally MacLeod	1977–78	17	7	5	5	41%
Jock Stein	1978–85	61	26	12	23	43%
Sir Alex Ferguson (part-time)	1985–86	10	3	4	3	30%
Andy Roxburgh	1986–93	61	23	19	19	38%
Craig Brown	1993–2002	70	32	18	20	46%
Berti Vogts	2002–04	31	8	7	16	26%
Tommy Burns (interim)	2004	1	0	0	1	0%
Walter Smith	2004–07	16	7	5	4	44%
Alex McLeish	2007	10	7	0	3	70%
George Burley	2008–09	14	3	3	8	21%
Craig Levein	2009–	4	2	1	1	50%*

* to 1 October 2010

Other international teams managed by Scots

Armenia – Ian Porterfield 2006–07

Australia – Eddie Thomson 1990–96

Belgium – William Maxwell 1910–13 and 1920–28; Doug Livingstone 1953–54

Bahrain – Danny McLennan 1973

Botswana – Peter Cormack 1986–87

Canada – Tony Taylor 1988–89

Fiji – Danny McLennan 1990–92

Holland – Billy Hunter 1914

Iceland – Alexander Weir 1957; Duncan McDowall 1972

Iran – Danny McLennan 1973–74

Iraq – Danny McLennan 1975–77

Jordan – Danny McLennan 1978–80

Libya – Danny McLennan 1992–93

Mauritius – Danny McLennan 1965–68, 1986–88

Malawi – Danny McLennan 1983–84

Maldives – Roy Aitken 1998

New Zealand – Ian Marshall 1990–93, Bobby Clark 1994–96

Oman – Ian Porterfield 1997–98

Philippines – Danny McLennan 1963–64

Republic of Ireland – Doug Livingstone 1951–53

Solomon Islands – George Cowie 2000–03

Trinidad & Tobago – Ian Porterfield 2000–01

Turkey – Billy Hunter 1924–26

Uganda – Bobby Williamson 2008–

Uruguay – John Harley 1909–10

USA – Robert Millar 1928–30; David Gould 1933–34; Bill Jeffrey 1949–52, Andrew Brown 1947–48

Zambia – Ian Porterfield 1993–94

Zimbabwe – Danny McLennan 1968–73, John Rugg 1973–75 and 1977–79; Ian Porterfield 1996–97

Bibliography

Alex Ferguson: Managing My Life by Sir Alex Ferguson (Hodder & Stoughton, 1999)

The Ally MacLeod Story (Stanley Paul, 1979)

Ally McCoist: My Story by Ally McCoist and Crawford Brankin (Mainstream, 1992)

The Book of Football Quotations by Peter Ball and Phil Shaw (Stanley Paul, 1984)

The Boss: The Many Sides of Alex Ferguson by Michael Crick (Simon & Schuster, 2002)

Craig Brown: The Autobiography by Craig Brown and Bernard Bale (Virgin Books, 1998)

The Cult of the Manager by Jeff King and John Kelly (Virgin Books, 1997)

Dalglish by Stephen F Kelly (Headline, 1992)

Dalglish: My Autobiography by Kenny Dalglish with Henry Winter (Coronet Books, 1996)

The Don of an Era by Alex McLeish with Alastair MacDonald (John Donald, 1988)

Dundee: Champions of Scotland 1961-62 by Kenny Ross (Desert Island Books, 2003)

Eddie Turnbull: Having a Ball by Eddie Turnbull with Martin Hannan (Mainstream 2006)

Father of Football: The Story of Matt Busby by David Miller (Pavilion Books, 1994)

The First 100 Years of the Dons by Jack Webster (Hodder & Stoughton, 2002)

Football: A History of the World Game by Bill Murray (Scolar Press, 1994)

The Football Manager: A History by Neil Carter (Routledge, 2006)

The Football Managers by Johnny Rogan (Queen Anne Press, 1989)

Gaffers: The Wit and Wisdom of Football Managers by Phil Dampier and Ashley Walton (The Book Guild, 2009)

God is Brazilian: The Man who Brought Football to Brazil by Josh Lacey (Stadia, 2005)

The Green Line by Alan Green (Headline, 2000)

Gritty, Gallant, Glorious: A History and Complete Record of the Hearts by Norrie Price (Price, 1997)

Hail Cesar by Billy McNeill (Headline, 2004)

The Head Bhoys by Graham McColl (Mainstream 2002)

Heart of Midlothian Football Club: A Pictorial History by David Speed, Bill Smith and Graham Blackwood (Heart of Midlothian FC, 1984)

Hearts: Great Tynecastle Tales by Rob Robertson and Paul Kiddie (Mainstream, 2005)

If You're Second You Are Nothing: Ferguson and Shankly by Oliver Holt (Macmillan, 2006)

Illustrated History of Aston Villa 1874-1998 by Graham McColl (Hamlyn, 1988)

Into The Light: A Complete History of Sunderland Football Club by Roger Hutchinson (Mainstream, 1999)

Inverting the Pyramid: The History of Football Tactics by Jonathan Wilson (Orion, 2008)

Jock Stein: The Definitive Biography by Archie Macpherson (Highdown, 2007)

Jousting with Giants: The Jim McLean Story with Ken Gallacher (Mainstream, 1987)

McIlvanney on Football by Hugh McIlvanney (Mainstream, 1994)

Mr Stein: A Biography of Jock Stein by Bob Crampsey (Mainstream, 1986)

My Story by Tommy Docherty (Headline, 2006)

One Hundred Years of Scottish Football by John Rafferty (Pan Books, 1973)

The Only Game by Roddy Forsyth (Mainstream, 1990)

The Quiet Assassin by Davie Hay (Black & White, 2009)

The Rangers Miscellany by Robert McElroy (Vision Sports, 2009)

Rangers: The Managers by David Mason (Mainstream, 2009)

The Real Mackay by Dave Mackay (Mainstream, 2004)

The Sack Race: The Story of football's Gaffers by Chris Green (Mainstream, 2002)

Scotland: The Complete International Football Record by Richard Keir (Breedon Books, 2001)

A Scottish Football Hall of Fame by John Cairney (Mainstream, 2004)

Scottish Football Quotations by Kenny MacDonald (Black & White, 2009)

Shankly: My Story by John Roberts (Trinity Mirror Sports Media, 2009)

Shanks: The Authorised Biography of Bill Shankly by Dave Bowler (Orion, 1996)

Silversmith: The Biography of Walter Smith by Neil Drysdale (Birlinn, 2007)

Sir Bobby Charlton: My Autobiography by Sir Bobby Charlton (Headline, 2007)

Slim Jim Baxter by Ken Gallacher (Virgin Books, 2002)

A Strange Kind of Glory by Eamon Dunphy (Mandarin, 1991)

Talking Shankly: The Man, the Genius, the Legend by Tom Darby (Mainstream 1998)

To Barcelona and Beyond, the Men Who Made Rangers Champions of Europe by Paul Smith (Breedon Books, 2006)

Triumphs of the Football Field by Archie Hunter (Sports Projects, 1997)

Willie Maley: The Man Who Made Celtic by David W. Potter (Tempus, 2004)

Index